CONTENTS

PREFACE TO THE ENGLISH EDITION

The original manuscript was ready for the printers in July 1970, i. e., before the Lusaka Conference and even before the Preparatory Conference in Dar Es Salaam. I have therefore felt that a short postscript would be in order. In it the outcome of the Lusaka Conference is compared with the views expressed in the last section of the book. The documents at the end of the book have also been brought up to date by the inclusion of the two Lusaka Declarations. The other final documents are not included because they do not introduce significant new substance.

I am also indebted to the Publisher Oceana Publications for their friendly cooperation in the publication of this book in English.

Belgrade, November 1971

L. M.

PREFACE TO THE FIRST
SERBO-CROATIAN EDITION OF 1971

Nonalignment, rather the individual or collective action of the nonaligned countries, influenced greatly the last twenty five years of international relations. The number of books and of other publications on world politics covering nonalignment, if only passingly, is increasing steadily. Nevertheless, the literature on this specific phenomenon is still scarce. This book is an attempt to fill the gap.

This circumstance offered advantages, but it also caused problems. Nonalignment is a phenomenon which could and which should be illuminated from many angles, showing its several facets. Thus, in the very beginning of my work the question arose: whether to treat only one aspect as specialists prefer, or to venture a more or less rounded approach, covering most of the essential elements of nonalignment?

I decided to follow the latter course, conscious of the complexity of the undertaking and of the many shortcomings inherent in such an approach. In view of the limitations of a book, I had, further, to shorten or to omit some elements of the argument and make other arbitrary decisions and selections, which may not meet with other people's approval. The author of a book, however, has no other choice, but to follow his own judgment and leave it to others to fill the lacunae and correct the short-

7

comings of his effort. The subject matter in this case anyhow requires further exploration and more complete presentation.

In preparing this book, I have heavily drawn on my personal experiences. Some of my past positions and assignments had been closely connected with the problems and the development of nonalignment. The quoted works of others are but a fraction of the existing literature on nonalignment and related problems, and they have assisted me in my endeavours or helped me to form my own views and understanding of the underlying theoretical problems, as well as the general social and political environment in which nonalignment originated and developed.

In my work on this book I had the benefit of many contacts and discussions with friends and colleagues in my own country and abroad. I owe a debt of gratitude to all of them, scholars, political leaders and statesmen. In the final shaping io the book, I had the invaluable assistance and advcfe of Professor Jovan Djordjević of the Belgrade University and Ljubivoje Aćimović of the Institute of International Politics and Economics in Belgrade. Without this help given generously by friends and colleagues this book would have come to the reader with still more deficiencies.

Belgrade, 3 May, 1970.

L. M.

INTRODUCTION

Nonalignment is considered in this book as a phenomenon which arose from the specific conditions after the war in international relations and in individual countries and parts of the world. No attempt will, therefore, be made to describe, analyze or interpret this phenomenon as a universal category which would presume to be valid for all times or at least to have been applicable for some time prior to the twentieth century. Nonalignment will be discussed as a phenomenon of post-war trends in the world, since the material basis and consciousness of this movement was a direct result of immediately preceding events. It would be difficult, and hardly worth trying, to find a direct connection with events in earlier centuries.

The discussion of nonalignment does not dwell or insist only on the interpretation of the term nonalignment, i. e., on the otherwise important fact that the nonaligned countries have never been, and do not wish to be, aligned with any bloc. This fact was, of course, of extreme importance and in given circumstances appeared as an unavoidable element of the policy and ideas of the nonaligned countries. Finally, the fact that the statesmen and other leaders in these countries without hesitation or qualification adopted the term nonalignment and insisted upon it must be regarded as highly significant. It was a component part of nonalignment in international relations, and so their attitude to the blocs and the cold war must be starting point for every discussion of nonalignment, although the analysis must not end there.

Defined in this manner, nonalignment is completely different from the concept of neutrality and neutralism. Nonalignment is not simply a modern form or specific derivative of neutrality or neutralism. In fact, neutralism has existed alongside nonalignment, and countries from these two categories have sometimes even attempted to establish closer relations with one another, but without any notable success. Apparently the reason for this lack of success was not only the far broader foundations of nonalignment on conceptual elements which are outside the sphere of political international relations of the cold war, but also differences in the sphere of practical international activities.

Any consideration of nonalignment, in whatever context, must begin with an analysis of the basic characteristics of contemporary events and of what is specific in the development of the modern world. For this reason, a detailed examination of each act or policy of the nonaligned countries or an exhaustive list of historical data would not bring us any closer to the real essence of this phenomenon. The best approach would be to consider the most important facts and discuss their connection with the specific trend which produced them.

The forthcoming discussion must therefore be based on certain assumptions which, taken all together, should outline the main characteristics of our times. They are here summarized in seven points, which cover the period between the years just prior to the First World War and today. Naturally, certain of these phenomena relate to specific years in this time span. Nevertheless, it has been assumed that they have been present throughout this entire period either as actual facts or as tendencies, and that they show signs of gaining in significance.

1. Modern development in the material sphere has made possible, and inevitable, a rapprochement and better acquaintance among peoples, who previously had very little, if any, contact with one another. In the twentieth century the world began to shrink, and the intensity and volume of contacts among people and their institutions increased at an imprecedented rate. This increased interaction brought an increased interdependence, but conflicts also began to show a greater tendency of becoming universal. Two outstanding manifestations of this trend were the world wars and the world organizations of the League of Nations and the United Nations.

2. This new state of affairs gave completely new and much greater dimensions to the foreign policy activities of all countries and the role of this activity also gained in importance. Thus, events beyond the borders of a country began to influence much more decisively every aspect of the internal development of that country. This dependency is present not only in economic life, but also in all realms of human activity, including the formation, development and orientation of political and other trends and movements in various countries. These movements therefore show an ever stronger trend towards transnational contacts and ties.

3. The intensification of transnational activities in the world led to a rapprochement and to direct contacts among a large number of individuals in a number of ways other than through state and institutional channels. People living in different societies began to have closer ties, but antagonisms also began to arise between them. Greater proximity, more intensive contacts and better acquaintance increased the awareness of differences and inspired aspirations which earlier did not exist or which were held only by a narrow strata of society in countries which were in a subordinate or unfavorable position vis-à-vis others.

4. Naturally, all this had to lead to a drive for a more complete emancipation of man's personality from the taboos and myths inherited from the past. People began to reject inherited inequalities and injustices, whether based on race, nationality or any other special grouping, and there is particularly opposition against submission to economic exploitation or colonial subordination. Thus very significant revolutionary movements were begun in all societies, although they became most conspicuous where the challenge was the greatest.

5. These changes faced statesmen and governments with situations which were new and inexplicable in terms of old ideas. There was an exceptionally rapid and unexpected radical change in positions, alliances, alignment and in general in the foreign policy of states and particularly of the large and more important powers. Alignment in the First World War did not correspond to the pre-war constellation of alliances, and alignment in the Second World War still less. The about-turn in world policies

11

between 1929 and 1939 has no parallels in history in the dimensions and significance of the changes and in their influence on the further course of the history of mankind.

6. The great powers, which had previously been the protectors and guarantors of a certain stability and order in the world, became the main source of rising insecurity, and their behavior gave the impression that they were playing with the fate of nations and of all mankind. The period before the First, and even more so before the Second World War, with its list of cynical and short-sighted political and material acts of aggression against weaker and smaller countries and nations discredited and completely destroyed earlier myths about the reasonableness, if not wisdom, of the great powers. This largely undermined the authority and political influence of the great powers, but also increased the self-confidence of smaller countries, not only in so-called civilized areas, but also in the colonies.

7. Although progressive ideas could arise only in certain environments, where there were conditions for them, they, as well as products of material progress, spread and were adopted in areas where they never could have been developed because of the level of development, and where they were often absorbed and adopted only with considerable distortions. Thus the social development in many parts of the world, if not everywhere, took on a chaotic appearance. Even long-established social and political institutions were shaken. The instability which was thus created and which developed was particularly evident where there was not sufficient flexibility and where conflicts and crises were the most intense, i. e., where the need for change was felt most strongly, either because of the inacceptability of existing institutions or because of material difficulties and poverty.

Through the combined effect of all or some of these factors, the modern world has passed through grave crises in international relations and in the internal relations in all countries and on all continents. Never before in history has the map of the world changed so rapidly and so radically. Empires have fallen, colonial systems have broken up, and the way of life, both materially and socially, has changed fundamentally in all countries of the world, from the most backward to the most advanced.

But two processes deserve special attention in all this fermentation: the loss of authority of the great powers and the destruction of the myth about their role as protectors of peace and order in the world, and the breaking up of the colonial systems. The first chapter of this book will be devoted to these questions, so that the origins and development of the independent role of the previously passive majority of mankind can be shown not only as a specific case of the general trend for emancipation, but also as a completely concrete reaction to the loss of political and moral authority of those powers which until then had truly directed events in the world and determined the course of history by their joint or individual actions, agreements or conflicts.

PART ONE
THE ORIGINS OF NONALIGNMENT

CHAPTER ONE

CHANGES ON THE WORLD POLITICAL SCENE AND THE EMERGENCE OF NONALIGNMENT

A. RELATIONS AMONG THE GREAT POWERS

CHANGES IN THE LINE-UP OF FORCES ON THE EVE OF WORLD WAR II

The Allied victory in the Second World War failed to create those conditions which the Allies had promised while the war was in progress and in which they probably believed at that time. Cracks in the Allied ranks had started to show up even before the war ended. The most glaring of these, though not the only one, was the mutual antagonism between the Western Allies and the Soviet Union. It is very difficult to say with any certainty how much of it could be traced back to earlier suspicions and ill-will, and how much resulted from the conflicting plans for the post-war period, from the anticipation of rivalry in organizing the post-war world.

This question will probably never be answered, because even if any statements or documents from either side do eventually come to light in the future, it is hardly likely that they will disclose the manner and circumstances in which some of the crucial decisions were made. Documents and the news published at that time clearly show that there had been a certain amount of friction, although at first subdued, between the two partners in the great coalition throughout the entire war.

Past grievances could have had much to do with this, because before the war relations between the West and the Soviet Union had almost always been strained, and they came to a breaking point when the Soviet Union was expelled from the League of Nations on December 14, 1939, because of the Soviet-Finnish war. This decision by the League of Nations council[1] climaxed the steady corrosion of relations which had begun when the U.S.S.R. signed a non-aggression treaty with Hitler's Germany on August 23, 1939,[2] following the failure of negotiations between the Soviet Union and the Western Allies.

In the spring of that year the Soviet Union had expressed its dissatisfaction with the policies and attitudes of the Western states, whose signing of the quadripartite Munich agreement had demonstrated their lack of determination to oppose aggression. The first serious hint of this dissatisfaction appeared in a speech by Stalin at the opening of the Eighteenth Congress of the C.P.S.U. on March 10, 1939, and the first open and direct warning to the Western states was voiced by Molotov at a joint session of the two chambers of the Supreme Soviet on May 31.[3] Finally, after several months of unsuccessful negotiations between the U.S.S.R. and Great Britain and France, the non-aggression pact between the Soviet Union and Germany was concluded.

Agreement on the partition of Poland and a friendship pact between the Soviet Union and Germany followed, together with an agreement on economic relations, calling for deliveries of raw materials from the U.S.S.R.[4] Next came the Soviet Union's brief war with Finland, which lasted from December 2, 1939, to March 16, 1940, when a peace treaty was signed.[5] This war was the direct cause of the Soviet Union's expulsion from the League of Nations. But as far as the Soviet Union was concerned, it

---

[1] Société des Nations, Journal Officiel, XX-ème année. Nos. 11—12 (2-ème partie): Cent septième séssion du Conseil, Document A. 46. 1939, VII, pp. 506 *et seq.*

[2] See the text of the pact in: *Droit international et histoire diplomatique*, Documents choisis par Claude-Albert Colliard, Ed. Domat Montchrestien, Paris 1948, p. 369.

[3] *Keesing's Contemporary Archives* 1937—1940, p. 3591.

[4] Droit international et histoire diplomatique, *op. cit.*, pp. 370—371.

[5] *Ibid.*, pp. 372—374.

accomplished a number of tasks: the borders with Poland and Finland had been moved further to the West, and, in the diplomatic sphere, relations with Germany had been settled.

As can be gathered from the above-mentioned speeches, all these acts were inspired by the Soviet Union's resolve to safeguard its interests at all costs, indeed at any cost. After the Western Allies abandoned Czechoslovakia at Munich in 1938,[6] and openly sided with Hitler in his pressure against Prague, Stalin went into collusion with Hitler against Poland, which on that occasion was described as the "ugly product of Versailles". The Soviet government claimed those measures to be justified and prompted by the behavior of the Western states.

In London and Paris, this interval in European history was, of course, viewed differently; the agreements with Hitler were considered as a sell-out to an enemy who had caused a new world war. But in any case each side showed a deep distrust of the other. As a result of this antagonism between the U.S.S.R. and the West, the triangular structure of European politics produced in 1939 a rapprochement between two sides which until then had seemed to be irreconcilably hostile to one another, as witnessed by the anti-Comintern pact of 1936.[7]

THE FINAL LINE-UP OF FORCES
AND FRICTION AMONG THE ALLIES

The Soviet-German alliance was short-lived because on June 22, 1941, Hitler attacked the Soviet Union. The Soviet Union and Great Britain rapidly came to terms, and soon afterwards a tripartite coalition was formed when the U.S.A. entered the war after the Japanese attack on Pearl Harbour on December 13, 1941. Already in the early months of the war Moscow began to doubt whether the Western Allies really wanted to relieve the heavy pressure which Hitler's armies were exerting on the Russian front. Stalin demanded a second front in Europe as

---

[6] *Ibid.*, pp. 358—359.
[7] *Ibid.*, pp. 344—345.

soon as possible, to force the German command to transfer some of its forces from the Eastern front to the West.[8]

Therefore the effect which the events immediately preceding the outbreak of the Second World War had on the main protagonists during and directly after their collective military efforts in the Second World War should not be underestimated. The statesmen of the countries involved did not judge this previous behavior in terms of sympathy, friendship or ethical principles; nevertheless these events, even if viewed rationally, must have had a strong influence on the forming of opinions. They showed also that there were two sides which tried to form combinations with Hitler's Germany based on the permanent antagonism between them, an antagonism pre-dating Hitler's regime in Germany.

In the pre-war years, each side made temporary use of Hitler to strengthen its hand against the other, so it was understandable that when the third party ceased to exist, old hatreds had to flare up again. Actually, even while the war was on, each side accused the other of putting its own selfish interests first. To the very last day, Hitler believed that the Allies would start fighting among themselves and that this would save him from final ruin.

This hope, of course, was founded on the sum total of antagonistic relations between the two Allied camps, but also on the assumption that before the war ended there would be a clash between the different ambitions and aspirations in exploiting the victory and organizing the post-war world. Whereas at first relations among the Allies were troubled by the problem of the opening of a second front in Europe, after the turning point in the war, i. e., after the victory at Stalingrad and El Alamein, it was the question of the organization of the post-war world and influence within it that became the over-riding issue.

Allied statesmen had made their feelings on this matter clear even in the first half of the war. The first declaration to contain explicitly formulated war aims was the Atlantic Charter,[9] pro-

---

[8] The first demand for a second front was made as early as July 18, 1941. "It seems to me, therefore," wrote Stalin to Churchill, "that the military situation of the Soviet Union, as well as of Great Britain, would be considerably improved if there could be established a front against Hitler in the West — Northern France — and in the North — the Arctic." Winston S. Churchill: *The Second World War*, Vol. 3, *The Grand Alliance*, Houghton Mifflin Company, Boston 1951, p. 383.

[9] *United States State Department Bulletin*, 16 August 1941, p. 125.

mulgated at a meeting of the heads of the U.S.A. and Great Britain on August 14, 1941. This document served as a basis for a much broader declaration proclaimed as the Declaration of the United Nations[10] on January 1, 1942. These were the first steps taken towards creating a comprehensive conception of the post-war world. It acquired more concrete features in the Moscow Declaration,[11] signed on October 30, 1943, by the foreign ministers of the Soviet Union, Great Britain, the United States, and the Chinese ambassador in Moscow.

The immediate precursor of the United Nations Charter, i. e., of the final stage in the building of what was supposed to be a new and harmonious world of peace and security, was the Dumbarton Oaks proposals prepared by the four great powers in Washington. The Dumbarton Oaks conference, lasting from August 21 to October 7, 1944, was held in two stages, the first without China and the second without the presence of the Soviet Union.[12]

The post-victory world, as envisioned by the great powers during the war, was to be constructed on two basic premises: first, the victory over fascism had created all the necessary conditions for the preservation of a stable peace, and all that was necessary was for the international community to guard against a renewal of German militarism, and, second, peace and cooperation could be guaranteed only by the great powers, which would continue the close cooperation which they had instituted during the war. Both of these premises were wrong, as was soon demonstrated by further developments in international relations.

These premises were echoed in all the documents which preceded the United Nations Charter and in virtually all statements and other communications intended for the Allied countries as well as in those directed to nations under enemy occupation during the war. At first, when the main task was still to mobilize popular resistance against the aggressor, the outlook for the future was for the most part outlined in general and vague terms. However, as the war drew to a close, and particularly immedia-

---

[10] *Ibid.*, 3 January 1942, p. 3.
[11] *Ibid.*, 30 October 1943.
[12] See: *Yearbook of the United Nations 1946—1947*, pp. 4—9.

tely preceding and during the San Francisco Conference, which produced the definitive text of the Charter, these ideas were given a more precise formulation.

The new world organization, the United Nations, was founded on the belief in a harmonious cooperation among the great powers which headed the war coalition. But instead of cooperation there arose a conflict between the East and the West after the war. Nevertheless, in the face of the obvious lack of unanimity and the increasingly sharp dissensions between the great powers, lip service was still paid to the fiction that the United Nations rested on cooperation among them. Similarly, the West insisted, albeit less and less, that the main danger to peace continued to be a possible resurgence of aggression by those powers which were defeated in the Second World War. It is interesting that the conflict between East and West gained momentum at the same time the two sides were holding the Nuremberg trials of war criminals.

The main contenders in the arms race, which began after the war, were primarily the former allies, particularly the United States and the Soviet Union, and it was their differences from the time of the war rather than cooperation which dominated their mutual relations. However, such misunderstandings and friction among allies are not an unusual occurrence in modern or even ancient history of international affairs. There have been, many cases in the past when former allies became bitter enemies and even waged war among themselves after having won a war. We do not have to go far to find an example of this; witness the development in the Balkans after the First Balkan War.

Nevertheless, the case in point has certain special features which set it apart from other examples of conflicts among former allies. For a better understanding of the situation after the Second World War, it is necessary to throw some light on a few special features of the East-West confrontation, notably the cold war developing from it. First of all, the role played by the ideological conflict between the Soviet Union and the West should be examined.

At first glance this factor would seem to be very important, because, after all, the Second World War was fought largely on an ideological basis, as a war against an exclusive conception of racial supremacy and fascist ideology. But this was so only in appearance. The dealings of the West and the Soviet Union with Hitler on the eve of the outbreak of the Second World War are the best evidence of the extent to which ideological differences were subordinated to national interests, such as were conceived by the holders of power.

DIFFERENCES IN IDEOLOGY AND POLITICAL PRINCIPLES DID NOT PREVENT AGREEMENTS WITH HITLER

At one time or another both sides in the Allied coalition tried to reach an agreement with Hitler, even after his actions in Germany and the countries he had already occupied and the character of the "new order" he was preparing for Europe and the entire world had become well known. Neither side felt inhibited from doing so on ideological grounds. Efforts to achieve a lasting cooperation with Hitler failed only because at a given moment Hitler decided to take a further step towards achieving supremacy in Europe and in the world, and no longer considered cooperation with either side necessary.

It is in this light that Molotov's address to the joint session of the chambers of the Supreme Soviet on October 31, 1939, should be read. Molotov had said: "What this amounts to is that the British, together with the French, proponents of the war have proclaimed something of an 'ideological' war against Germany, that is reminiscent of the religious wars of past times. In fact, religious wars against heretics and religious opponents were once in vogue. As we know, they had disastrous results for the masses and led to the economic breakdown and cultural decline of nations."

Further on in his speech Molotov accused the leading circles in Great Britain and France of wanting the Soviet Union to revert to the days of "religious wars, superstition and cultural backwardness". According to Molotov, there was "absolutely no justification for such a war." "One may accept or reject the ideology of Hitlerism," continued Molotov, "just as any other ideological system — this is a matter of political attitudes. But everyone must realize that ideology cannot be destroyed by force, that it cannot be eliminated by war." But the punch-line is certainly in the next sentence: "Therefore it is not only senseless but criminal to fight... a war 'to destroy Hitlerism' under the guise of a struggle for 'democracy'."[13]

Molotov's remark about an ideological war was completely unwarranted, because at the last moment, on the very eve of the outbreak of the war, London and Paris tried to avoid it. They elected to fight only when they had realized that there would be no war between the Soviet Union and Germany, no "ideological" war as they had hoped and expected in terms of the tone and ideological phraseology of the anti-Comintern pact. Molotov's words were calculated to place responsibility for the outbreak of the war at the door of the Western countries and to press for the cessation of hostilities and the recognition of new *status quo* created after the partition of Poland.

By this time the Soviet Union had already gone a long way in fostering friendly relations with Germany. Molotov's speech was far from reflecting the real state of affairs in international relations, but it gave a true picture of the situation that had arisen in relations between the U.S.S.R. and Hitler's Germany. The speech was in keeping with the obligations assumed under the Declaration and Agreement signed in September 1939. In these documents the two countries undertook to make all efforts "jointly and in agreement with other powers" to bring about a cessation of the war between Germany and the Western powers. The agreement also laid down the "areas of interest" in occupied Poland, and Article 4 gave long-range prospects of mutual relations: "The two governments consider this agreement as a sound basis for developing and promoting friendly relations between their peoples."[14]

Whereas Hitler himself used the ideological phraseology of the anti-Comintern pact on numerous other occasions, he was always willing to make temporary agreements and alliances, be it

---

[13] *Keesing's Contemporary Archives* 1937—1940, p. 3780.
[14] *Droit international et histoire diplomatique, op. cit.*, p. 370 and 371.

with the West or with the Soviet Union. So it was that both sides of the latter-day alliance against Hitler at one time or another felt betrayed and deceived by him. In his speech of July 3, 1941[15] Stalin complained of perfidy and deceit, after the world had heard similar bitter words from Neville Chamberlain in his speech to the House of Commons on September 1, 1939.[16]

Later on in the war, ideological themes cropped up again with increasing frequency in speeches and statements by Allied statesmen, whose obvious aim was to move into action and encourage to greater efforts the peoples in the occupied countries and in the Allied rear. Reference is made to direct ideological propaganda, not to other types of propaganda, such as, for example, reports on Nazi terror and enslavement. However, towards the end of the war, the actions of the Allies, in contrast to their war propaganda, again superseded ideological consideration.

In this atmosphere, curious agreements and temporary alliances were made which patently ignored ideological barriers. Probably the most bizarre among these was the abortive friendship between the Soviet Union and the Rumanian king, Michael, who on July 19, 1945, received the "Order of Victory", at that time the highest Soviet decoration, from the hands of Soviet Marshal Tolbukhin. Later the Western powers succeeded in coming to terms with him, so the U.S.S.R. dropped him, and he was forced to abdicate on September 30, 1947.

The Western attitude to this entire problem of ideological coloration of international relations in our times was characterized by Winston Churchill in the introduction to his war memoirs: "One day President Roosevelt told me that he was asking publicly for suggestions about what the war should be called. I said at once 'the Unnecessary War'. There never was a war more easy to stop than that which has just wrecked what was left of the world from the previous struggle."[17]

The behavior of the great powers in the years of the war, as during the diplomatic prelude to the war, was aimed at gaining

---

[15] Vneshnaia politika Sovetskogo Soiuza v periode otechestvenoi voiny, OGIZ, Moskva 1944, p. 25.

[16] *Keesing's Contemporary Archives* 1937—1940, pp. 3703—3704.

[17] Winston Churchill, *op. cit.*, Vol. 1, *The Gathering Storm*, p. iv.

as favorable a position as possible in the world and at achieving their own aspirations and goals. The fact that both the Soviet Union and, somewhat later, the West realized that the Versailles system was untenable and that it must be changed played an important part. The Soviet Union had openly attacked this system from the very outset, and in the West the system of reparations had been rapidly modified and there was a willingness to give ever greater concessions to Germany. As Hitler's rise proceeded apace, relations deteriorated to such an extent that the more and more flexible attitudes of the West, after their initial rigidity, only increased Hitler's appetites instead of appeasing a disgruntled Germany. Both the West and the Soviet Union are much to blame for whetting Hitler's aggressive appetites and his hopes for success. Their mutual relations, and their relations with Hitler on the eve of the war, are certainly a convincing example of a disregard for ideological differences but also of shortsighted schemes.

THE ORGANIZATION OF THE POST-WAR WORLD, THE COLD WAR AND THE COLONIAL QUESTION

After the war, ideologically slanted statements reappeared and took on a role similar to the one they had in the past. Again the object was to win over the population living on the other side of the "front". Ideological phraseology was calculated to gain the sympathies of the populations living in countries on the other side of the new demarcation line between the East and the West in Europe. The conflict between the former Allies intensified in inter-governmental relations, but it also extended to internal affairs, where each side tried to sow dissension in the political life of the countries on the other side and thus to achieve the support of at least a segment of the population.

At first after the war a peculiar combination of two essentially irreconcilable and contradictory attitudes took shape. The United Nations was set up on the basis of cooperation, but at the same time a bitter conflict began to develop within it. Disputes about the organization of the post-war world, and especially of Europe, proliferated. Uncompromising stands were taken, and all material and political forces were mobilized in the mutual struggle. But at the same time the structure was being built of a world organization which rested on the assumption of an existing and functioning directorate of these same great powers which were increasingly at daggers drawn. This leaning towards a directorate was particularly strong in the draft of the Charter prepared by the great powers at Dumbarton Oaks in 1944. The idea of world rule by a directorate of great powers was watered down and modified in the final text of the Charter at the insistence of a number of small and medium-sized countries from the ranks of the Western camp.

According to the original proposals drafted by the great powers at Dumbarton Oaks, the equal role of all member countries on matters of peace and security, which had still existed, at least formally, in the League of Nations, would be abolished. Leland M. Goodrich and Edward Hambro warned against this in their commentary of the Charter: "Under the Covenant (of the League of Nations) the Assembly and the Council were equally empowered to deal with 'any matter within the sphere of action of the League or affecting the peace of the world'. The Proposals (from Dumbarton Oaks) attempted to delimit the functions of the two organs by making the General Assembly primarily the body for discussion and for dealing with matters of general welfare, and the Security Council the body for action in the limited field of maintaining international peace and security."[18]

This "limited field" would give the Council and its permanent members a complete authority in regard to world political affairs. In San Francisco the role of the General Assembly was strengthened, and other important changes were also made in the proposals of the great powers. Perhaps the best example of the generally accepted belief that cooperation among the great powers could continue is the provision on voting in the Security Council. Eventually this provision was changed, when it was agreed that the abstention of one of the great powers would not

---

[18] Leland M. Goodrich and Edward Hambro, *Charter of the United Nations*, Second Edition, Stevens & Sons Limited, London 1949, p. 8.

prevent the taking of decisions in cases in which the Charter called for the "concurring votes of the permanent members".[19]

The conflict of interests which pervaded even the years of collective warfare was bound to appear in a more blatant form after the defeat of the common enemy. In the post-war scramble for positions, both sides began an ideological mobilization of all possible social and political forces on their own territories and in the countries on the opposite side of the new front. Hostility mounted and included struggles within each individual country and the exploitation of all possible social, economic, and, of course, above all political possibilities to win over new allies.

As different parts of the world developed much closer contacts, these efforts inevitably spread to other continents, and they engendered a new type of universal political conflict. The great powers strove to extend their influence throughout their overseas possessions, colonies, and dependent countries. The Western powers tried to use their prerogatives of trusteeship to bring the colonies of defeated Italy under their sway and struggled to keep a firm grip on all their other positions in various parts of the world. As part of this manoeuvring to broaden its existing areas of influence and create new ones, in September 1945 the Soviet Union submitted a demand to become trustee of a part of the Italian colonies.[20]

Generally speaking, the attitude towards the colonies at that time was completely different from that which evolved later under the pressure of national liberation movements and which led to changes in various positions in debates in the United Nations. Therefore we should first examine the policies on colonies at the time when the great powers were trying to agree on a new post-war organization in the world.

The Dumbarton Oaks proposals made no mention of the colonies. The general approach taken was very simplistic in

---

[19] *Charter of the United Nations*, Article 27, paragraph 3.

[20] In a press interview on September 18, 1945, one newsman asked whether it was true that the U.S.S.R. wanted trusteeship over Tripoli and was interested in Eritrea. Molotov answered that there was "an element of truth in the report". This interview was reported at the time in the world press and is quoted here from *Keesing's Contemporary Archives* 1943—1946, p. 7469.

comparison with the final text of the Charter: executive political authority was to be handed to the Security Council, and the General Assembly would be primarily a debating forum and would be concerned with questions of general welfare. Furthermore, the International Court of Justice and the Secretariat were also envisaged as principal organs of the future organization. The Economic and Social Council was assigned a secondary role and did not rank with the principal organs, while the Trusteeship Council was not provided for at all. There was no mention whatsoever of equality "without distinction as to race, sex, language or religion." These words were added in the suitable places only at San Francisco. There the Economic and Social Council was promoted to the rank of a principal organ, and provisions were made for the Trusteeship Council.[21]

However, even there the colonial question *per se* was not presented as an obligation to emancipate the colonies. Chapter XI, bearing the title, "Declaration Regarding Non-Self-Governing Territories", was inserted into the Charter to cover the colonial question, but it contains no definite legal obligations except for conscientious administration of the colonies. The concept of independence does not exist in this text. Independence is envisaged only for trust territories, which are the subject of the next chapter, "International Trusteeship System". The former mandate territories of the League of Nations and the colonies of the defeated adversaries from the Second World War were included among these territories. The mandate system of the League of Nations after the First World War comprised the colonies of the defeated enemies in that war.[22]

In short, at the end of the Second World War, the great powers and the other countries that they had invited to San Francisco did not essentially change the concepts of the League of Nations in regard to the colonial question. The general formulations on equal rights and human rights without distinction

---

[21] Cf. the text of the proposals of the great powers in the *Yearbook of the United Nations* 1946—1947, pp. 4—9.

[22] Compare Article 22 of Covenant of the League of Nations, *Droit international et histoire diplomatique, op. cit.*, p. 163 with the Dumbarton Oaks proposals and Chapter XI of the United Nations Charter.

as to race, sex, language, or religion changed nothing in this respect, because the rights of the peoples in the colonies were specially defined and very clearly limited in Chapter XI of the Charter.

In fact, efforts were redoubled to consolidate positions in overseas areas. Even during and immediately after the war, Great Britain did everything in its power to maintain its hold on India and its other colonies;[23] France first entered negotiations with Ho Chi Minh and then took up arms against the national liberation movements in its possessions in Indochina; and the Netherlands, first with the assistance of the British army and then with its own forces, doggedly fought to maintain its authority in Indonesia. At that time there were still no extensive movements for independence in Africa. However, in the Near and Middle East, the English and French gave up their occupation of Syria and Lebanon only under the pressure of public opinion aroused in the world during the debates in the Security Council, and the Soviet Union withdrew its occupational forces from part of Iran's territory in similar circumstances.[24]

The zeal with which these countries vied to extend their influence in the world was no longer inspired so much by traditional economic interests in expanding markets and procuring sources of raw materials. Economic considerations increasingly gave way to an overriding ambition to acquire global footholds in the cold war. Although raw materials and oil had been of prime importance during the war, and although immediately after the war they were still considered very important, already in these first post-war days the cold war logic began to take precedence.

A situation thus arose that was prejudicial to the aspirations of the colonial peoples. Their aspirations encountered opposition from the old colonial mentality that had even been preserved in the United Nations Charter, as well as from the efforts of the two former allied camps to spread their influence and to strengthen their positions in the global confrontation which had arisen between them.

---

[23] W. Churchill, *op. cit.*, Vol. 4, *The Hinge of Fate*, pp. 204—221 et passim.
[24] *Yearbook of the United Nations 1946—1947*, pp. 327—345.

THE BEGINNING OF THE ANTI-COLONIAL MOVEMENT

From its very inception, the confrontation between the blocs was characterized not only by conflicts between countries taken as a whole, but also by efforts to secure maximum support within the opposing country through ideological slogans and attempts to make use of whatever forces could be mobilized. This strategy was, of course, also applied in the overseas areas, i. e., in the colonial empires and later in the emancipated countries.

Concomitant with this development of relations among the great powers, the liberation struggle in the colonies and especially in Southeast Asia took on momentum. The first wedge was driven into the colonial empires when Great Britain was forced by India's resistance to grant it independence. But an important factor in the successful development of anti-colonial movements was the fact that during the war the colonial powers had not been able to maintain control over many overseas areas. This was particularly true of the colonial possessions in the Far East and in Southern Asia, which had fallen under the occupation of Japan.

After Japan's defeat, the national liberation movements were no longer willing to exchange their liberation from the Japanese for a return to the domination of the old colonial power. The upheavals of the war had undermined the foundations of the colonial empires, but their statesmen were slow to realize this. While they were drafting proposals for the Charter and drawing up a political map of the post-war world in which they foresaw just one danger, just one possible conflict, and that was a renewal of German militarism, the world was actually developing along completely different lines. A new and fierce conflict in the very ranks of the Allies was coming to a head, and a new force had appeared on the world scene, the force of awakened nations, first in Asia, and then in Africa and all the other places where colonies existed.

These new forces of the anti-colonial movement were faced with a situation after the war which gave them no choice but to pursue their goals and aspirations through persistent struggle. The conflict which was developing among the advanced industrial states was outside the domain of their immediate interests, while both sides in this conflict showed a lack of concern for the true aspirations of these peoples for emancipation. The leaders of the anti-colonial movements quickly realized that the Allied victory in the war had not solved all their problems, but at the same time that the exhausted condition of the colonial powers provided a good opportunity to wage a resolute struggle for emancipation.

Thus three groups of countries appeared on the world stage after the Second World War: the divided former allies, between whom a confrontation was shaping up later to be known as the "cold war", and the third force, represented first by the liberation movements in the colonies followed by the newly emancipated countries which refused to join either of the two sides in the cold war. This third side of the triangle was not the product of non-involvement at the time the conflict arose, i. e., during the war, but only appeared after the cold war had already begun. During the war it had not even existed, and insofar as a liberation movement was extant, it did not have a clear policy on international relations, much less in regard to the war and the great powers which were the main protagonists in it.[25]

The new countries came into being after a long struggle which had little to do with the changing relations among the advanced countries, and particularly among the great powers right before and during the Second World War. When these countries took their place as independent factors in world affairs, the new relations among the great powers and among the advanced countries had already been formed. They entered a situation in the world in which they had to find their bearings and decide on a policy with an eye to their immediate political and economic interests as well as their long-range interests, in accordance with their general position as new, relatively weak and, most important, economically underdeveloped countries.

---

[25] In *The Hinge of Fate*, Churchill describes the differences between Nehru and Gandhi in their attitude on Great Britain and its military efforts in the war with Japan. Nehru was inclined to assist the British war effort, whereas Gandhi insisted on an uncompromising stand towards the British, reasoning that an independent India could better defend itself against the Japanese. In his book, *The Discovery of India*, Nehru maintains that there was no disagreement between himself and Gandhi on this point, but he does cite differences between them on whether to incite mass actions during the war which could hinder the war effort.

They were also faced with already formulated principles of international cooperation and the finished structure of the new world organization, so that they had no choice but to enter into its framework. They found a situation in which it was completely normal for advanced countries to change their political orientation and their partners according to need and always to find justification by invoking their proclaimed "higher" interests.

At the same time, they could not help realizing that trade and economic relations were serving more and more as weapons in political disputes. Whether it be from internationally regulated sanctions, group decisions, boycott or blockade, or other more subtle forms of using economic relations in the political struggle, the new countries understood that they were exposed to great dangers. Economic weakness was not only a source of danger from direct military attack and aggression, but it could be used against them even without open hostilities. Their powers of resistance to such measures were even less than their ability to withstand armed attack militarily. The guerilla wars in Indochina and Indonesia immediately after the war showed that there were even considerable possibilities in this respect. It is therefore understandable that one of their main concerns had to be a rapid economic development and the strengthening of their economic position in the world, along with an improvement in relations in the world market.

Nevertheless, from the very beginning of their existence, the new countries had to take an active part in international affairs; in the interest of their own survival they had to try and fashion a new world in which they could develop and overcome their weaknesses and poverty. They themselves were the product of great changes which in turn generated further changes for which they prepared the ground. They resulted in an ever increasing number of new countries in the material sense and, in the moral sense, in the awakening of hundreds of millions of people in parts of the world which until that time had submitted to the colonial system.

These new countries and their role in the world had not been anticipated in the post-war world system designed by the great powers before the end of the war. They had to force their way into this system with great difficulty. It had been generally accepted that the First World War marked the end of the era in which Europe was the center and in which ascendancy in Europe automatically implied ascendancy in the world. The world community now expanded to include advanced countries outside Europe, first of all the U. S. A. and Japan.

THE CREATION OF A POST-WAR GLOBAL SYSTEM OF INTERNATIONAL RELATIONS

The coalescence of international relations in various parts of the world into a global system only began to take place after the Second World War. By then the structure based on relations among the three factions in Europe (the Western powers, the Soviet Union and the Rome-Berlin-Tokyo Axis), which had dominated in the years before the war, ceased to be paramount. An era of new world relations was opened in which the countries of the so-called third world kept aloof from the structures and combinations organized and led by the great powers. This new part of the world, which changed the character of the political background against which the confrontation between the blocs and great powers was being played out, became an increasingly important new element in international relations. Its role, of course, went much further than just providing a new and heretofore unknown ground for the activities of the great powers; the third world became an active participant in world affairs, and it is on this point that we should dwell for a clearer understanding of the role of nonalignment in international relations.

Nonalignment emerged as a third element in what had been virtually a bipolar setup of international relations. This bipolarity developed very rapidly along the line East-West and remarkably thoroughly wiped out the division which had led to the war and which cost mankind so many human and material losses. In other words, the end of the Second World War had changed the world beyond recognition and instituted new patterns often resulting from radical internal changes in various countries, and so, understandably, it marked the beginning of extreme general insecurity and an intensive arms race which at times was attended by very bitter local armed clashes.

Special mention should be made of the internal weaknesses in many countries, which resulted from a decline in economic activity or war devastation, as well as from the disruption of world trade patterns. The general economic instability in those parts of the world which suffered the direct effects of the war and serious economic disability led to an uncommon dependence and feeling of insecurity both from an assumed external threat and from internal disruptions fomented from the other side of the cold war barrier.

POST-WAR DISTURBANCES IN THE WORLD ECONOMY

The economic disruptions in the world are best illustrated if the participation of various parts of the world in the general world GNP in the last normal pre-war years is compared with that in 1949 after the immediate aftereffects of the war had been overcome. According to U. N. statistics, the share in the world GNP of the advanced regions not directly affected by the war (the U. S. A., Canada, Australia and New Zealand) rose from 29.6 per cent to 44.4 per cent, whereas the share of Europe as a whole, including the Soviet Union, dropped from 46.6 per cent to 38.7 per cent. The remainder of the overall world GNP was accounted for by the underdeveloped continents, which had been severely affected by the advanced regions' concentration on the war effort, or even by war operations (particularly in the case of Asia). Their share fell from 23.8 per cent to 16.9 per cent.

It is interesting that the share of the United States alone rose from 25.9 per cent to 40.9 per cent, whereas the share of the other countries in this group (Canada, Australia and New Zealand) remained virtually unchanged, with a negligible drop from 3.7 per cent to 3.5 per cent.[26] According to these U. N. statistics, which must be taken with certain reservations in view

---

[26] *Materijali o kretanju u svjetskoj privredi i trgovini* (Data on Trends in the World Economy and Trade), Ed. Slobodan Branković, Institute of International Politics and Economy, Beograd 1964 (mimeographed), p. 14.

of the difficulty of making a comparison of this kind for a period of great upheavals, certain basic trends are nevertheless visible. The United States emerged from the war considerably stronger economically in comparison with the rest of the world. America's success had a very adverse effect on Europe, especially Western Europe, which prior to the war had had a major role in the world economy in general and in world industrial production in particular. It fell behind during the war and never recovered its former position again.

The U.N. statistics on world industrial production also show that between 1938 and 1948, industrial production in the U.S.A. increased some 70 per cent, whereas West European industrial output had by 1948 barely reached its level of ten years earlier.[27] In later years the ratio of industrial output changed considerably in Europe's favor, so that North America (the U.S.A. and Canada) accounted for 48 per cent of world industrial output in 1962, in comparison with 47 per cent in 1938. Over the same interval Western Europe still did not reach the volume of its pre-war output, since its share fell from 39.5 per cent to 35.6 per cent.[28] Although these figures are incomplete,[29] they can nevertheless serve as a basis for assessing relative economic capability and changes in the balance of power between Western Europe and North America.

As a corrective to these figures it should also be taken into consideration that all the countries in Western Europe were outstripped by West Germany, which had been particularly hard hit by the war and whose industrial production in 1948 barely exceeded 50 per cent of its 1938 production.[30] The trends in other countries were somewhat more favorable, but in view of later development, the above outline gives a fairly accurate picture of the general situation in Western Europe after the war, i. e., in the period relevant to this consideration.

Eastern Europe emerged from the war as a significant factor

---

[27] *Monthly Bulletin of Statistics*, Statistical Office of the U.N., July 1948, pp. 32—35.

[28] *Materijali o kretanju u svjetskoj privredi i trgovini, op. cit.*, p. 42.

[29] There are no figures for the COMECON countries, the People's Republic of China, North Korea and North Vietnam.

[30] *Materijali o kretanju u svjetskoj privredi i trgovini, op. cit.*, p. 105.

first and foremost in the political domain. Its share in the world economy was not large, but it is significant that notwithstanding the extensive destruction, the Soviet Union recovered its position at the same time as Western Europe decreased its share in the world economy. The Soviet Union's share in overall world income rose from 8.1 per cent in 1938, to 11.2 per cent in 1948.[31] But the fact should also be taken into account that after the outbreak of war in Western Europe, the Soviet Union carried on normal economic activities for nearly two years (from September 1, 1939, to June 22, 1941).

The role of the Soviet Union and the countries closely linked with it grew in the years after the war, owing to rapid economic development and particularly the fast rate of industrialization of those areas which had been traditionally poorly developed. This development greatly increased the political importance of this area during the post-war years. The initial economic weakness of these countries did not substantially affect relations within Europe, because in Western Europe, too, the economic situation was critical and required exceptionally great efforts to overcome the problems of economic slowdown and obsolete equipment and organization and to create conditions for a steady growth.

On the basis of all this we can roughly describe the world situation in the early post-war years as the beginning of a new era in international relations. As has been mentioned, a world pattern had evolved, comprising three categories of countries: the advanced countries of the West, including Oceania (Australia and New Zealand) and Japan, then the countries grouped around the Soviet Union, at first only in Europe but later in Asia as well,[32] and, finally, the third world, which had become a distinct element in world affairs, especially after the successful decolonization in Southeast Asia, and which took on even greater importance with the inclusion of Africa.

This division can also be defined according to the type and character of the economies of these categories of countries. The advanced countries of the West have a capitalistic system

---

[31] *Ibid.*, p. 14.

[32] China is included here, since the conflict between China and the Soviet Union took on importance only in the 1960s and gave a new turn to the course of international relations.

dominated by private ownership over the means of production; the socialist countries grouped around the Soviet Union have state ownership of the means of production and a state monopoly in foreign trade, whereas the third world is primarily characterized by its low level of development, in respect to both labour productivity and social structures. Furthermore, this part of the world is not homogeneous, for there are very large quantitative differences in it,[33] as well as extreme variations in respect to the character of social and economic relations and particularly in respect to political institutions.

However, all countries can also be categorized by the fact that some are already more or less formed as modern nations and rank as modern societies with modern, although differing, institutions, whereas others are still in the process of general modernization in every respect. It is clear that the first category should include the countries of both the East and the West (in terms of the cold war division), whereas the second group should include the countries which were recently emancipated in the process of decolonization as well as those older countries in the same areas which had retained their titular independence but which differed very little in internal systems, level of development and social structures from the new countries. The latter would include, for instance, Ethiopia and Liberia in Africa and Thailand in Asia.

This classification is of course not based on the political orientation of various countries or their governments, but rather on the nature of their internal problems and the difficulties they face in international relations. In this respect they appear somewhat distinct from the countries of the first category, and they seem to be a group having certain common interests and problems. In regard to common and similar problems, it should again be stressed that the similarity lies in the essential nature of the problems and not in concrete issues. Thus, for example, two countries in this category may have completely different concrete problems arising from their different levels of development and

---

[33] In the 1950s, the GNP per capita of Burma was around 50 dollars, while in Venezuela it was 700 dollars. See: *Materijali o kretanju u svjetskoj privredi i trgovini, op. cit.,* p. 19.

types of basic economic activity, as well as some other factors, but nevertheless they have the similar basic problems of having to compete with highly advanced countries on unequal terms.

The mutual relations between these categories evolved in different and specific ways. As has been shown, the countries of the East and West in the advanced world crossed swords immediately after the end of the war in a large and unique conflict. This in turn gave rise to a rigid discipline in the two blocs and to the cold war. Since the countries directly involved in the cold war controlled over 83 per cent of the world income in 1949, their mutual conflicts naturally had a strong impact on events in the entire world. The preponderance of these countries in armaments was even greater, since practically all the modern weapons were in their hands. At that time there was still no armed force worthy of mention outside this area. However, military-strategical considerations aside, there still remained a large difference in economic development.

Per capita income is usually taken as a yardstick for measuring differences in economic development. This indicator, however, is not sufficiently reliable for a number of reasons. First of all, it is calculated on the basis of current prices of goods and services in different countries, and these prices in most of the underdeveloped countries are far from being freely formed in competition with supply in the world market. Furthermore, prices are most often reduced to a common denominator, i. e., the U.S. dollar, on the basis of an exchange rate which in the majority of cases, too, is not freely formed in the world market. Thus there is a double distortion in these comparative calculations. These distortions often add up to give a numerically more favorable picture than is really the case.

It is perhaps still more important that the resulting average incomes do not present a realistic picture in any case, since the distribution of income is carried out in different ways in the advanced and the poorly developed countries. Guy-Willy Schmeltz warns against this in his trilogy on the world economy prepared for *Institut des Sciences et Techniques humanes*. How income is distributed is best shown by the figures in the table published

39

in this work. Whereas in the U.S.A. working people earn three times the amount that is earned on capital investments, and in Great Britain this ratio is almost four to one, in the poorly developed countries the average ratio is one to one, and there are even cases when income from investments is greater than earnings acquired from work.[34]

Nevertheless we should mention that according to rough estimates, the average per capita income in the advanced countries at the beginning of the 'sixties was about $ 1,000, and in the poorly developed countries $ 100, with a maximum of $ 2,500 at one end of the scale, and $ 35 at the other.[35]

This pattern changed somewhat over the years; the economic strength of the countries involved in the cold war grew steadily, whereas increased emphasis on nuclear and other superweapons put the Soviet Union and the United States, the only two superpowers which boasted of the entire range of these weapons, into a class by themselves. In descending order came the countries having some nuclear weapons (Britain, France and China), and finally countries with modern conventional armaments. The new countries of the third world found themselves in an even more unenviable position because of their backwardness in this respect as well.

Another important characteristic of this development was that from the military aspect, although not also economically, the two sides in the cold war struck a kind of equilibrium between them. In other words, political, economic and military development may have been motivated in all these countries by the cold war, but it is nevertheless at a level and in a category which are beyond the reach of the underdeveloped countries of the rest of the world.[36]

In contrast with the development of the advanced countries, the third world was primarily concentrating on liberating itself

---

[34] Guy-Willy Schmeltz, *L'economie du tiers monde*, La Colombe, Paris 1965, pp. 25 and 26.

[35] *Materijali o kretanju u svjetskoj privredi i trgovini*, *op. cit.*, pp. 29 and 30.

[36] A certain exception in this respect is China, which by virtue of its size, large population and internal system managed to achieve a limited military nuclear potential in the 1960s. Of course China has still not achieved an offensive military potential measuring up to that of the superpowers, but it has shown that it is capable of doing so and also that it possesses an extraordinarily large defensive military potential.

from colonialism and on solving the basic problems of internal development, mainly accelerated economic growth. But this problem, which was given top priority after the gaining of independence, brought in its wake a host of other problems. All of them faced the problems of the modernization of society, since otherwise economic growth was not possible. Industrialization cannot take place either in a feudal or in a tribal or caste system.

Economic development taken alone created new problems. It made possible improvements in public health and social services, in living conditions and in the control of disease. In fact, a prerequisite for rapid economic development was improvement in these services and energetic measures to eradicate the diseases, such as malaria and various intestinal disorders, which greatly sapped the working ability of the population as a whole. Economic development would not have been possible without the eradication of these illnesses, but this at the same time disturbed the balance between the birth rate and mortality in all the underdeveloped countries of the world.[37]

These public health and social measures particularly reduced infant mortality, with a resulting sharp rise in the population growth rate.[38] Thus the sudden population increase not only put a drain on food supplies, but also produced a very strong pressure on all social services and the economic infrastructure, which in any case were deficient. In some areas, particularly in Southeast Asia and the Far East, there was a considerable increase in population density, which in the majority of the countries in this area had always been relatively high. In all these countries, however, the rapid growth in the population was not accompanied by an equivalently rapid economic growth, so that stagnation set in and the growth rate of per capita income dropped off.

These problems and the processes of development which they set into motion were also greatly hindered by the frictions between different nationalities and disputes about boundaries, which in most of those countries had been drawn by the colonial powers. The conflicts arising from this were not restricted to

---

[37] Carlo Cipolla, *The Economic History of World Population*, Penguin Books, London 1965, pp. 80—81.
[38] *Ibid.*, p. 83.

internal affairs, but also affected relations with other, especially neighboring, countries.

The insecurity and instability of the general world situation could not, therefore, be attributed to the same reasons, nor do they have the same character in the developed and underdeveloped parts of the world. Whereas the internal problems of the industrially advanced world were due to different social and political systems based on modern economics and social structures, the underdeveloped countries faced completely different problems which resulted from their backwardness. Whereas the relations in the North were sharply polarized (especially in the critical first years after the war), relations in the South were diverse and of a local character, because of unsolved internal problems of development and because social processes there had only entered the era of the creation of modern societies. In short, in the North there was a confrontation between societies which had passed through the many phases of development and were materially advanced, whereas in the South enormous efforts were made to make up for the time lost under colonialism. The battle for supremacy in the North was offset by the struggle for survival and the minimal advance that was necessary in the South.

*

* *

The dramatic events which led to the outbreak of the Second World War and to the post-war grouping of countries deeply shook the foundations of international relations. Shock waves were felt both in the internal affairs of various nations and in international relations. Already shaken by the great disturbances of the First World War and movements resulting from it, the system of social values underwent further, fateful changes in the period of the Second World War.

It is no exaggeration to say that the acceptance of hierarchical patterns in social and political relationships had been challenged still during World War I; this challenge led to a thorough revision of values and existing systems, particularly following the events of the largest war in history. The changes brought about by the Second World War considerably altered the way of life, social relationships and political climate in countries in all parts of the globe.

What we are mainly concerned with here is the loss of confidence in and the refusal to accept the special role of the great powers as political leaders and their hegemony in international affairs. Their behavior and the damage they inflicted on one another in the political, diplomatic and military spheres while stripping each other's ideological and political facades, encouraged a novel aspiration towards equal relations in the world. However much the post-war history may have vindicated these aspirations, their appearance certainly did bring about deep and far-reaching changes in international relations.

On the ruins of the broken and discredited moral values of the great powers, which had previously served as the basic criterion of social and political values in the world, there arose the new self-confidence of the previously oppressed nations, which expected to take part in the creation of values and to decide on their own ideals and aims of political and social development. The emancipation of the colonies was the first goal to be achieved through the thus awakened consciousness. However, as we shall see further on, this is just one of the elements of the development which was to spread to all continents.

The general suspicion that no one won the Second World War was soon borne out in reality. Neither international peace nor any of the aims for which the war had been fought were achieved, except for the defeat of the states grouped around the Berlin-Rome-Tokyo Axis. The most significant aspect of this strange situation was not the fact of a new confrontation within the war coalition, but rather the breakdown of the entire system of relations in the world. The authority and prestige of the great powers had suffered a decisive blow.

All the previous empires and systems of relations were founded on the material supremacy of the leading powers. Nonetheless, they did not apply their force in everyday problems, nor did they threaten to use force if any state did not respect the rules of the game. They were able to survive primarily because they were accepted, either as a necessity, or as the least of all possible evils, or simply out of awe for the powerful and their superiority, which after all was also characteristic of previous hierarchical social systems on a national scale. This acceptance of the hierarchical structure of international relations broke down as the result of the events and behavior of the great powers in the Second World War. The world found itself faced with an acute revolutionary crisis in international relations. The overwhelming majority of mankind rebelled against the existing order and began to dismantle the colonial empires.

B. DECOLONIZATION AND THE EMERGENCE OF "NEW COUNTRIES" NATIONAL LIBERATION MOVEMENTS IN SOUTHEAST ASIA AT THE END OF THE SECOND WORLD WAR

The Second World War did not solve the problem of relations among the great powers, nor did it create conditions for harmonious cooperation among the countries which had fought together in it. In a certain sense it could be said that the war simply did a political reshuffle and thus created conditions for new conflicts or, more precisely, for a continuation of power politics and preparations for a new war with a different alignment of powers. However, this would not be quite true, because the war also had other, more far-reaching consequences: it profoundly affected all the states and political systems and structures which rested on the domination of one nation over another and upset the internal social relationships in all the countries which in some way had been involved in it.

These developments caused the breakdown of political systems in a number of countries, principally in Eastern Europe, and heralded the end of the colonial system. The latter of the two phenomena is of particular interest, because it resulted in the formation of a large number of new and independent states, among which the nonaligned movement has its most active supporters. The intensive decolonization after the Second World War was not only the background against which the policy of nonalignment evolved, but was in fact the point of departure for this movement. As shall be shown later, the demand for complete decolonization was the first policy on which the non-aligned countries initiated their own organized, international action.

The first successful drive against colonialism was begun in Southeast Asia. This was understandable, because the Second World War made the strongest impact on the political development in this area of the colonial empires. During the war Japan occupied French Indochina as well as Burma and Malaya, which belonged to Great Britain. Dutch possessions in Indonesia were likewise under the Japanese occupation. Japanese divisions also penetrated the territory of British India, at its easternmost point bordering on Burma.

The breakup of the colonial empires in Southeast Asia during the war did not lead to emancipation and independence, but rather to Japanese occupation. But this occupation was a temporary military expedient and could not have evolved into a lasting structure of colonial power. The time was too short, and the final status of these areas remained unsettled, depending on the final outcome of the war. What is more, Japan had a great need for its war effort of the raw materials abundantly available in those areas. Confronted with an anti-colonial mood, Japan was as tolerant as possible of the national liberation movements in these countries.

Political crisis came to surface in virtually all these areas after Japan's defeat, when the European powers tried to restore their former colonial authority. But the crisis also gripped India, which had not been occupied by Japan. Actually, it set in while the war was still on. In his war memoirs, Churchill vividly described the situation that had come about: "The atmosphere in India deteriorated in a disturbing manner with the westward advance of Japan into Asia. The news of Pearl Harbour was a staggering blow. Our prestige suffered with the loss of Hong Kong. The security of the Indian subcontinent was not directly endangered." Churchill then proceeded to describe the political situation which had arisen since India "was threatened for the first time under a British rule with large-scale foreign invasion by an Asiatic Power. The stresses latent in Indian politics, grew. Although only a small extremist section, led by men such as Subhas Bose, were directly subversive and hoped for an Axis victory, the powerful body of articulate opinion which supported Gandhi ardently believed that India should remain passive and neutral in the world conflict... The peril to India might possibly only consist in her link with the British Empire. If this link could be snapped surely India could adopt the position of Eire. So, not without force, the argument ran".[39]

The description of prevailing political views and moods, given by Jawaharlal Nehru in his book, *The Discovery of India*, somewhat differs from that by Churchill. Nehru wrote as a British prisoner in the fortress of Ahmadnagar, where he spent almost three entire years, from August 9, 1942, to March 28, 1945. "There were many trends in public opinion," says Nehru, "as was natural in such a vast country and at such a time of crisis. Actual pro-Japanese sentiment was practically nil, for no one wanted to change masters, and pro-Chinese feelings were strong widespread. But there was a small group which was indirectly pro-Japanese in the sense that it imagined that it could take advantage of a Japanese invasion for Indian freedom. They were influenced by the broadcasts being made by Subhas Chandra Bose, who had secretly escaped from India the year before."[40]

Nehru was referring here to the situation which had arisen after Japan had already entered the war, i.e., at the beginning of 1942, when the British sent the Stafford Cripps mission to convince the Congress Party to cooperate in the war effort in the face of the great danger of the Japanese invasion of India. Nehru expressly stated that "in spite of past history and all that had happened, we were eager to offer our co-operation in the war and especially for the defense of India, subject necessarily to a national government which would enable us to function in the co-operation with other elements in the country and to make the people feel

---

[39] W. Churchill, *op. cit.*, Vol. 4, *The Hinge of Fate*, pp. 205 and 206.
[40] Jawaharlal Nehru, *The Discovery of India*, The John Day Company, New York 1946, p. 478.

46

that it was really a national effort and not an imposed one by outsiders who had enslaved us. There was no difference of opinion on this general approach among congressmen as well as most others...".[41] Furthermore, he expressly denounced Churchill's Great Britain for trying to preserve British domination in India at all costs. "But what could we do unless some door was open for honorable cooperation," complained Nehru.[42] He went on to decline responsibility for deteriorated relations with London and showed how Churchill's harsh and uncompromising policy led to the break in talks and how the wrongful arrest of the Congress leaders provoked spontaneous demonstrations which were then suppressed in blood.[43]

Great Britain managed to retain its positions in India, partly through cruel repressions against the Congress Party activists and partly owing to the successful military action against the Japanese in the border region with Burma. There a successful offensive was begun in the early months of 1944 and was continued in the following year.

As Churchill himself admitted, the majority of politically active Indians had decided in favor of nonalignment as early as during the war.[44] But these policies could not be put into practice at that time. The Congress Party and all other organizations representing Indian public opinion were under strong pressure from British authorities, and the majority of leaders were interned or confined in places from which they could not instigate intensive activities. The intensification of political life could only come after the war.

The history of this period is sufficiently well known, and there is no need to repeat it here. However, for an understanding of later policies and the influence of India among the nonaligned countries and in the world, it must be pointed out that the Congress Party had always had clear ideas about the future orientation of its foreign policy. This is shown by a statement made by Jawaharlal Nehru on September 24, 1946, when he was Vice-

---

[41] *Ibid.*, p. 450.
[42] *Ibid.*, p. 450.
[43] *Ibid.*, pp. 494—501.
[44] W. Churchill, *op. cit.*, *The Hinge of Fate*, pp. 214—221.

Premier and foreign minister in the last British government in India. The following excerpt from the statement is particularly eloquent:

"In the sphere of foreign affairs, India will follow an independent policy, keeping away from the power politics of groups aligned one against another. She will uphold the principle of freedom for dependent peoples and will oppose racial discrimination wheresoever it may occur. She will work with other peace-loving nations for international cooperation and goodwill without the exploitation of one nation by another. It is necessary that with the attainment of her full international status India should establish contact with all the great nations of the world, and that her relations with her neighbouring countries in Asia should become still closer."[45]

Although India was still under British rule, it was a transitional period leading to full independence. In view of this, and because of the close relationships between Great Britain and the United States dating back to the time of joint war efforts in this area, India had a kind of quasi-diplomatic relation with the U.S.A. A similar situation applied in respect to relations with China, with which there also had been close cooperation during the war. In his last sentence, Nehru alludes primarily to the establishment of relations with the Soviet Union and with countries of the Near East.

After gaining independence on August 15, 1947, India began to implement the policies laid forth in the above statement. It goes without saying that in addition to the countries mentioned, India established diplomatic relations with the rest of the world. However, relations with the Soviet Union and countries of Eastern Europe as a new quality in international affairs, were especially important for India's foreign policy orientation, and so were its relations with the Arab countries of the Near East. After the war these countries acquired full independence, although their position as Category A mandate territories even before the war was different from the status of classical colonies;[46]

---

[45] *India Office Bulletin*, quoted in *Keesing's Contemporary Archives* 1946—1948, p. 8169.
[46] See Article 22 of the Covenant of the League of Nations, particularly paragraph 4.

their independence was an important step towards the creation of a post-war "third world".

The emancipation and independence of the Arab countries of the Near East did not at first produce any major changes in their internal social and political systems, but some of them soon began to press for genuine equality and more favorable conditions in the world market and in international relations. India's relations with these countries were the first diplomatic contact and international cooperation among countries which gained independence after the Second World War. Subsequent changes in some countries of the Near East, and particularly Nasser's accession to power in Egypt, led to very close relations between the Near East and Southeast Asia, two areas where nonalignment, as a universal movement of new countries, made its first steps.

This relationship, however, had its own serious problems. The Arab countries were very militant Moslem states, in which Islam was the state religion and had a very strong influence on public life. At this time India was in the midst of a fierce struggle between the Moslems and Hindus, which even resulted in the forming of a special Moslem state of Pakistan at the time when independence was granted. The Indian government had to use all its skill and tact to maintain and foster friendly relations with the Moslem countries of the Middle East at a time when it itself was in conflict with one of the largest Moslem countries in the world, Pakistan.

At the same time India tried to develop close relations with its immediate neighbor to the east, Burma. Friendship in this quarter was important to relieve the situation in the eastern part of the country, where relations with the eastern part of Pakistan were strained. This friendship was possible because in Burma, as well as in Indochina and Indonesia, at the end of the war there was very strong opposition to the return of the old colonial rule.

The national liberation movement in Burma developed under conditions differing from those in India. Burma had been occupied by the Japanese and attained independence after the vicissitudes of occupation, war on its own territory, and the refusal to accept again the pre-war *status quo*. In the dramatic events at the end of the war, the leader of the national liberation movement, Aung San, was killed together with the majority of the leaders of this movement on July 19, 1947, at the time when India was preparing for full independence. The first prime minister of independent Burma was U Nu, who succeeded Aung San, and independence was declared on January 4, 1948. The first comprehensive statement on foreign policy was made on June 17 of the same year. This statement was made by U Tin Tut, first minister of foreign affairs, and the following excerpt is of special significance:

"What the Government seeks is to extend its political and economic relationships with the outside world. Burma has no desire to be entangled in any alignment of world Powers, and wishes to be in friendly relationship with all other countries. She desires to adhere to the friendly relationship already entered into with the U.S.A., the U.K. and other countries in Western Europe and China. These countries are themselves in friendly political and economic relationship with Russia and other countries under the "new democracy", and in seeking to do the same. Burma hopes her relationship with the Western democracies and with China will in no way be impaired."[47]

This and Nehru's statement are the first foreign policy pronouncement by the new countries of Southeast Asia at the time when they gained independence. The national liberation struggle in the other countries of this area was much more complicated and greatly under the influence of developments in the world in general, and of the cold war in particular. In Indonesia there was a long drawn-out and bitter struggle against the British troops which soon after Japan's defeat had come to the aid of Britain's ally, the Netherlands, since it was not able at that time to send armed forces to Indonesia. Later Dutch forces continued the struggle, but full independence was eventually gained in 1949.

Indonesia expressed its basic principles in the very first phase of its long armed and diplomatic struggle for full independence and recognition. The Indonesian government sent the

---

[47] *Burma Information Bulletin*, Rangoon, quoted in *Keesing's Contemporary Archives 1948—1950*, p. 9428.

parliament a political statement on September 2, 1948, which stated in part: "Have the Indonesian people fighting for their freedom no other course of action open to them than to choose between being pro-Russian or pro-American? Is there no other position that can be taken in the pursuit of our national ideals? The Indonesian Government is of the opinion that the position to be taken is that Indonesia should not be a *passive* party in the area of international politics but that it should be an *active* agent entitled to decide its own standpoint... The policy of the Republic of Indonesia must be resolved in the light of its interests and should be executed in consonance with the situation and facts it has to face... The line of Indonesia's policy cannot be determined by the bent of the policy of some other country which has *its* own interests to service."[48]

As is known, Indonesia was not in a position immediately after this proclamation to put its intentions into practice — to implement the policy of independence and non-submission to any great power whatsoever. The new republic still had to contend with military intervention and wage a long struggle. But when the country was finally freed, its policy reflected the same basic tenets which had been proclaimed simultaneously with the statements made in Burma and even earlier in India. Thus in those countries which were the first to succeed in achieving their independence after the war a foundation was laid for a policy which virtually all the emancipated countries in Asia and Africa were to follow later on.

In Indochina there was also an armed struggle, since France was not willing to recognize the national liberation movement as representative of the people and also did not wish to renounce its position as a colonial power. Here the struggle for independence was the most difficult and it is still going on today, twenty-five years after the defeat of Japan. This protracted armed and political struggle has given its stamp to the internal development and international relations in all of Indochina, and particularly in Vietnam.

It is a characteristic of these countries that the movement

---

[48] Mohammad Hatta, *Indonesia's Foreign Policy*, "Foreign Affairs", No. 3, 1953, pp. 441—452.

which led the struggle for national independence also formulated the policy of the new sovereign state. The countries in which neither the victory nor the defeat of the liberation movement was achieved — like Vietnam — have had a different experience, which has been extremely difficult, drawn-out and bloody. India was the first in the world to achieve its goals. However, in all the countries of Southeast Asia the gaining of independence was attended by great upheavals and acute crises.

Whereas the crisis of Indochina, especially in Vietnam and to some extent in Laos, was due to outside intervention, which was also a feature of the independence struggle in Indonesia, in India the problem was the outbreak of internal conflicts and bloodshed as a result of conditions inherited from the past. The division of British India into India and Pakistan was followed by fierce and mass clashes in which many Moslems and Hindus alike lost their lives. This bloodshed and migration of millions who fled across the newly drawn borders between the two states after independence greatly handicapped the two new countries.

Burma and Indonesia were also torn by internal conflicts and even armed struggle between embattled political movements. These countries spent a great deal of energy in putting their internal affairs into order and equipping themselves to take an effective role in world affairs. Foreign intervention in Indonesia began immediately after Japan's defeat, when the attack by British troops was later joined by Dutch units, which took over the fight. In Burma strong foreign intervention took place after the success of the revolution in China, when various defeated units of the old regime transferred to Burma and joined with movements against the Rangoon government. This situation lasted for several years, and Burma brought it before the United Nations for discussion in 1952.

In the other countries of Southeast Asia the national liberation movements were sooner or later put down, but the *status quo* was never restored. All the countries in this area gradually achieved their independence unless, as Thailand, they had already been formally set up as independent states before the war. However, national governments were formed not after an open and successful rebellion, but in the course of a gradual evolution under the control of the colonial power. Power was not taken by revolutionaries, but rather by representatives of those groups and classes which had cooperated with the authorities of the foreign rulers.

Thus there were considerable differences, both in internal development and in foreign policy orientation, between these two categories of newly liberated Asian countries. Whereas India, Indonesia, Burma and Cambodia had followed the policy of nonalignment from the very beginning, Ceylon, Malaya, Singapore and the Philippines retained their ties with the West. This classification however is not so simple; Pakistan also aligned itself on the side of the West, since the tradition of the Moslem League differed from Congress policies before as well as during the war, although antagonism with India, and particularly disputes over Kashmir, probably played the most important role. A sharp division occurred in Vietnam, where parts of the country aligned themselves with the opposing sides in the cold war, as had been the case in Korea.

DECOLONIZATION IN THE NEAR EAST AND IN AFRICA

Formation of independent states in the Near East marked the first step towards decolonization in the world. Demands for independence had already been heard in Asia during the war, and ferment in India had its roots in activities immediately after the First World War. However, independence was achieved only in 1947. Such trends, and particularly the development of political philosophy and the activity of the Indian Congress, are of inestimable value in examining the movement for emancipation in the countries of Asia and Africa and shall therefore receive more detailed consideration further on.

The formation of independent Arab states in the Near East was the first step in a broad and intensive anti-colonial movement which at that time had not been recognized either by the statesmen of the colonial empires or by the fighters against colonialism themselves. The struggle to create independent Arab states in this region began during the First World War, when the Arabs rebelled in 1916. The Entente promised them liberation from the Ottoman Empire and independence when the war was over. After the war, instead of granting independence, the countries of the Entente attempted to implement their plan to carve up the Ottoman Empire and impose their influence in the Arab world of the Near East.

Between the two world wars the Arab states gained independence one after another. During the Second World War the authority of European imperial powers in this region did not completely break down, but it did weaken under the blows of the Hitler war machine. This gave new impetus to those who wanted to do away with the League of Nations mandate system in this area. While the war was still on, preparations were made to do away with the influence and domination of Great Britain and France and to set up a common Arab state. These plans were later changed, and instead of a common state, the Arab League was formed.

Immediately after the war the West European powers were openly challenged when they attempted to reestablish the old pre-war system. The dispute was ended when British and French troops were withdrawn from Syria and Lebanon, but Britain's other strongholds remained untouched. Full victory in the struggle for independence was blocked by another problem which had existed in this region since the First World War, the problem of the creation of Israel as the homeland of the Jews. It was promised in the Balfour Declaration at the time of the First World War, and the matter was revived during the Second World War as an effect of the Nazi persecution and extermination of the Jews.

Furthermore, the Arab states were headed by the governments and politicians who had in the past cooperated with Paris and London and were wary about revolutionary coups d'état in their countries, since these would threaten the special interests of those circles and classes from which these politicians stemmed. Thus the process of emancipation progressed in fits and starts until the end of the Second World War. Later, in new circumstances, this process was continued and will probably go on for

54

some time to come. All we can do at present is mark important events, such as the revolution which overthrew the monarchy in Egypt in 1952, the fall of the monarchy in Iraq in 1958, and the revolutionary coups d'état in Syria, Sudan, Yemen and Libya.

Except in Egypt, where after initial restiveness a relatively stable government was established, all other countries experienced new upheavals and frequent changes of government. Yet, in very general terms, the state of political relations in the Near East did not undergo any fundamental changes as a result of this restlessness following emancipation. The shaping of foreign policies and the building of a platform of nonalignment in these countries, although not so much subject to government instability, were nevertheless strongly influenced by the Palestinian problem.

This last issue helped to increase the already strong influence of Islam on the political life in these countries and at the same time to subordinate all other questions and interests, first to opposition against the creation of the state of Israel, and, once it was established, to the struggle against it. In the twenty-five years following the end of World War II, three wars were fought between Israel and the neighboring Arab countries, which left a very deep mark on Middle East relations. Significantly, even nonalignment and the concrete policies and actions of the Arab countries were constantly overshadowed by this central issue in their foreign policies.

While World War II was still ragging, renewed efforts were made to create the state of Israel, and the mass immigration of Jews to Palestine elicited strong protests from the Arabs. They were particularly hurt by the official support for the Jewish immigration from President Harry Truman, which denied the Arabs a potential ally in their efforts to weaken the British and French positions. An even more difficult situation arose when all the great powers endorsed the creation of the state of Israel, which was proclaimed on May 15, 1948, by a United Nations resolution.

In the wars which ensued, all the major powers helped Israel at one time or another. In the first war of 1948—49, Israel was helped by the U.S.S.R.; in the second war Israel went into military cooperation with Great Britain and France, whereas in later years and immediately before the June 1967 war, Israel enjoyed very strong support from the United States. In the first war the Arabs were backed by Great Britain, whereas in the second war both the U.S.S.R. and the United States sought in the United Nations the withdrawal of the British and French troops. The weapons used by the Arabs in the third war had been mostly received from the U.S.S.R., which gave the Arabs very significant material and diplomatic aid before, during and after that war.

The policy of nonalignment was formulated in the Middle Eastern countries gradually and under the strong influence of all the enumerated factors. Like India when she gained her independence, they also turned inwards to face their own problems, although in a different way and in different circumstances.

The process of decolonization in Africa south of the Sahara started later. The first breakthrough was the proclamation of Ghana's independence in 1958, followed by Guinea's secession from the French Union and by the French withdrawal from their other colonies on this continent, and finally by the evacuation of the remaining British colonies. This process took place at the time when the cold war was at its height, but also at the time when nonalignment had already made its appearance on the international scene. Consequently, these movements cannot be regarded as the original phenomena which helped to shape the platform of nonalignment. This also applies to the colonies elsewhere which have a relatively small number of inhabitants living mostly on small islands.

Furthermore, decolonization in its later years was concomitant with the third world's efforts to improve the economic position of the countries whose political problems were aggravated by an inherited economic backwardness. It was this last-mentioned circumstance that caused some of the newly formed countries to get together, seeking a remedy to the economic ills which followed immediately upon their independence.

The process of decolonization was, consequently, a prerequisite for the development of nonalignment on a world scale, inasmuch as this process engendered and multiplied those forces which embraced the policy of nonalignment, and it also served as a political school which helped countries to understand those problems that form the basis of the policy of nonalignment. The behavior of the great powers in trying to establish a new world order which would eliminate aggression coincided with their efforts to preserve their positions as colonial powers.

Consequently, decolonization, as a general rebellion against hegemony and power politics, was highly influential in shaping the foreign policy conceptions of the new countries. One of the tough problems which these countries soon had to face was their economic backwardness, which kept them in an unequal position in their relations with the more developed countries. Underdevelopment and slow economic growth caused internal instability and political problems which afforded opportunities for pressure from outside influences and even for open forms of intervention and interference in these countries' internal affairs.

During their conflicts and struggle for world supremacy, the great powers not only compromised themselves, but also lost the ability of impressing the colonial peoples with their superiority. The colonial rule and the dominant role of the great powers in the world were based on their material superiority and on the readiness of their underlings to accept their rule as a necessity if not as a product of inferiority. The military defeats in the Far East and in much of Southeast Asia increased dissatisfaction and sparked off a new and increasingly powerful world movement against colonialism. The hierarchical structure of world relationships suffered another heavy blow, which changed the course of world history.

C. THE INDIAN CONGRESS'S OWN ROAD IN THE STRUGGLE FOR INDIA'S INDEPENDENCE

India has special distinction in this study not only because it is the largest of the nonaligned countries or because it was first in the post-war wave of decolonization to acquire independence, but also because a continued liberation struggle in India lasted from the First World War until its independence in 1947 and inspired anticolonial movements in many other countries.

During the decades of struggle for independence, in peace and in war, India experienced all the basic problems of a liberation movement. In other words, India is undoubtedly the best example on which we can study in detail the ideological, political and economic problems of the struggle for independence and the gradual maturing of the conception of nonalignment.

It is, of course, not possible to give here a comprehensive or even a brief review of the overall activities and intensive intellectual efforts in one of the most significant epochs in India's history. However, we cannot touch on this experience without trying, even inadequately, to throw light on some especially significant developments. For this purpose we shall make a very brief reference to certain elements in the struggle of the Indian Congress which was the most important political force of British India and subsequently the political base of the new Indian state.

THE INDIAN CONGRESS
BETWEEN THE TWO WORLD WARS

The Indian Congress is the oldest and the most articulate anti-colonial movement, not only in Asia but in the world as a whole. It very early formulated both the policies of internal evolution, which meant in the first place breaking loose from the colonial power, and those for external relations. In his book, *The Discovery of India*, Nehru said that, "the Congress gradually developed a foreign policy, which was based on the elimination of political and economic imperialism everywhere and on the cooperation of free nations." This process started already in the 'twenties. "As early as 1920, a resolution on foreign policy was passed by the Congress, in which our desire to co-operate with other nations, and especially to develop friendly relations with all our neighboring countries was emphasized."[49]

Although other nations bordering on India did not follow the road of nonviolence mapped out by Mahatma Gandhi, still the imposing activity of Congress and its persistent struggle

---

[49] Jawaharlal Nehru, *The Discovery of India, op. cit.*, p. 422.

for independence wielded an influence in the entire area of Southeast Asia and well beyond in the whole world. India had some remarkable minds, which in politics as well as in culture stood out head and shoulders among the colonial peoples and reached the highest peaks in the world. Gandhi, Rabindranath Tagore and Nehru are undoubtedly among the greatest personalities of the twentieth century. It is therefore reasonable to study the evolution of nonalignment from the example of India, which made the first breakthrough in the liquidation of the colonial system and was the first stronghold of nonalignment.

We must, of course, always bear in mind that the movement in India was also defined under the strong influence of the very rich and highly original historical heritage of this great and complex country. If we attempted to study the evolution of the liberation movements with an historian's pretensions, we would have to study each country separately and in detail. However, our aim is much more limited. What we are attempting to do here is to show the extent to which the war-time upheavals influenced post-war foreign policies and to shed light on the political problems and conflicts which emerged during the war and which brought the colonial peoples into confrontation with two mighty powers fighting for supremacy.

It was a situation in which it was not easy to apply the maxim that my enemy's foe is my friend. True enough, there were individuals among the leading politicians, such as Subhas Chandra Bose in India, who attempted to follow this prescription through to the end. There were others who did so more subtly, and with much more reserve, and there were also moments when entire movements in Southeast Asia sought some kind of *modus vivendi* or temporary tacit and even explicit understandings with the Japanese invaders. All this is undoubtedly highly interesting for an historian, but it does not enter the framework of this study.

What is important for our purpose is to establish what the dilemmas were in India, how they created a difficult situation, and how this situation was handled by the politicians there. It is, namely, frequently said that the policy of nonalignment evolved from the struggle for independence and that subsequent independent governments were a continuation of the activities and policies of the liberation movements. This at first glance can be accepted as an obvious and acceptable description of the course of events. However, it must not be accepted uncritically, without research, that the policy of an opposition or a revolutionary movement will necessarily be continued by the government which later evolves from it. For instance, Congress's hostile stance vis-à-vis Great Britain gave way after independence to a relatively successful cooperation and friendship and even to continued membership in the British Commonwealth, without recognition of the British crown as a symbol of sovereignty. Accordingly, concrete policies and their evolution prior to and after accession to statehood shquld be examined.

A clear distinction must be made between Congress's struggle for independence in the years before the war, its policies during the war, and, finally, the policies formulated after independence, when Congress was no longer an opposition force, but the government of the newly created, independent state of India. There is no need to go into details about the first phase, when India's foreign policies were formulated in the pre-war years. At that time, problems appeared in the light of a clear and simple situation — the struggle for independence and the abolition of British rule in India.

As has been mentioned, the first articulate policy of Congress was made as early as 1920. At that time, after the First World War, Congress's renewed activities had taken on new breadth and vigor.[50] At first the movement concentrated on internal Indian problems, i. e. the struggle for independence. Gradually a platform was also developed to serve as a basis for policies on events in the outside world.

The evolution that Congress's 1920 policies had undergone seven years later is significant. As early as 1927, Congress debated its policy in the event of an outbreak of another large--scale war in which Great Britain would be involved. It was at the time of Locarno — before Hitler's rise to power, before Japan's invasion of the continent, before Italy's aggression in Ethiopia, and before the civil war in Spain — that Congress

---

[50] *Ibid.*, pp. 358—421.

considered it necessary to define its policy on an eventual war, and it shows just how much this question preoccupied the leaders of the Indian anti-colonial movement. They gave much thought to this problem, because it could cause new difficulties and repression as well as offer new opportunities for achieving independence; it could put India into an even more untenable and humiliating position, but could also strengthen its position vis-à-vis the colonial power.

The policy defined by Congress in 1927 reflected a situation which held out no immediate prospects for its taking power and assuming responsibility for administering the country. With reference to these decisions and later policies, Nehru said that Congress "declared that India could be no party to an imperialist war, and in no event should India be made to join any war without the consent of her people being obtained. In the years that followed, this declaration was frequently repeated and widespread propaganda was carried on in accordance with it. It became one of the foundations of Congress policy and, as it was generally accepted, of Indian policy. No individual or organization in India opposed it."[51]

This first stage in the shaping of a foreign policy was based on general assumptions regarding a possible war. It had more to do with bitter memories of India's humiliating position in World War I than with policy-making in response to a concrete threat of war. In a way, it could be described as a set of principles to be presented to the masses and to provide a comprehensive policy on all the problems of the political life of the movement and the country. It was an abstract policy, and it had to be reconsidered in the event of any concrete threat of war, particularly in the light of the increasing possibility for Congress to succeed and become a government.

This situation arose in the late 'thirties, when there was actually a genuine danger of war. War was no longer a hypothesis but an imminent reality, and Congress's activities in the new circumstances were able to change easily from general propaganda and protest into actions with immediate consequences

---

[51] *Ibid.*, pp. 423—424.

for the future of the country and the population. The problem of a war began to take on new dimensions. Policies were no longer black and white, and the horizon was darkened by mounting problems and doubts which soon advanced to the very centre of the stage.

"War between England and Germany," wrote Nehru, "became probable; and if this broke out, what then would our policy be? How would we reconcile the two dominating trends of our policy: opposition to British imperialism and opposition to fascism and nazism? How would we bring in line our nationalism and our internationalism? It was a difficult question in the existing circumstances, difficult for us, but offering no difficulty if the British government took a step to demonstrate to us that they had given up their imperialist policy in India and wanted to rely on popular good will."[52]

Even in retrospect,[53] Nehru considered the heart of the dilemma as ideological, a dilemma between nationalism and internationalism, even though the question was becoming an increasingly political matter of taking sides in a dispute liable to burst into an open war. Later, in the middle of the war, the political aspect of the problem became overriding. But more should be said about the ideological aspect before considering its political implications.

Congress was under the strong influence of Mahatma Gandhi's ideas, and his ideological views played a very important role early in the war. It is only in the last stage just before the banning of the Congress party and arrest of its leaders that the political aspect gained ascendancy. This aspect became, however, paramount only at the time of the government take-over and afterwards. But before the war and in the first years of the war, the ideological treatment of this dilemma led to disputes within Congress and to a disagreement between Nehru and Gandhi. A reconciliation took place, as is usual in such situations, on the level of political considerations and not through the victory of either side or even through an ideological compromise.

---

[52] *Ibid.*, p. 424.
[53] This text was written sometime during 1944 or at the beginning of 1945 while Nehru was imprisoned in the Ahmadnagar fortress in India.

THE INDIAN CONGRESS'S DILEMMAS AND SEARCH FOR NEW POLICIES DURING THE SECOND WORLD WAR

Events did not wait for a settlement of these internal disputes in Congress. War broke out, and the Congress Working Committee, after "long deliberation", published a resolution on September 14, 1939, in which it avoided giving an answer to the real dilemma and instead reported the existing dispute and placed the question before the public. "If the war is to defend the status quo, imperialist possessions, colonies, vested interests and privilege, then India can have nothing to do with it. If, however, the issue is democracy and a world order based on democracy, then India is intensely interested in it."[54] Such an attitude resolved nothing, because it only confirmed a general theoretical approach to the problem and gave no hint as to how to act in given circumstances.

In his writings while in prison, Nehru also called attention to the passage calling upon the British government to "declare in unequivocal terms what their war aims are in regard to democracy and imperialism and the new order that is envisaged, in particular, how these aims are going to apply to India and to be given effect to in the present. Do they include the elimination of imperialism and the treatment of India as a free nation whose policy will be guided in accordance with the wishes of her people?"[55] He goes on to say that this statement was published after"anxious deliberation" and with the intent of achieving a breakthrough in relations with England "so as to find some way to reconcile our eagerness to join in this world struggle with popular enthusiasm behind us and our passionate desire for freedom."[56]

Thus at the beginning of the war, Congress had a "dual policy", as Nehru himself called it. It has already been mentioned that behind this indefinite policy an ideological debate went on which was responsible for the vagueness about the basic problem of the moment. Gandhi was a firm and unwavering champion

---

[54] Jawaharlal Nehru, *The Discovery of India*, op. cit., 433—434.
[55] *Ibid.*, p. 435.
[56] *Ibid.*, p. 435.

of the methods of nonviolence, and he opposed any form of aggressive struggle for the goals of Congress. He extended his policy even to the situation arising from the Second World War. He came into conflict with the other leading politicians of Congress even before the war on questions regarding military training. His stand was an expression of deep and sincere humanism, which put the interests and future of mankind as a whole in first place. In accordance with these views, which had been developed before the war, the fate of India could never be placed above the higher interests of the principle of nonviolence and the broad interests of mankind.[57]

The crisis which took place in Congress over these dilemmas was temporarily pushed into the background by the arrest of the main leaders, but it again came to the fore when they were released in December of 1941. At that time, in the face of the threat from Japan, Gandhi insisted on a full commitment to nonviolence. This was the last ideological debate on the question of the war policy and on Britain's war effort. According to Nehru, Gandhi never raised this question again. "In later months, leading up to August 1942, Gandhiji's nationalism and intense desire for freedom made him even agree to Congress participation in the war if India could function as a free country."[58]

So ended an ideological debate which was understandable at a time when the general policies of the anti-colonial movement were being elaborated, but which necessarily led to confusion and hindered action at a time of crisis. "The practical statesman took precedence over the uncompromising prophet."[59] It should not be forgotten that at this time negotiations were already in progress between London and Congress and that, albeit with very strict limitations and without sufficient authorization and guarantees, the British government was willing to acknowledge

---

[57] On page 426 of *The Discovery of India*, Nehru quotes Gandhi's following words: "My idea of nationalism is that my country may become free, that if need be, the whole of the country may die, that the human race may live... I do want to think in terms of the whole world. My patriotism includes the good of mankind in general. Therefore my service of India includes the service of humanity." On pages 452 and 453, Nehru further illustrates the consistency of Gandhi's views, adding: "Very few persons in India accept in its entirety his doctrine of nonviolence or his economic theories yet very many have been influenced by them in some way or other."

[58] *Ibid.*, p. 455.

[59] *Ibid.*, p. 455.

Congress as the potential government of India. In his account of these twin discussions, within Congress and with the British, Nehru increasingly appears in the role of statesman and leader supplanting the earlier role of "prophet", ideological leader and revolutionary agitator of the masses.[60]

Thus the dilemma changed into a political issue to be resolved on the basis of expediency, an issue with no inherent value which takes on meaning only if it leads to a desired goal. The evolution of Congress took an important " leap", from the role of "prophet" to the role of "leader". At the same time, politics became a matter of statesmanship, and it is here that we can look for those elements which were later to develop into India's post-war policies and which developed into the policy of nonalignment. The question of nonviolence and the concepts connected with it were never again raised in Congress. "When later Sir Stafford Cripps came with his proposals, there was no question of nonviolence."[61]

In fact, mass actions during the war were always extremely restrained in India. "During the three years of war (until the dissolution of Congress in August 1942 — author's note) we had deliberately followed a policy of nonembarrassment, and such action as we had indulged it had been in the nature of symbolic protest".[62] What is more, according to Nehru, Congress was ready to cooperate for minimal concessions from London, but it was not prepared to completely renounce its demand for an independent role in the war effort. The question of the future of India after the war as opposed to its role during the war was never raised in this context at all.[63]

But Congress was still racked with painful internal discussions. The dilemma shifted to the political level. It was clear that in the given situation, as the rift with London and its emissary Sir Staf-

---

[60] It is interesting that in this part of his book on the development of India, in a discussion of the problems facing the Indian Congress during the war, Nehru quotes from a book on the art of war. He cites a paragraph from Liddell Hart's *The Strategy of Indirect Approach* on the relationship between politics and "truth". The following sentence from this quotation is particularly interesting: "The prophets must be stoned; that is their lot, and the test of their self-fulfillment. But a leader who is stoned may merely prove that he has failed in his function through a deficiency of wisdom, or through confusing his function with that of a prophet."

[61] Jawaharlal Nehru, *The Discovery of India, op. cit.*, p. 455.

[62] *Ibid.*, p. 482.

[63] *Ibid.*, p. 468.

ford widened and immediate danger from a Japanese invasion increased, India's salvation did not lie in passivity. Passivity would have furthered the interests of Japan and would not have resolved the dilemma between two possible courses of action, all-out struggle for independence or participation in the war for democracy against fascism on the side of Britain. Congress leaders, and most of all Gandhi, realized this. "Inaction at that critical stage and submission to all that was happening had become intolerable to him. The only way to meet that situation was for Indian freedom to be recognized and for a free India to meet aggression and invasion in co-operation with allied nations. If this recognition was not forthcoming, then some action must be taken to challenge the existing system to wake up the people from the lethargy that was paralyzing them and making them easy prey for every kind of aggression."[64]

But these conclusions, even though the result of a sober appraisal of the situation, clashed with another logic which also had an indisputable basis in a realistic assessment of the existing situation. Together with many other Congress leaders, Nehru developed views which differed from those expressed by Gandhi and which had an important influence on many politicians of the anti-colonial movement. Nehru himself commented on this awkward state of affairs in the ranks of Congress. "Some of us were disturbed and upset by this new development, for action was futile unless it was effective action, and any such effective action must necessarily come in the way of the war effort at a time when India herself stood in peril of invasion. Gandhiji's general approach also seemed to ignore important international considerations and appeared to be based on a narrow view of nationalism.[65]

These differences in views and the constant vacillation in stressing first one and then the other principle did not leave a particularly visible mark on political action because none was possible at that time. They are important as evidence that while the war was still in progress, i. e., when all contradictions had reached their fullest intensity in view of the emergency, Congress

---

[64] *Ibid.*, p. 481.
[65] *Ibid.*, p. 482.

66

had already begun to show statesmanship in its political assessments and made decisions in the light of political considerations. In accordance with this new approach, Congress had to discard the simplistic black-and-white assessments of earlier decades and face reality in its impending decision whether to support Britain in the struggle for democracy against fascism — for how otherwise could India help the other Allies — or to carry on fighting Britain regardless of the effect on the war effort.

India and Congress, which by then had become the country's main spokesman, were in a terrible predicament because they could not identify with either side. No extreme solution was possible. The war was being fought by powers having their own scores to settle. They had a reason to fight, regardless of how progressive or reactionary they were in terms of historical development. India could find support for its aspirations with both sides, but they remained essentially alien to India's basic interests.

In the 'twenties, Congress gave no quarter in its struggle against Britain and the Commonwealth. "The racial discrimination and treatment of Indians in some of the British dominions and colonies were powerful factors in our determination to break from that group."[66] England, the British Empire and the British Commonwealth with its dominions were abhorrent and could command neither consideration nor sympathy. The feeling was mutual, because at that time and in the beginning of the 'thirties Congress was regarded as a foe to be stamped out, although it was sometimes necessary to negotiate with it owing to its influence among the people.

This was the simplified situation as Congress found itself arrayed for a showdown with England, when the rest of the world seemed a mere backdrop for this struggle. A new element appeared in the position of Congress and the anti-colonial movement during the war, when the struggle for independence became part of the broader conflict among the great powers. In this new situation the struggle for independence had to seek its own path, apart from the warring factions, but could not find it. In the first half of the war, India came to grips with the general problems and

---

[66] *Ibid.*, p. 427.

situations which later were to determine the general lines of action of the nonaligned countries. Already then, India was in a certain sense nonaligned.

Its position and problems were primarily due to certain specific circumstances. First of all, Congress was then a very strong and influential political movement in India, which spoke on behalf of a very large portion of the population. Even before the war it asserted itself as a real political force in various provincial governments, and, therefore, in a moment of crisis could reasonably expect to participate in an all-Indian government. Secondly, from the end of 1941, the war was no longer a remote event having no immediate effect on the fate of the country. Invasion was an immediate threat, and the Japanese had even actually entered a small part of Indian territory. Finally, India and its possible contribution to the war effort in men and material was of paramount importance for England.

Without dwelling upon other arguments and subjective feelings or the special features of Gandhism which were mainly based on nonviolence, we can see in India's example how the policies and views which later became the basis of the platform of nonalignment emerged and developed. We may recall that as early as 1941 nonviolence had definitively ceased to be a subject of internal discussions in Congress, at least insofar as wartime tactics were concerned. Therefore, this special and typically Indian phenomenon did not play an important part in later discussions. Nehru pointed out the basic change that took place in Gandhi's views during discussions on the attitude to the war. Whereas earlier Gandhi had firmly stuck to his tenets of nonviolence, even in respect to international war,[67] a significant evolution took place in the course of 1942, before the banning of Congress and the big round-up of its leaders.

"These were obvious difficulties, and we discussed them at length with Gandhiji without converting each other. The difficulties were there, and risks and perils seemed to follow any course of action or inaction. It became a question of balancing them and choosing the lesser evil. Our mutual discussions led to

[67] *Ibid.*, p. 450.

a clarification of much that had been vague and cloudy, and Gandhiji's appreciating many international factors to which his attention had been drawn. His subsequent writings underwent a change, and he himself emphasized these international considerations and looked at India's problem in a wider perspective."[68]

Of course, this does not mean that Congress remained passive. In fact, Congress demanded for India to be acknowledged as an equal partner in the war effort, a demand which the English did not accept. But Congress's position could not be put into practice in the given circumstances, because it did not have any authority in the country. Thus this period of trial and tribulations only served to crystallize views and create a foundation for a later definition of nonalignment. This process had been imposed by the war events, but it would not have been possible had there not been a basic platform in the 'twenties to serve as a starting point. This platform underwent great changes, and it could not be mechanically applied in the new situation of increased responsibility. But this is natural and always occurs as revolutionary programmes evolve into statesmanship.

Although the original, pre-war platform was too simple and unrealistic, it was an unavoidable necessity. Without it, opportunistic views could have compromised the main objective of the movement, which was independence. The manner in which Nehru expressed the basic political dilemmas was perhaps itself a product of certain simplifications inherited from the past. These simplifications completely vanished when the Indian government began to formulate and define the policy of independent India. The lack of clarity in the formulation of Congress policy during the war also derived from the fact that Nehru's thesis on Congress's shift from extreme nationalism to strongly emphasized internationalism in its policies was only partially correct. It would be more nearly correct to say that the shift implied a stronger emphasis on the national interests of the Indian people and a more immediate concern for the well-being of the nation, which are not essentially internationalist arguments.

---

[68] *Ibid.*, p. 482.

What this evolution actually implies is the abandonment of certain forms of internationalism and nationalism, founded on the simplified ideologies of the revolutionary movement, in favor of the practical considerations of political leaders who were already exercising the functions of statesmen. Or, to use Nehru's words, the "prophets" turned into "leaders"[69].

The impingement of international events on discussion gave rise to two contradictory considerations. The victory of Japan and Germany would have meant a victory of latter-day invaders and enslavers, the spreading of a political movement which was not acceptable to India. But, there was another way of looking at things, and it did not escape Nehru's notice. He wrote that "before the advancing Japanese armies the British colonial empire cracked up with amazing rapidity. Was this proud structure, then, just a house of cards with no foundations or inner strength? Inevitably, comparisons were made with China's long resistance to Japanese aggression in spite of her lack of almost everything required for modern war. China went up in people's estimation, and though Japan was not liked, there was a feeling of satisfaction at the collapse of old-established European colonial powers before the armed strength of an Asian power. That racial, Oriental-Asiatic feeling was evident on the British side also. Defeat and disaster were bitter enough, but the fact that an Oriental and Asiatic power had triumphed over them added to the bitterness and humiliation. One Englishman occupying a high position said that he would have preferred it if the *Prince of Wales* and the *Repulse*[70] had been sunk by the Germans instead of by the yellow Japanese."[71] All of this was of great importance for Indians, because it indicated a better opportunity for the dream of independence to come true at last, but it could also imply new dangers.

The central question was that of the immediate and future interests of the Indian people and the realization that there were other dangers in the world to India's freedom besides the British

---

[69] *Ibid.*, p. 456.

[70] These ships were the nucleus and main striking force of the British Navy in Asia and were two of the best ships that England had at the time. The Japanese sank them on December 10, 1941, after destroying the U.S. Pacific fleet at Pearl Harbor.

[71] Jawaharlal Nehru, *The Discovery of India, op. cit.*, p. 457.

Empire. It was clear that on the eve of possible triumph the movement was already forced to assess events and factors in the light of their future role as a responsible government. This transformation from a liberation movement into a government began in India earlier than in other areas, since well before the war Congress succeeded in exerting its influence on state affairs, if not on a national scale, at least within various provinces.[72]

Naturally enough, later on, when discussions already had started on transferring power and proclaiming India's independence, Congress devoted even greater attention to a study of all the circumstances liable to affect Indian foreign policy. Although the policy taken in response to the threat of Japanese invasion was a milestone in the evolution of Congress's foreign policies, all questions connected with foreign policy had not become matters of practical politics and statesmanship.

Whereas during the war and before the crisis in relations with London in 1942, Congress treated the British government as an irreconcilable enemy, relations became much easier and more tolerant after the war. In his notes made during his imprisonment, Nehru recounted the stands taken by London, and particularly by Churchill, whom he described as an "uncompromising opponent" of Indian independence, who had stated, "Sooner or later you will have to crush Gandhi and the Indian Congress," and who considered India "that most truly bright and precious jewel in the crown of the King."[73]

Nehru also considered inevitable the breaking of all ties with the British Commonwealth,[74] because racial discrimination was an insurmountable obstacle to membership in this group. However, when the time came for independent India to decide on its relations with Great Britain, the policies of the Indian government, under the strong influence of Nehru, were much more moderate. It can also be assumed that in England as well, attitudes on relations with India underwent some far-reaching changes. Both sides were compelled to view their mutual relations within the context of the overall world situation. This approach was a new

---

[72] *Ibid.*, pp. 361—374.
[73] *Ibid.*, p. 445.
[74] *Ibid.*, p. 427.

one for the leaders of Congress, who found themselves in the novel role of statesmen confronted with problems which they could not even have dreamed of in the earlier phase of their activity as fighters for independence. Finally, and this is of special importance, the internal problems after independence were responsible for some of India's foreign policies.

As relations with Great Britain lost their emotional elements and former antagonisms, greater attention was paid to the country's immediate needs. Particularly in the first few years, the overriding problem was the unrest caused by the partition of British India into independent India and Pakistan. In the difficult situation immediately after the partition, when serious economic and political consequences of the bloodshed and mass migrations were strongly felt, Indian policy was primarily concentrated on internal problems and on relations with its immediate neighbors. India generally kept aloof from large international problems. In international affairs, and particularly in the United Nations, India energetically pressed for solutions to those problems which were of direct interest to the Indian public, for instance questions of racial discrimination against the population of Indian origin in South Africa.[75] India was also active in the United Nations in opposing the inclusion of the former mandate territory of South West Africa into the Union of South Africa.

Speaking before the Indian parliament on March 17, 1950, Nehru felt the need to explain this period of Indian foreign policy. "Ever since India became independent, we have been interested in these various happenings all over the world. Indeed, we were interested in foreign affairs even before. But the first thing that we kept in view was to build our own country on solid foundations and not to get entangled in matters which did not directly affect us. Not that we are not interested in those matters but the burden of these entanglements would be too great and, as the House knows, the problems we had to face in our own country were big enough for any country to face."[76]

In view of his earlier clearly pronounced interest in world

[75] GAOR, No. 136 (A/205 and A/205 Add. 1), pp. 1006—1062.

[76] Jawaharlal Nehru's Speeches 1949—1953, The Publication Division of the Ministry of Information and Broadcasting, Government of India 1954, p. 141.

affairs,[77] Nehru felt the need to show the parliament that his reticence was not unusual or without a precedent. He delved into the history of the eighteenth century. "About a hundred and fifty years ago, the Western world was breaking up on account of all kinds of imperial and revolutionary wars. Having achieved independence by breaking off from the British Empire, the United States was naturally affected by these upheavals; nevertheless, it avoided being involved in the chaotic situation of Europe — although it doubtless had its particular sympathies — because that was the natural thing for a nation in that state of affairs to do. Now, this analogy, although it may not be a particularly good one in the circumstances of today, has a bearing and I wish to point out to this House that for a country that has newly attained freedom and independence, this is a natural policy to pursue."[78]

It is quite obvious that all these analyses by Nehru were based on India's special situation immediately after attaining independence, and that those circumstances did not have such a great effect on India's later behavior. Yet, it is highly significant in our study of nonalignment to take note of this transient period of withdrawal and the acceptance of a kind of isolation. This attitude stems just as naturally from the earlier experience as it later logically gave rise to the much more active policy of nonalignment.

Let us then end here our consideration of the evolution of policies in India in the last stage of its struggle and in the early moments which followed its independence. As we have said earlier, a more detailed examination of this case was indicated both by India's role in third world developments and by the fact that some policies and conflicts manifested themselves in India much more articulately then elsewhere in the early period of the struggle for independence. At any rate, India was the first among the Southeast Asian countries to attain independence following World War II.

---

[77] In *The Discovery of India* on page 427 Nehru noted: "When we talked of the independence of India, it was not in terms of isolation. We realized, perhaps more than many other countries, that the old type of complete national independence was doomed and there must be a new era of world co-operation."

[78] *Jawaharlal Nehru's Speeches 1949—1953, op. cit.*, pp. 143—144.

In the struggle for independence, India more than any other country had to face and deal with problems arising from the colonial and pre-colonial past, as well as with problems which derived from the contemporary international political, economic and social conflict. When we say more than any other countries, we refer to the diversity and number of problems as well as their magnitude. Grappling with all these difficulties, trying to overcome its past and to find its own place in the present in order to be able to make a blueprint for its future, independent India found itself in the unfavorable position of an underdeveloped country which faced its most difficult tasks immediately after overcoming all the obstacles on the road to its independence. It came face to face with the problem of determining its relations with the great powers and of taking a side in the conflicts which for those powers were a matter of life and death, but for India only a new burden and a source of new perils. India felt no allegiance or need to identify itself with the policies and rivalries of the rich and powerful, who were and remained alien to it. Just as the other nonaligned countries, India understood very early that it belonged to a separate category of countries which have a specific interest in general isssues even though they might not have identical specific problems and needs.

D. FORMATION OF THE MOVEMENT OF NONALIGNMENT

THE BEGINNING OF THE MOVEMENT OF NONALIGNED COUNTRIES

Although the acquisition of independence by some colonies, first in Southeast Asia and then elsewhere, created a basis for nonalignment, the policy of nonalignment itself gained substance and became a factor in international relations only in stages. What mattered was not the number of the nonaligned, but the fact that these countries were only gradually able to abandon their own internal or immediate preoccupation and form their own policies and modes of international activity. The new countries became nonaligned first in the consciousnesses of their political leaders and statesmen and only afterwards in the practice of their international behavior. They were, in fact, nonaligned from the very first day of their real independence, but became known as such only later on.

BEGINNINGS OF INTERNATIONAL COOPERATION

The term nonalignment came into usage only late in the 1950s in newspapers and government statements. Some believe that the term became accepted even earlier. Thus, for example, Krishna Menon said in his review to the *Times of India* that he believed the term had appeared as early as in the beginning of the 1950s.[79] It is difficult to establish the exact date because it had already been used in verbal statements of which there are hardly any written traces.[80]

The policy of nonalignment did not come about as the result of previous analyses or implementation of a well-designed and fully evolved theory. Therefore, both in its definition and application in international relations it was subject to constant changes. Irrespective of its deeper meaning and its historical roots, its outward manifestations depend very much on current situations and fears or aspirations which at a given moment may be particularly significant.

The policy of nonalignment also signified a tendency toward independence and an answer to the formation of two antagonistic blocs. By its appelation it is defined negatively, i. e., as a policy of non-participation in bloc groupings, military alliances or political blocs. Whatever term we may take in different languages, it

---

[79] *The Times of India*, September 30, 1968.

[80] The term "nonalignment" in English appeared rather late in official statements and documents. At the tripartite meeting on Brioni in June 1956 (Tito, Nehru and Nasser), this term was still not used. However, in the communiqué on the meeting between Tito and Nasser which was also held on Brioni immediately preceding the tripartite meeting, the expression "nonalignment with blocs" was used. The text of the Brioni meeting is given in the Appendix.

always contains a negation, aloofness from these cold war constructions.[81] ✓

The expression was mainly used in official documents as a term denoting the nonaligned countries rather than their policies, the definition of their orientations, or their basic demands. The policy was frequently described in terms of independence, autonomy, or active and peaceful coexistence. However, as time went on, nonalignment appeared more and more frequently to signify the policy of the nonaligned countries.

Important in this sense was the Conference of the Heads of Nonaligned Countries in Belgrade in 1961. It then became customary to refer to nonaligned countries and to the policy of nonalignment, or simply to nonalignment.

Different analysts and politicians variously treated nonalignment as a kind of peacetime neutrality, as a policy of fence-sitting between blocs, or as an endeavor to keep equidistance between the blocs. These views of the policy of nonalignment were, of course, not always due to a misunderstanding or superficiality, but very frequently to deliberate disparagement or attempts to underrate it.

The latter should be especially emphasized, because the attempts to obscure or misrepresent the aims and substance of the nonalignment policy were a favorite method of fighting this anti-bloc effort during the cold war. The powerful bloc-inspired information media indulged in it for many years, and this had a definite effect in some quarters.[82] One of the effects was the attempt among the adherents to the policy of nonalignment to treat it as a new and original comprehensive view of the world. This attempt was in a certain sense a reaction to detraction on the part of bloc critics.

---

[81] The term "nonalignment" as used by the statesmen of various nonaligned countries has very different implications, but it always refers to an active policy. For instance, in his more important speeches on foreign policy in the 1950s, Nehru stressed the active quality of nonalignment (cf. *Jawaharlal Nehru's Speeches 1949—1953*, op. cit., pp. 143—144, 231 et passim.). Prior to the Belgrade Conference, Tito often referred to the "so-called nonaligned countries" (Tito: *Govori i članci*, Vol. XVI, Naprijed, Zagreb 1962, p. 34). Tito also used this term without qualifying it (Ibidem, p. 38). In those years statesmen most frequently used the term "nonalignment" or "noninvolvement" to refer to actions, and not to a characteristic of nonaligned countries.

[82] Confirmation of this can be found in world newspapers on the days immediately prior to, during and after the conference, i. e., from the second half of August to mid-September 1961.

This more often than not gave rise to what can be described as "ideologization" of the policy of nonalignment. Namely, as a reaction to attempts to expose this policy as a tactical move or skillful diplomatic game, some protagonists tried to present it as a new contemporary ideology and give it a separate ideological foundation. However, far more significant was the tendency to exclusivity among the governments of the nonaligned countries as seen in attempts to strictly limit participation at the conference of the nonaligned to a narrow circle of the orthodox. This happened during the preparations for both the Belgrade and the Cairo Conferences, when it was discussed which countries to invite or admit to the Conference. These tendencies did not fully triumph, and so the circle of participating countries increased from one conference to the next, embracing an ever widening spectrum of countries as regards internal systems and specific national foreign policies.[83]

Invitations to the conference were each time an object of discussion, and they were subjected to strict criteria which reflected a certain exclusiveness. The unwillingness of some countries to participate was occasionally due to political expediency, but in other cases it was based on the unwillingness to approve a comprehensive platform covering almost all contemporary problems. The first case was particularly evident in the opposition of some nonaligned countries to the admission of those of their neighbors with whom at that time they had open political disputes.

Such acts and views facilitated and encouraged attempts to show up the policy of nonalignment and cooperation among its protagonists as an attempt to form a third bloc. They were, however, not particularly successful, because neither was the creation of such a bloc feasible nor did the practical behavior of the nonaligned countries encourage such beliefs.[84] It should be noted that a bloc character was frequently insisted on by critics, especially when renewed efforts were made to strengthen the cooperation

---

[83] Cooperation in spite of the differences in the concrete foreign policy of various countries is mentioned as early as in the communiqué after the tripartite meeting on Brioni in June 1956. See the Appendix.

[84] See: *Jawaharlal Nehru's Speeches 1949—1953, op. cit.*, p. 231, where a speech held on February 17, 1953, states the futility and inacceptability of creating a third bloc.

among nonaligned countries. Yet these claims would soon give way to opposite assertions, namely that the third-world countries were only engaging in tactical maneuvering.

Such inconsistencies in the treatment of nonalignment in political public discussions, and especially in the press, do not apply to this question alone. Nonalignment has been receiving different kinds of treatment according to given situations. Nevertheless, attempts to credit the nonaligned countries with shrewd tactics of playing one bloc against another in order to gain advantages for themselves deserve special attention. The nonaligned countries, as a matter of fact, have never intended, nor have they been able to achieve any material gains by playing the big powers and blocs against one another. They were frequently attacked by one or the other side in the cold war, or even by both sides simultaneously. If they received any aid or enjoyed support from a great power or a bloc, it was only because their interests happened to coincide with the bloc's tactical requirements. There was, for example, a coincidence of interests in the case of Yugoslavia's resistance against the Cominform, and in the case of India's conflict with China. There was a similar situation when the U. S. A. and the U. S. S. R. acted jointly in the United Nations to stop the aggression against Egypt in 1956.

As can be seen from the above, the policies of the observers and even of the protagonists of nonalignment themselves have been very diverse but they also changed in different situations. There is, after all, nothing unusual in this, because it is obvious that a significant international political phenomenon must inevitably produce diverse reactions in those circles which it affects or which may feel affected by it. What is far more interesting is that over the years there have been different interpretations and definitions of nonalignment even among its champions. Here we do not mean those changes which relate to the current assessments of the international situation or to the changes in attitudes or policies in a given situation. They are understandable and indispensable if a consistent action is to be carried out in situations which alter from time to time. What we mean here is different conceptions of the term nonalignment.

The views among the adherents oscillated from demands for

the creation of a more or less institutionally built up international organization having regular meetings and membership, to the proclamation of principles of nonalignment as a general concept which should also be applied among the nonaligned. Consequently, there had to be difficulties in drafting common platforms. These differences appeared for the first time at the meeting of the nonaligned countries in Cairo in 1964.[85] Then obviously it was no longer possible to prevent some of the participants from putting in something of their own ideology. Yet the common platforms, even after the inevitable compromises, were not emasculated or bereft of significance for the international communite.

It is certainly highly significant that the nonaligned countries have remained strongly dedicated to their platform. The circle of nonaligned countries went on increasing without there being any defections. Even in the case of an extremely drastic differentiation, as in the case of Indonesia at the time of the Cairo Conference, there can be no question of defection in the full sense of the world. Even in the countries where the governments which endorsed nonalignment were overthrown, the new governments continued being faithful to this policy.[86]

This constancy did not preclude changes in emphasis or in the behavior and foreign policies of various countries. Foreign policies within nonalignment may reflect conflicts of interests and not only differences. At international conferences of nonaligned countries, joint policies frequently were presented and defined in deference to concrete issues of special interest only for some countries.[87] Such endorsements for the policies of one or several participants produced differences which were resolved by compromises, as is clearly shown by formulations in the final conclusions of conferences. However, the treatment of these issues in official documents clearly shows that these questions had not been dis-

---

[85] Cf. the unabridged texts of the speeches made by participants at the conference. Various divergences in views are left out in the abridged texts published in "Review of International Affairs" and in the majority of other information media.

[86] Compare the attitude of Indonesia before and after Sukarno's overthrow, as well as the behavior of Ghana, Sudan, Mali and other nonaligned countries where there were coups d'état. In Indonesia, Ghana and Mali, the policy of nonalignment took on renewed force after the coups.

[87] For instance, the questions of the Congo, the Near East and the French bases in Tunisia as treated in the Belgrade Declaration adopted at the end of the Belgrade Conference in 1961. See the Appendix.

cussed as basic problems and that they were rather an appendix than a constituent part of the platform.

Mutual cooperation and coordination among nonaligned countries must be taken only as an activity based on the agreement on basic aims and aspirations, but this by no means implies that those countries are necessarily conducting a fully consonant foreign policy, as in the case of countries members of an alliance. The foreign policy of each country, especially if it is not a great power, is very largely predetermined by political circumstances in its immediate environment. Unless a determined effort is made to coordinate the acts and foreign policies of countries whose experiences are different, they will respond differently to similar situations and problems in their relations with the outside world. It would seem that the tendency to react differently is more accentuated in the underdeveloped countries. For various reasons, which will be mentioned later, internal conditions strongly influence the foreign policies of the nonaligned countries, and this invariably produces the above-mentioned disparity.

Although studies of foreign policy are usually concentrated on one specific country or group of similar countries, their conclusions are often generalized to apply to the entire category of nonaligned countries. Statesmen are especially fond of taking the experiences of their own countries, such as they see them, as a basis for generalizations. It is therefore no wonder that in scientific analyses, and especially in policy statements presented by the statesmen of the nonaligned countries, we can find highly divergent views and assessments about nonalignment. They account for the widely differing definitions of nonalignment that have been published or uttered.

It is not unreasonable to say that there are as many definitions of nonalignment as there are nonaligned countries, and possibly even more. Most probably every statesman of these countries believes his own version to be the most adequate definition of the concept of nonalignment. For this reason, the compilation of a list of nonaligned countries before each conference is always a difficult job, even when no attempts are made by a participating country or group to bar another country.

In a certain sense it can be said that the policy of nonalignment has permanently been undergoing definition, reexamination and criticism, while resisting arbitrary assessments. The leading statesmen of the nonaligned countries have been at it at all their meetings; proclamations and action programs have been formulated, earlier policies have been enlarged upon or amended in the light of current developments, and statements have been made or repeated refuting allegations that a third bloc was being created.[88]

All this is understandable since the movement of the nonaligned countries is something new in international relations, not only because of a common platform, but also because of the form of cooperation among a large number of generally dissimilar countries. Countries have usually formed associations in order to carry out a joint foreign policy with regard to a concrete problem or in a determined political situation, on the basis of a community of political interests.

This form of cooperation can obviously not be applied to the joint action of the nonaligned countries; it is also outside the framework of the second category of international association and cooperation — that of regional groupings. These groupings are based on assumptions that the countries of a region have certain overall common interests and aspirations and that their concerted action may contribute to a successful implementation of their aims. Such groups are created for a region to conduct a common foreign policy vis-à-vis the rest of the world. Since the nonaligned countries are distributed over all the continents, it is impossible to expound their community of interests or their joint action through a union constituted on a geographical basis.

SOCIO-POLITICAL COMPONENTS OF NONALIGNMENT

The gradual development of international cooperation among the countries which embraced nonalignment was not

---

[88] Particularly interesting in this respect are the discussions at the conferences of nonaligned countries held in Belgrade in 1961 and in Cairo in 1964.

possible without a common ideological basis for joint action in the event of problems. Cooperation ensued under the impact of current international problems and in the situations which developed in the tension-racked post-war period of the cold war. These external influences and pressures produced corresponding reactions and determined the policies of the newly liberated countries. The similarity of these reactions, spontaneous and individual at first, made for a rapprochement and cooperation which gradually turned into a separate international movement, a community of like-minded nations.

Although it originated in the sphere of practical political and diplomatic cooperation and coordination, the movement cannot be assigned exclusively to political expediency, because then we have the unanswered question of how in the first place assessments of current affairs happened to coincide among countries which are geographically distant and very different in other characteristics. What is obviously needed is to try and find those common elements which are basic to the conceptions of all these different societies.

One of the first thoughts that comes to mind is that all these countries are economically underdeveloped and that this fact obviously plays a significant role in their international relations, and in the shaping of their foreign policies. But, this is still no satisfactory answer to our question, because it is clear, and can be tested in contemporary events and in earlier history, that the economic needs of a country affect its political behavior in international relations in different ways. Economic underdevelopment in itself cannot provide the basis for insisting on independence and nonalignment. It is in fact easier to assume that the underdeveloped countries would conduct a less independent policy than those that are at a higher level of economic development.

Economic factors, therefore, do not explain the behavior of the less developed newly liberated countries, former colonies, in contrast with the observance of bloc discipline by the majority of very highly developed countries. The bloc division of the world which began regimenting the developed countries immediately after the Second World War encompassed only a few of the third world countries. The majority of them remained outside bloc alignment, at the moment of their independence, they usually proclaimed their intention to keep aloof from any combinations and to conduct their own policy, which subsequently was called nonalignment.

As we have seen, for example in India, nonalignment emerged from a conception of relations with the outside world developed during the national liberation struggle. It was the outcome of a firm resolve and required much perseverance and determination in opposing attempts to spread bloc control over the whole world.

At this juncture we may ask to what extent this attitude should be ascribed to subjective factors, i. e., to the conceptions and aspirations of individual leaders or leading groups within the nonaligned countries, and to what extent nonalignment can be regarded as a permanent aspiration of the basic political forces of a given country. In other words, is nonalignment a temporary orientation or behavior of a country, subject to the internal or international balance of forces of the moment, or is it a product of the mentioned aspiration and of revulsion against the state of international relations?

The majority of Western authors treat nonalignment either as a view which reflects the wishes and aspirations of nonaligned nations, or as a set of foreign policies related to the cold war.[89] There are, of course, other views, including Robert L. Rothstein's strong emphasis on the social origin of the policies and orientations of these countries. His assessment runs as follows: "The behavior of the nonaligned countries differs from the behavior of the older generation of Small Powers not only because the environment in which they live is different but also because they are, in many respects, a different kind of Small Power. It is not simply that they are weak, inexperienced, beset by regional conflicts, nationalistic, and unstable domestically; the same characteristics could be used to describe the first generation of "new" Small Powers, the successor states to the Austro-Hungarian

---

[89] For more on this subject, see Bojana Tadić, "Nonalignment — A Conceptual and Historical Survey", published with other symposium papers in *Nonalignment in the World of Today*, Institute of International Politics and Economics, Beograd 1969, p. 113 et seq. The author gives a comprehensive review of the works of John W. Burton, whose paper is also published in this compilation. His most important work on nonalignment is *International Relations — A General Theory*, Cambridge University Press, 1965.

Empire. The critical difference does not lie so much in their external circumstances as it does in the fact that many of the contemporary nonaligned states lack any identification with, or attachment to, the traditions of the Western state system".[90]

Some authors consider the same problem rather in terms of the direct political aims of the nonaligned countries or countries at a lower level of economic development. Leaving aside those who would see in nonalignment only fence-sitting and running after benefits by playing one great power against another, we should mention the ideas of Robert Osgood, who views nonalignment as an avoidance of alliance. This puts him close to the views on non-identification, but he at the same time sees in this policy an attempt to gain economic benefits from both sides.

"Nonalignment," states Osgood, "reflects the tendency of the new and weak states to be far more concerned with their internal problems, and in some cases with local conflicts and rivalries, than with the cold war, which they view as a distraction. They would like the dominant currents of international politics to revolve around the issues of anticolonialism (or anti-neocolonialism) and economic development rather than around the power competition between communist and noncommunist states."[91] This view is also interesting because it coincides with Nehru's thought as he criticized Western countries from exactly the same position.

As far back as in 1954, Nehru contrasted two similar theses about events in the world — as seen by the highly developed countries and great powers compared to the views of the underdeveloped world. "Probably in the United States," Nehru says, the crisis of the time is supposed to be Communism *versus* Anti-Communism. It may be so to some extent. But the crisis of the time in Asia is Colonialism *versus* Anti-Colonialism. Let us be quite clear about it."[92] One year later, Nehru was still more explicit at the conference in Bandung. He took up this thesis again, but in a sharper form, saying that "it was an intolerable

---

[90] Robert L. Rothstein: *Alliances and Small Powers*, Columbia University Press, New York 1968, p. 243.

[91] Robert E. Osgood, *Alliances and American Foreign Policy*, Johns Hopkins Press, Baltimore 1968, p. 87.

[92] *The Hindu*, August 27, 1954.

humiliation for an Afro-Asian country to degrade itself as a camp follower of one or the other side."[93]

Soviet writers generally use the term "neutrality" in regard to nonalignment, and this, especially in early years, helped to simplify the content of this school of thought. In more recent times it has been realized that nonalignment is a product of the social situation and legacy in these countries. Thus the great collective work, published by the *Institute for World Economy and International Relations*, about post-war international relations, emphasizes the significance of the specific social development of the third world countries and positive elements in the platform of nonalignment as applicable to colonialism, to the struggle for equality and to economic development.[94]

As regards development in the third world, Soviet authors dispute the possibility of any autonomous development and foresee a division along the line of the rift which occurred within the developed world. Thus S. I. Tjul'panov of the Lenin University sees a possible prospect of economic development only on the basis of a choice between those two roads "when one and a half billion people living in the new states witness the interaction and struggle of two formations: capitalist in its last stage and the communist in its first stage. Each one of them is more progressive than those socio-economic systems in which the majority of the population of those countries live. Historical experience has shown that both ways of development are objectively possible."[95]

This stand represents a substantial evolution, considering the earlier views that could be found in Soviet literature on this subject. We are, therefore, only referring to works published during the 1960s. Similar views can also be found in the studies by Rymalov and Tjagunenko,[96] as well as in an earlier work by

[93] "Spoljnopolitička dokumentacija" (Foreign Policy Documentation), Institute of International Politics and Economics, No. 10, 1955, Belgrade.

[94] Mezhdunarodnye otnosheniia posle vtoroi mirovoi voiny, Vol. II, Ed. A. A. Lavrishchev and D. G. Tomashevski, Izdatel'stvo politicheskoi literatury, Moskva 1963, p. 203.

[95] S. I. Tjul'panov, *Ocherki politicheskoi ekonomii razivaiushchikhsia stran*, Izdatel'stvo "Mysl'", Moskva 1969, p. 14.

[96] V. Rymalov and V. Tjagunenko, *Slaborazvitye strany v mirovom kapitalisticheskom khoziaistvu*, Izdatel'stvo sotsialno-ekonomicheskoi literatury, Moskva 1961. See also V. C. Tjagunenko, *Problemy sovremennykh natsionalno-osvoboditel'nykh revoliucii*, Izdatel'stvo "Nauka", Moskva 1966.

Tjul'panov about economic and political problems of the new countries.[97] Equally interesting is the contribution by I. I. Potekhin in a compilation of works about African socialism, which was published in the U.S.[98]

Other authors who have dealt with these questions include John W. Burton, who undertook to explain the phenomenon of nonalignment as an integral part of the entire system of relations in the world, and Jean Ziégler,[99] who undertook to make a sociological analysis of the behavior of these countries, especially in Africa. Ziégler based his assessments and analyses partly on György Lukacs's work, *History and Class Consciousness*, which was published in 1923.[100]

Ziégler attempted to interpret the socio-political transformation wrought by the anti-colonial liberation struggle, by applying the theory and experience of the social changes in Europe during the first half of the twentieth century and particularly the models of the socialist revolutions of that period. He placed the rebellion of the masses against the colonial rule into the narrow framework of political movements and conflicts between various groups within the narrow stratum of quasi-European structures created under the influence of the colonial rule. Thus he overlooks the fact that colonial power is authority imported from abroad and dependent on the might of a distant metropolis rather than on the balance of forces within the colonial society.

Attempting to interpret the anti-colonial movement as a replica of the social revolutions in Europe, he necessarily arrives at the conclusion that "the anti-colonial revolution according

---

[97] S. I. Tjul'panov, *Ekonomicheskie i politicheskie problemy novykh suverennykh gosudarstv*, Izdatel'stvo Leningradskogo universiteta, Leningrad 1964.

[98] I. I. Potekhin, "On African Socialism: A Soviet View" in the book *African Socialism*, Stanford University Press, Stanford 1964, pp. 97—112.

[99] Jean Ziégler, *Sociologie de la nouvelle Afrique*, Gallimard, Paris 1964.

[100] It should be mentioned that later György Lokacs abandoned the views that he took at that time and expounded in this work in particular. The changes in his viewpoints can be seen in the interview which he gave to Albert Reif, published in "Die Zeit" in issue 15 of the 25th edition, Hamburg, on April 10, 1970. In this interview Lukacs's following words were quoted: "'In the 'twenties I tried to adopt Marxism *(History and Class Consiousness* was written in these years), later I realized that in a certain respect the line in *History and Class Consciousness* was incorrect, and so I also left *History and Class Consciousness* behind me.'" In the same interview, Lukacs explains the turning point he underwent in 1918 when he took up Marxism and abandoned the ideas put forward in his books, *Spirit and Forms* and *Theory of the Novel*.

to the system of Marxian theories is a senseless act."[101] He, of course, does not realize that he is trying to fit a square peg into a round hole. The senselessness, as conceived by Ziégler, is in the fact that the anti-colonial revolution happened before the old society developed the conditions necessary for the creation of a new one. However, something else is at stake here; namely, within the colonial system political consciousness had advanced so far that conditions were ripe for an open struggle for independence and formation of an autonomous state, i. e., for the abolition of the rule imposed from outside.

The task of the revolution was not to overthrow one class in order to establish the rule of another, because the colonies were subject to the state authority of the overseas power which was not established and which could not be changed by any act or even by any revolutionary transformation in the colonies. The only thing that was possible was to expel the alien power. This for Ziégler was not a "revolutionary opportunity", simply because he did not see in Africa true colonial relationships but rather a synthetic picture of the European model of social revolutions which presuppose the existence of an autonomous society in which there is a conflict between the forces produced by and dependent on the balance of forces in that society.

In his analysis of concrete cases he remained true to his one sided interpretation of political events. In his opinion, for example, Nkrumah's shrewd move in Ghana was to include the demand for independence in the program of his party during the colonial rule and to "appeal to the national pride of the Ghanian people."[102] In the case of the Belgian Congo, he could not explain the Belgian decision to withdraw from that colony. Examining the political movement only from within the society of a colony, he overlooks the general conditions in Africa and in the world and the impact of the anti-colonial movement, which influenced the destinies of some colonies if even indirectly.[103] Here, of course, it should be borne in mind that it is precisely because there had been no unified and powerful anti-colonial movement in the

---

[101] Jean Ziégler, *Sociologie de la nouvelle Afrique, op. cit.*, pp. 40 and 41.
[102] *Ibid.*, p. 77.
[103] *Ibid.*, p. 173.

Congo that the Belgians believed they could retain their influence and their interests. The truth of this was shown in the years of intervention after the granting of independence. Their aim, of course, was not to restore colonial relationships but to protect their economic interests and to bring the necessary pressure to bear on the Congolese government to safeguard these interests.

It is understandable, although completely contrary to historical experience, the anti-colonial revolutions are in the end proclaimed by Ziégler as failures because they did not succeed in "breaking down the state".[104] The author fails to perceive that what was essential in the colonial system was the rule from the overseas metropolis; once this rule was broken the revolution did succeed. This, of course, did not resolve everything, not even the most important problems of society. In the given situation the best the revolution could achieve was to open up the historical process of an autonomous social development which had been suppressed if not completely smothered by the imposition of external rule, a rule which far exceeded the intervention of an occupational force in a war between states with comparable social structures. It tried more or less openly to subject and keep in subjection the social structures of the colony, to put to profit its advantages as a modern state and to prevent any progressive social action.

Among the newer studies, especially in recent times in the United States, attention is being focused on the specific problem of the creation of states in the former colonies. Dankwart A. Rustow[105] lists this as a special case in his categorization of the general process of state formation. He distinguishes four different categories: firstly, post-dynastic states in Western Europe and some other parts of the world; secondly, linguistic states of Central and Eastern Europe and the Near East; thirdly, countries brought into existence as a result of overseas migrations; and fourthly, post-colonial states in Asia, Africa and Latin America. This categorization is interesting for our considerations, particularly because it emphasizes the fact that the post-colonial states

---

[104] *Ibid.*, p. 374.
[105] Dankwart A. Rustow, *A World of Nations*, Brookings Institution, Washington D. C. 1967, p. 62.

do not necessarily coincide with language groups and are not steeped in the traditions of a remote past which hold together the Walloons and Flemings in Belgium, the English, Scots and Welshmen in Great Britain, etc.

The new countries had to forego the customary preliminary process of social development towards statehood. Instead, they had to satisfy themselves with their physical definition, which they inherited from their colonial past, and to insist on the borders which the colonizers had drawn up. Although in Africa the new states frequently changed the names that had been given them by the colonizers, they held sacrosanct something which was a far more brutal expression of the arbitrariness of the uninvited colonizers, namely the borders of the colonial empires and their administrative units.

Rustow notes this circumstance, which leads him on to consider the attempts of altering this state of events by means of union. He pointed out that the attempts at mergers into larger units had failed, notwithstanding the language or any other factors that were designed to assist this purpose.[106] The only successful cases were those of annexations of territorially and population-wise quite insignificant areas to larger units which absorbed them after granting some kind of acknowledgement for the special identity of the absorbed portion.

The attempts to change the existing state boundaries from within on the basis of the right to self-determination were also brutally suppressed within the countries and roundly denounced within the continent. Thus Biafra's attempt at secession produced a particularly violent and cruel civil war, and the creation of Biafra was condemned by the majority of the African states. The support by the majority of the African states for the central government in the civil war in Nigeria best shows to what extent the undermining of the integrity of the territorial units created by the colonial rule was considered dangerous. However, it should be remembered that for the new African states there was hardly any other choice, because the abolition of the inherited borders or a challenge of their validity would create a completely chaotic

---

[106] *Ibid.*, p. 69.

situation in the continent and would most probably throw all the countries into an unrestrained internecine fight. What is obvious after the consideration of these two views is that it is extremely difficult to create a socially well-founded state structure upon the ruins of a colonial empire.

As we can see, contemporary authors and scholars hold varied and frequently opposing views and assessments of nonalignment. There is relatively little literature about this phenomenon, and apart from the symposium organized by the Institute of International Politics and Economics in Belgrade in January 1969[107] no scientific meeting has been held especially dedicated to nonalignment. Nevertheless, nonalignment has survived as a foreign policy orientation, and the nonaligned countries continue showing the willingness and ability to present themselves as a movement of like-minded countries, despite all the changes in the international arena during the last two decades.

All the attempts to find a place for nonalignment in the present world contain certain elements which must be taken into consideration, but there is still to be made a complete and full definition of nonalignment. Researchers aiming to comprehend this phenomenon thoroughly have a wide-open field before them. There is no doubt that literature about nonalignment will increase in due course and that many still obscure problems will eventually become clearer. What may be lacking today is the necessary distance in terms of time, since the phenomenon itself is still in the stage of an intensive evolution.

From what has been done so far in the field of scholarly research, we can only conclude that we are confronted with a specific contemporary problem which was prompted and is determined by the general contemporary social evolution, which implies increasingly active endeavors to achieve man's maximum emancipation. These efforts have created the means for this emancipation and have developed the necessary political consciousness but all this has been done within the framework of social structures which tend to restrict the full development of personality. The development of large systems and modern methods of produc-

---

[107] A list of participants is supplied in the above-mentioned compilation, *Nonalignment in the World of Today*, Institute of International Politics and Economics, Belgrade 1969.

tion have helped man's liberation from want, but have at the same time become the hampering elements for the development of his personality. "The problem which faces the modern world," wrote Bertrand Russell as far back as 1917, "is the combination of individual initiative with the increase in the scope and size of organizations."[108] Since then this question has been treated in various ways in theory and in governmental or social practice, but it still remains unresolved.

It would seem that evolution in the underdeveloped countries, especially in the areas which until recently had been under colonial rule, should be examined within the framework of this general trend. Although it is obviously unreasonable to use specific forms of social and political processes of the developed world as models for the interpretation of events in the third world, there is no doubt that this evolution also is an integral part of the general trend. As a matter of fact, even specific ideas and well defined political aspirations stemming from a developed environment where they were derived in locally prevalent conditions, are being transplanted today into remote areas and are accepted there. These ideas and aspirations thus became the propelling forces and guiding principles in societies where they could not emerge by themselves, since the levels of development and concrete problems of those societies had not matured that far, just as the ideas of the nineteenth century Europe could not appear as political factors in the social conditions of earlier centuries.

Of all the approaches in examining the essence and social substance of nonalignment, the most important is that which studies the social rationalization of that phenomenon. It is, of course, not possible by either that or any other method to throw light on the totality of the elements making up nonalignment. However, it should be borne in mind that nonalignment grew out of a fundamental social transformation of its own kind which took place in the process of liberation from colonialism as a basic expression of the aspiration for emancipation. However, this liberation was not simply a political emancipation, nor was it a classical social transformation comparable to similar revolutionary or

---

[108] Bertrand Russell, *Political Ideals*, George Allen & Unwin, London 1963, p. 75. The first edition was published in the U.S.A. in 1917.

evolutionary changes in the developed industrial societies. Consequently, defining a basic policy governing relations of the nonaligned countries with the outside world is not a normal process by which a social and political body reacts to a comparably constituted world. The nonaligned countries are completely new structures created in specific conditions that came into being in a way which is different from the ways in which the states of the developed world came about, as shown by Dankwart Rustow in the aforementioned study.

By attempting to penetrate deeper into the essence of the problem, we must be aware that the analyses will necessarily lay a greater emphasis on certain fundamental components and that many specific problems will not be equally treated, because they should be explained by other methods. However, research into the social determination of nonalignment is the element which may be useful in any other research as a point of departure and as a basis for other special investigations.

CHAPTER TWO

SOCIO-POLITICAL CHARACTERISTICS AND DEVELOPMENT PROBLEMS OF THE NONALIGNED COUNTRIES

A. SOCIO-POLITICAL CHARACTERISTICS OF NONALIGNMENT

SPECIAL STATUS OF THE NONALIGNED COUNTRIES IN THE INTERNATIONAL COMMUNITY

At the time of the colonial rule, social relationships and the oppressive political regime afflicted the broad strata of the people, who also lived in great poverty and complete indigence. In the eyes of the masses, the responsibility for their misery and disenfranchisement lay, as truly was the case, on the colonial rule and the organs and institutions which it created or supported. Consequently, any demand for a change in economic conditions, political status and social relationships boiled down to an anti-colonial political struggle.

It is characteristic that all the liberation movements and political organizations, of which some were in the last years of colonialism permitted to operate and even to take a hand in the administration, were predominantly engaged in this kind of struggle. The scope of a purely trade union struggle, as in the developed countries, was much too narrow, and the possibility of effective pressure against employers was much too limited. Yet, even in the cases when such a struggle did promise success, usually the intervention of the authorities on behalf of the employers transferred the conflict to a political, anticolonial terrain. It is understandable, consequently, that even the leftist trade unions of the mother countries conflicted with the unions in the colonial possessions in Africa during the 1950s, failing to understand the basic differences in the social relationships and situations in the mother country and the colonies respectively.[1]

In these conditions it was necessary to propagate the idea that once the colonial power has been eliminated, all the evils which caused the liberation movements to open struggle would also be eliminated. These ideas were encouraged by the propaganda of these movements themselves, which, for understandable practical reasons, always denounced colonialism as the main enemy and the cause of all evils. This greatly simplified the actual situation; in other words, it reduced to the simplest possible terms the far more complex causal relationships between the colonial system and the miserable condition of the colonial peoples.

Liberation was usually at first followed by a great elation and expectation of the long-awaited improvement of overall conditions. However, before a genuine improvement could happen, it was necessary first of all to develop economic activities and this, obviously, was a slow process which was hampered by many difficulties, some of which have already been mentioned. It is particularly necessary to bear in mind the difficulties appearing in relations with the developed countries and generally the difficulties which arose in the world market.

The undeveloped forms of social relationships and structures which survived the pre-colonial times also hindered the development of an expanding and efficient economic activity on the large scale that is indispensable for a speedy economic development. Furthermore, there is also the lack of working habits, as well as a low level of education and little inclination for collective and organized work with a division of labor, all of which are a prerequisite for the modernization of economic activities. The efficient

---

[1] See Sekou Touré, *Congrès Général de L'U.G.T.A.N.*, Presence Africaine, Paris 1959, pp. 7—15.

economic activity of the population was sometimes also hampered by such stumbling blocs as traditional privileges, division of the population into social formations inherited from a remote past, as well as a number of other prejudices and taboos.

On the economic level new troubles soon arose as a result of the departure of experts, weakened organization of production and working discipline, and increased difficulties in foreign markets.[2] Although all these troubles were temporary, they were significant because their effect coincided with the first expressions of impatience on the part of the masses, who had been expecting quick and tangible results after the liberation.

Consequently, the government was under increased pressure, because the masses as a rule expected the government to bring improvements. This pressure prompts fast action to produce some concrete results quickly, but the government apparatus is usually not sufficiently experienced to handle the problems facing the country, which very often differed from those in the developed countries. Certain objective factors are also responsible, such as climate, soil, availability of the sources of energy and labour, communications, etc. Thus very often not even well-meaning experts from the developed countries can find satisfactory solutions easily and quickly.

Finally, a suitable social framework for accelerated economic development, which means satisfactory social relationships, and the elements necessary for the building of modern social structures were being developed very slowly, and in some places they were not even adequately started. Social development had been distorted during the colonial regimes much too long and far too efficiently, and the negative effects could not be removed or put right so easily and quickly.

A way out of this situation is sometimes sought in forcing the construction of modern and frequently even grandiose economic projects, carried out by foreign experts using financial resources obtained from abroad and operated by a small number of highly qualified workers and technicians. These projects,

---

[2] These negative consequences were particularly severe in countries where the general atmosphere created by the bitterness of the struggle for emancipation caused technical personnel to leave more quickly, as was the case in Algeria.

inasmuch as they might satisfy some national needs, invariably absorb large quantities of hard-earned foreign exchange, and very often their amortization and efficiency in the world market depend on a number of factors which are hard to foresee. At best they promise returns in a far-off future, whereas in the short-run they usually consume much foreign exchange without substantially hastening the country's economic and social development.

These weaknesses and problems apply generally to the most underdeveloped countries which became liberated from colonialism, above all to the majority of the African countries. However, in a modified way these very same or similar problems also appear in all the underdeveloped countries. Among these, India inherited from the colonial times a relatively progressive, although quantitatively very limited industry. It also had rudimentary but highly skilled cadres of technicians and engineers and intellectuals. Nevertheless, these problems and regional troubles greatly retard the expected improvement and economic progress.

Furthermore, India has to wrestle with a very fast population growth, which creates exceedingly difficult social and economic problems. A similar situation obtains in Pakistan as well as in Indonesia. Some effects of these troubles are seen in the political instability and military coups in Pakistan and Indonesia, and in India there are signs of the waning influence of the Congress Party and of internal dissensions within it.

What has just been said should not be taken as a criticism of the policies in those countries, but only as an example of how economic and social underdevelopment of a country inevitably aggravates its problems precisely at the moment when it is politically most necessary to produce some results. Furthermore, this should help us to understand the internal and external acts and policies of the governments of the newly liberated countries.

Efforts to overcome all these difficulties branched into three directions: persistent endeavors to eliminate them by means of internal measures in the social, economic and political spheres; prevention of too strong expressions of dissatisfaction and of this dissatisfaction growing into anti-government actions; and, finally, intensive efforts to hasten economic development

96

by means of favorable agreements with the outside world, and particularly with the developed countries.

We are mainly interested in this last domain of action, but there is no doubt that it must always be viewed in conjunction with the other two domains, which both involve the government's internal policy. Models for resolving one's own social problems are frequently sought in other countries. In those of the new countries where the influence of the colonial ruler had been more intensive and pervasive, as in India, this apparently did not even arise as a problem because the British models were utilized almost automatically. In some other countries, however, especially in some of the newly liberated countries of Africa, various foreign models were used in addition to those of the mother country, which in some respect remained present in every former colony. At the same time, there is an increasing number of ostentatious rejections of foreign patterns and their replacement with original solutions, with a strong proviso that in addition to political independence from foreign countries, especially from the advanced countries, there should also be ideological independence.[3] This occasionally gives rise to endeavors to "ideologize" the foreign policies of nonalignment and make them a component part of a new ideology formed in those countries.

In a certain sense one cannot deny the originality of these ideologies, because very frequently the ideas developed elsewhere were applied in completely different and novel circumstances. However, it is far more important that statesmen do place so much emphasis on originality. They try to take full advantage of all the achieved successes in order to strengthen their political position in the country and to shift responsibility for difficulties onto factors outside the government's control, which include unfavorable terms of relations with foreign countries.

This orientation is understandable because these relations are indeed what hampers most the solution of internal problems. Irrespective of the significance of external factors, there is a strong tendency to emphasize them as much as possible.

---

[3] Compare the articles by George Padmore, Julius Nyerere, Mamadou Dio, Tom Mboya, Kwame Nkrumah, and Leopold Senghor in the compilation *African Socialism*, Ed. William H. Friedland and Carl G. Rossberg, Jr., Stanford University Press, Stanford 1964.

Continually under pressure to strengthen its position in the country and wrestling with multiple internal and external difficulties, the government of a newly liberated country naturally tries to protect itself from any external influence, and particularly from the influence of those countries whose economic power is liable to threaten its positions, and possibly even its independence. The government's sensitiveness on the question of independence soon after its inauguration results from a feeling of insecurity, since it must struggle against great odds to preserve the country's independence before it can attempt to solve its difficulties. However, it must at the same time yield to the pressure of its own people who, as time goes by, become more and more impatient.

In addition to animosity growing between the government and the people because of their rising expectations which it is practically impossible to meet, we also come across some other problems liable to raise difficulties and affect political stability. Sometimes it is inefficiency in governing the country, particularly in dealing with economic problems; elsewhere it is exaggerated corruption and estrangement from the people, and in yet other cases it is incompetent and prejudicial maneuvering in international relations, which provide arguments for those who may wish to use force in order to bring down the government. However, it is relevant here not to consider in detail all the defects of the regimes in the underdeveloped countries, but rather to throw light upon their economic weaknesses. Finally, all the above-mentioned failings can in the last analysis be traced back to one single essential cause — underdevelopment.

It is important to state this, because the impossibility of satisfying internal demands and of diminishing the resulting political pressure makes it ever more imperative to seek help from abroad to create favorable conditions for economic development. Since most of the difficulties of these countries stem from their disadvantageous position in world markets, it is understandable why their governments are so heavily involved in world actions concerning the problems of development and trade.

With reference to the inclination of the newly liberated countries toward nonalignment, it is interesting to recall the kind of nonalignment practiced by the United States early in the nineteenth century, after it had put an end to Britain's efforts to reestablish its authority in America.[4] At that time the U.S.A., just as the countries which liberated themselves after the Second World War are doing now, insisted on nonalignment and on non-interference from outside. The United States also assisted the movements for decolonization in America, in order to strengthen its own international position and to keep up in the country the mood and impetus of the anti-colonial struggle. Consequently, in addition to the understandable solidarity of the new countries, they also have quite realistic political motives for their anti-colonialism. These motives, of course, do not lessen the significance of solidarity; what is more, they give this policy a firm and rational base, which benefits the peoples in the colonies and their liberation movements far more than if they only had to count on the symphaties of some politicians or statesmen in neighboring countries.

The foreign policies of the nonaligned countries are also influenced by the political forces which come into existence very soon after liberation. In fact it is only after the abolition of the colonial rule, which acted as a power above society, that the normal process of social development may begin. The traditional social patterns are revived, such as the tribal system which had been somewhat inhibited under the colonial rule, although it was frequently granted some latitude in order to prevent the development of more contemporaneous social structures. On the other hand, as labor relations advanced from the very backward forms of exploitation which existed at the time of colonialism, and as they extended over broader strata of the population, the numbers of working people increased and a working class developed as a new element in the structure of society with more and more pronounced progressive social aspirations.

These processes, of course, vary greatly from one country to the next. Some of them had a fairly well-developed working class even before liberation. In others, the tribal institutions either compromised themselves during the revolutionary struggle or were

---

[4] See the excerpt from *Jawaharlal Nehru's Speeches, 1949—1953, op. cit.,* p. 143, quoted in Chapter One.

altogether nonexistent. Elsewhere, next to the tribal systems there were also various other systems based on primitive means of production dating back to pre-colonial times.

Internal political life in the newly liberated countries gradually became polarized. It was mainly the working class and intelligentsia that championed progressive actions channeling the country's development towards socialism, whereas the upholders of conservative aspirations were the representatives of the pre-colonial society, certain elements of the colonial society and landowners (wherever they exist) and the newly created bourgeoisie (which in some of the most underdeveloped countries still does not play an important role).

Thus class antagonisms increasingly began to enter the picture, although sometimes obfuscated by the presence of archaic social elements. As a result these societies entered a stage of greater instability, and their political institutions became increasingly subject to upheavals or forcible overthrow. This is where foreign interventions have a particularly important role. They are justified by internal polarization which the champions of the cold war represent as "infiltration" from the other side. The insistence on this real or imagined threat intensifies the attempts at interference from either side, thus increasing the tendencies of transferring the cold war onto the terrain of the new countries.

As the intensity of the cold war abated, the big powers began jostling each other at various points in the world, taking advantage of internal weaknesses in the new countries. Intervention acquired especially drastic forms wherever contradictions eventually led to open conflicts. Very frequently, intensive and brutal interference caused sharp deterioration in internal relationships, as was the case in Vietnam after the Geneva Agreement of 1954, and later in the entire area of former French Indochina.

Open interference, increased difficulties in world markets and at home, a tough struggle in the remaining colonies and racialism in Southern Africa — all these combine to steer the new countries toward nonalignment, i. e., toward independence from the blocs. This course implies the struggle for their own interests, for a complete decolonization and racial equality, and for the abolition of the blocs or of whatever encourages their formation.

Impelled by these internal and external factors, at the time of a rampant cold war, the nonaligned countries developed a tendency of keeping aloof from the cold war and of trying to help put an end to it or at least alleviate it. This tendency spread over practically all the existing countries of the third world, as was evidenced by the composition and the final documents of the 1955 Bandung Conference. The terms of reference of this conference clearly demonstrated that the countries of Africa and Asia were aware that they constituted, notwithstanding the foreign policies of some of them, a separate body, a separate category of countries. It is significant that this was in the first place a political conference, and the awareness of its particularity was based not so much on the low level of economic development but on the internal being and the external basic interests of these countries.

It matters not to us how faithful some countries were then or later to this conception of singularity and non-identification with the existing blocs. After all, the later evolution has shown that at least in some of the cases the joining of the blocs had been judged opportune in connection with some of the direct problems in their closest neighborhood,[5] hence there is no point in dealing with exceptional cases. Instead we shall continue assuming that the nonaligned countries are factually representatives of the third world, especially those which liberated themselves from colonialism after the Second World War.

The nonaligned countries in due course developed their particular identity in the world, and with their activity and joint foreign policy proclamations[6] set themselves up as a category of countries on the basis of their separate social being, alienated from bloc interests and conflicts among the blocs, trying to ease the world situation in the belief that their aspirations will be more easily carried out in peaceable conditions. Their special endeavor is to strengthen their own international status and to allay the

---

[5] During the Bandung Conference and up until the most recent war with India in 1965, Pakistan was closely connected with a policy and organizations which relied on the United States. After the armed conflict with India, Pakistan fostered relations with China and the Soviet Union, which supply its armaments, but at the end of the 1960s, Pakistan asked to be invited to the new conference of nonaligned countries.

[6] See the material in the Appendix on the activities of the nonaligned countries.

101

danger arising from a low level of development and the resulting internal weaknesses.

This policy is therefore committed to the maintenance of peace and a further development of international relations in order to facilitate the abolition of inequalities which still exist in the world because of drastic differences in economic development and international status. Its aim is to implement the basic principles of coexistence, but its practical activity can hardly transcend those limitations which are imposed by the body social of these states. It may help to resolve world problems only inasmuch as this solution directly involves the solution of their own problems. This is very largely true in regard to the economic problems of today's international community, although this action of the nonaligned is especially designed to deal with the problems of the underdeveloped countries and only in passing touches upon the problems which primarily affect the developed countries. Thus the outstanding problems in economic relations among the highly developed countries remain outside that sphere. So far not even the interested countries have succeeded in resolving them, which complicates the problem of relations between the developed and underdeveloped countries.

The nonaligned countries have shown little interest for those political problems in relations among the developed countries which do not affect them directly. This helps to explain their relative inactivity regarding nuclear armaments outside that part of the problem which concerns them directly. The policy of nonalignment has shown itself to be constant in an otherwise fluid internal and international position of the nonaligned countries. It does not reflect the image which is created about this policy outside the nonaligned countries. It can only be understood as an expression of the interests which have arisen and developed following the profound and even painful changes in the countries supporting nonalignment.

The policy of nonalignment may consequently be described in a positive sense as a policy stemming from the difficult international position of these countries mainly due to their internal difficulties and problems. In trying to resolve their own problems, these countries must also consider some of the general ones of

102

the international community. Their interest in these general problems originates from their internal troubles and weaknesses, and it is just as constant as the problems themselves.

Their claim to speak on behalf of the interests of the entire community is nevertheless justified, because the division into the developed and underdeveloped countries is undoubtedly a general problem for the entire world. These countries and their aspirations can therefore not be treated as particularism on the world scale. Whereas the developed countries have succeeded in maintaining their growth rates despite the lagging behind of the underdeveloped countries, and in resolving their problems without bothering about the fate of the less developed countries, the latter have no prospect at all of resolving their own problems unless relationships in the world economy as a whole have been amended. Since they have no sufficient material force they are forced to seek their own security by strengthening the stability of peace and security in the entire world.

EFFORTS TO STRENGTHEN INDEPENDENCE

Viewed from the standpoint of power politics, nonalignment came into existence as the result of a spontaneous desire to remain aloof from the conflict between the group of countries aligned around the two greatest world powers of the post-war period. Hence this policy was frequently described as "neutrality" and regarded as a purely passive attitude to world problems. This was especially evident at the beginning of the Korean war. One might accept the statement by Krishna Menon in an interview to the *Times of India* that it was he or another diplomat who used in the United Nations the term "nonalignment" in order to counter the affirmations that the nonaligned countries had a passive attitude to the world problems.

At the beginning of the Korean war, India and Yugoslavia, as well as some other countries which at that time were closest to what is known as nonalignment, frequently abstained from voting. In these conditions passivity was an expression rather of impotence than of principle. As Nehru said in 1946, and as it was reaffirmed by the leaders of Burma, Indonesia, Yugoslavia and some other countries, nonalignment was an active policy, which in given situations required opting out or abstaining, but which always, whenever major world problems were at stake, called for an active position and initiative.

The unexpected outbreak of war in Korea, the rapid deterioration of relations between the two blocs, and the small number of countries prepared to follow an independent course of nonalignment prevented more active pursuit of the policy, at least temporarily. However, as soon as an opportunity arose to end the war and to transfer the dispute from the battlefield to the conference table, the nonaligned countries actively participated in negotiations, and India in particular became a highly significant factor in efforts to end the war and stabilize the situation in Northeast Asia.

Even in the initial activities of the nonaligned countries it was evident that there was no formal organization or grouping. There was no organized voting bloc of the nonaligned countries. They voted individually, according to their own inclination and not according to any instructions or a rigid pattern. In the U. N. General Assembly in 1950, seven delegations expressed an attitude of nonalignment by abstaining from the voting on proposed resolutions,[7] but India's amendment, which followed more or less the same line, received 24 votes. Later on the nonaligned countries as a rule received significant support for their proposals, including the votes of countries having very different political orientations.

We have taken the Korean war as an example of the behavior of the nonaligned countries, because in the early years of nonalignment this conflict was in the focus of international attention. It not only affected the current policies of almost all the countries in the world, but also influenced the entire development of international relations and helped the United Nations to improve its instruments and methods of making and keeping peace. However, this case is not representative of the activities of the nonaligned countries. It was too early in the day, and nonalignment had not yet come into its own.

---

[7] Egypt, India, Lebanon, Saudi Arabia, Syria, Yemen, and Yugoslavia.

Even at that stage the concept of nonalignment meant something more than a passive attitude. The aim of these countries was not just to avoid involvement in a conflict, but also to mobilize forces against the outbreak and escalation of conflicts and against the formation and strengthening of the blocs. The usual phraseology has been to prevent the use of or reliance upon force in international relations. This position was based on the United Nations Charter. It should not be taken as naivety on the part of statesmen who set unattainable goals, nor should it be used to criticize the Charter on that score. International relations can be affranchised from the use of force only if some very far-reaching social and political changes, which are not realizable in an immediate future, are effected. In this case, however, the presentation of such a demand implies the desire to channel the development in the world towards that remote goal.

Early in the 1950s, the crux of the policy of nonalignment was to oppose power politics and the use of force or reliance upon it, and to maintain international peace and security. As a result of the limited strength of the policy of nonalignment and the inexperience of its protagonists, these countries were not able to formulate specific and concrete political goals and still less to independently undertake definite actions in this respect. It was also necessary to rally as many countries as possible under the banner of nonalignment. The most suitable basis for this policy was a general formulation which everyone was willing to adopt.

This generalized and sometimes even vague stand of the leaders of nonaligned countries on the political problems in the early post-war years reflected the general situation in world politics at the time. The cold war was on, and tension between the two sides was very high. The number of independent countries adopting the policy of nonalignment steadily increased, but was still quite insignificant. It was difficult enough to think of ways to establish less strained relationships, never mind cooperation between the main antagonistic powers. The highest tensions and the most dangerous conflicts of the cold war were still to come.

During the Korean war, the nonaligned countries acquired early experience in concrete activities aimed at resolving a specific conflict, and they did not trouble much about the basic problem of how to improve the unsatisfactory state of international relations. But soon afterwards, the policy of nonalignment produced some general and comprehensive platforms for regulating international relations as a whole. At that time its most significant contribution was the creation and expansion of the zone of nonalignment, which prevented the two blocs from dividing the entire world into two spheres of influence, into two antagonistic armed camps.

In the course of time, the number of nonaligned countries increased, mainly thanks to the disintegration of the colonial empires. It is today difficult to establish accurately how many countries belonged to one of the two blocs at the beginning of the cold war and subsequently abandoned them and joined the nonaligned countries. Often the allegiance of the countries which were not within the very nucleus of the blocs was rather uncertain. It seems beyond a doubt that prior to 1948 Yugoslavia owed allegiance to a bloc, but it is more difficult to tell whether Egypt had also been aligned with a bloc, in the sense in which the concept of alignment is customarily understood today. This is understandable in view of the general structure of relationships at the time when the blocs were in the stage of formation.[8]

On the other hand, the countries which acquired independence after the Second World War made up a large portion of the world population, even if we only count those which won independence in the very early post-war years. In the course of time more countries became independent, so that the number of nonaligned countries greatly increased in Africa, and the movement extended its orbit even as far as Latin America. The colonial background of most of the nonaligned countries and the mounting wave of anti-colonialism throughout the world had a strong effect on the spreading and formulation of the policy of nonalignment. This influence was no less significant than that of

---

[8] The foreign policy of Egypt, as of other Arab countries which were nonaligned at that time, was under the strong influence of political developments in the Near East, particularly the efforts to found Israel as a separate country. After Israel's formation, it was constantly affected by clashes with this state. In the first conflict, Great Britain was on the side of the Arabs, while the United States expressed sympathy for Israel. The Soviet Union gave full assistance to Israel in this war, in war material and in the diplomatic sphere.

the cold war. Anti-colonialism for more than a decade set the tone for the activities of the nonaligned countries.

The disintegration of the colonial empires of Great Britain, France and the Netherlands in Southeast Asia inaugurated the final crisis of the colonial system. In the quoted statement by Nehru made in September 1946, we already find strong accents of anti-colonialism. Later on anti-colonialism became the most important force of nonalignment, with very far-reaching effects. The first major gathering which heralded the subsequent conferences of nonaligned countries was the Bandung conference of Asian and African countries.[9]

This development brought to the surface another problem which until then had not been much in evidence owing to the structure of the colonial empires. The newly independent countries started life as poorly developed countries. Their economic problems now became problems of international significance. Early in the 1950s the problem of economic development became one of the major issues in the United Nations.

In view of the increasingly tense atmosphere of the cold war and the tendency of the blocs to spread by absorbing as many new countries as possible, the economic weaknesses of the poorly developed countries became a political problem since they provided excellent opportunities for external pressure. On the other hand, the blocs started using economic aid and even normal economic relations more and more as instruments of cold war policies. Consequently, the development of the policy of nonalignment should not be viewed exclusively as the political behavior of countries anxious to avoid being drawn into the conflicts between the two blocs, but rather as a reaction to an involved complex of trends and conditions in a fast-changing world.[10]

It is true that the real significance of changes can be evaluated only in retrospect. It was not easy to fully comprehend their ramifications at the time, namely, in the early post-war years,

---

[9] The communique published after the tripartite meeting on Brioni expressly cited the Bandung Conference held a year earlier as the precursor of the joint cooperation among the nonaligned countries which was promoted by this tripartite meeting.

[10] The first action for substantial assistance to the underdeveloped countries was initiated in the United Nations by the nonaligned countries, and over the years this politically most active group in the third world became the nucleus and initiator of all actions in this realm.

and those who were active in politics must have viewed with astonishment the magnitude and speed of changes, the outcome of which they could not foresee with any certainty. It is, therefore, not surprising that the ideas and statements from that time — not to mention attempts at defining nonalignment — should be full of inconsistencies, differences and even controversies.

The new independent countries of the third world first concentrated their efforts on maintaining, strengthening and elevating their status in the world, a status that was being seriously threatened by ruthless economic competition and the cold war. The feeling of pride in newly-acquired statehood, as seen in a strong insistence on sovereignty, marked their basic approach to international relations. It made a strong and lasting imprint upon their foreign policies.

Consequently, nonalignment can be defined as a policy strictly based on independence, conducted by states which experience a strong feeling of insecurity but are not able to cope with events in their environment. It is substantially a defensive policy, but one that is at the same time imbued with fervent nationalism.

Opposition to the policy of toeing the line generally stems from the fear that by joining a bloc the country would lose its freedom of action, both in international affairs and in internal policies. This does not imply that aloofness from the blocs is not at the same time inspired by the rejection of the idea of bloc policy. In fact there is no contradiction between those two motives, because the global policy of a bloc cannot help conflicting with the policy of a country which insists upon its independence. The global policy of a bloc is generally, if not invariably, directed by the leading power in the alliance.

It is obvious that none of these statements should be taken at their face value. There is no such thing as "full freedom of action", because confrontation with the environment necessarily limits this freedom. This applies just as much to the great powers, even the superpowers, as it does, of course, to the smaller and underdeveloped countries. These last-mentioned countries do not have much choice in critical situations, but they treasure the freedom they do have highly.

They are frequently forced against their will to act in a determined manner or to put up with behavior from others which they may consider objectionable and even unacceptable. Standing outside of blocs they occasionally have to renounce their freedom of action, whereas joining a bloc would mean for them a permanent and general loss of that freedom. Moreover, it should be remembered that underdeveloped countries, as members of a bloc, have fewer opportunities for independent action within the bloc organization, should an improvement in international relations permit such a possibility.

Consequently, the dilemma is to choose between an independent stand in foreign policy, which implies inevitable compromises under the pressure of circumstances beyond the control of that country, and submission to a discipline which permanently and totally limits free decision-making. This dilemma loses its drastic character when a country considers that its interests are so coincident with those of the bloc, or of the country heading that bloc, that renunciation of independent decision-making gives no feeling of subordination. Furthermore, there is substantial difference between a young and economically underdeveloped country and a trully developed country. The latter, relying upon its economic position and international status, is much better equipped to claim a greater freedom of action should there be any divergences in interests or should a rigid discipline inside the bloc be felt unnecessary.

The success of some developed countries in gaining greater freedom of action within the Western bloc, especially at times when tension between the blocs has abated, is a good example in support of this thesis.[11] The probability of greater freedom varies from case to case and depends on the general level of development and strength of each country. It is considerably greater in Western Europe than in the rest of the world.

This development also shows that the role of the dominant power within the bloc cannot be fully defined. The degree of domination and the ability to influence the policy of an alliance

---

[11] In this connection compare the opposition by various NATO member countries to the plan presented by the U.S.A. on the formation of multilateral nuclear naval forces, as well as the refusal by Denmark and Norway to allow nuclear weapons to be placed on their territory.

vary from case to case. They depend on numerous factors, the most important among which is the degree of strain, i. e., assessment of the danger threatening from outside, as well as on the ability of the leading bloc power to maintain its position within the bloc without openly hectoring the other members. Conversely, whenever it has been necessary to restore bloc discipline by cracking the whip, it resulted in increased tension between the blocs.

The nonaligned countries, economically underdeveloped and sensitive to external pressures, decided to protect themselves against a possible loss of independence by remaining outside the blocs and by resolutely opposing any encroachment on their sovereignty, except when it might be for the benefit of the international community.

The stifling of free action in international relations was always challenged whenever a major national interest was at stake, for example demands or rejection of demands to alter the borders inherited from the colonial period. In most cases, whether the issue concerns the borders or something else, the roots of the conflict go back to pre-independence times when foreign powers were still in charge.

The nonaligned countries have often very energetically insisted on the satisfaction of their direct demands, and especially on the correction of the situation inherited from the colonial past. Indonesia for many years aided resistance against the Dutch authorities in West Irian and against the British authorities in Borneo, whereas India used force to establish her sovereignty over the Portuguese colony of Goa. At the same time they insisted on a peaceful solution of disputes among the great powers. They defended their acts by claiming that the issue was the final liquidation of colonialism, or unwillingness of the colonial power to withdraw before the expressed will of the people.

This behavior will seem more rational if we accept that nonalignment's main motive is to maintain and promote independence, to eliminate the feeling of insecurity and to abolish the gap between the underdeveloped and the developed countries. The generalization of this principle and formulation of the platform of nonalignment are based upon national experiences which are

110

compared and coordinated with the experiences of other countries, and not on a generalized, theoretically defined premise. In other words, nonalignment is the result of the political programs of individual countries, inspired by their conditions and needs. The elaboration of precepts and principles, and the formulation of a general platform came later, as an outgrowth of practical action.

The same applies to alliances. While strongly opposing the existing blocs, i. e., alliances of a global character, the nonaligned countries have always accepted alliances of a local character. Sometimes this policy produced negative results and got the nonaligned countries involved in local wars, although they continued being nonaligned in the sense which they themselves attribute to this term and which truly represents the essence of their policies.

EFFORTS TO INCREASE SOCIAL STABILITY

Closely connected with the political motives of nonalignment is its economic content. The nonaligned countries are trying to speed up economic development and improve their position in world markets because they realize that otherwise they cannot achieve internal political stabilization. Economic development is not only an element of internal policy; one could rather say that it is mainly motivated by the international situation. It arises from the need to maintain and strengthen national independence. We have already pointed out that the desire to preserve independence is the prime consideration in formulating foreign policy in general. It has been shown that the low level of economic development has always been the main limiting factor in regard to foreign policy. It is therefore understandable that countries are anxious to overcome their underdevelopment, which prevents them from formulating and implementing a less constrained foreign policy, by accelerating their economic development.

However, efforts in that direction can only produce results on a long-term, and even very long-term basis. Since the earliest beginnings of the policy of nonalignment, the economic factor constituted one of the main motive forces and later became the strongest motive which impelled the nonaligned countries to cooperation and joint action. Indeed, actions in the economic domain brought most of the countries together under the banner of nonalignment.

Nonalignment could also be defined as a policy designed to improve the prestige and influence of a country in the international community, enabling it to participate on an equal footing in the life of that community. This would be in accordance with the earlier definition, because independence can be exercised only if a country possesses the means necessary to do so.

In some instances, especially in the early years of nonalignment, statesmen and politicians of those countries tended to overemphasize the political element, failing to show a commensurate interest in international economic problems. This was most probably the result of an exceptionally tense political situation and high sensitivity to direct political dangers. However, in those cases too, one should not jump to the conclusion that the policies of those countries were not largely determined by economic necessities.

The political activities of the governments and leading political organizations of the nonaligned countries should be viewed in their totality. If a political issue overshadowed all others at a given moment, it does not mean that the leaders had lost sight of the need to alleviate the poverty of their own people. They may always have had economic vicissitudes uppermost in their mind, but on occasion these were given less emphasis in the conduct of their foreign policies. Finally, it should be recognized that in some cases the playing down of the economic element of nonalignment was the result of poor judgement, or of overestimating the possibilities of achieving results exclusively by political efforts.

Except for rare exceptions, the governments and leading political parties of nonaligned countries generally regarded the policy of promoting economic development as a defensive policy designed to preserve internal political stability. The most serious and direct threat to the political stability of these countries is violence against government to which any well-organized group can resort, taking advantage of the people's dissatisfaction with the slowly rise in living standards. Internal stability is often threatened not only by the inadequacy of the socio-political system but also by the low level of economic development or by the inadequate distribution of the available fund of goods and services. It may also be menaced by high capital investments, an inefficient utilization of resources, or by a misguided policy of economic development. It is quite futile to recommend efficiency to the governments of the less developed countries, because one of the characteristics of underdevelopment is precisely that efforts in the economic domain are poor and inadequate.

Consequently, in the majority of these countries internal stability is shaky, and more or less violent coups d'état are a frequent occurrence.[12] Hence efforts are being made to alleviate the situation by providing external economic aid, which is another device in the general effort to ensure internal stability. Irrespective of whether it is made through an international organization, bilaterally, or within regional groups, this effort is always boosted when dissatisfaction becomes rife in the country.

However, it would be wrong and irrational automatically to relate the level of political stability to the level of economic development. First of all, political stability cannot be identified with political and social relationships. It does not depend only on the excellence of a socio-political system, but is more directly the function of the level at which the population accepts that system. These subjective assessments, however, change not only in the course of centuries but also at shorter intervals, especially in our times of rapid and deep changes.

Every attempt to establish a functional link between economic development and political stability is necessarily an approximation which is qualified by specific circumstances and assumptions. It should be assumed first of all that the acceptance or rejection of a given system will be proportionate to the sacrifices demanded from, or benefits accrued to, that section of the population which is a potential force for overthrowing or supporting the system.

---

[12] Coups d'état and even counter coups took place in a number of nonaligned countries in Asia (Burma and Indonesia) and in Africa (Ghana, Sudan, Nigeria, Mali, Congo, Syria, Algeria, Libya, etc.). Similar occurrences are of course typical for other countries in the region of the underdeveloped countries.

A consideration based on economic development can do no more than show, more or less accurately, to what extent a given state of the economy calls for sacrifices and/or how much it satisfies monetary expectations.[13]

This dependence cannot be expressed by means of a simple formula. It is obvious that the same percentage of the national income allocated for administration, defense and economic growth does not unduly burden the population where per capita income is at a high level, as it does in countries with a very low income. Within the limits of existing conditions in the present-day world, the political effect of a given rate of investment and government spending is likely to be greater where the general level of income is lower. Furthermore, the rate of government spending and investment in some advanced countries would not be at all possible in countries having the lowest per capita income, for it would jeopardize the basic subsistence needs of their population. On the other hand, in some very highly developed countries even relatively high levies on consumption are still tolerable and permit a standard of living which exceeds that of other developed countries, not to mention the less developed ones.

This means that in a given country a parallel rise in national income and public expenditure and investment has a positive effect on political stability. However, this presupposes the amount of these savings from consumption to be sufficient to cover the needs of the administration, defense and investments needed to ensure the envisaged economic growth. If this amount is inadequate, as is largely the case in the poorly developed countries, and if the rate of economic growth is to be speeded up in order to achieve a sufficient progress in view of the low absolute income, there is immediately a tendency to reduce consumption. This upsets the stability of the political system or at least of the political

---

[13] H. Mynt made a very interesting remark in connection with these considerations in *The Economics of the Developing Countries*, Hutchinson University Library, London 1967. On page 19, the author states: "On the one hand there is what may be called the objective problem of poverty which can be measured by the absolute level of per capita income. On the other hand, there is the subjective problem of the discontent of the underdeveloped countries with their present economic status which far transcends this simple measurement. For this arises not only from their inability to fulfil economic desires, such as the desire to imitate the high standards both of private consumption and public social welfare, but also from the psychological and political drive to raise national prestige and obtain equal status with the developed countries.«

institutions. The effect will be felt most severely when the political system is inelastic and when avenues are not open for citizens to influence government policies.

Stability is understood here as the ability of society and its institutions to adapt to new needs. This, of course, does not mean that in a stable society existing institutions do not have the ability to maintain themselves and withstand pressure. They in fact maintain themselves either by resisting changes, or by absorbing innovations into the system, which thereby changes but preserves its essence and thus can more effectively resist the pressures aimed at negating the system as a whole.

Such a definition of stability also implies that the level of democracy and personal freedom of citizens will be approximately proportionate to stability. This statement echoes the well-known assertion that the feeling of insecurity in any political system tends to make the authorities more repressive, whereas self-confidence arising from stability allows much greater tolerance of non-conformism.

The influence of economic development on a political system and its functioning is only one of the factors which determine political trends in society and should not be taken as a formula which explains more than just one of the functional relationships which give a conclusive result only when taken all together. This aspect is interesting for us because this formula throws light on one of the most important contradictions in the aspirations of the less developed countries.

By trying to speed up economic development these countries are frequently jeopardizing their own political stability, but they are forced to do so because they are thus strengthening that factor which helps to create stability, i. e. the factor of economic development. In other words, in order to promote political stability through economic activity, they are forced first to jeopardize this very stability by forcing economic development.

Any decision to speed up economic development must not only take into account the internal effect of this drive, but, most important, recognize the fact that the poorly developed countries are both relatively and absolutely lagging behind the highly advanced countries, and that their international position is therefore deteriorating. Thus it becomes compellingly urgent to ameliorate this situation and reverse the trend as much as possible and as soon as possible.

In the internal development of a country, economic development and the political aspects of its internal life and growth of its institutions have a reciprocal effect on one another. Acceptance or rejection of the regime does not depend solely, and often not even predominantly, on the burden that economic development and poverty inflict on the citizens. The already mentioned inadequacies in administration, wrong decisions, and even the personal qualities or shortcomings of the leading statesmen and politicians may play a very important role. Of course, these specific factors greatly depend on the overall political system in a given country. The character of that system and the character of social relationships may soften or sharpen the effects of the general economic situation and the mentioned inadequacies. In short, the political climate of a country affects the willingness of its citizens to bear sacrifices and accept hardships, and also influences the results of economic efforts.

Without going into a detailed discussion of these interrelationships, we shall content ourselves with the statement that political and economic activities are linked and that there can be no success or failure in one of the two spheres without repercussions in the other. Thus the nonaligned countries' insistence on actions aimed at improving their lot should not be treated as a separate economic activity or a separate aspect of the policy of nonalignment, but rather as a part of the very definition of this political activity. Such activity is just as political as actions to defuse the cold war or to liberate the colonies. If its immediate goals are to gain economic advantages or to accelerate development, it should be remembered that this is the aim and expected result of every action taken by these countries, including even those which are purely political in their immediate aims.

116

THE IRRELEVANCE OF THE CONFLICTS AMONG THE ADVANCED COUNTRIES FOR THE NONALIGNED

Nonalignment has shown a vitality that is truly impressive. In spite of the deep upheavals and crises which some of the nonaligned countries have experienced in their relations with neighboring countries or in their internal development, their number has steadily increased, and no country has ever left the ranks of the nonaligned for good. Some countries have hesitated and vacillated in their foreign policy orientation when faced with difficult crises, but equilibrium was always finally restored, and nonalignment was reinstated.

This loyalty of the nonaligned countries to their general line in relations with the outside world should not be taken as a unique and exceptional phenomenon. Just as nonalignment is generated by the essence of the social processes in these countries and their position in the international community, the policies of the countries within the blocs have also been conditioned by circumstances beyond their control. This phenomenon is the sequel to a deep change taking place over the last few decades: foreign policy has ceased to be the secret game of a small number of political groups and cabinets.

Although foreign policy is still today formulated in an often understandable and sometimes necessary secrecy, and is even more often shrouded in unnecessary mystery, basic international policies are inconceivable in any contemporary state without the knowledge and acquiescence of the broadest strata of the population. This does not reduce the possibility of relatively rapid and often unexpected changes, particularly in critical situations, but such tactical moves — aside from their historical importance — must be distinguished from the shifts in the direction or nature of the policy.

In an essay on foreign policies, F. S. Northedge[14] correctly pointed out that there was no reason to expect that a change of government or ideology or even a revolution in a country would

---

[14] *The Foreign Policies of Powers*, edited by F. S. Northedge, Faber & Faber, London 1968, p. 12.

alter the manner in which it handles its foreign relations, i. e., that a change in diplomatic approach necessarily implies a change of policy. Of course, this observation should be regarded as a long-term assessment. Even in cases of very radical internal changes or deep social transformations, certain constants appear after a certain time; they are in fact values which change so slowly that they may be assumed as constants over time spans which can be summarized and understood as historical periods.

In the case of very deep transformations, departures from the norm may last somewhat longer, particularly in the case of important ideological issues. But these views are also subject to changes, since "in foreign affairs, the view of the road changes when one moves from the passenger's into the driver's seat."[15]

However, changes in the countries of the third world happening as a result of government overthrows, democratic elections or a shift in the balance of forces within the ruling elites do not usually produce such deep divergences in viewpoints as to disturb stability in foreign policy.

The consistency of the nonaligned countries in their foreign policies is therefore not an exceptional phenomenon in the present-day world. In this respect nonalignment does not differ from other orientations; it is a truly fundamental policy and not just tactics. The stability of a policy in international relations is the best proof of its social relevance and importance in the life of a nation, particularly at a time of rapid and sweeping changes which often call for radical measures and shifts in tactics.

If we are to explore the reasons for the stability of this policy despite its variable concepts and the vicissitudes of the international situation, we must investigate the basic elements in the social structure underlying its changing surface. In other words, we must investigate the foundation on which the foreign policies and options of the nonaligned countries are based.

There is no doubt that opposition to the cold war and the rejection of the alternative which it imposed provided the initial

---

[15] *Ibid.*, p. 13.

impulse for a redefinition of foreign policy and adoption of the policy of nonalignment. This occurred in different circumstances and at different times, i. e., in situations of varying intensity and scope of the cold war hostilities. Furthermore, it took place during various phases of national life, soon after independence or following national emergencies, as was the case when the monarchy was overthrown in Egypt in 1953 and replaced by a new, republican political system.

Leaving aside for the moment the matter of the internal convulsions or external troubles of the countries adhering to the policy of nonalignment, we shall concentrate on the cold war itself as the ever present factor in every new proclamation of nonalignment. We shall not analyze this factor and the characteristics of its various phases, but shall try to find what is permanent in this phenomenon and liable to produce a similar reaction in countries at different levels of underdevelopment.

The cold war arose within the advanced portion of mankind, in an area which over many centuries had acquired and maintained a dominant place in the world, i. e., the countries of Europe and of North America. As the conflict spread, other countries were drawn into the cold war, but two groups remained in the centre of the strife: the North Atlantic Pact and the Warsaw Treaty Organization.

Although all the countries in this area are not economically developed to the same extent, this region should nevertheless be treated as developed. After all, under a political assessment of development, countries are not categorized according to strictly economic indicators, but rather according to the role which they really play in international affairs. This evaluation must include the economic, military, and political potentials of a country. Finally, this area is particularly significant because whoever gains the upper hand in it could dominate the entire world.

The role that Europe once played in international relations (until the First World War) has now been taken over by this area, which extends from the eastern confines of the Soviet Union to the western coast of North America. All the other countries of the world have until recently been subordinated to the countries of Europe and North America, or have been extensions of them (Australia, New Zealand and South Africa). The only exception in the twentieth century is Japan.[16]

The cold war, accordingly, originated and was waged primarily among the countries of the region which had the dominant place in world affairs and in which the fate of the entire world had been decided. If we went to extremes and tried to represent the potential of a region exclusively in terms of military strength, then the predominance of this part of the world would be even greater, but this would be too one-sided a picture. We mention this only as a reminder that the military power of the blocs in the early post-war years was the foundation for their foreign policies.

Clearly, the cold war could not have had the same significance for the countries of the European and American continent as for those outside this area. For the former, it was their own conflict, in which they had a stake to win or lose. In other words, their survival depended on its outcome, and in the beginning hopes of a victory were nurtured on both sides in the cold war. It was only later that the unreality of this concept became apparent to everyone.

The picture looked quite different to the countries in other parts of the world; the victory of either side did not hold out the promise of any essential changes for them. This does not mean that some political currents in one country or another did not hope to gain an advantage from the victory of a side in the European-American sphere. The bourgeoisie in the new countries could expect benefits if the West won, and the socialist movements, insofar as they were formed in the first years after the war, could ancitipate advantages if the East won. However, in neither case would their overall position change overnight; in no case could they depend on the points won or lost by a side in the cold war.

What is more, the practical policies of the Soviet Union under Stalin could not be much of an inspiration for the left-wing

---

[16] Later, in the 1960s, China emerged as a special and increasingly important factor in international relations and as the first nuclear power outside the area designated above. However, at the time that nonalignment appeared and developed, i. e., from the end of World War II up to the beginning of the 1960s, the description given above of the specific role of the border area connected with Europe and North America holds true.

forces of these countries. The position of these countries did not depend on the good will of the two groupings in the European-American region, but rather on real relationships based on social and economic differences. Finally, whatever consequences the outcome of the cold war might have for the poor countries, they certainly did not seek this way out of their difficulties. They did not count on the outcome of the war at all, reasoning that the lack of prospects that it would end in a foreseeable future was a sufficient reason for keeping out of it.

In short, the countries of the less developed parts of the world looked upon the cold war as a conflict in another world, a world which was outside their realm of interests and with whose way of life and level of development they could not catch up for a long time to come.

They therefore could not identify themselves with the cold war. Even when they became involved in it, it went against the grain and they were liable to change their behavior unexpectedly, as was the case with Pakistan which subordinated its relations with great Powers to the interests in its own border conflict with India.[17]

Thus there was no identification in the third world countries with either of the opposing sides in the cold war in contrast to Europe and North America, where there were clearly defined social structures which gave a special stamp to the cold war. For a country to join one of the blocs, there must be a certain similarity in views and social systems. This similarity existed in the opposing groups in the developed part of the world, but it did not end there. There was a certain amount of identification in other parts of the world too; in the case of Japan, and of some Latin American countries in which the European element maintained a majority or was firmly in power. Identification with the East, for example, became evident in Cuba's foreign policy orientation after Fidel Castro's take-over. A number of right-wing regimes in the countries of Central and South America were clearly on the side of the West.

---

[17] Pakistan went the farthest in this respect. After a short military clash with India in September 1965, Pakistan began to procure more and more war material and weapons from the Soviet Union, but this did not prevent it from developing relations with China as well. The direct cause of this turn-about was the U. S.'s halting of arms deliveries.

THE DEVELOPMENT AND MODERNIZATION
OF SOCIAL SYSTEMS

The policy of the nonaligned countries cannot be viewed merely as a policy based on the negative principle of refusing to join the blocs. The nonaligned countries have been very active in international relations, and this activity has given a positive content to nonalignment. Nonalignment and non-cooperation with blocs imply the need for an independent policy definition and not reliance on collective beliefs of a group of countries or, as is most often the case, on the stands of the bloc leader. The nonaligned countries' active stand on world events is therefore rooted in their own needs and in judgements based on their specific interests.

Unlike the advanced countries having established social structures and developed institutions, the underdeveloped countries could not even try to impose their systems on others nor are they interested in doing so. They do not act as protagonists of formulated concepts which they wish to export to other countries. In fact, they resist such attempts by the developed countries and are in search of new ways and models of economic and social development. When they succeed in retaining their identity and in resisting the efforts of the developed countries to foist upon them their own systems and policies, they become nonaligned and determined to reject any interference in their internal affairs. The policy of nonalignment thus implies not only political independence and autonomy, but also the search for individual modes of internal development.

By defending their individuality, these countries at the same time take an active hand in international affairs, but their activity is primarily motivated by the desire to preserve their individuality. This does not mean that they follow no principles, because already at the time when they were being formed they were directed by the idea of abolishing colonialism and they had to solve economic problems. Their activity is designed to radically change the picture of the world, but here as well they are guided by their internal needs and not by a wish to impose their solutions on others.

This characteristic of the nonaligned underdeveloped countries reflects their special role and the specific features of their policy, as opposed to the policy of neutrality of some European countries. Furthermore, this characteristic precludes them from forming their own blocs. Neither can they join the existing blocs, nor can they form blocs among themselves. In today's conditions, at any rate, the forming of a bloc calls for a certain proselytizing approach.

In the cold war confrontation the countries are not merely participants in an international conflict, but also centres of political and social activities within the two blocs. The cold war is not fought just between groups of states, but also within each individual state. The transnational concatenation of political forces imparts to the confrontation an intensity and ferocity characteristic of civil wars. The victory of a side means the victory of its concepts and social system. The propagation of one's own model of society is, therefore, one of the essential elements of the conflict.

Of course, chances of attaining this goals by means of the cold war are practically nonexistent. Since a direct inter-bloc military context could not lead to a victory, because war as an instrument of settling scores had become unacceptable, the strife between the two blocs grew into a protracted state of political tension. In practical terms, the principal aim of each bloc is to coordinate the foreign policies of its members, since their survival depends on a common foreign policy and similarity in internal systems.

It would be difficult to imagine how new countries could create international organizations based on a joint foreign policy to the extent to which the blocs have. Their cooperation is possible only on the basis of common platforms agreed upon for each specific situation. Their common platform can and must be defined and redefined from time to time, and cooperation cannot be institutionalized by entrusting a permanent organization to determine the joint foreign policy of its member states.

A bloc-enforced cooperation demands identification which is not possible among the underdeveloped countries for the reasons that have been mentioned earlier, and most of all because of the fluid internal conditions arising from their imperfect social structures. This is best shown by the fact that no attempts on any scale and in any geographical region to set up some sort of ideo-logical-political organization of the new countries involving a joint active foreign policy have so far succeeded.[18]

The failure of any such efforts indicates not that there is no desire or need for close and lasting cooperation, but rather that there are no possibilities or real justification for bloc coalitions among these countries. Cooperation of another kind, on concrete issues such as decolonization and economic problems, has pro-duced some truly significant results. Thus emphasis is not on whether cooperation is possible, but rather in what sphere it is possible. This of course defines both area and the problems in which a lasting and systematic cooperation can be achieved. This point is important because it helps us to outline the active aspect of the policy of nonalignment in order to arrive at its positive definition.

For this purpose it is necessary to investigate the basic pro-blems of internal development typical for these countries and the pressures they exert on foreign policy, or conversely, how foreign relations affect their internal problems. Their overriding national concern, at a first glance, appears to be the need to secure foreign currency necessary to buy those products and services which are indispensable for a rapid economic development and which are not available in their own countries.

This is a vital problem indeed, especially for the countries in a more advanced phase of industrialization which have no suitable export produce, such as oil or some minerals. However, it would be unreasonable to think that this alone is material to the correlation between internal problems and international rela-

---

[18] The Arab countries showed a relatively high degree of cohesion, but they cannot be taken as a unified group, except in connection with the dispute with Israel. After the June war of 1967, however, differences have arisen among them even on this issue which have proved to be a serious impediment to any collective actions and even to agreement on a joint platform at the meeting of Arab leaders in December 1969.

It is difficult to bracket the Latin American countries in a separate political group with a common foreign policy, since the unity achieved in various instances through the Organization of American States is qualified by the dominant influence of the U. S. A. This organization is more accurately seen as an auxiliary organization of the system of alliances linked with the North Atlantic Treaty Organiza-tion. Initiatives on problems of development, for instance at meetings of UNCTAD, do not fall under the category of collective foreign policy, because there is a general platform here which allows co-operation even among countries that are otherwise in open conflict with one other, e. g. India and Pakistan, both active participants within the group of underdeveloped countries in UNCTAD.

tions. Internal affairs in underdeveloped countries and world affairs are also linked in other ways.

The economic interdependence of all the countries in the world, however remote they might be from each other, has considerably increased. Greater national output and improved transport facilities and communications have contributed to this enormous expansion of the world market. This is common knowledge but so is the fact that the rate of production growth has not been uniform either in the world as a whole or in various branches of economic activity. But dependence on the world market has a different effect on highly advanced countries and on poorly developed countries. This dependence does not have the same character in both cases, nor does it create problems that are similar.

This is not the place to go into this question in detail, but we must nevertheless consider the special position of the underdeveloped countries in this respect.

Their economic development, and this primarily means modernization of their economies by improvement of agriculture and acceleration of industrialization, is taking place in a world dominated by highly advanced technology. The developed economies and advanced production methods dictate relationships in the world markets. If there are any exceptions applying to the traditional methods of production of some exotic products, they only confirm this general rule. In consequence, the first basic form of the dependence of the underdeveloped countries is dependence on the centres of contemporary science and technology.

Furthermore, there is a mounting dissonance between modern technology's demand for mass production and the slow and inadequate development of the internal market in the underdeveloped countries. Modern mass production is a product not only of increased technical opportunities, but also of mass consumption resulting from increased living standards of the population. Mass consumption is not possible in the underdeveloped countries because it is only through industrialization that they would eventually expand and intensify their internal consumption. Consequently they become dependent on foreign markets for the sale of their new industrial products to such an extent that it weakens their position in the world market. Finally, the economies of the underdeveloped countries are not able to keep up with the increasing demands for investment caused by the ever more expensive and complex instruments of modern production. These expensive instruments, equipment, means of transport, apparatuses and machines of various kinds, as well as fuels and chemicals, are developed quickly, but some of them also become soon obsolete. Their own capital for reconstruction and modernization is obviously not adequate, and hence they come to be dependent on external financial resources.

These three forms of dependence — in the domains of technology, production and financing — are not the only weak points of the underdeveloped countries, nor does the above fully reveal the acute and far-reaching nature of each one. For example, the unfavorable position resulting from their need to stimulate foreign trade and from the inferiority of their foreign trade organization, as well as difficulties in competing against renowned producers, the unfavorable structure of imports and exports, etc. are only some of the additional points which have not been touched upon here and which aggravate the position of the underdeveloped countries in the world market and make their economic development dependent on the behavior and trends in the world.

We have said earlier that the new countries are in the stage of developing their social systems, even in the stage of national formation and definition of national territory. This internal social and political transformation coincides with efforts to overcome economic backwardness and with all the difficulties arising therefrom. This process is taking place in a world where states with well-formed political institutions wield a strong influence in the world market.[19] As a result, the new and economically underdeveloped countries are exposed to very strong external pressures.

External influence in itself should not be regarded as something undesirable, but here we are dealing with the impact of

---

[19] The term "world market" is used here and elsewhere as defined by contemporary economics. Of course there is no such thing as a single, united market in which economic market laws operate. The existence of sovereign states and the very sophisticated modes of governmental intervention shatter the "world" character of the market into a number of national markets in which market laws operate more or less freely. Therefore the world market is a complex concept which subsumes the operation of market laws and the existence of national barriers and intervention.

power from far mightier states, states on which those countries are economically dependent. However, there were also other external impulses. Independence movements in those countries were strongly influenced by the developed part of the world. Revolutions, revolutionaries and literal ideas and trends crossed the seas and national borders and encouraged liberation movements in the third world.

This does not diminish the historical role of the movements against foreign domination which arose spontaneously in some parts of the world, such as for instance the movements against foreign domination in India and in China in the 19th and early 20th centuries respectively. However, the actual liberation of these countries took place mostly on concepts and in the spirit of the ideas which emerged in some parts of Europe, from the Magna Carta in Britain and the French Revolution to socialist revolutions.

Nor did any of the European nations achieve its unification and socio-political formation without foreign influence or interference in their autonomous internal development, yet their position was different from that of the countries which now find themselves in a similar stage of development. This is not to say that the situation of the new countries is in every respect more difficult, but there is no doubt that their internal development is subject to very particularly strong external influences. It is evident, for example, that the independence of some African colonies was achieved as a result of successful anti-colonial movements in some other African colonies and the general movement against colonialism in the world.[20] This fact is used as an argument that some colonies had been given independence "voluntarily". There is also no doubt that struggle for independence in the remaining colonies in Africa helps to keep up political mobilization in the independent African countries and that the latter aid the liberation movements, out of solidarity as well as for internal political reasons, and in order to strengthen their own independence.

---

[20] The example of Guinea, which voted for independence in the 1958 referendum and managed to hold its own against France, encouraged the majority of former French colonies in Black Africa to demand their own independence.

Finally, border disputes and nationality problems, characteristic for the early stage of national formation owing to separatist and hegemonist or unitarist tendencies, make relations with neighbors in some new countries almost inseparable from their internal relations. In some cases it is even difficult to distinguish internal problems from external ones, because the definition of what comes under the spheres of foreign or internal policies is not always clear or is under dispute.[21]

The prime mover in the political life of the new countries is the people's aspiration to improve their material and social position as quickly and as radically as possible, as well as the desire of their governments to meet this pressure, unless they choose to curb such aspirations with force. In this last instance there can obviously be only temporary equilibrium, because in such conditions it is not possible even to think of resolving the basic socio-political problems. The country in which such a policy prevails must, therefore, rely on factors outside society for its survival, which practically means reliance on external forces having sufficient resources and interest to back the regime in being. We are not going to consider these cases because they are obviously outside the scope of this study.

It is therefore understandable why the nonaligned countries are keenly considering the question of the development of social relationships and the formation of new and materially and historically acceptable institutions. These endeavors are very frequently related to socialism. This is evidenced by the declarations on internal social and political developments in most of the nonaligned countries in Asia and Africa.

Nonalignment is therefore gradually acquiring the character of a movement which aspires towards social transformation, but which is composed of countries that, while swearing allegiance to socialism, envision and carry out this transformation in very different manners. What is more, there are also internal differences in some countries or political movements as to the method, pace and direction of changing the existing conditions. It is beyond a doubt that this situation should indeed be changed.

---

[21] Examples of this are the conflict over Kashmir between India and Pakistan, the civil wars in Congo-Kinshasa and Nigeria, and some aspects of the relations among Arab states in the Near East.

The complexity and diversity of attitude among the non-aligned countries are due not only to the specific conditions prevailing in each country, but also to various influences from outside. The predominance of an influence frequently affects the policy orientation of that country more than the internal factors themselves. Consequently, the countries having otherwise similar social and economic problems frequently take very divergent roads.

Yet, despite these differences, there are nevertheless certain common features. Modernization is carried out under the compulsion of two major motives: to promote stability and to strengthen their international position. It is not dependent on the subjective predilections for modernization and changes of individual statesmen and politicians. Yet at the same time, desire for a change and unanimity about a goal do not necessarily imply unanimity about methods and directions of action, nor agreement as to the pace at which transformation should be made.

Consequently, in terms of the development of social institutions and relationships, nonalignment may be regarded as a socio-political tendency which seeks modernization and is resolved to achieve it. Nonalignment is not yet developing towards unified ideological conceptions or views about the ways and means of further social development. Neither in that respect nor in respect of foreign policy do the nonaligned countries constitute a conformist community of thought, but they have common basic desires and general goals which form the basis for cooperation typical of the foreign political activities of these countries.

The policy of nonalignment in the sense of non-adhesion to blocs, in other words in its negative sense of standing aloof from the cold war, springs from the very being of those countries whose past and social realities keep them outside that sphere of international relations within which the cold war is being fought. It is at the same time significant how poorly and vaguely the acceptance of the policy of nonalignment is formulated. In the majority of these countries it hardly goes beyond very generalized statements about their refusal to align themselves with the blocs.

The elaboration of policies and the construction of a unified political conception was the product of a limited circle which from very outset established itself as a dynamic nucleus of nonalignment.[22] These countries inspired and organized all the actions of the nonaligned countries. When this nucleus functioned, the entire movement was galvanized, when it was passive, handicapped or absorbed by other problems, there was passivity in the entire nonaligned community.

Whereas the principle of nonalignment, in the sense of being apart from the blocs, could develop in those communities which wanted to stand behind the sidelines in any dispute among the countries which are socially alien to them, the principle of coexistence could be elaborated only from a progressive view of the world and presupposes a well developed social structure in the country[23]

This, of course, does not exclude the possibility that individuals in any country might, through intellectual effort, arrive to similar points of view. However, we are not dealing here with proclamations or theses of different politicians or scholars, but with foreign policies which no personality can permanently impose on a country if they do not safeguard the social interests of those strata which shape national policies in the given country.

The attitude to the policy of nonalignment in the countries which have adhered to it shows that there is in fact a deep relationship between the internal conditions and needs of a society and its foreign policy orientation. However, it is necessary to emphasize the role of the government as the policy-maker of a country, all the more so since some of the new countries seem to prefer relying on a bloc in dealing with international issues.

In the countries which won independence after the Second World War, or, like Ethiopia, liberated themselves from foreign occupation, governments have come into power by one of three methods: they emerged from the liberation or anti-colonial movements after the successfully completed anti-colonial or liberation struggle; they continued the administrations which existed in the last stage of colonialism as local governments or indi-

---

[22] India, Egypt and Yugoslavia make up this nucleus.

[23] For more on this problem and on the nonaligned countries' lack of identification with the issues and protagonists in the cold war, see the article by Leo Mates, "Društvena uslovljenost politike nesvrstavanja" (Social Factors Conditioning the Policy of Nonalignment), *International Problems*, Beograd 1966, No. 3.

130

genous elements in mixed administrations; they came into power by means of a coup, having brought down the government which had come into being in one of the two mentioned ways.[24]

It is, therefore, understandable that the degree of representativeness of governments may vary considerably from one case to the next. What is more, the method of accession to power does not hold the key to representativeness. Government policies in some of these countries place them well within the scope of the blocs. The question arises whether in such cases these policies may be treated as acts of a non-representative government, or if we should seek in this behavior deeper motives and revise the earlier statements about the representativeness of the governments which adhere to the policy of nonalignment?

If we take a closer look at these countries, we shall find that they are generally very undeveloped and dependent on the aid which they receive and that they follow the guidance in foreign policies of the country granting this aid. Of course, by far the greatest benefit from this aid, as regards direct personal interests, goes to those circles close to the government or upon which it relies. On the other hand, among the bloc-oriented countries many are in a more or less open conflict with their immediate neighbors, are not sufficiently strong to cope with the situation alone, or their ruling circles cannot maintain themselves without external help.

It is also important to note that the great majority, in fact almost all, of the permanently bloc-oriented countries in Asia and Africa are located in the zone of the Pacific, where immediately after the war there were very strong and intensive revolutionary movements and heavy armed conflicts, particularly in Indochina and Indonesia, and to a lesser extent in the Philippines. Finally, we also find bloc orientations in the divided countries in that area (Korea and Vietnam), where the physical presence of the great powers determined political developments after the war.[25]

---

[24] Sometimes there are even combinations of these categories, especially when the representatives of national liberation movements took part in the last phase of colonial administration, as was the case in India and Ghana.

[25] A characteristic instance in this connection is the statement by the Provisional Revolutionary Government of South Vietnam upon its formation in 1969 that when the war is over it intends to adopt the policy of nonalignment.

It is certainly not accidental that the socially most developed countries in Asia and Africa declared themselves as nonaligned and are following that policy in a manner which truly corresponds to their concrete interests. On the other hand, in the most developed countries of Latin America there has been a more or less constant and hard struggle ever since the war between the popular masses organized in different parties against military dictatorships which are in favor of alignment.

We are led to conclude from the foregoing that nonalignment is a stable policy based on non-identification with the policies of any of the blocs. This, of course, does not mean that wherever the possibility of identification exists it must automatically happen. The countries whose internal structure and ideological formation place them in one of the camps may well, by following their own special interests, refuse to join a bloc. This is sometimes clearly stated, as in the case of Switzerland, and elsewhere there are only some intimations in that direction, as in the case of France.[26]

The only thing that can be concluded from the adduced arguments is that there are deep and lasting reasons which led the countries of the underdeveloped world generally to opt for nonalignment. The motivation which was under scrutiny here applies to the pronouncedly negative aspect of that policy, which is to keep outside the bloc conflicts, to base one's own foreign policy on the demand for freedom of action vis-à-vis each of the blocs and to resist any compulsion to follow bloc policies. This means in practice protection against external interference and involvement in any dispute between states belonging to the developed world, i. e., among the great powers and power blocs.

---

[26] We have in mind here the occasional statements by the French government against the policy and existence of blocs rather than its withdrawal from the military organization of NATO. This last step does not separate France from the bloc, because it remains a member of the Pact.

B. PROBLEMS OF SOCIAL AND ECONOMIC DEVELOPMENT

THE FORMATION OF POST-COLONIAL STATES

The ability to identify and readiness to cooperate with blocs are not only a function of the degree of economic development or of a country's general position in the world; there should also be an additional kinship of social systems. In this respect there is a substantial difference between the countries of Europe and North America on the one hand, and the underdeveloped world on the other. The former have a common past which is reflected in the cultural, social and scientific-technical heritage from the past centuries.[27] On the strength of this affinity and the differences which developed following the revolutionary trans-formations in Eastern Europe, two types of social systems came into being after the war, sufficiently clearly defined to serve as a basis for identification. Identification does not necessarily imply a full inclusion into a bloc. Some of the very "Western" countries, as for instance Sweden, have never countenanced military links with the North Atlantic Pact. They are West European neutrals, as they frequently call themselves. On the other hand, France refused to participate in the military organization of the North Atlantic Pact, but it remained a member of the military alliance and undoubtedly identifies itself with the West on all basic issues.

As for the countries of the underdeveloped part of the world, there is no question of any common historical links with the countries of the European-American sphere, nor are there social structures resembling those in Europe or in North America. In contrast to the clearly defined social systems and structures with firmly constructed elements, societies in the new countries

---

[27] The common heritage of these countries is reflected not only in the sphere of culture and general economic and social development, but also in the sphere of political thought. Marxism arose in Western Europe and spread East, where it was of crucial importance in the formation and develop-ment of revolutionary movements.

are in the stage of formation, in the phases of the crystallization of structures and social elements.[28]

These two worlds came into intensive contact during the era of European colonization. The most characteristic products of these contacts were certainly the colonial societies in some areas of Black Africa. It was not only military conquerors and administrators that penetrated into these primitive social systems at the height of colonization, but also the social patterns of the mother country. In accordance with their primitive means of production, tribal societies developed economic activities and relationships which throughout the centuries maintained stable social structures and ideologies, including primitive religions. The only significant breakthrough prior to European colonization was the Arab penetration into a wide area of Africa south of the Sahara, which brought Islam into those societies but little else.

The European colonization penetrated far more deeply into the indigenous way of life than the Arabs had and imposed completely new political relationships and, to a varying extent, new economic activities and economic relationships. European colonizers first appeared as representatives of an alien society which penetrated ever more deeply into the pores of the existing social fabric and into the way of life and thinking of individuals. Whatever numbers of immigrants from this alien society came, they always imposed the legal and social system which promoted the interests of the colonization, while making use of the local social elements and structures combining them with the imported elements which were frequently maladjusted and deformed reflections of home conditions.

The result of the colonial rule was consequently a complex of relationships and imposed institutions which were not the product of domestic social forces or of autonomous development of local societies. The entire system relied on imported might which openly and squarely stood outside and above the colonized society. Consequently, there were not only deformations of the existing social order, but also deformed, externally dictated de-

---

[28] Although European influences have been strong in this modern formation of social structures, it must be kept in mind that the previous systems of social relations in Asia and Africa considerably differed from those which in Europe resulted in modern capitalist or socialist societies.

velopment in the newly created colonial system of society. The resulting harm has done more to hamper development after decolonization than even the low level of economic development or the consequences of economic exploitation.

In some areas which were subjected to intensive economic exploitation indeed, the colonial government was forced to introduce more progressive social relationships, including wage-labor in the place of the slave labor or feudal and tribal relationships. True enough, these more progressive relationships were never brought to the levels attained in the colonizer's home countries developed under pressures of organized workers' movements. Nevertheless, in the colonies where major investments were made, these investments created a relatively more favorable basis for the further development than in less developed colonies. The latter are the most tragic product of colonialism, because neither did the colonizers have much use out of them, nor did they, after gaining independence, have a base to rely on in their efforts to develop their economies.[29]

After independence, the colonies obviously could not continue to exist in the social framework created during colonialism. They equally well could not return to the situation preceding colonization. They had no choice but to make what use they could of the remnants of a broken social order to construct a new edifice of social relationships and political institutions.[30]

Quite understandably, efforts were made to put to the best possible use, and most frequently to copy, the achievements of the other developed countries as regard political institutions and social system. This particularly applies to those institutions which can be created relatively quick and through subjective action. The basic elements of a modern social organization, which can be formed only during the process of economic development, did not exist, nor were they adequately developed and activated. This is how difficulties arose in the internal development which are still enduring to this day.

---

[29] Whereas according to U. N. statistics the per capita income in Ghana after independence was $ 150, in Chad it was $ 40 and in neighboring Togo $ 50.

[30] In the majority of cases in Africa, not only various colonial institutions but also personnel from the colonial period were retained some time after independence. This refers not only to technical services, but also to armed forces, the judiciary, teachers and police.

On the one hand, state institutions and organs of government were created after liberation in all the former colonies. However, in many young countries, in Africa in particular, these institutions, including even political parties, did not overcome traditional tribal attachments and loyalties. Thus on the surface there is a facade of European-modelled political structures, beneath which the traditional patterns of a remote past continue to live on. Only in some areas where modern economic activity is more strongly developed have they been corroded by the new spirit generated from it. However, even here we should guard against exaggerated expectations in regard to the social and political effects of the modernization of economic relationships. All they do is create a base for a further development in the sphere of politics and general behavior in public affairs, whereas the actual modernization of political life is proceeding very slowly.

Even the setting up of a new state is a feat under the given conditions. Here we should distinguish several particular problems. First of all, there is the problem of integration into the international community, i. e., breaking the pattern of foreign relations of colonial past. Next comes a number of extremely difficult internal problems. The process of building a state follows a course which is fundamentally different from the way in which the modern states of Europe had been created, those very states which now serve as a model for the political leaders of the former anti-colonial movements who are now trying to become statesmen and builders of new states. This problem has still not been sufficiently elucidated in literature, but there have been some rather important contributions already.

Thus, for example, Dankwart A. Rustow believes that the "founding of a new state in the process of transition from colonialism to independence is one of the most arduous and most delicate tasks of political leadership."[31] He enumerates five separate factors which should be taken into consideration in addition to the normal tensions which always appear in a politically undeveloped society and which arise from conflicts between the followers of a movement and their leader as they endeavor to build

---

[31] Dankwart A. Rustow, *A World of Nations, op. cit.*, pp. 153—156.

political institutions, between different tendencies among the followers themselves, as well as between realities and aspirations within the movement. The factors which Rustow especially emphasizes are, firstly the need to work fast, and yet to ensure a lasting result; secondly, the most important questions are at the same time the most urgent ones, which hinders the application of the democratic process of decision-making, as it usually happens in stable states only in emergencies which, there too, create similar situations; thirdly, there is a transition from the state of rebellion against authority to the state of creating a government; fourthly, the leaders must be above disputes and rivalries, and yet they must follow them closely and have a good knowledge about them; fifthly, at the moment of the downfall of the old and the creation of the new institutions, the role of leader is extremely difficult and important because it is through the leader that continuity, which the general transformation wants to upset, is ensured.[32]

This analysis of the problems affecting political life in new states is highly interesting, but it does not take sufficient account of the special circumstances arising from the need to create modern states in an environment whose social development had not reached the level comparable to that when modern states were created in Europe. This creates an additional difficulty or specially aggravates the earlier mentioned problems. As they have been given, these factors can also apply to revolutionary transformations or secessions or unions in socially developed environments such as Europe. These factors are common to all the deep changes in regard to statehood, and, although not reflecting the entire range of problems, are also applicable to the creation of post-colonial states.

Political instability which is the sequel to the mentioned problems frequently leads to usurpations of power which may temporarily resolve a tension but do not create bases for stability. Not only does a coup d'état not solve the basic problems requiring long-term efforts and favorable conditions in the country and in international relations; it is also a source of instability reproduced

---

[32] *Ibid.*

in a more acute form. As Rustow correctly points out,[33] referring to Max Weber and some earlier authors, when changes in institutions are introduced, while they are still new and vulnerable, stability depends on the leaders' charismatic influence. The toppling of a leader and the usurpation of power by the leader of the rebellion leads to the weakening of the charisma. The new leader can hardly invest the sullied and torn cloak of "liberation", and also the force of the charisma relies on originality, on a leader's ability to open up new roads, to create miracles, because he succeeds without trying to impose authority, counting on new sources of strength in the enthusiasm of millions whose aspirations he embodies. These qualities can hardly adorn the shield of a successful leader of a coup after the accomplishment of independence, no matter how much at a given moment he might express the general dissatisfaction with the prevailing state of affairs.

It is only in the states in which the new institutions, i. e. the new government and its mechanism, had become stabilized before the coup that relatively enduring new relationships may be expected, and even a temporary stabilization of the new regime. Hence the government overthrows soon after independence tend to lead to a general chaos. The best example in this respect is the Congo. Stabilization may then be induced by the appearance of a new leader or a group who will save the country from disaster and attain a stature resembling that of a leader of a liberation movement. The state of chaos usually leads to increased external intervention, as is again shown by the example of the Congo, and this enhance the feeling of insecurity, misery and oppression which dominated in the colonial era.

It is quite understandable that circumstances may differ from one country to the next, depending on the pre-colonial situation, on the duration of the colonization and on the degree of the colonial power's intervention in the internal life of each colony.[34] Another important factor in the post-colonial life was

---

[33] *Ibid.*, pp. 157 and 165.

[34] In addition to outside influences, strong tribal feelings also added to the bitterness of the internal conflicts that rent Congo-Kinshasa after the gaining of independence. Somewhat later tribal conflicts caused an extremely bloody civil war in Nigeria as well.

the amount of natural resources each country had for its economic development, and its geographical and climatic features. Yet, despite all the differences, these countries may be treated as one single, although very broad, category in comparison with the countries of Europe and North America. This categorization, as we have said, does not apply only to economic and technical but also to social and political characteristics.

Another significant factor is that in the majority of these countries, no nation in the modern sense of the word had been formed either during the colonial or pre-colonial times. This has especially aggravated the situation wherever linguistic and other ethnical differences exist within the borders of one state. The fact that national boundaries had been inherited from the times of the scramble for colonial possessions is grievously felt today by some newly formed states in Africa and Asia. National borders frequently cut across ethnical territories. As a result, within the borders of one country there are ethnical elements which find it difficult to cohabit with other groups or to fuse into a national whole, while the members of the same ethnical group are left on the other side of the border. This tends to create tense relations between some neighboring countries.

Border disputes in particular may very easily bring about difficult situations wherever national consciousness, embracing an entire population or its bulk, has developed within a state. The conflict on the borders between India and China is probably the most notable dispute of that kind. However, all over the underdeveloped world, and particularly in Africa, such disputes are frequent. Particularly critical are those situations where internal strife breaks out at the same time, so that the international aspect appears to be the sequel to an unresolved national question within one or several countries, as in the case of the borders between Ghana and Togo.[35]

All these factors, in addition to the other social, political and economic problems, produced a permanently unstable internal equilibrium in the societies of these countries. In other words,

---

[35] Both these countries contain as a minority group part of the Ewe tribe, which has such a developed sense of identity that it is doubtful that members of this tribe could become assimilated in the process of nation-building which is being energetically pursued by both these countries.

they were social formations which were only in the process of being created, and hence their lives were characterized bv dramatic changes. Here we have formally constituted states whose constitutions and legal acts frequently make them appear as a product of mature social development. There is a semblance of a completed crystallization, of sufficiently durable relationships and structures which could serve as a skeleton that would reliably support a stable form of statehood. However, viewed over a longer period of time, these new states reveal themselves as a fairly thin disguise of a body politic which is in a state of ferment and occasionally produces some convulsive upheavals. When the outer shell breaks down, it discloses internal instability masked by a semblance of order which had been maintained by means of an imported administrative and political apparatus that did not emerge from internal processes and trials of strength by politically conscious social forces.

The former colonies, having liberated themselves and started along the road of independence and building of their own state, generally try to make a great leap forward which must make up a lag of sometimes as such as several centuries in development. What they want to accomplish with this effort is to pull themselves out of their predicament, to assert their identity on the world scene and at the same time vigorously to throw off the rags of their immediate colonial past and replace them with modern garments of a modern state.

The trouble is that in most cases these garments do not fit the societies of these new countries. Whereas it is relatively easy to inaugurate new institutions and proclaim a new order, it is extremely difficult to change social realities. It is particularly impossible to alter socio-political relationships as long as the material base of society remain traditional and primitive, promoting precisely those relationships which are being thrown off as retrograde.

Dankwart A. Rustow rightfully points out that Europe's experience is different from that which the post-colonial societies must gain in their progress to modernization, especially when creating their own states. His formula for the process of creating states in Europe is: unity — authority — equality.[36] In this formula, "unity" marks the initial phase of social formation and amalgamation, i. e., the emergence of social structures which create cohesion and shape the fragmented mass into a single social body. Then comes the phase "authority", when this body organizes itself, having adopted a general government system through social evolution and contest within an already united body politic. The third phase is the cultivation of the social system and socio-political relationships in order to achieve democratization and emancipation of the human personality. Rustow uses here the term "equality" only as a symbol of political progress and not as egalitarianism.

The author goes on to suggest that the process of the formation of a nation in the former colonies should be represented by the same formula but in an altered sequence. He believes that the process in fact goes in this order: authority — unity — equality.[37] The sense of the altered order of sequence is that in these societies authority came first, formed either through a peaceful transfer when there had already been a nucleus of indigenous government in the last stages of the colonial government, or through winning power when, as in Indonesia, decolonization was effected through an uprising or another form of open struggle.

After the establishment of authority, there is the problem of building that unified social body which in the early beginnings of the process in Europe preceded the stage of the creation of a modern state. It is only after this internal transformation has been carried out, in fact only after a modern substance has been infused into the new state structure, that one can go over to the next stage of developing and perfecting the political and social system.

Rustow therefore believes that all the new countries should be divided into three categories. The first includes those countries in which there is an immediate need for a responsible authority and a reliable public service. The second incorporates the countries which have in their bureaucracies or party organizations (or both) an efficient instrument for national unification, but have

---

[36] Dankwart A. Rustow, *op. cit.*, pp. 275—280.
[37] *Ibid.*

not yet come to an acceptable definition of their geographical identity. The third includes those which had resolved the problems of authority and unity and are therefore capable of concentrating on the questions of the political and social equality. There is the additional remark that in those countries in which the problems under one and two have not yet been resolved, the choice is only between a more or a less efficient dictatorship (personal, military or party).[38]

This analysis strikes at the root of the basic problems of internal political development. It is incomplete because it does not take into consideration that modernization in these cases cannot be limited only to the socio-political sphere. It is not only the uncompleted historical tasks, i. e., the reverse order of resolving those historical tasks in the sphere of socio-political evolution, that acts as a brake to the further development. In order to develop modern socio-political relationships, it is necessary to create the material base of society upon which alone these relationships may rest. The trouble is, however, that to force this development, as was shown in the previous chapter, is to threaten political stability and, consequently, the achievement of the final goals shown in the model.

In other words, the post-colonial states, in contrast to other types, are inherently unstable, because their development inevitably goes through a period of great instability almost during the entire process of formation of a modern society. On top of that they augment this instability even further by accelerating economic development in order to come out of the situation which engenders and perpetuates instability. This, of course, is more easily done by maintaining the enthusiasm and collective will to prepare through sacrifices and self-renunciation for a better future.

Thus statesmanship goes through a hard time because the required mood can be sustained only if successes follow one another and if a correct balance is struck between a rapid pace of development and the satisfaction of the population's basic needs. It may not be amiss at this point to recall President Tito's words, spoken on several occasions, about the need for "the

---

[38] *Ibid.*, p. 276.

coming generation to continue the task" and thus "reduce this burden a little"[39] for the present generation. However, it is not easy to carry out this requirement in practice, especially in the conditions of an extremely low level of development.

It is therefore no wonder that in the underdeveloped countries of the world it is difficult to find sympathy for the disputes, peculiar to an altogether different social environment, arising from contradictions alien and often incomprehensible to the peoples of the underdeveloped countries. The lack of this identification is, therefore, not entirely due to differences in the levels of economic development.

INFLUENCE OF ECONOMIC UNDERDEVELOPMENT ON RELATIONS WITH THE EXTERNAL WORLD

Nonalignment coincided with the emergence of the problem of underdeveloped countries in the years of decolonization, appearing first in Southeast Asia and the neighboring countries. Since then, as the movement spread over the economically least developed continent, Africa, the economic situation of the nonaligned countries has had an extremely significant role in determining their foreign policies. We have already seen that the low level of development and efforts to accelerate it also determined internal relationships and predispositions for the policy of nonalignment.

Now we should take a look at another facet of the same problem. The unsatisfactory level of development is not just an accidental or solitary phenomenon in just some of the nonaligned countries. It is a universal phenomenon in these parts of the world, going back to the past centuries. As a phenomenon of immediate international significance, it became conspicuous only after the success of decolonization in the years which followed the Second World War. However, these same areas had been underdeveloped even before decolonization, while they still formed part of colonial empires.

---

[39] Tito, *Govori i članci* (Speeches and articles), Naprijed, Zagreb Vol. X, p. 236.

While these territories were ruled by the colonial powers, their economic problems were of an internal nature, providing a rallying cry for anti-colonial movements, and the principal political stimulus was the desire to achieve statehood and independence. When they became independent, the new countries came into a difficult position vis-à-vis the much better developed industrial states in the world market. The problem of underdevelopment thus became acute, and the United Nations undertook actions to increase technical and economic aid to these regions.

We should, however, guard against the simplification of splitting the world into two categories — the developed and the underdeveloped countries. Neither is the level of development in the so-called developed world uniform, nor are all the underdeveloped countries underdeveloped to the same extent or in the same way. In order to obtain a somewhat clearer picture, we should make a brief review of the history of the problem of underdeveloped countries.

We are today accustomed to looking at North America as the most advanced part of the world, followed immediately by Western Europe. This classification applies only to a very recent past. Modern development began with the industrial revolution, which started in England in the 18th century. The first steps in that direction, as is known, were the development of the textile industry following important inventions of textile machines in the period between 1733 and the end of that century. The pace and significance of the social transformation which came in the wake of the industrial revolution received a strong, new impulse with the development of the steel industry, which in the first half of the 19th century made a fundamental change in the social structure of England.[40]

As the industrial revolution spread, first in France and the other countries of Western Europe and in the United States, and then (in the second half of the 19th century) in Germany and Central Europe as a whole, the zone of industrialization widened. The first wave of the industrial revolution was limited to the broad area of Western Europe and North America and was

---

[40] T. S. Ashton, *An Economic History of England: The Eighteenth Century*, London 1955.

marked by the utilization of steam energy in the machines which dominated the industrial production of that time. The mentioned area thus became the leading part of the world in economic development, as well as the cradle of modern social theories and political transformations which followed changes in social structures.

It should be remembered that before the beginning of this revolutionary change, China, for example, was at least as developed as Europe in regard to artisan production and military equipment, as well as in military theory. Some other regions were also able to hold their own in competing against Europe in the market place as well as on the battlefield. However, in the world of that time there were areas which lagged considerably behind in their development. These include most of Africa as well as some regions in Asia and Oceania.

Differences in the levels of development, whenever sufficiently large, were resolved, in the event of a direct confrontation, by occupation and colonization of the less developed areas. The industrial revolution in Western Europe resulted in mass migrations overseas of the British as well as of other nationalities, which brought about extermination and disenfranchisement of the indigenous populations in North America, Australia and New Zealand more than anywhere else. These areas were attractive because of their temperate climates as well as their natural wealth, which was necessary for a successful economic development.[41]

Of all the countries outside the area of the original industrial revolution, Japan alone succeeded in joining the modern industrial evolution and in gradually pushing itself into the leading group. What is more, in a foreseeable future Japan is likely to outstrip in development all other countries except the United States.

In Eastern Europe, industrialization in some places started before the First World War, but undoubtedly the crucial moment for this area, and especially for Russia, was the victory of the socialist revolution of 1917. Following an extremely rapid indus-

---

[41] The colonization of Africa brought a large number of Europeans to the south of the continent (the Republic of South Africa and Southern Rhodesia) and to climatically favorable East Africa, whereas the Atlantic coast (above and below the equator) remained without any European colonization worth mentioning.

trialization in the years preceding World War II, the Soviet Union created a base which made it one of the two superpowers in the world. Economic development in the other East European countries, except in Czechoslovakia, also followed upon the internal changes which took place after World War II.

Industrialization in other parts of the world began either later or at a considerably slower pace than the development in Eastern Europe. Thus in China a significant breakthrough was made only after the victory of the socialist revolution, although in some centers industry had been developed even before. In India, industry is restricted to a few large cities, whereas the broad expanse of the country is still far from being included in this process.[42]

This brief review of an otherwise well-known and exhaustively studied period in modern history was necessary here to show how unacceptable and incorrect the very widespread classification into developed and underdeveloped countries is. Furthermore, it also serves to remind us that different levels of development had once been responsible for confrontations and very sharp conflicts. These conflicts were in fact far more brutal than anything that is happening today in relations between the developed and underdeveloped countries.

The slave trade from Africa, to supply suitable labor for the production of cotton and other industrial crops in the United States, the Indian wars in the 19th century in the U. S., extermination of the aboriginal population in Australia, are only the best known examples of wholesale brutalities which took place during that era throughout the world. We should, namely, bear in mind that the means of transportation developed together with the development of production, especially after the number of railways and sea-going steamships increased. It made possible a broader and more intensive contact between the developed societies of the industrial regions and overseas areas which stood apart from this development.

---

[42] Alvin Hansen in his book, *Economic Issues of the 1960's*, McGraw-Hill, New York 1960, pp. 151—154, states that urban India, according to population estimates at that time, numbered 60 million people and represented a separate structure in which the greatest wealth existed side by side with extreme poverty. However, this part of India made up of "islands" in the sea of rural India, is where economic development takes place and represents a "medium developed area".

The development gap kept widening, more so between Europe and the rest of the world than between individual European countries. Thus, for example, despite its very modest industrial base, Russia was able to expand its territory in Asia and the Far East in the 19th century, taking advantage of the very low level of economic development in Central Asia and the Far East, which in addition were very sparsely populated.

Having spread over the whole of Western Europe and North America by dissemination of knowledge and know-how, the industrial revolution expanded further through the domination by industrially advanced countries over the other, underdeveloped countries and areas. This domination was imposed either through open colonization, e. g., in the large cities of China, or through economic penetration, as in the case of Russia before World War I, and the other countries of Eastern Europe prior to the socialist revolution. Thus there was a narrow community of countries called "civilized", with a gulf between them and the other nations.

There are, however, some other elements marking differences between individual countries. The level of economic development is not a simply defined magnitude which can be expressed by a quantitative index. Despite its high per capita income, Kuwait clearly cannot be put on a par with the West European countries having a similar index. Important advances in per capita income of a truly underdeveloped country are hardly possible unless some major changes are made in their social patterns. These patterns sometimes resist such changes even more stubbornly than the economic system and it is harder to change them than to accelerate economic growth. The classification of countries according to a rule of thumb has therefore no great practical value, because development is a complex process, and there are also differences between countries within regions. For example, classification of countries according to per capita output is an imperfect indication of the true differences which divide them into categories, and just as unsatisfactory is the classification on the basis of geographical location.

As we have said earlier, confrontations between the developed and underdeveloped countries were resolved most frequently through domination and colonialism. Only some insignificant cases of underdeveloped and weak countries, which could not possibly be regarded as autonomous factors in the world, escaped this finality. Yet there were also cases which cannot quite fit the same classification. An example is Imperial Russia's economic dependence on West European firms which controlled every major Russian industry, or the countries of Latin America which were in a similar, and some in an even worse predicament. In both cases the countries involved were either a large European state or a number of overseas countries in which government was held by the descendants of European settlers.

The gulf between the economic developments of the Western and Eastern parts of Europe very largely explains the most recent history of that continent. Dramatic stirrings during the present century climaxed in the two world wars. In fact, historically viewed, World War II was the continuation of World War I, and the entire period between 1914 and 1945 may be regarded as a period of preparations for great social transformations. Prior to this period, there were no independent states in Eastern Europe except for the three empires (the Russian, Austro-Hungarian and Ottoman) and a few small and weak states that had just emancipated themselves from their subjection to Turkey.

The area of what is today Eastern Europe, with the sole exception of Bohemia, was economically retarded. The division of Europe into East and West, as we can see, dates back to the time when the expansion of the industrial revolution by peaceful means stopped and the acquired industrial advantages were used to subject the less developed countries and nations. This at the same time shows that the division of Europe into East and West stems from basic historical conditions, i. e., from retarded economic development and the use of a higher level of development for the purpose of domination and subjection.

Reactions to this state of affairs and the results of efforts to remove this inequality were varied. Countries in Eastern Europe, having made some progress in developing industry — although it was in the hands of foreign capital — were able to take advantage of the resulting new social structures to carry out social transformations by means of revolutions as a prelude to a considerably accelerated economic development. A favorable circumstance for them was that they developed within the framework of general European historical and social processes, so they were able to fit into the process of modernization of Western Europe without great adjustments and changes in inherited habits as had been necessary in environments which in the past developed completely apart from Europe.

These countries, excepting Yugoslavia and Albania, became part of the bi-polar political constellation of Europe following the Second World War, which made them participants in the cold war. Hence the course they took differed from that which the countries of Southeast Asia and Africa followed some time later, owing to different levels of development, and to the existence of different political affinities and the resultant allegiance to blocs.

These differences purport to show first of all that the efforts of the underdeveloped overseas countries to catch up with the West have produced very poor results so far. The gap in the levels of real income, as a result of the poor absolute growth of the gross national product and mass poverty due to the inequitable spread of wealth, increased considerably. In the majority of countries it was further widened by a rapid growth of the population as a sequel to decreased mortality coupled with high natality.[43]

The poorly developed countries have consequently entered the new era of their history — the era of independence — heavily handicapped.[44] The developed countries of the West made great strides ahead, and even the less developed countries of Europe embarked upon an accelerated development, while being inward-

---

[43] For more on this subject, see Gaston Bouthoul's *La surpopulation*, Payot, Paris 1964. The author discusses in detail the effect of rapid population growth in the underdeveloped countries (pp. 72—98 and especially pp. 147—150). One of the interesting observations in this book is that the acceleration of economic growth in the underdeveloped countries tends to encourage faster population growth by natural increment and the feeing of the labor force as a result of the modernization of economic activities. "Thus," says Bouthoul, "the depressive overpopulation devours itself, negating the progress that has been made so painfully."

[44] See the discussion on pages 10 through 22 in H. Mynt's *The Economics of the Developing Countries, op. cit.* The author points out the difference resulting not only from the position of the new countries in the world market, but also from the fact that the economic processes in them are not such that the theory developed at the beginning of industrialization in the "older" countries could be applied. In this connection the author gives special attention to the "take-off" theory elaborated by W. W. Rostow in *The Stages of Economic Development*, Cambridge University Press 1963. See especially pp. 17—58.

looking and deeply involved in the cold war. The countries which slowly emerged as a result of the disintegration of the colonial empires therefore had to face difficult problems in the world market.

DETERIORATION OF THE INTERNATIONAL ECONOMIC POSITION OF THE UNDERDEVELOPED COUNTRIES

Having appeared in the world market, the new, developing countries had to reckon with realities inherited from a time when they still did not exist as independent factors in international relations. Their legacy was their relative economic backwardness, but they also met an unfavorable situation in the world market which was dominated by countries that had gone far ahead in labor productivity and generally in technical progress. Even the character of the world market was formed in the past, when such pronounced differences in levels of economic development either did not exist, not on the present geographical scale anyway, or did not so deeply affect the life interests of nations.

World trade has long ceased to be a simple exchange of goods or even a combination of multilateral relations based on the purchase and sale of goods. Thus there is a complex system of economic relations in which trade, in the classical sense of the word, was only one element. In the place of imports of a small number of luxury articles and overseas products and exports of local surpluses, a vigorous activity developed on which the welfare and rate of economic development of various countries depended more and more[45].

In addition to trade, some countries engaged in much more far-reaching and durable relations. The world market developed into a market of capital, labor and technical know-how. This is

---

[45] The role of world trade and the formation and development of conditions in the world market were in the center of attention of the underdeveloped countries at the very beginning of their action in the United Nations at the Sixth Session of the General Assembly (see the resolution adopted at the meeting held on January 12, 1952). In recent years this interest has been reflected in the formation (1964) and later in the work of the United Nations Conference on Trade and Development (UNCTAD).

where the world division of labor is operated and cooperation and integration are negotiated, which besides trade and credit operations also include the sphere of production. As relationships diversified and internal economic processes became increasingly dependent on events in the outside world, so the market expanded outward.

Thus, the line between the "national" economy and the problems of the world economy became increasingly blurred, and the entire world is today encompassed by an interdependent system of international economic relations. The changes in the world after the Second World War played a prominent part in this expansion of the world economic system.

When the United Nations was founded in 1945, its membership consisted of 51 founding nations. In terms of continents, its composition was as follows: Europe 14, America 22, Asia 9, Africa 4 and Australia and New Zealand 2. For our purposes, these figures should be somewhat corrected, because some countries were not members although operating independently in the world market. Some of them even started playing an increasingly significant role in political relations without being admitted into the world organization. Furthermore, the Ukraine and Belorussia should be counted with the U. S. S. R. as one state. If we make this correction and include all the countries which appeared in the world market in the early post-war years, we have the following figures: Europe 26, America 22, Asia 11, Africa 4, Australia and New Zealand 2.[46]

Taking the situation in the U. N. General Assembly in 1963 (a total of 113 countries), and after making the above-mentioned corrections, we get the following picture: Europe 28, America 24, Asia 25, Africa 35, Australia and New Zealand 2.[47] Two new states appeared in Europe, Iceland and Cyprus, and three remained outside the United Nations — the two Germanies and Switzer-

---

[46] The two German states are included in this calculation, even though at the time no German state formally existed, this area being a zone of occupation.

[47] The number of countries at the General Assembly in 1963, preceding the second conference of the leaders of the nonaligned countries, shows the rapid increase in U. N. members in the years of nonalignment's rise to a world movement. Since that time, of course, the movement has continued to grow, and the number of U. N. member countries is constantly increasing as new countries are formed.

land. In Asia, Korea and Vietnam did not become members of the U. N. Consequently, in Europe the number of independent countries increased from 26 to 28, in America from 22 to 24, whereas in Asia this number jumped from 11 to 27, and in Africa from 4 to 35.

Whereas in 1945 there was in Asia, Africa and America a total of 32 underdeveloped countries (the developed countries included Japan, South Africa, the U. S. A. and Canada) in 1963 this number increased to 82. As a result of this development, the circumstances in which the newly liberated countries found themselves changed substantially and so did international political and economic relationships. Until then the territories of many of these underdeveloped countries had been a part of the economic systems of the colonial powers. The problem of underdevelopment did exist, but it was played down and did not directly appear as an international issue. This could take place because they were economically closely tied to the colonial metropolises and because their peoples were not able to act independently on the world scene.

It is obvious that many former colonies even after independence were not able immediately to develop their international economic relations. Trade as a rule continued long after independence to flow along established channels through which the economies of those countries had been connected with the world markets. They started operating more independently only gradually. They first created their own trade organizations and set up their own networks in other countries for exports and imports. This was followed by the diversification of trade partners and a more equitable distribution of trade among an increased number of countries, with which direct trade relationships were established.

This process unfolded at varying speeds in different newly liberated countries. In the first place it depended on the degree of political independence which the country had secured as it achieved its formal independence.

Furthermore, it depended, and still does, on the type of commodities available for export. Finally, the speed of this process greatly depended on the ability of the newly created national trade organizations, on a reasonably sound trade policy and on the national economic policy in general. This last mentioned factor is important because it governs the quantities and qualities of goods available for export and salable in foreign markets.

As these factors vary from one country to the next, the overall results present a confusing picture. The underdeveloped countries are trying to increase the number of their trade partners and to distribute business among them more equitably, although generally they mostly trade with the developed Western countries. Consequently, distribution of trade over a large number of partners has not produced the geographical structure of economic relationships that would be both politically and economically most favorable for the developing countries.

A breakdown of the trade of the developing countries taken as a whole shows that approximately three quarters is with the developed countries, and only one quarter among themselves.[48] Their trade with the socialist countries is still very limited and not much more than five percent of their total foreign trade. Since the markets of the developed countries were already organized into large integrated areas, the position of the developing countries weakened even more.[49]

It is therefore obvious why the terms of trade, the ratio between the prices of the export products of the underdeveloped countries and those of the developed countries, kept deteriorating. In the years between 1950 and 1960, when the policy of nonalignment was taking shape, the price ratio in the trade between the developed and underdeveloped countries, according to figures provided by the United Nations yearbooks, deteriorated by 15 per cent at the expense of the underdeveloped countries. Since then this tendency has generally continued, and unless the international community seriously intervenes, it is not likely to turn for the benefit of the underdeveloped countries.

---

[48] These figures, as well as all the other economic data in this chapter, have been taken (and rounded off to simplify presentation) from tables in the mentioned publication, *Materijali o kretanju u svjetskoj privredi i trgovini*. They mainly relate to the decade of the 1960s, the period in which nonalignment grew into a world-wide movement. It is our intention to show the economic conditions and trends in this vital period.

[49] The development of world trade shows that it flourishes best not among countries at different levels of development, not on the basis of complementarity between the industrialized and non-industrialized countries, but rather among highly advanced countries at a similar level of development.

153

This unfavorable ratio of prices mainly arises because primary products, foodstuffs, raw materials and fuels provide the bulk of exports. Primary products account for about 90 per cent of the exports of these countries. This, however, is not the only reason. What also affects the price ratio is the fact that the same or similar products fetch different prices, according to the countries of origin, invariably at the expense of the products originating from the underdeveloped countries.

Another unfavorable circumstance is the considerably faster growth in the exports of finished products in comparison with those of primary products. Whereas during that same period the exports of finished products in the world grew at an annual rate of about 8 per cent, the exports of primary products increased annually by only about 3.5 per cent. This picture becomes even more bleak if we take into account that the growth in the exports of primary products from the developed countries increased twice as fast as that of the underdeveloped countries.[50]

The total effect of this trend was a continuous decrease in the participation of the underdeveloped countries in world trade. Thus, according to the United Nations yearbooks, the share of the underdeveloped countries dropped between 1950 and 1960 from 30.0 to 20.4 per cent, whereas the share of the Western developed countries during the same decade increased from 59.8 per cent to 66.0 per cent. Consequently, the world trade between the underdeveloped and the developed countries is continually conducted at the expense of the former. The cumulative negative effect of this situation is reflected on the economies and living standards of these countries even more than the above figures show, because of the relatively high population growth there.

In addition to the annual 3.6 per cent growth of exports in the decade 1950—1960, we should also reckon with the annual population growth of over 2 per cent. However, this average value does not reflect the situation in some of the regions, where we find a low growth rate of exports and a high population growth

---

[50] Nevertheless, Mynt's observation is relevant that the underdeveloped countries were hurt even more by the fact that they were not able to lower production costs of primary products and thus have better chances of marketing them in the world market and earning greater profits. *The Economics of Developing Countries, op. cit.*, pp. 150—156.

rate. Furthermore, these are generally the regions where the volume of exports is in any case relatively small, so that the starting point is a very low one. A considerable increase in exports in such conditions could be achieved only by increasing the exports of raw materials, because even a fast increase in industrial production could still not very greatly affect the volume of general exports, since the share held by industry in these countries is a small one, especially in export surpluses. In the existing conditions in the world it was also not easy to achieve a sizable and rapid increase in the volume of exports of raw materials from the underdeveloped countries. During that period already, the total exports of raw materials from the industrialized countries were greater than the corresponding exports from the underdeveloped countries. Thus the diminishing consumption of raw materials for the same output in the industrial countries, coupled with mounting production and export of raw materials from there, rendered the position of the underdeveloped countries even more difficult. As regards industrial products from the underdeveloped countries, they encountered great difficulties in the markets of the developed countries. What inhabits a sizable increase in exports to other underdeveloped countries is the low purchasing power there and competition from developed countries.

In the given situation, the only way out was to improve trade with the COMECON countries.[51] This meant that the latter should consume more export articles from the underdeveloped countries and increase the exports of those products which are needed by those countries, mainly capital investment and industrial consumer goods. However, the general volume of exports, especially in those categories, from the COMECON countries was fairly limited. The latter's foreign trade is developing very dynamically, but its low level, even if considerably augmented, permits only the anticipation of future improvement, but not the solution of immediate problems.

As regards the trade between the COMECON and the underdeveloped countries, no sufficient experience is available on the

---

[51] COMECON — The Council for Mutual Economic Assistance — is composed of the following countries: Bulgaria, Czechoslovakia, Hungary, the German Democratic Republic, Rumania and the Soviet Union.

basis of which we could anticipate the structure of that trade when it is several times greater than the present. It will very largely depend on the character and structure of investment and personal consumption in the COMECON countries when they achieve a higher level of economic development and living standards.

However, the position of these countries, like that of all the underdeveloped countries, is difficult and has been showing signs of further deterioration. This deterioration is seen in the poor effects of trade and a slow pace of economic development, as well as in a mounting indebtedness which threatens the further development of trade. It also reduces the ability of these countries to make use of credits and loans, because they burden even more their balances of payments. This situation, quite obviously, decreases the flow of private capital into those countries.

As the economic gap between the underdeveloped parts of the world and the industrialized highly developed countries increased, it became the cornerstone of the policy of the newly formed countries. Their orientation in the world — determination of their behavior vis-à-vis other countries, the industrialized countries in particular — was strongly affected by the above-mentioned factors and internal pressures which arose very soon after the gaining of independence.

The policy of the nonaligned countries was therefore mostly determined by their economic position, as well as by the social and political circumstances which developed from economic under-development. This rather than merely the wish to draw economic benefit from relations with the outside world is what explains the special behavior of the nonaligned countries in international relations. They were preordained to act in their specific manner independently of concrete diplomatic actions and of the post-war pattern of power and tensions among the great powers.

PROBLEMS OF DEVELOPMENT

Political differentiation and the gradual formation of two blocs had a definite bearing on the concrete policies and foreign

156

political moves of the underdeveloped countries. Some opted for the bloc policies as a result of external influences and internal weaknesses. This differentiation and bloc alignment could not, however, inhibit their fundamental and vital interests, which urged them to cooperate with other countries in order to jointly safeguard their economic interests. This has enhanced the attractiveness of nonalignment for them. Their difficult economic situation brought them closer to the policies and actions of the most active protagonists of nonalignment.

The crucial economic problem of most of the underdeveloped countries — acceleration of development — is being dealt with in the face of a very high percentage of population increment. Thus they come up against two new problems. First of all, they must raise the rate of economic growth high enough to make its per capita effect sufficiently elevated to ensure the expected rate of development. Subsequently, as the economy is modernized, it is necessary to increase the production of food and investments into social services in order to ensure normal nutrition and to decrease inflationary pressures combined and exacerbated by increased demands for food in the domestic market. This, however, makes it difficult to maintain the level of exports in cases where food is a major item in the structure of exports, without threatening vital needs of the population.

We should not expect a diminished population growth rate in an immediate future. Population increment is the direct result of better living conditions and especially of the progress of welfare and medical services, which help to reduce child mortality and lengthen the average life expectancy. High natality is a legacy from the times when high mortality was rife. Experience has shown that the process of conscious or unconscious adjustment to new living conditions is fairly slow, so that Asia, Africa and Latin America are undergoing a period of sharp population increase, which in some of these areas has certainly not yet reached its peak.[52]

Increased food production and improved social services are

---

[52] See the findings of the United Nations Family Planning Mission to India, United Nations General Distribution ST/SOA/SER.R/11, November 24, 1969.

therefore — at least for another generation — one of the principal tasks. Conditions for their realization are not equal. In the densely populated areas of Asia it is obviously necessary to insist on intensive soil cultivation, whereas in some of the less thickly populated areas of Black Africa the cultivated areas can still be extended by forest clearing. But in either case, what is needed is the importation of equipment which is not being produced in the country.

Wherever there is a possibility of extensive development, demands for equipment are, obviously, lower, but in those countries as a rule the possibilities of importing these implements are relatively poor. In other words, even the importation of the most elementary equipment for extensive agriculture may be an exceedingly difficult problem for the country having an extremely low national income and a very favorable pattern of exports which serve as a source of foreign exchange. Consequently, this problem has more or less similar relative dimensions for some of the underdeveloped countries. This, *mutatis mutandis*, equally applies to our present consideration, and it is therefore hardly necessary to repeat it everywhere.

Agricultural equipment, fertilizers, plant disease control and other aids and additional equipment should be available in the domestic market in sufficient quantities and at an economical cost to be accessible to agricultural producers. This last demand is particularly difficult to fulfil, because the economic level of farmers normally does not permit long-range investments, irrespective of whether or not they might be justified or assumed to be profitable. Furthermore, the educational level of farmers is usually not sufficiently high for a successful utilization, sometimes even for comprehension of the benefits offered by the improved means of production.[53]

---

[53] In his extremely interesting book, *L'Afrique noire est mal partie*, Edition du Seuil, Paris 1962, René Dumont points out the shortcomings in the basic orientation of the leading circles in Africa. He criticizes the imitating of a "consumer society" and the exaggerated efforts to accelerate industrialization, while the specific conditions and possibilities of Africa are not used to their fullest advantage. See in particular pp. 87—107 and pp. 221—238.

Albert Hirschman in *The Strategy of Economic Development*, Yale University Press, New Haven 1964, mentions a similar problem. On page 209 he states the harmfulness of setting rigid priorities in the development of the underdeveloped countries in general.

Consequently it is necessary to provide more favorable financial terms for the purchase of modern means of production, and at the same time to design a national economic policy, and especially an agricultural policy, that will promote the modernization of agriculture and increased production. As a result, of course, the entire fiscal and organizational activity of a country must in a certain sense be adjusted to the needs of agriculture, and practice has shown that this requires a very long-range and concentrated effort, which very largely burdens not only the state apparatus, but also the sources of national finances. Especially if we add to this the great educational effort and technical advisory services and the cost of soil improvement and soil study. The latter is particularly important whenever new crops or completely new methods of cultivation are to be introduced, owing to the lack of that normal experience which gradually, without special effort, accumulated in the countries where agriculture had been developing for centuries.

This already immense problem is enlarged by the fact that the entire effort to advance agriculture within a short time is racing agains the population increase. Furthermore, this effort requires a parallel advance along a very broad front to overcome the general backwardness in health, education, living and especially in consumption, including nutritional habits. Sometimes these efforts are inhibited by prejudices and traditions which may be overcome only by a general effort to raise the economic as well as cultural and political levels of the entire population. This problem is heightened by the fact that in these countries a preponderant number of the economically active population are engaged in agriculture, and thus agricultural problems become national problems.

The enormous resources necessary for this gigantic effort in practically every single underdeveloped country cannot be earned from the existing agricultural output. Not only can agriculture hardly cope with the problem of feeding the growing population; it has such low productivity that it cannot produce sufficient means even for its own development at the pace demanded by the needs of the country. What is more, initial progress does not help matters very much, because the concurrent growth of national needs continually places upon agriculture new and ever more difficult demands, for greater quantities and higher productivity of labor.

Agriculture thus cannot get ahead of the general economic development; it always runs behind and is constantly under pressure. This, of course, is due to agricultural development's inherent lag behind industrial development, especially since in the underdeveloped countries agriculture makes up by far the greatest share of economic activity. For the same reasons, any progress it might make considerably accelerates development in the remaining sectors.[54]

The underdeveloped countries cannot, however, limit themselves to developing agriculture alone, because that would produce even greater difficulties and insoluble problems. First of all, in order to purchase equipment and other industrial products from the developed countries, they must increase the flow of foreign exchange, for which, as we have seen, agricultural products are not convenient commodities. It is furthermore necessary to create jobs for that part of the population which will be set free for other occupations with agricultural development. This applies particularly to the intensification of agriculture, but no less to the enlargement of cultivable surfaces. Of course, this enlargement in itself implies normally a considerable increase in labor productivity in comparison with the very primitive traditional agriculture. In some countries of Central Africa, for example, a large portion of the population is engaged in agriculture which has hardly progressed beyond the organized gathering of fruits.

The development of industry (and artisanship in many

---

[54] On page 52 of *The Economics of Developing Countries*, H. Mynt states that the possibilities opened up by the development of agriculture for effective and profitable exports and for a stimulus to general economic growth should not be overlooked. He warns, however, that the necessary investments must be made for this line of development. The author recognizes all the problems involved and therefore recommends a multidimensional approach with consideration given to the specific conditions and possibilities of each separate country (pp. 147—164). This argument in fact merely reaffirms the existing difficulties and the impossibility of laying down a uniform development and foreign trade policy based on strict adherence to set priorities. In this connection see the arguments presented by Vladimir Dragomanović in his article, "Pravci industrijalizacije i spoljni uslovi ekonomskog razvitka" (Trends in Industrialization and External Factors Influencing Economic Development), International Problems, 1963, No. 2.

underdeveloped countries) in itself requires great organizational and special educational efforts, as well as an increased amount of financial resources and considerable imports. This, together with the efforts required by agriculture, increases the pressure on foreign exchange. The entire development of these countries is constantly torn between demands for the importation of equipment and other elements necessary for agriculture, and the development of other activities, such as industry and artisanship, transport, the infrastructure and essential services.

Here again the situation hardly improves after a few initial steps. The development of industry invariably requires imports of raw materials. The dimensions of this problem depend on the structure of the economy and geographical conditions, but imbalances are inevitable, even with the most careful planning. Then there are the increasingly new and more costly demands in the investment activity itself. The process of accelerated economic development calls for a sustained, if not accelerated rate of growth. The development of the internal market demands higher labor productivity, which cannot be speedily achieved without new and greater investments requiring imported equipment.

This phenomenon of the reproduction of similar problems at a higher level explains the similarity of the basic problems in the countries at different levels of development. It is only much later, when the country is already getting out of the situation of the relatively low development, that things begin to run more smoothly.[55] This, of course, does not imply an end to economic problems, because these exist in all the countries in our time, a time of exceptionally rapid economic growth. We should note that it is not possible to accurately define the boundary where underdevelopment stops, because this boundary continually moves along with the general development in the world.

As we compare the problems arising in the field of agricultural and non-agricultural economic activities, we come to the conclusion that one sector expects help from the other, and that neither is capable of resolving its own problems. It may

---

[55] Compare H. Mynt, *op. cit.*, p. 20.

look like a vicious circle, but in the development of mankind, including the development of individual nations, there are no vicious circles from which there is no way out. This applies here as well. The problem appears to us very much like a vicious circle because we have viewed it separately and only from one, the economic, aspect. The experience of achievements in the world has shown that there is no situation from which a nation cannot raise itself, so to speak, by its own bootstraps.

The fact that the development of the underdeveloped countries is running in a vicious circle which at times may appear unbreakable is well known and has been abundantly discussed in the literature on economic development. There is, therefore, no need to enter into a closer consideration of the theoretical aspect of this question. However, we should refer to the book by the Yale University professor, Albert Hirschman, *The Strategy of Economic Development*, in which the author underlines "the importance and creative virtue... of pressures, tensions and disequilibrium."

"Actually the argument is no more, Hirschman states, than an extension of the familiar view which makes economic growth dependent on a continuing outcropping of profitable opportunities. These are, after all, also disequilibria which induce a constructive action. But our extension of the concept of disequilibrium to include situations replete not only with opportunities to be grasped but with hindrances, difficulties and other types of tension, raises the question whether the response to such situations is not at times going to be destructive and whether the process that has been sketched is not therefore a rather risky affair." He continues with the answer that this is what makes the "cushion" of foreign economic aid necessary.

Hirschman believes that "for a number of reasons" it is neither necessary nor desirable to abolish tensions. "In the first place, he writes further on, underdeveloped countries already operate under the *grand tension* that stems from the universal desire for economic improvement oddly combined with many resistances to change. Much is to be said for breaking down this grand tension, a highly explosive mixture of hopes and

162

fears, into a series of smaller and more manageable tensions."[56]

The real problem of mankind, of all mankind in fact, consists in a much more accurately defined task: to help to draw the underdeveloped countries out of their backwardness with *as few sacrifices* for the nations of these countries, with as few upheavals for the international community as possible. In other words, this means to facilitate a progressive evolution for the underdeveloped countries. This, of course, implies that not only the interests of the underdeveloped countries are involved, but also the correctly understood long-range interests of the developed countries, including the most developed ones.

The underdeveloped countries of Asia, Africa and Latin America, including the Asian socialist countries, were responsible in the years of the emergence of nonalignment for approximately two thirds of the world population and only about one fifth of the world gross national product. On the other hand, the most advanced countries, meaning those in Western Europe and North America, had just over one sixth of the world population and just under two thirds (60 per cent) of the world gross national product. These figures are rounded off in order to obtain easily comparable quantities. Insistence on exact percentages does not give greater accuracy in any case, because the methods of calculation, and especially of conversion to a common denominator, are complicated and delicate. Hence so many differences in the figures being quoted by different authorities in the world.

These approximate figures show us that per capita national income in the most developed countries was more than ten times higher than the average in the underdeveloped countries. The extreme cases were, of course, much greater. That ratio goes as high as 1:50 between the United States and some of the most underdeveloped countries of Africa.[57]

If we take into consideration the yawning gaps in the levels of development between the great mass of underdeveloped countries and the highly developed countries of Western Europe and North America — the predicament of the underdeveloped

---

[56] Albert Hirschman, *The Strategy of Economic Development, op. cit.*, pp. 208—209.

[57] All these figures are based on U. N. material in the compilation: *Materijali o kretanju u svjetskoj privredi i trgovini, op. cit.*

countries in the world market is glaring. These figures also show that these countries in the world market is glaring. These figures also show that these countries must cover a long and arduous road of accelerated economic development if they are to reach a level comparable with the achievements of the now developed countries. Without that they cannot count on a permanent and complete equilibrium in the world market and particularly in international trade. This in other words means that at the time when they need most to draw a maximum out of their international trade, the achievement of favorable conditions is either impossible or only partially feasible when these countries are already past their greatest need.

The rate of growth of national income in the underdeveloped countries consequently has been increasing very slowly. The annual increment of the national income in the countries with the lowest GNP was in the period 1950—1958 — 3.8 per cent, whereas in those same countries the population increased at the rate of 2.0 per cent per annum. Thus the per capita national income increased at a rate of only 1.8 per cent. However, it should not be thought that this is a steady and continual growth. Its fluctuations in the past years produced drops in per capita national income, both as a result of poor production and sudden population increases.

The Dutch economist Jan Tinbergen, for example, calculated that — allowing for fluctuations over decades — the national income per head of population in Southeast Asia in 1957 was only 5 per cent above the figure of 1913. According to these figures, if we take 1913 as index 98, in 1957 the index would be only 103. In the same period (1913—1957), the national per capita income in the United States doubled.

The effect of these figures on the level of economic development and living standards is, of course, much heightened by the fact that in the developed countries each percentage also increases income, because of the large amount to which that percentage relates. With the underdeveloped countries having a much lower income, an even more impressive percentage still does not mean very much. If the absolute amount is low and the rate of growth also low, and especially if it is coupled with a considerable pop-

164

ulation increment, the final result only very imperceptibly changes the conditions and bases for a faster economic development. This situation actually prevails in the majority of the underdeveloped countries.

Here again we come up against a vicious circle. Wherever there is a particular need to accelerate economic growth — in order to reduce the development gap — the conditions necessary for such an acceleration are lacking. The developed countries, on the other hand, possess a much better ability of increasing their national income growth rate. Furthermore, their growth is not cancelled out to such an extent by population increment.

This, of course, does not mean that there is no way out of the existing situation. As we have already said, there is no such thing as a completely closed circle. Our study so far has shown that the situation in the underdeveloped countries cannot be expected to improve by itself and that the market and economic laws will not automatically fill the gap between the rich and the poor nations which has developed in the course of recent centuries, especially in the decades of intensive industrialization.[58]

Such pronounced differences have arisen first of all because the industrial revolution began and brought initial fruits within the narrow sphere of what are today the developed countries. This initial international division of labor created conditions for the ever faster development of these few countries, whereas the rest of the world lagged behind. The European population of some British overseas possessions (Canada, Australia, New Zealand and South Africa) capitalized on their kith-and-kin ties with the mother country and established close economic cooperation. In that manner those countries succeeded in achieving a considerably faster economic growth, and today their European populations fully enjoy the fruits of the economic development. These fruits are limited to the European population in these countries, what is particularly flagrant in South Africa, where

---

[58] Many writers think that there is little likelihood of this gap being closed even in the distant future. Fourastié, in his study, *Le grand éspoir du XX siècle*, Gallimard, Paris 1963, believes that according to the logic of development the gap must be overcome in the very distant future, but that in the meantime the underdeveloped countries can improve their position only by providing various kinds of services to the advanced countries (pp. 254—264).

the native population lives in conditions that are frequently worse than even in the most backward colonies.

Another favorable circumstance assisting the rapid development of some countries is undoubtedly the higher level of education of the European population in comparison with that of the natives. This factor should not be overestimated, because none of those countries have produced scientific or technical achievements giving them possibilities of fast development. On the contrary, they overcame their backwardness in spite of the very low level of general education of the immigrant population, mainly because they were backed by highly efficient ties with the home country and its achievements. These living ties, including the movement of people and free access to the centers of higher education in Europe, played a decisive role and contributed to the creation of a corresponding human base for economic evolution.

On the other hand, the economies of those countries were never isolated from the economies of the mother countries, even after acceding to the dominion or full independence status. They have always enjoyed preferential treatment which offers them relatively more favorable terms of trade and even the achievement of high prosperity based on agricultural activity. Possibly the best example for this is New Zealand, although it very much applies also to Australia, Canada and South Africa. We should add, of course, that the customary figures about per capita national income for South Africa do not reflect the true situation, because they are calculated on the basis of the entire population. This is one of the absurdities to which formal statistics lead, since the native population participates very little in the creation, and still less in the utilization of this high level of income.

In addition to that category of countries we should also consider two special cases — Japan and the U.S.S.R. These two countries, in the period since the First World War increased their per capita national income at an exceptionally fast rate, despite a high population increment. During that interval, Japan trebled its per capita income, although the population growth remained high. This fast development, which began towards the end of the 19th century, brought Japan to the rank of a great power in the early years of this century. After the Second World War, Japan's economic development continued at an exceptionally high rate, whereas the population increment was reduced. Japan's accelerated development began after the radical socio-political changes which took place in the last decades of the 19th century. Furthermore, Japan preserved its full independence and resisted attempts of foreign domination. The mentioned social changes were a prerequisite for the preservation of independence and for faster economic development.

The fast economic development in the Soviet Union is also a notable phenomenon. In the mentioned period the per capita national income was quintupled. It is true, though, that the starting point had been extremely low. In 1913 it was on the par with the level of per capita national income of Latin America. Accelerated development in that country only began in the third decade of this century, after a drop in income owing to the war and the civil war. Here the change in the social and political structure of that country played an even more important role. It is also significant that this development took place under exceptionally unfavorable conditions — boycott and open hostility on the part of the developed Western countries and a high rate of population growth. After World War II, development was again boosted, especially in the early years of reconstruction. After that, economic growth levelled off, but the rate of population increase also gradually dropped.

There is no doubt that the possession of many essential natural resources was responsible for this outstanding feat. But in this consideration it is not significant, because today's conditions do not create such problems as the Soviet Union had had to overcome, especially in the first and most difficult years of its forced development.

These three categories of examples of accelerated economic development apply to countries which did not participate in the original industrial revolution and in that process of development which has brought about today's differences in the world. There is no doubt that conditions have very much changed, but the lesson from those examples is certainly a precious guide for

167

today's underdeveloped countries, because all these examples have certain common elements.

First of all, a precondition for an accelerated development in all those countries was the existence of a social system which aided the development of productive forces at a given stage of social development. In the first two instances, in the 19th century and early in the 20th century, it was the capitalist system. The example of the Soviet Union later revealed exceptional possibilities of development following the victory of the socialist revolution. Furthermore, we should also mention the accelerated development of certain less developed countries in Eastern Europe, including Yugoslavia. These are, of course, much shorter periods, but indications are sufficiently clear and justify our reference to these countries.

When using the Soviet example, we must of course take into consideration the development in that country which during the years after World War II achieved exceptionally important successes in the field of natural sciences and their application in economic activities by the introduction of streamlined methods of production. In this manner the economy of the Soviet Union became clearly a differentiated combination of a highly developed and a considerably less developed economy within the same state. This peculiarity created mounting difficulties to which the administrative management of the economy made a special contribution. However, the study of that period of development and of its problems does not fall within the terms of reference of this work.

As has been shown by examples all over the world, what is necessary for the acceleration of the economic development of the underdeveloped countries is social relationships which stimulate a collective orientation towards a general interest or, as Hirschman describes it, "group orientation,"[59] in contrast to orientation toward one's own exclusive interest. An extreme orientation towards personal gain must act destructively and constitute one of the great problems among the underdeveloped countries.[60]

The example of the Soviet Union is particularly significant

---

[59] Albert Hirschman, *The Strategy of Economic Development, op. cit.*, pp. 11—13.
[60] *Ibid.*, pp. 14—20.

here, in fact even more so than the mentioned instances of the British Commonwealth, because there were no developed economic, political and other ties with the advanced areas in the world. These factors also played a highly significant role in Japan's rapid development. In that country, one element of change at the end of the 19th century was the establishment of lively exchanges with Europe and America. Consequently, the present-day underdeveloped countries must strive to develop such ties under conditions as favorable as possible for them.

Another factor of rapid development was the fact that the nations in question had from the beginning been capable of freely developing their economies. This freedom, of course, was not given to the indigenous population in the British possessions, but the European population there was able to develop its economy autonomously. Allowances for the needs of Great Britain and the Commonwealth were compensated by the benefits which the association offered, mainly financial and commercial.

Among all the above-mentioned factors, independence certainly has the greatest role. The example of the Soviet Union shows that it was more important to preserve its independence, and with it its own internal system, than to use the advantages offered by international economic relations. This example brings home even more forcibly the fact that the political and social conditions in which economic development is taking place are a decisive factor. In other words, the "insoluble" economic problems are beginning to appear under an entirely different light if the totality of social factors are comprehended as a whole. The problems of rapid economic development of the underdeveloped countries cannot be resolved unless the social and political problems are simultaneously dealt with. One of the first political problems is the regulating of relations with the outside world.

THE ROLE OF FOREIGN POLITICAL ACTIVITY IN SPEEDING UP ECONOMIC DEVELOPMENT

It is understandable why the underdeveloped countries, whenever they succeeded in winning the freedom of independent action together with political independence, insisted from the very beginning on a definite foreign policy — on the policy of nonalignment. In fact, even before this freedom was achieved, some leaders in Asia and Africa presented foreign policy programs following the pattern of nonalignment. These new, economically underdeveloped countries were the first nucleus of the movement of nonalignment; they were and remained the protagonists of the principle of peaceful and active coexistence and the abolition of colonialism, as well as of any other form of foreign domination or interference in internal affairs.

In international actions organized within or outside the United Nations, the leading role among the underdeveloped countries was played by the politically most active and the most independent countries — the nonaligned countries. Their political convictions were formed in the context of the international situation and post-war tensions. They are the political inner circle of the underdeveloped countries. The extension of their circle is therefore nothing but a manifestation of the expansion and strengthening of political consciousness within the ranks of the underdeveloped countries.

We should also bear in mind the objective conditions inherited from the times of the past war or arising in the post-war unsettled international relations, which inhibit some countries in Asia and Africa, and particularly in Latin America from taking a clear and definitive orientation towards nonalignment. The fact that an increasing number of countries, despite these objective cold war difficulties, is taking an active part in the undertakings of the nonaligned countries is certainly a very important element which may influence the solution not only of the current political problems but also of international economic issues.

The economic position of the underdeveloped countries was one of the extremely significant factors which affected their foreign policy orientation in the post-liberation years. Notwithstanding the considerable differences is structures as well as in social relationships in some of the countries and parts of the world, they had certain common interests and common problems which created a consciousness about these common interests.

First of all they had a common past in the sense of economic

170

dependence, which in the majority of cases was heightened by a complete political dependence in areas formerly belonging to colonial empires. It gave them a strong impulse towards economic independence, notwithstanding any specific theoretical consideration of the advantages which could arise therefrom. Experience acquired in the political field was to be automatically transferred to the economic sphere. At any rate, in many cases the penetration of the colonies by economic organizations preceded military and political subjection, i. e., the imposition of overseas rule.

Another common point was the desire to carry out the industrial revolution and speed up industrialization and to build up heavy industry. Such ambitions were particularly strongly pronounced wherever there was mineral wealth or where it was believed to exist. One strong impulse in that respect was the need to employ an increasing number of citizens who became available following modernization of agricultural activities. This modernization was sometimes only rudimentary, but nevertheless created a great pressure on the labor market.[61] Consequently, the importation of technical know-how, capital and equipment was only an apparently equalizing common demand of all the underdeveloped countries.[62]

Finally, all these countries have always suffered very unfavorable terms of trade in the world market. Whether exporting raw materials and food or manufactured goods of their young industries, they met difficulties in finding customers or meeting world prices, which cancelled out a large part of the anticipated profit from foreign trade with the developed countries. However, since their trade was directed precisely to those countries, the entire effect of foreign trade was unfavorable.

---

[61] Fred Cottrell in *Energy and Society*, McGraw-Hill, New York 1955, points out on page 129 that the modernization of agriculture in India would free some 30 million workers for whom jobs outside agriculture must be found — the equivalent of half of the work force employed in the U.S.A. Since 1955 there has been a large increase in India's population, and this problem has become even more acute.

[62] The difficulties which began to appear at the first session of the 1964 U.N. Conference on Trade and Development in Geneva later proliferated and showed that the problems of development and the interests and demands arising therefrom were not the same for all the underdeveloped countries. Recognition of the special interests of the most poorly developed countries thus followed. See the *Algiers Charter* in the Appendix.

The total result of all these factors was increased indebtedness to the highly developed countries, which hindered business, and internal development dependent on foreign trade.

The creation of favorable conditions which would help solve internal economic problems through increased world trade was not possible by just economic measures or efforts. The only way to achieve anything in that direction was through political activity in international relations. The need for such activity created a strong base and stimulus for collective actions both within and outside the United Nations to improve world market conditions to suit the needs of the underdeveloped countries. That action was from the beginning the strongest and the most reliable element holding together the nonaligned countries.

Nonalignment can therefore be considered as a political endeavor of a part of mankind which found itself in the middle of the 20th century on the sidelines of development which precisely at that time acquired fantastic and until then unimaginable dimensions. One of the achievements of that accelerated development was the outstanding development of communications and transportation of men and goods, providing increased opportunities for material and ideological contact among all parts of the world.

More drastically than even before, differences in conditions prevailing in different parts of the world have become evident. Technical development calls for the creation of large systems and integration on a global scale, but in practice it has both produced an unprecedented difference in the levels of development and at the same time has created means of making it more obvious. In this manner a significant element of discord was introduced in the international community which heightened the already existing feeling of alienation of the underdeveloped world from those countries which, swept by scientific and technical progress, struck out on their own towards the realization of a trully affluent post-industrial society.

The recent political experiences, the aftermath of the two world wars as well as the experiences of the colonial past have thus been complemented by the bitterness of the feeling that despite all efforts the prospects of catching up with the developed

172

countries and participating in their material progress are becoming a more and more remote vision, if it can at all be described as a vision rather than utopia.

The deep impression which this situation has made on the politicians and statesmen, as well as on the broader population strata in the underdeveloped part of the world, have produced different reactions, especially as regards the ways and means of overcoming the legacy of underdevelopment and the present difficulties by means of internal measures. On the international level, the underdeveloped countries began to feel that they were bound by a similar if not common fate. This similar fate arose from the common fact that they were behind in development and consequently in an inferior position within the international community; hence differences and antagonisms between them lose very much in significance.

This similar destiny was translated into a common action on the basis of the feeling that the acquired independence and the autonomy of internal development were being threatened. This feeling not only did not evolve from a rational assessment of the situation in the present world of technology, science and economy, it has been encouraged mostly by the concrete political and sometimes even military acts of the great powers and the powerful developed countries against the countries of the third world. Whether these acts were designed to bring the cold war into that part of the world or were the acts of interference by the great powers, they encouraged cohesion among the underdeveloped countries in political actions on the world scene aimed at protecting their threatened positions and at creating favorable conditions for their improvement.

Although nonalignment arose at the time when the cold war began to spread, this political movement cannot be explained only as a desire of participant countries to stay outside a conflict due to preoccupation with their own problems, as a desire to draw a direct benefit out of neutrality and good relations with both sides in the dispute, or as taking tactical advantage of a situation which offers short-range benefits. The nonaligned countries would essentially have found themselves in a similar position even if there had been no cold war. It is possible that conditions

173

would have been more favorable for their needs but they would in any case have to constitute themselves as a separate part of the international community.

The political action of nonalignment is substantially an active response to the present situation of the third world countries and an attempt to attain their basic aspirations. It is consequently not simply a by-product of the conflict between the two protagonists in the cold war. It is a movement which is clearly defined by its positive demands on the international community and which has been inspired by positive desires stemming from their low level of development, their internal problems and from the awareness of the gap separating them from the developed countries and from the fear of being threatened which is generated by all these disadvantages.

CHAPTER THREE

THE YUGOSLAV
POLICY OF NONALIGNMENT
TAKES SHAPE

Since the mid-fifties Yugoslavia had been an active participant, and often an initiator in all the actions of the nonaligned
countries, but nevertheless she holds a special place among them
because of her geographical position and because of the basic
characteristics of her society, her specific history and the difference in social structures. Finally, for Yugoslavia World War II
was not mainly an opportunity to get free from foreign domination
but a historical moment in which a revolutionary transformation
of society was made.

It is therefore understandable why there are similarities as
well as differences between Yugoslavia and the majority of the
countries which, after World War II, adopted nonalignment.
Nonalignment in Yugoslavia did not follow immediately in the
wake of the revolutionary transformation but came only later
and gradually under the impact of relations with the outside world.
During the first three post-war years, Yugoslavia was undoubtedly
aligned in the sense and in the manner in which many countries
in those years were aligned.

Furthermore, Yugoslavia had inherited from her past the
tradition of European civilization. She was consequently predis-
posed to seek her identity and interests within the European political pattern. In the event of a division into two camps, it was
logical for Yugoslavia to opt for one of the two sides.

175

Finally, Yugoslavia is economically less developed than the European average, especially in comparison with the overall level of development in the Western part of the continent. She is behind in her social structures and its potentials, in educational levels and psychological dispositions, and in the process, begun still well before the war, of modernization of economic activity. Neither should one forget the rich traditions of political activity in her past, and the transcending of pre-capitalist social relationships.

In view of this it is necessary to consider the special role and the road of Yugoslavia within the context of nonalignment. This consideration should embrace two domains of research: firstly, the character of relations with the outside world and experiences acquired in that field, and secondly, the peculiarity of internal development as an influence in the shaping of foreign policies. These two domains of research cannot always be strictly separated, because they are often interrelated. Understandably enough, a special emphasis will be placed on external factors, because their explanation will give us an insight into the determination as well as motivation of the country's concrete action in relation to the outside world, in other words, within the framework of the activity of the nonaligned countries.

SPECIFIC CHARACTERISTICS OF YUGOSLAVIA'S INTERNATIONAL POSITION FOLLOWING WORLD WAR II

a) ALIGNMENT

In contrast to other nonaligned countries, Yugoslavia came out of the war as an active participant and member of the victorious Allied side in the war. Consequently, on the strength of her international status, from the very beginning she maintained direct and close relations with the countries which soon afterwards became confronted in the cold war. In that respect her status substantially differed from that of the other countries which proclaimed themselves as nonaligned after the war.

Consequently, for Yugoslavia the conflict between the Allies was not a conflict in an alien and remote world, but rather an event in which she herself was an active participant. This is the first substantial difference which places Yugoslavia in a special category of nonaligned countries from the very outset. Yugoslavia, in fact, belongs to that world with which the nonaligned countries neither could nor wanted to identify themselves from the start. Still in the early days of the cold war, Yugoslavia, voluntarily and with a full conviction in the correctness of her act, took the side of the Soviet Union and considered herself attached and aligned with it in its confrontation with its former Allies from the West.

Yugoslavia's decision in no way diminished her desire to act independently. She regarded her relationships with the Soviet Union as a relationship of equal cooperation and an expression of solidarity rather than a relationship of subordination. The conception upon which Yugoslavia's policy of friendship for the U.S.S.R. concurrent with her insistence on autonomy and independent internal development was based is best reflected in an article which at the time had a programatic and ideological significance. That was an article by the Prime Minister and Secretary General of the Communist Party, Tito:

"Owing to the existence of the great Soviet Union with its socialist system and owing to its great successes, within a short period and in all domains of social activity, conditions have been created within a short span of time which are based on a rich experience gained in the construction of the great socialist country, and which have permitted the broad working masses in other countries to come to the understanding that it is not only necessary but also possible to achieve in each country a better and more just social system. But the road to achieve this should not and cannot be everywhere exactly the same as had been mapped out by the great October Revolution. To put this question dogmatically would be un-Marxist and un-dialectical. These roads may and do have many common points, but the specific conditions and nature of each country's internal development determine the specific nature of the road toward a better social system, in the concrete case, in this country, toward the achievement of a true people's democracy."[1]

As this quotation shows, internal development in the Soviet Union was never regarded as a model to copy, but it certainly did play a very important part in shaping Yugoslavia's internal and foreign policies after the war. Yugoslavia felt closely attached to the Soviet Union, as a brotherly socialist country, and there were hopes that this brotherhood would develop. Yugoslavia relied on her own assessments in making use of the Soviet experience. There was no intention of abandoning autonomous political decision-making in Yugoslavia, but yet this decision-making had been greatly influenced by a desire to adjust as much as possible to the common policy of the family in which the Soviet Union as the largest country certainly did play a decisive role.

This pro-Soviet foreign policy orientation of post-war Yugoslavia was based upon three basic reasons. The first was the conviction that there was similarity in aspirations towards the common goal — socialism, if not in all the details of the form or the means and ways. This reason, as we have already said, played an important role despite the determination to preserve independence and full freedom of national development.

In the domain of international relations, concretely in connection with Yugoslavia's vital interests in external relations, the Soviet Union was a natural ally, and it is upon this that the other two reasons for Yugoslavia's foreign political alignment were based: in the last stages of the war the Soviet Union had given Yugoslavia a most precious assistance in considerable quantities of war materials and in the cooperation between the Soviet Army and the Yugoslav People's Army, including cooperation in joint military operations in the northeastern parts of the country and in the battle for Belgrade.

Finally, the Soviet Union had offered very significant diplomatic support to Yugoslavia's demands relating to the settlement of some post-war problems and involving the country's vital

---

[1] Tito, *Govori i članci, op. cit.,* Vol. II, p. 369 (The quotation is from the article "Temelji demokratije novog tipa" first published in "Komunist", No. 2 for 1946).

interests. This support was based on the fact that the internal development in Yugoslavia had flouted the hopes of the Western powers of seeing the old Yugoslavia reestablished and headed by a government that would closely ally itself with them. At the same time this support increased pressures from the West and created an even greater need for the Soviet backing.

Whereas the first two points, the feeling of kinship for the Soviet Union as a socialist country and gratitude for its war-time assistance, were subject to erosion, the third point, support in current difficulties with the West, gained in importance. The erosion was particularly visible in connection with the feeling of affinity based on similarities in social systems. In regard to war-time help an understandable psychological reaction of exalation about the victory and about the magnificence of one's own effort, contributed to the continuation of euphory but as to the feeling of closeness, daily experience produced continually dissonant notes.

After the war, much more than during the struggle itself, there developed a powerful feeling of pride and conviction that Yugoslavia did not owe anything to anybody, because she had given more than her share to the joint victory. These feelings had been present during the war, too, but then they were repressed by the need to give even more, to make an even greater effort in the last struggles on which the settlement of one of the most sensitive questions depended so much, that of the Western borders.

It was quite clear to most people, including soldiers and civilians that frontiers were at all times drawn on the basis of the balance of forces created by military power or by means of other pressures. All the former frontiers of Yugoslavia were so created, in a period which was still validly remembered. That fact had been constantly emphasized during the war. However, after the war it was necessary to shift the emphasis to the diplomatic terrain and prepare for the signing of the peace treaty. The mood which was then prevalent can best be recalled by the speech which Prime Minister Tito held at the first public meeting in liberated Zagreb on May 21, 1945:

"In the course of this struggle, we became the most combative and the strongest European ally of the democratic powers in the war against the common enemy of all the United Nations. We have given in this struggle 300,000 young lives.[2] We have fought in order to liberate our country, to make it a better and happier community, but also in order to liberate those of our brethren who had been subjugated for more than twenty years to an alien power. Now the peace conference should bring a definitive settlement about the definite annexation of these parts of our country to our state. By liberating, or as they call it, occupying those regions we did not put anybody before an accomplished fact. It is by the force of our arms that we arrived on the Isonzo and into Furlania, just the same as the Allies, by the strength of their arms, had vanquished the enemy in Africa and arrived at the Isonzo. We have not usurped anything by pursuing the enemy to the point where we have arrived.[3] It would therefore be wrong and a great injustice to accuse us of putting anybody before an accomplished fact, and of having taken by the force of arms anything which was not yet granted to us by international law. We have not come to Istria, Trieste and the Isonzo to place our Allies before an accomplished fact and to appropriate these regions, but we have come to annihilate and help destroy the greatest enemy of civilization — Germany. A great injustice would be done to our people if they were now accused and asked to leave, not taking into account that Istria, Trieste and the Slovenian Littoral cost us 8,000 dead during the last ten days of fighting. We have a right to remain there as allies, because we want recognition of our allied rights, just as we have acknowledged our own duties which we have fulfilled one hundred per cent and are still doing so."[4]

The signing of the treaty of friendship and cooperation with the Soviet Union was described in the same speech as a "great event", as "brotherhood strengthened in the common struggle", but also as an "act which we have signed in order to safeguard ourselves against any future eventualities." Of special significance was the stress on safeguarding against "any eventuality", but it

---

[2] This figure refers only to the number of those partisans and Yugoslav People's Army soldiers (then the National Liberation Army) killed in combat.

[3] This is an answer to the assertions and articles of the press in the West.

[4] Tito, *Govori i članci*, Vol. I, *op. cit.*, pp. 270—271.

was not presented as a mere dependence on the Soviet Union or solicitation of the protection of that great power.[5] "We have established firm links with the Soviet Union," Tito said, "because it is in the interest of our country and in the interests of both the Allies". In his speech he also emphasized his wish to develop relations with the other Allies as well, and with the countries that had been occupied during the war.[6]

The treaty of friendship and cooperation with the Soviet Union was to mark the beginning of the building of post-war relations which were to extend to all aspects of cooperation.[7] The treaty was ratified by the presidency of AVNOJ on June 10, 1945, when it was again described as a great historical act and a "result of the people's long-standing aspirations."[8] Subsequently in August of the same year, in his speech at the third session of AVNOJ, Tito again referred to that treaty:

"The most significant foreign policy act in the history of new Yugoslavia was made on April 11, 1945 in Moscow, when the Treaty on Mutual Aid, Friendship, Economic and Cultural Cooperation with the Soviet Union was signed. This great historical act was enthusiastically greeted by all our peoples. This act has long and steadfastly been desired by all our peoples. But it is only now, twenty-six years after the establishment of old Yugoslavia, only after the great catastrophe which overcame our country in 1941, only after the peoples of Yugoslavia in their liberation struggle had taken their destinies into their own hands and removed anything that hindered the rapprochement with the brotherly Soviet nation — it is only after all this that finally the centuries-long aspirations of our peoples have been realized and an indestructible link established with the peoples of the Soviet Union, which will be the guarantee of our security and a great benefit for the development of our country."[9]

---

[5] The treaty was signed on March 7, 1945, in Moscow by Prime Minister Tito for Yugoslavia and Minister of Foreign Affairs Molotov for the Soviet Union.

[6] Tito, *Govori i članci*, Vol. I, *op. cit.*, pp. 272—273.

[7] For the complete text of the agreement see *Official Gazette*, No. 40, 1945, p. 341.

[8] Tito, Vol. I, *op. cit.*, p. 291. The abreviation AVNOJ stands for Antifascist Council of National Liberation of Yugoslavia, the main political representative body of the Liberation Movement in Yugoslavia during the war.

[9] Tito, *Govori i članci*, Vol. II, *op. cit.*, pp. 16—17.

The leaning towards the Soviet Union was consequently not only a reflection of Yugoslavia's actual relations with the outside world and her feeling of affinity and recognition for past help, but also the most important external factor in ensuring security and realizing national aspirations in the future. Yugoslavia was indeed aligned, prepared to treat this alignment as an immutable foundation of her foreign policy, although even then, at the height of enthusiasm, she made sure that the country's needs in regard to the development of relations with the rest of the world should be realistically assessed. Interesting in this connection was the interview granted to a correspondent of the Soviet newspaper *Krasnaiâ Zvezda*, in which, in addition to the Soviet Union's help, which was already beginning to come through, Prime Minister Tito also stressed the need for aid from other countries, "and especially from America."[10]

Yugoslavia thus differed from the majority of the latter-day nonaligned countries not only by being a socialist country, but also because in the early post-war years she was a part of that system of states within which there was a rift and alignment on two sides. The consciousness of belonging to this system did not arise only from Yugoslavia's geographical position but, above all, from her total and intensive involvement in the war which had been waged for four years on her territory, and during which the socialist transformation of society had taken place.

In this connection we should not lose sight of the fact that the revolution in Yugoslavia was not modelled after the October Revolution, when power was taken over by a coup d'état effected on November 7 in Petrograd and other centers, as a prelude to the real revolution, to a fundamental transformation of society and creation of new revolutionary institutions. At the moment of taking over control early in the afternoon on November 7, 1917, Lenin proclaimed at the meeting of the Petrograd Soviet of Workers' and Soldiers' Deputies: "The workers and peasant revolution, about whose inevitability the Bolsheviks have been speaking all the time, has been effected." A little later he explained the situation which had just arisen. "From now on a new epoch

---

10 Tito, *Govori i članci*, Vol. I, *op. cit.*, p. 254.

182

starts in the history of Russia and this third Russian revolution should in its final outcome bring about the victory of socialism." Lenin concluded his brief speech with the following words: "We in Russia must now devote ourselves to the building of a proletarian socialist state."[11] In other words, at the given moment the question of central power was resolved, and everything else was only to come.

The revolution in Yugoslavia unfolded quite differently. In his statement made before the second session of AVNOJ on November 29, 1943, the supreme commander, Tito, who at the same session was elected President of the National Committee of Liberation of Yugoslavia (Provisional Government), divided the course of the revolution (national liberation struggle) into four stages:

"First, the capitulation of Yugoslavia and the beginning of the popular uprising, which in its beginning had acquired the form of numerous partisan detachments for the struggle against the invaders;

"Second, the growth of the partisan detachments into regular military units, battalions, brigades and divisions and the creation of the National Liberation Army of Yugoslavia;

"Third, the transformation of the national liberation committees into the genuine popular government, and the creation of the Anti-Fascist Council of National Liberation of Yugoslavia; and

"Fourth, the stage in which we are now, and that is — the transformation of the Anti-Fascist Council of National Liberation of Yugoslavia from a general political body into the highest legislative body, and the creation of the National Committee of Liberation of Yugoslavia as a provisional people's government."[12]

Thus the formation of the government on March 7, 1945, in Belgrade was the final step in the formation of the new state which was preceded by a deep social transformation begun in the smallest territorial units. This, of course, did not preclude a further evolution after 1945 and, after 1948, a new fundamental social

---

[11] Lenin, *Sochineniia*, fourth edition, Vol. 26, Moskva 1944, pp. 208—209. The text is translated from the Russian by the Author.

[12] Tito, *Govori i članci*, Vol. I, *op. cit.*, p. 150.

transformation. However, Yugoslavia did appear as a new state with already established institutions and as a social entity fundamentally different from the pre-war Yugoslav society.

Although the last mentioned circumstance was of exceptional significance for the formation of the first political platform in relations with the outside world, it, however, did not distinguish Yugoslavia so much from the other nonaligned countries at the moment when nonalignment had begun to take shape in the ideas of individual leaders in Southeast Asia. The main difference stemmed from Yugoslavia's alignment and her intimate relationship, first with the wartime alliance, which at that time was frequently called "the United Nations", and later on with the Soviet Union, when relations with the West were cooling and gradually deteriorating.

b) SIMILARITIES WITH THE NONALIGNED COUNTRIES

We have seen that what distinguished Yugoslavia in the early post-war years from the other countries which later on cooperated with her as nonaligned countries, was her alignment. However, it was already obvious then that Yugoslavia had specific characteristics which distinguished her from the other countries aligned with the Soviet Union and which made her similar to those of her later friends and co-militants in nonalignment. This can be seen from her earliest foreign policy statements.

Let us first take a closer look at the specific features contained in the body politic of Yugoslavia, in her revolutionary struggle and transformation during the Second World War. The socio-political content of that transformation has already been emphasized, and it was this more than anything else that prompted identification with the Soviet Union. However, the fact that this transformation was occurring in a completely different sequence than the revolution in Russia, caused some other significant effects.

The old order, together with its state apparatus, had been

destroyed in the war under the blows of the enemy. It was first the central government authority that broke up in a panic flight in 1941, together with its entire military and civilian apparatus. The political factors and organizations which before the war had constituted the political fabric from which the political apparatus of the state had been woven also disappeared.

As regards the governmental and political institutions which legally existed in the old pre-war state, there was a complete vacuum. Only two factors remained on the scene: first, the occupation forces with their apparatus and the attached quisling institutions and organizations, some of them imported from among the emigrees or raised by the enemy to an importance which alone they could never hope to achieve; second, the resistance movement which in the early days had two centers, partisan and chetnik, but which soon, owing to the cooperation of chetniks with the enemy, was reduced to the partisan movement alone.

This movement was the offspring of the Communist Party, illegal before the war, which took up the challenge of the newly arisen situation and opposed the occupation and the fragmentation of the country into various occupational territories.[13] The Communist Party was numerically small at the beginning of the war, but it had two advantages: very soon it remained the only political force which opposed the enemy, and its cadres possessed the resolution, capability, knowledge and military training necessary to organize armed resistance which would grow into an uprising and a massive regular military action.

These advantages were acquired through the political action of the communists before the war and their training, both in underground activity against the old regime, and in the participation of a large number of activists in the civil war in Spain; some received training in the schools for reserve officers within the framework of the general military service, and the movement was joined by a small number of career officers. However, the most important of all was the organization and resolution of

---

[13] After the collapse of the old Kingdom of Yugoslavia, the country was divided as follows: Slovenia was partioned between Germany and Italy, the quisling "Independent State of Croatia" was set up, the following zones of occupation were established: Hungarian, Italian, Bulgarian and German, and other parts of Yugoslavia were annexed to the above countries.

this relatively small body of men to rally the people to the struggle, and to increase the readiness of the people to resist.

The efforts of the Party resulted in a gradual, and later on increasingly fast and intensive political reorientation of the broad popular masses. Although the Communist Party during the war placed the emphasis on the struggle for liberation of the country rather than its ideological premises, still its influence on ideological orientation became stronger and stronger from one year to the next. The strengthening of its influence and its leadership in political life can be represented as a threefold process: firstly, political goals and the formulation of day-to-day policies were completely in the hands of the Communist Party, because there had been no other significant political factors of resistance; secondly, since the local organs of government had broken up very quickly, provisional organs of authority on the liberated territory were formed under the influence of the Communist Party, and they undertook to deal with current problems for which the socialist conception in given circumstances was certainly the most suitable, if not the only possible one; thirdly as instigators of resistance and political action in the struggle for independence, the communists assumed as a matter of course the leading positions in all spheres of activity, and the policy and the dynamism of the Communist Party daily attracted hundreds and later on thousands of new members who became some of the most active participants of the liberation movement.

At the time when regular and internationally recognized organs of authority were formed after the war, that is to say, at the moment of formal assumption of power, the revolutionary movement had behind it four years of armed struggle during which a powerful regular army was created, and throughout the whole country a new revolutionary government was already under way, supported by the population. In other words, the new government did not emerge from a civil war, did not have to sign an unequal peace treaty, as had been the Brest-Litovsk Treaty, and did not have to resist foreign intervention.

In brief, the revolution in Yugoslavia, although essentially a socialist revolution, was at the same time a liberation war, a struggle for independence, similar in one way or another to the struggle of the liberation movements in the colonies which later on as independent countries took up nonalignment. It is precisely this dual character of the political and armed struggle in Yugoslavia during the war that has imbued new Yugoslavia with a sympathy and understanding for the liberation movements in the colonies, and towards the new countries of the third world.

As we have already said, the inclination toward alignment with the Soviet Union tipped the balance in the early months after the war, but there was a firm resolve to preserve the country's independence. The earliest document which refers to this problem comprehensively is Prime Minister Tito's address to the National Assembly on April 1, 1946, in which we find the following important statement:

"Our foreign policy so far has been based — and must also be based in the future — on the following principles:

"First, to work with all our might for the strengthening of peace in the world.

"Secondly, to work with all our might to win for Yugoslavia her rights, those which had been denied her after the First World War — i. e. to regain the wrongful loss of her territories such as Istria, the Slovenian Littoral and Trieste, the Slovenian part of Corinthia, etc. — as well as those rights deriving from this war, which are based on the enormous sacrifices and losses which our country and our peoples have suffered;

"Thirdly, to work for the strengthening of cultural, political and economic relations, in the first instance with the brotherly Slavic peoples headed by the Soviet Union, and also with other countries, particularly with those with whom we have jointly fought for four years against the same enemy;

"Fourthly, to work with all our might to safeguard our country, her security, her peaceful development, in short — to do everything in order to prevent a disaster similar to that of 1941."[14]

It would be exaggerated to claim that this policy was identical with that which Nehru outlined five months later, but there is no doubt that it was compatible with the then possible definition of

---

[14] Tito, *Govori i članci*, Vol. II, p. 189.

the policy of nonalignment. It contain the following elements, which were also contained in the early proclamations of the policy of nonalignment: first, insistence on the development of relations with all the Allies, which means with the Soviet Union (especially) and with the Western countries; secondly insistence on peace and independence (the tragedy of 1941!); thirdly, solution of the question of frontiers (which was the problem of practically all the new nonaligned countries); fourthly, the basing of the national policy on the tradition of the liberation movement.

*
* *

This comparison of similarities and differences between Yugoslavia in the early post-war years and her later friends from the movement of nonalignment has shown that Yugoslavia, even at the time of her alignment, was sympathetic to the aspirations and preoccupations of those countries. An additional circumstance is that she, too, suffered a relative economic backwardness and that one of her first and most difficult tasks was to heal the terrible wounds of the war and start an accelerated economic development. In fact, the two disparate components influencing her internal and foreign policies were not in a state of static equilibrium; over the years greater emphasis was placed on the policy of nonalignment as misunderstandings with the Soviet Union proliferated. A counter balance to this tendency, however, was the inclination towards increased reliance on the Soviet Union as a result of the cold war and which threatened to draw Yugoslavia into the vicious circle of increased dependence on the Soviet Union and deteriorated relations with the West.

THE PROBLEM OF BORDERS AND CONFRONTATION WITH THE WEST

The borders of Yugoslavia after the First World War were drawn on the basis of the existing balance of forces and the general world situation as reflected in the peace conference. In fact, Yugoslavia even after the conference had to resign herself to the loss of Rijeka (Fiuma), which was taken away forcibly after the Yugoslav border with Italy had already been legally established. There was particular dissatisfaction because Italy obtained Zadar and Rijeka, together with the whole of Istria and the Slovenian Littoral.

During the Second World War this question again came into the public eye as a specific problem of Yugoslavia. It would probably have arisen in any case, because it involved a fairly large territory and a considerable number of Croatian and Slovenian inhabitants. Furthermore, Italian sovereignty over Zadar in the center of the country's coastal belt was a source of constant irritation. The question became even more acute when Italy tried during the war to appropriate a considerable portion of the Yugoslav coast and to place Croatia under her tutelage. The Duke of Spoleto was even named the King of Croatia.

It is therefore understandable that still during the war, especially in Croatia and Slovenia, the question of borders was raised very strongly. The National Anti-Fascist Council of National Liberation of Croatia — ZAVNOH,[15] as well as the Slovenian National Liberation Council — SNOO,[16] proclaimed the annexation of the territories inhabited by the Croats and Slovenes, i. e., Istria and the Slovenian Littoral with Trieste, to Croatia and Slovenia. These decisions were confirmed and endorsed by the Anti-Fascist Council of National Liberation of Yugoslavia.[17]

Thus while the war was still in process the policy of new Yugoslavia in regard to her borders was proclaimed. The above-

---

[15] *Hronologija oslobodilačke borbe naroda Jugoslavije 1941—1945* (Chronicle of the Liberation Struggle of the People of Yugoslavia), Military History Institute, Beograd 1964, p. 551.

[16] *Ibid., p.* 560.

[17] *Ibid.,* p. 595.

mentioned acts could not have a legal effect, they could only be regarded as a counter to the further Italian pretensions and as a formulation of demands which after the war would be presented at the peace conference. If we take into consideration how cautious formal statements were about the post-war system of the country and about future foreign policies, such an energetic approach to the question of the borders certainly shows how lively and politically active this issue was, especially in regard to Italy.

In the last days of the war the Yugoslav armed forces made a special effort and displayed exceptional skill and resolve in penetrating deep into the rear of the German front, bypassing the German defensive lines before Rijeka. In that operation, considerable German forces were destroyed and all of Istria with Rijeka, and the Slovenian Littoral with Trieste, were liberated.[18] The Allied forces, which were advancing northwards through Italy, were met near Monfalcone at the mouth of the Isonzo, on the western border of that territory which still during the war had been proclaimed as a constituent part of Yugoslavia.

The meeting at the mouth of the Isonzo brought about the first dramatic confrontation between new Yugoslavia and the Western Allies.[19] The Allies were certainly anxious to limit as much as possible the westward push of a country which was already regarded as a member of the rival formation headed by the Soviet Union, and they also wanted to avoid a precedent in view of the fast advance of the Soviet armed forces into Germany which could facilitate a *de facto* delimitation there too. They wanted at all costs to prevent the automatic application of the rule that every ally may hold under his occupation the territory which he takes during military operations.[20]

This attitude of the Western Allies caused much discontent in Yugoslavia, although it was accepted that border questions should be settled around the table of the peace conference. In

---

[18] *Ibid.*, p. 1110.

[19] The Allied Command and later the governments in Washington and London energetically demanded the withdrawal of Yugoslav troops from west of Trieste and from the city of Trieste and the handing over of these territories to the Anglo-American units. See: *Hronologija, op. cit.*, pp. 1105—1106.

[20] In Germany there actually was a considerable correction of the line resulting from military operations, as there was also in Czechoslovakia.

the already quoted Zagreb speech of May 21, 1945, Prime Minister Tito underlined that "it would be a great injustice to accuse us of having put anyone before an accomplished fact and of having taken by the force of arms anything that had not been approved by international law."[21] But in this speech, as in all his earlier and later speeches, Tito underlined the right of Yugoslavia to those territories and emphasized the great sacrifices that had been made in order to liberate them.

During the first three years after the war, relations between Yugoslavia and the West were constantly overshadowed by this first confrontation, as well as by a series of incidents which took place in the strained atmosphere. Those incidents included the shooting down and forcing to land respectively of two U.S. Army transport aircraft in the northwestern part of the country. The aircraft belonged to a regular military line over Yugoslav territory, although the right of flying over it had been specifically denied.[22] From year to year the atmosphere worsened, partly as a result of the ever sharper confrontation on the frontier questions, and partly because of the deterioration of the general atmosphere in Europe, in other words, because of the cold war.

The diplomatic struggle over the Trieste question was conducted within the framework of special agreements among the four great powers which had assumed the responsibility of settling post-war international issues and the system of peace. This task consisted of two parts. The first, direct task, was to prepare the text of peace treaties and the other to control in the meantime the former enemies. This also included the responsibility of convening the peace conference once the texts were ripe for presentation to this broad forum.

Since the question of Trieste had been a component part of the peace treaty with Italy, that question was then dealt with at quadripartite meetings. Consequently, Yugoslavia was not able to participate directly in the elaboration of the texts which would decide on her borders. So as not to be excluded altogether, she was forced to lobby the representatives of the four great powers in order to be heard in the quadripartite meetings, without

---

21 Tito, *Govori i članci*, Vol. I, *op. cit.*, p. 271.
22 *Keesing's Contemporary Archives* 1946—1948, *op. cit.*, p. 8086.

the right to vote and even without fully participating in the discussions. Equal rights had been given to Italy. At the final meetings of the peace conference there was little likelihood of changing anything that had already been decided among the four in the preparatory phase.

At that time it seemed that the decision of Pula and Trieste was an extremely important strategical and economic question, and so a very sharp division occurred among the great powers. Thus the question of Trieste became a bone of contention between the two blocs as the cold war suddenly developed. Negotiations ceased to be discussions between allies and became a contest of force between two rival great powers. The situation degenerated to such an extent that in 1947, when the peace conference finally took place, it was impossible to find a generally acceptable solution.

The peace conference in Paris therefore met in an atmosphere which resembled more the tense climate preceding a war than the state of serenity expected after the conclusion of a war. The main problem at the conference was to find a solution to relations not so much between the victors and the vanquished, as between the disunited allies themselves who had won the war but had succumbed to increased tensions. Thus a temporary solution was arrived at regarding the borders between Italy and Yugoslavia. Neither side was able to enforce its own solution, and the answer was found in a compromise. A separate free territory was provided for, embracing the city of Trieste and its immediate surroundings.[23]

The city of Trieste in Zone A, the coastal belt connecting it with Italy, came under Anglo-American occupation, and Zone B, south and east of the city, under Yugoslav occupation. This situation was provisional, because the entire territory was to be administred by a governor. But the two sides could not agree upon any one person, the provisional situation continued even after the peace treaty had come into force, and the prospect of a solution diminished as tensions between the East and the West increased.

---

[23] *Službeni list* (Official Gazette), 1947, No. 74, p. 1001.

Finally, in March 1948, a new turnabout took place, showing to what extent the Trieste issue had become a part of the cold war in the early post-war years. The London Declaration was issued by Great Britain, the United States and France. On April 18 of the same year, Italy was to hold elections which were to be decisive for the country's future. In Italy, as in France, popular fronts had been broken up, the Communists dropped out of governments, and on the eve of the parliamentary elections there were speculations whether the Christian Democrats led by De Gasperi would preserve their majority, or whether there would be a great swing to the left and possibly a left coalition or even a Communist government.

In the London tri-partite declaration, published on March 20, 1948, the three Western great powers proclaimed their desire for the peace treaty to be revised, and for zones A and B, i. e., the entire free territory of Trieste, to be definitively handed over to Italy. This meant that both Zone B with the towns Kopar, Porto-rož, Piran, Buje and Novi Grad, and Zone A which included Trieste and the territory today under Italy, should go over to Italy.[24] The three great powers could not evidently revise the peace treaty without the U.S.S.R. and therefore, as they published the declaration, they sent a note to Moscow asking the U.S.S.R. to agree to the revision of the Italian peace treaty, claiming that it had not been possible to agree on a governor and that the anticipated solution had become unfeasible. This was in fact an invitation to reopen the entire question of the frontiers between Yugoslavia and Italy. The peace treaty depended on the will of the four great powers, and it could be changed only following an agreement among them.

Relations between Yugoslavia and the West came into a crisis for two reasons. The confrontation on the borders was the continuation of the old struggle for national territory which had ended unfavorably after World War I, because at the time Yugoslavia had been a new state without a strong international position and suffering from great internal weaknesses. On the other hand, the Allies had obligations towards Italy, arising from

---

[24] Department of State Bulletin, March 28, 1948, Washington D. C., p. 425.

the London pact concluded in 1917. As much as they might have been immoral and legally invalid in the newly arisen situation, those obligations nevertheless played an important role in the drawing of the borders.

After World War II, Yugoslavia no longer acted as a weak and insignificant new country in dispute with one of the big Allies, but rather as a country which in the course of the war had created for itself an important international position, facing across the table a vanquished Italy. However, that which gave Yugoslavia prospects of a favorable outcome in her border dispute at the same time constituted an obstacle to their realization. A strong Yugoslavia was undesirable from the West's point of view, because she would tip the balance in favor of the Soviet Union, the rival in intra-Allied relations. Since this rivalry was increasingly turning into hostility, this circumstance was becoming more and more decisive.

This ill-will towards Yugoslavia was especially significant in connection with Italy, which had been regarded as socially and politically unstable in view of the upheavals and the unclear internal political constellation following the defeat in the war and the downfall of fascism. As the population in the disputed territory energetically endorsed the Yugoslav demands, resistance grew in the West against the satisfaction of the Yugoslav aspirations. Thus the U.S.S.R.'s role in the peace talks became more and more pivotal.

The reversal marked by the London Declaration in the Western attitude on the Trieste question was unfavorable for Yugoslavia, not only because of what the Declaration contained, but also because it formally placed the decision in the hands of the Soviet government. In this situation Yugoslavia was not able to prevent the reopening of the question of the peace treaty. The only thing she could do was to resist as a sovereign state the imposition of outside decisions.

By publishing the Declaration, the West's intention was to challenge the U.S.S.R. to a negative answer and to use this negative answer to the maximum in international relations, especially in the electoral campaign in Italy. In the prevalent state of hostility, there was no hope of an agreement between the West and the Soviet Union about a revision of the peace treaty with Italy, certainly not in a direction that would be contrary to Soviet interests. This implied, of course, that the delimitation between Italy and Yugoslavia was still a delimitation between two Allied camps, in fact that it was the frontier between the two sides in the cold war which had just begun.[25]

The actual state of affairs which arose as the Western great powers changed their minds about the solution of the Trieste question provided by the peace treaty was however altogether different. Soon after the proclamation of the London Declaration the dispute between Yugoslavia and the U.S.S.R. came to a head and escalated into a conflict with all the countries affiliated in the Cominform, the Information Bureau of the Communist Parties, which was founded in 1947. Thus Yugoslavia found herself between the devil and the deep blue sea. March 1948 was the critical point in Yugoslavia's post-war history, which vitally affected the shaping of her foreign policies. She was in dispute and confrontation with both sides in the cold war, not only because of the foreign political pretensions of the two parties, but also because of the basic concepts of the internal development in Yugoslavia. It was a crucial point which at the same time deeply influenced the internal development of Yugoslavia, which in turn influenced her stand toward the outside world.

CONFRONTATION WITH THE COMINFORM COUNTRIES

The confrontation between Yugoslavia and the Soviet Union started immediately before the publication of the London Declaration, in fact during the two preceding days. The first acts were the telegrams in which an immediate withdrawal of the

---

[25] The year 1948 marked the eve of the first large clashes in the cold war. In addition to the events involving Yugoslavia, in February of that year there was a coup d'état in Prague, and later in 1948 the Berlin crisis broke out, which led to the final division of Germany. At the beginning of the following year the North Atlantic Treaty Organization was formed.

Soviet civilian and military experts from Yugoslavia was announced. These telegrams were sent to the Yugoslav government on March 18 and 19, 1948. They were followed by an exchange of letters between Belgrade and Moscow, and finally by Yugoslavia's expulsion from the Cominform and by the proclamation of its first resolution directed against Yugoslavia.[26]

These two steps by the Soviet government caused astonishment in Yugoslavia, although it was known that in the course of years, during as well as after the war, there had been differences in views and disagreements in some international as well as in a number of internal questions. What was most unusual was the manner in which the dispute started. The first step was to cut off cooperation in the civil and military reconstruction of war-devastated Yugoslavia. Even before any arguments were put forward or a discussion started about a point of disagreement sanctions were taken, sanctions which were bound to have far-reaching effects. The recall of experts instantly interrupted cooperation in economic reconstruction as well as in the modernization of the armed forces. Subsequently this interruption became a full stop after all the relevant agreements and treaties had been cancelled.

In order to understand this act it is necessary to review the history of the development of relations between Yugoslavia and the Soviet Union, but it is even more important to throw light on the premises which had led to the open confrontation. Every single point which caused misunderstandings over the years could have been explained and could have been bridged over. What loomed large above all this was the very same question which dominated the relations later on as well, the question of the very nature and content of the relationship.

During the war the relations between the liberation movement in Yugoslavia and Moscow were limited to telegraph messages until the arrival of a Soviet military mission at the Supreme Headquarters of the National Liberation Army on February 23, 1944. Soon afterwards military missions were estab-

---

[26] A documented history of the beginning and development of this conflict is given in the *White Paper* prepared by the Yugoslav Ministry of Foreign Affairs in 1951. All the data in this chapter concerning this matter have been taken from *the White Paper* unless otherwise indicated.

lished in other headquarters in different parts of the country. That was mainly the period of the joint struggle against the common enemy, and in regard to this basic issue there had been no dispute. Yet there were in fact differences of views about the conduct of military operations, about the organization, character and size of units, and also about the political assessments of the internal situation in Yugoslavia.

As Belgrade was liberated and when military operations ceased on the entire territory of Yugoslavia, relations spread into the domains of cooperation in the reconstruction of the country and its internal organization and foreign policy. This cooperation was based on the achievements of the last months of the war, when the U.S.S.R. supplied Yugoslavia with considerable quantities of heavy military equipment, including trucks, artillery guns and tanks, and military aircraft. It seemed that this period of cooperation did not contain any elements of dissension. However, it should be noted that Yugoslavia had always insisted on full equality in treatment, and this insistence was reflected in the agreement which was concluded in order to legally define the role and action of the Soviet units which entered the territory of Yugoslavia towards the end of 1944.[27]

During the post-war years an increasing number of contentious questions cropped up, but the majority of them received very little publicity, and at the time when they appeared no special importance was attached to them in Yugoslavia. We should mention only two major examples of disagreement on questions in the domain of international relations; these were differences in connection with the solution of the Palestine question[28] and disagreement over a number of provisions contained in the first Soviet draft of the new convention on Danube navigation.[29]

---

[27] See the Agreement on the entry of Soviet Troops into Yugoslavia in 1944, *Peti kongres Komunističke partije Jugoslavije* (Fifth Congress of the Communist Party of Yugoslavia), "Kultura", Beograd 1948, pp. 120—121.

[28] Yugoslavia was the only country in the United Nations which, up to the final vote in the General Assembly plenum, thought that it was better to create an Arab-Israeli confederation in the area of Palestine. The overwhelming majority were in favor of the creation of a separate state of Israel. The great powers were all in agreement on this question, including the Soviet Union, which aided Israel in every respect in the first Israeli-Arab war. The Arab countries were opposed to any settlement which would mean the creation of any kind of Israeli state.

[29] Yugoslavia proposed a number of amendments to the draft of the Convention on the Danube, which was prepared in Moscow. Most important was Yugoslavia's insistence on maintaining sovereignty

These differences were partly aired in the correspondence of 1948. Despite all these differences, Yugoslavia endeavored throughout that time and with all available resources to preserve solidarity and cooperation with the Soviet Union as much as possible and observed her obligation under the treaty concerning friendly and mutual consultation. However, such a stand by Yugoslavia was evidently not sufficient. What was wanted was far more than that. And that was not immediately understood in Yugoslavia.

When the conflict broke out in 1948, it transpired very quickly that the concrete disputes from earlier years, as well as those which had just developed, were not of crucial importance. Hence it was not possible to resolve the entire conflict by giving in or compromising on those questions on which the differences or disputes formally arose. All these differences were only reflections, symptoms of a state of affairs, and did not directly make up the substance of the conflict. The development of the world situation contributed also to the sharpening of the conflict.

The U.S.S.R. began to build up its own bloc of states as the Western bloc was also taking shape. In that situation the Soviet Union wanted to create such relationships with its allies as would safeguard a monolithic coherence and tactical unity, in other words, the subordination of each state's behavior to the decisions which were taken in the center of the bloc. In fact it was an attempt to continue in a new setting the pre-war practice of the revolutionary movements aligning themselves with Moscow's policies. This practice eventually turned into the hegemony of the Soviet Union, as the party and the government blended still in the early years of Stalinism, and this situation became entrenched in later years.

Furthermore, the German question became acute, and tension was beginning to grow around it. The formation of the blocs occurred parallel with the build-up of political hostility on the German questions. Thus the cold war began to develop,

___

over that part of the Danube within the borders of the country. After initial opposition by Soviet representatives and representatives of other countries of Eastern Europe, the Yugoslav amendments were adopted at a meeting of the representatives of Eastern Europe in Moscow before the conference.

and it resulted in an armaments race. This race on its part contributed to a further escalation in the cold war between the East and the West.

The cold war resulted in higher tension on the Trieste question and in an extreme pro-Italian position of the Western great powers in the London Declaration, but at the same time the worsening of relations between the East and the West triggered off the Soviet Union's action against Yugoslavia. There is no doubt that relations between the Cominform countries and Yugoslavia were influenced by the former's conviction that an energetic and bold action would help to bring about Yugoslavia's capitulation and inclusion into the bloc, as well as her acceptance of full bloc discipline and abandonment of independent foreign policy-making.

The examination of the relations along these lines would be sufficient to explain Yugoslavia's determination to oppose the pressures from Moscow. However, in order to comprehend the further historical consequences of the situation that had arisen, we must view this confrontation also from the point of view of the internal development in Yugoslavia, namely the opposition to the imposition of unacceptable political, economic and social relations, institutions and forms of development.

Although the desire of Yugoslavia and her war-time and post-war leadership to develop close relations with the Soviet Union was based on the belief in their identity of views upon all major social problems, development tactics and the definition of final goals, it soon became clear that they did not see eye to eye. This became all the more evident when numerous advisers and experts in all fields of public activities came to Yugoslavia. They tried to transfer to Yugoslavia the experiences and solutions from the Soviet Union.

The job of these experts, as it was interpreted in Yugoslavia, was to give advice, whereas the responsible Yugoslav leaders and bodies should assess those recommendations and then accept them, modify or reject them. Thus it happened that a whole series of recommendations and opinions were not adopted and so from the very beginning there were different solutions to a number of extremely important questions. Particularly large

199

differences arose in connection with the agricultural and peasant problems, especially in regard to the nationalization of land and the method of organizing and operating work cooperatives.

Some of these problems were mentioned later in the correspondence which developed in the spring of 1948, following the withdrawal of the experts and advisers. From these subsequent polemics it can be concluded that there was a great misunderstanding in regard to the position and status of experts. Whereas they were accepted as advisers, in Moscow the rejection of many of their recommendations and the independence of the Yugoslavs caused great dissatisfaction. What is more, some decisions which were contrary to Soviet advice — and here we should again mention the agrarian problem — were regarded as a blatant abandonment of socialist principles.

Looking back now, the departure from the Soviet model at that time could be regarded as insignificant, and yet it produced deep reverberations and was reflected in the correspondence in the spring of 1948, in the Cominform resolutions and later on in the propagandist actions in the course of the worsening of relations. These acts, although only embryonic during the period 1945—1948, hinted at much more important independent moves in elaborating socialist conceptions and in developing social, political and economic institutions and relationships in Yugoslavia.

These differences did not stem from well-developed sociological or politicological conceptions, but they reflected the specific road through which the social transformation took place in Yugoslavia. Furthermore, we should also mention different traditions in Yugoslavia and Russia. Finally, centralism, which was one of the major hotbeds of statism, was not possible in Yugoslavia which was made up of units having different traditions and developed national feelings. However, a significant role may also have been played by a strong bond with the people during the years of the war and revolution, as well as by the spirit of democracy and humaneness in relationships within the leading political organization of the Communist Party of Yugoslavia.

For all these reasons the confrontation which took place in the spring of 1948 was not simply a dispute about foreign policies, or a sum of differences on various questions of social development, but a statement of disagreement on some of the basic questions of development and relationships, both in regard to internal problems and in regard to foreign policies. These differences brought about a conflict, because the Soviet leadership was not prepared to resign itself to the existence of these differences, but rather insisted on a monolithic unity, i. e., on a far more throughgoing acceptance of the Soviet pattern than Yugoslavia was prepared to tolerate.

Thus came the confrontation which began with the withdrawal of the advisers and experts and ended in the breaking off of all relations, excepting the minimum diplomatic contacts, and the breaking off of trade as well as of other forms of normal international intercourse. Just as the base from which this confrontation had sprung up was broad, so the effect of the break had repercussions in a very broad range of public activities. The conflict was extremely sharp, because the U.S.S.R. was in a hurry to break down resistance and establish its own influence in Yugoslavia in view of the development of the cold war.

The conflict could not be resolved by a simple adaptation in foreign policies, for this was not merely a case of foreign policy dissensions between friendly countries. Since the essence of the conflict consisted in the rejection of a subordinated status and aspiration towards an independent development of new forms of socialism, a way out could not be found by any peace-making or any formal acts. There were only two possible ways out: either for Yugoslavia to renounce her independence or for the Soviet Union to accept differences as being compatible with friendship. All the subsequent endeavors to regulate the mutual relations moved between these two possible solutions and thus even after the acute stage of confrontation frictions still continued.

THE STRUGGLE ON TWO FRONTS

Practically at the same time, almost coinciding to the day, both the great Western powers and the Soviet Union suddenly took a hostile attitude toward Yugoslavia. On March 18 and 19, the well-known historical steps were made which opened up the conflict with the East. One day later, on March 20, the London Declaration was made public.

At the time of the drafting of the London Declaration, the Western powers obviously had no information that it was precisely at the same moment that a historical Soviet demarche was undertaken which, naturally, was highly confidental and was at the time not made public. Even the fact that the representatives of the Soviet Union had visited Prime Minister Tito and communicated to him the contents of the two earlier-mentioned telegrams was not published. However, there is no doubt that this intervention was taken very seriously by Yugoslavia in the leading government and Party forums. On March 20 a reply was sent to Moscow in which it was possible to perceive a very resolute tone and an understanding of the gravity of the Soviet moves. There was no reason to suppose that the Soviet government had known that during those same days the representatives of the three Western powers had been sitting behind closed doors and had decided to publish the London Declaration and write the respective notes which were handed in Moscow after the Soviet demarches against Yugoslavia had already been made.

This should be emphasized, because all the circumstances seem to indicate that it was a matter of coincidence, so striking that it could appear not to have been all that accidental. However, there are no reasons at all to assume this, and by the same token, the behavior of both sides after those critical steps did not suggest that either side had been prepared for a move to be made simultaneously by the other side. The Western powers soon felt themselves caught in a trap of their own making. In the newly arisen situation they could not very well try to enforce its implementation, and the Italians did not permit them to formally retract it, but insisted instead on the British, American and the French governments' endorsing the validity of the Declaration.

Similarly, the Soviet Union hesitated until the autumn of the same year before replying to the note which the three Western powers had presented late in March, proposing the revision of the peace treaty. The belated reply by the Soviet government contained references to questions of procedure.

As regards the U.S.S.R., it should be remembered that Stalin did not think that there was a danger of Yugoslavia defecting to the West. He obviously believed that the Soviet positions in Yugoslavia, which were temporarily lost when the conflict broke out, would be regained. Furthermore, there could be no doubt that in its dispute with Yugoslavia, Moscow would be supported by the other East European countries, as well as by the Communist parties in Western Europe and elsewhere in the world.

From Yugoslavia's point of view, there could be no question of yielding to pressure in the hope that the dispute would be resolved honorably. Even a semblance of an honorable solution would be a capitulation. It was obvious that it would amount to the abandonment of independence and the transformation of Yugoslavia into a country subservient to Soviet domination.

Theoretically, of course, there was always a possibility that Yugoslavia might come closer to the West and take advantage of the dispute with the Soviet Union to obtain a favorable solution of the Trieste question, since hostility to the Yugoslav demands in the Trieste question had been mainly generated by the cold war. Such an attempt to soften and gradually invalidate the London Declaration would probably imply the consequence, if not the obligation, of entering a military alliance, certainly nothing less than close cooperation with the Western countries. Yugoslavia, while good relations lasted with the Soviet Union, did not resent the fact that this friendship made her position more difficult with the West. However, she was now able to act completely free of any obligation to the Soviet Union, which treated her in a hostile manner.

Both variants, involving surrender to pressure either from the East or from the West, were rejected out of hand. They were not rejected because their implementation would have been unrealistic. In the twentieth century. Europe had seen much more complex operations. Let us take as an example the 1939 treaty between the U.S.S.R. and Hitler's Germany, or even the earlier Soviet-German agreement or the Rapallo Treaty with

Italy at the time of the Genoa Conference in 1922. The above-mentioned variants were consequently not unrealistic, but the decisive argument against them was that they would mean subjecting Yugoslavia to the Western powers or to the Soviet Union. If this was the price to be paid for the modification of the Western powers' attitude on the Trieste question, it would in fact have forced Yugoslavia to undertake certain political mortgages which would somehow contrive to place Yugoslavia in a permanent state of dependence vis-à-vis the West. Yugoslavia would soon find herself in a position of not being able to survive without such support. Subsequently, if the West were to change or harden its conditions for continued support, those would have to be accepted, because her moral resilience would be considerably reduced. In either case she would assume a permanently dependent position vis-à-vis either side in the cold war.

The third possible solution was to reject the London Declaration and accept Stalin's challenge. This meant the continuation of a firm line toward Moscow and the starting of just as resolute a dialogue with the West after the rejection of the London Declaration and after the proclamation of Yugoslavia's firm resolve never to agree, at anyone's demand, to any changes in the peace treaty with Italy.

This was the policy which Yugoslavia then adopted. Not only did she continue her dialogue with Moscow, remaining quite unwavering on her own positions, but she just as firmly and inflexibly responded to the London Declaration. This attitude may be described as a temporary and voluntary isolation, because it meant that Yugoslavia was completely alone, without any friendly support or relation in the world. At the same time she found herself subjected to the pressure of all the great powers. Consequently, of all the possible attitudes this was the hardest. There were no mitigating circumstances, and, realistically speaking, no prospects of a favorable denouncement.

What made Yugoslavia's position all the more intricate was her exceptionally difficult economic situation. The described events were taking place shortly after the war, in the period when the basic reconstruction of the destroyed factories and transport systems had just about been finished. Even this process was not quite completed in some parts of the country. Naturally, in the course of reconstruction, modernization was introduced wherever possible, but Yugoslavia's economic activity had not yet reached its pre-war level. On the other hand, in the event of armed complications, the possibilities of waging a normal war were extremely small. Namely, if hostilities were to break out at that moment, Yugoslavia would have to reckon without her airforce, since the reserves of aircraft fuel were insignificant. Just as small were the reserves of other fuels, even if they could all be rounded up and rationally used, which was rather improbable. With the available stock there could be no question of any major military operations.

In other words, modern warfare, which requires motorization and aviation, was completely excluded. The only remaining possibility was partisan warfare, or what would be its more developed form, territorial warfare. This in other words implied the prospects of abandoning the capital city and most of the large towns, as well as the major part of the territory. It is only in the course of military operations that it would be shown whether Yugoslavia would accept any armed help and whether a front could be maintained until a reorganization could be made for a positional warfare, especially since Yugoslavia would have overwhelming forces pitted against her.

It would also be wrong to assume that Yugoslavia, having come into conflict both with the East and the West, was in a manner of speaking forced to adopt the policy of nonalignment. As if the policy of nonalignment were an easy and sure way out of a tough spot, Yugoslavia being simply pushed by both sides and forced onto the course of nonalignment. Nothing could be farther from truth. In fact, at that time Yugoslavia's policy of independence could not be described as nonalignment, but rather as a policy of isolation and acceptance of the challenge from all the great powers. The policy of nonalignment, such as had already been crystallized in Southeast Asia, did not yet exist as a concept in Yugoslavia.

Yugoslavia found herself in the worst straits imaginable, especially when it is borne in mind that it is a relatively small country, and that it was already economically crippled. It is true that the London Declaration did not prevent the development of trade with the West, but much of the trade had been oriented to the East and could not immediately be redirected towards the West. It was easy to find in the West anything that Yugoslavia needed, but it was difficult to sell Yugoslav products there. One should try and imagine the state of devastation and underdevelopment of the country in the spring of 1948. On the other hand, trade with the East had started suddenly to fall off because a boycott was imposed.

In view of the uncertain situation, Yugoslavia could not expect her struggle for the preservation of her independence to be of interest for the West, as subsequently proved to be the case. Yugoslavia's step was, indeed, regarded by the Western governments as a foolhardy attempt at resistance. At any rate, the West only knew about the dispute later on, after the publication of the Cominform resolution in June 1948. Only three months after its real inception the dispute became public.

Yugoslavia's independent foreign policy in the spring of 1948 was inspired by an unshakable faith in the country's resilience by the determination to place the basic interests of the country above the momentary interests of the state's survival. Such a decision, which is far from being a routine one, in fact constitutes a remarkable move, quite unparalleled in history. The decision was extremely hard to make. Everything that happened afterwards only reaffirmed the seriousness of the situation in which the country found itself.

Soon after the conflict became public an open economic pressure from the East was turned on full. Subsequently it gave way to military pressure and subversive propaganda, as well as to all possible forms of other pressure upon Yugoslavia. To top all this, and after the year 1949 has passed in extremely difficult conditions, the spring of 1950 brought an unprecedented drought which halved the wheat harvest. This then were the circumstances in which the Yugoslav policy of independence was formed, which subsequently developed into the policy of nonalignment. Just as Yugoslavia was being menaced by increasing military and economic dangers, there occurred a poor harvest. External pressure and a trade boycott could not be coped with by the development of satisfactory volume of trade with the West, and as pressure increased from the East, the scant reserves dwindled very fast.

The first agreement with three Western countries was made in 1950, concerning aid in food, especially wheat. The agreement was signed in 1950 at Bled. It marked the beginning of a systematic wooing of Yugoslavia, by offering her better organized and stronger support. Attempts were made to link Yugoslavia in some form or another with the North Atlantic Pact, which had been formed in the spring of 1949. The alternative of a link-up with the Western powers existed as a possible variant of the Yugoslav policy not only at the moment when it was necessary to choose a position, but even after Yugoslavia had taken up the challenge from both sides and embarked on a policy of independence. A discreet pressure was on all the time to bring Yugoslavia a little closer to the Western countries. In the end it was even pointed out that Yugoslavia's interests, her independence, integrity and frontiers would best be safeguarded if she were to join the North Atlantic Pact.

These overtures were being made practically all the time until a certain stabilization occurred and tension abated in relations between Yugoslavia and the East European countries. It should also be pointed out that when aid was granted to Yugoslavia, especially by the United States where aid is decided in public debates in the Congress, expectation for Yugoslavia to join the Western side in the cold war was fairly clearly expressed. From time to time Prime Minister Tito and other spokesmen of Yugoslavia made statements in which they publicly refuted the allusions, suggestions and direct proposals in that direction. It was then that Tito launched his famous phrase which became a kind of a slogan, that "we should rather go hungry and barefooted than sacrifice our independence."[30] The rejection of all these overtures by the West was based on the assertion of the country's independence. Any surrender to the West was rejected for the same reasons which influenced the decision in March of 1948, i. e., insistence on independence, regardless of its price. In a way, it was the continu-

---

[30] Tito, *Govori i članci*, Vol. V, p. 21.

ation of the position that was taken in 1948, which in the recent history of Yugoslavia can be compared with the attitude taken up by the Communist Party in 1941.

THE NONALIGNMENT OF YUGOSLAVIA

The policy of nonalignment in Yugoslavia began to crystallize under the influence of the confrontation with the two blocs, and after she became acquainted with the policies of the countries of Southeast Asia. The acceptance of the challenge from both sides and the resolve to protect her independence from pressures whatever side they might come from, could not permanently remain the basis of Yugoslavia's foreign policy. In addition to these negative and defensive aspects it was necessary to define the national foreign policy through a positive platform. Events in the world could not be gauged only by the yardstick of immediate interests and the needs of one's own country.

Furthermore, it became obvious that to wait until a direct threat appears was the worst possible policy for a small or medium-sized country. To reduce the possibility of such situations in the future and in order to meet situations in which danger knocks directly on the door, it was necessary to try to understand wider areas and channel the national policy along those general lines which are directed toward the preservation of general peace and security. This was also motivated by the natural desire to avoid isolation, which in itself is a source of danger and creates unfavorable conditions even when there is no direct threat to security and independence.

The first public definition of this policy was presented to the world public at the fifth session of the United Nations General Assembly in 1950, in a speech by the head of the Yugoslav delegation, Edvard Kardelj: "The peoples of Yugoslavia cannot accept the assumption that mankind must today choose between domination by one or another great power. We consider that there is another road, difficult possibly, but the necessary road of democratic struggle for a world of free and equal nations, for democratic relations among nations, against interference from outside in the internal affairs of the nations and for an all-round peaceable cooperation of peoples on the basis of equality...".[31]

At a different level, Yugoslavia became politically active in the early 1950s. Her policy soon began to crystallize, first through her support for the underdeveloped countries and soon after through the action of the nonaligned in connection with the Korean war. It is there that India appeared as a nonaligned country and, as is known, played an important role in negotiations leading to the armistice and its implementation. India supplied the chairman of the armistice commission in Korea. The commander of the units which were to supervise the exchange of prisoners and the implementation of the armistice agreement between North and South Korea was also an Indian. Yugoslavia began to cooperate with India, and thus in these early years after 1950, first in the economic and soon after in the political domain, the Yugoslav policy of nonalignment made its first strides.

Before Yugoslavia could take up this stand, it was necessary first to reduce the tensions between Yugoslavia and the great powers. The United Nations resolution adopted in 1951[32] marked the end of the most difficult crisis in the confrontation with the U. S. S. R. Soon afterwards the Trieste question started nearing its solution, and tension began to abate.[33] The period between 1951 and 1954 was one of relaxation for Yugoslavia. In this situation Yugoslavia's policies were no longer determined by the existence of a challenge and pressure, and there was no need to fight for the preservation of independence at any cost. Her foreign policy began to strike deeper roots. In the late 1950s and in the 1960s it was based on the reevaluation of the basic concepts

---

[31] United Nations General Assembly, *Offical Records*, Fifth Session, p. 69.

[32] General Assembly, *Official Record:* Sixth Session, Supplement No. 20(A/2119), p. 10.

[33] On October 5, 1954, in London an agreement was concluded between the governments of Italy and Yugoslavia and was also signed by the governments of the United States and Great Britain on the abrogation of the free territory of Trieste. The same day the representatives of the four governments signed a Memorandum on this question, which was ratified by the Federal Executive Council on October 7, and by the Federal Assembly on October 25 of the same year. For the complete text see the *Službeni list*, No. 43, 1954, p. 637.

about internal development and foreign policy and on the assessment of Yugoslavia's role in the international community arising from Yugoslavia's new international status.

At the end of 1954, close ties were developed with India, which by then was already playing an important role in the world. Yugoslavia's relations with the East and the West were by then already well developed, so that there was no longer any question of her isolation but rather of building up a platform of relations with the rest of the world, in contrast to the situation of 1949. In other words, at the end of 1954 Yugoslavia was already entering a new stage in her post-war relations, a stage of well-developed relations with all categories and groups of countries.

On his return from a trip in Southeast Asia, President Tito spoke at a meeting in Belgrade on February 12, 1955, about the role of the countries which he had visited in the struggle for peace and international cooperation: "It is precisely those nations which had gone through such tribulations that should come forward as the builders of peace — as those who work on the strengthening of peace and peaceful cooperation and coexistence among nations. The world is today divided into two blocs, but it is fortunate that in addition to those two blocs there is an enormous number of men and states who believe that it is a wrong policy to follow the line of division and not to do anything for the line of integration, for agreement among us and for a peaceable way of resolving problems which are not worth mankind's walking into new bloodshed and the most terrible catastrophe that it should ever experience."[34]

The new policy, which was not yet called nonalignment by name was being formulated in conditions when Yugoslavia was not forced into it by a particularly strong pressure from either side, or by a search for a way out of isolation. This formulation of the policy was being made at a time when it was reasonable to ask whether Yugoslavia was entering an adventure with her new friendships and her new relations with the big powers, abandoning the principles of her behavior from the previous years. In the same speech therefore, Tito referred to those mis-

---

[34] Tito, *Govori i članci*, Vol. X, *op. cit.*, p. 97.

givings and explained the difference between the tactics and the basic line of the Yugoslav policy:

"The question now arises — is this not a change in our policy, is Yugoslavia not now changing her policy? Now that she has started normalizing her relations with the Soviet Union, is she thinking of betraying the principles which have motivated her foreign policy? No! We are doing everything possible — precisely because of our principled attitude, for the sake of preserving peace and peaceful coexistence — to normalize our relations with all the countries wanting that, and to make these relations as good as possible. This has motivated us to normalize our relations with the Soviet Union and the other Eastern countries. If these relations go on improving every day, there should be no fear that we should abandon our good relations with the Western countries as well. We also want to have good relations with the Western countries. We are not in favor of the division of the world into two blocs. According to our conception, the world is one single whole. Ideological differences cannot be a reason for the countries to create bloodshed among them — unless someone possibly has some imperialistic aims, which is another matter. But ideological differences cannot be the reason for division of the world into blocs which would whet their knives, forge their weapons and pile up hydrogen and atomic bombs for their own destruction. I say: nothing in our foreign policy has changed. It has remained just as principled and consistent as it ever was."

"Obviously," President Tito continued, "the situation in the world is changing. The tensions are now greater, now lesser. For example, now the tension in the world has again increased. What are we to do now? Are we to reduce our efforts to ease this tension? No, we must strengthen them even more! And this motivates us even more never to join any of the existing blocs. This is because for as long as there are blocs and no new methods of solving international problems are being sought, the danger will always remain great."[35]

These new methods to suit the new situation were found

---

[35] *Ibid.*, pp. 98—99.

in rejecting bloc policies while at the same time associating with other countries having similar views in an active effort to improve international relations. A little further on, Tito said that explicitly: "No, we are not neutralists. We are very active indeed - we indeed say: do not rush headlong into a new danger. We indeed say and point the way to be followed by men and peoples in order to avoid that which is least wanted in the world today — a new war. Unfortunately, our voice is not sufficiently heard. But I think that everyday there are more of those who think as we do, not only in the countries which support our foreign policies, but also in the countries which belong to the existing blocs."[36]

Yugoslavia was thus for the first time regarded as a participant in a broad and new movement, which was based on a newly arisen situation, using all the opportunities which the new situation offered and opposing all the dangers that were being generated or aggravated in it. The policy of cooperation with the countries of the third world already existed and his voyage to India and Burma was not accidental or without the knowledge of the basic lines of development in those countries and of their views on international issues. At any rate, while efforts were made to obtain an armistice in Korea, Yugoslavia was cooperating with India in the United Nations.

Departing on his trip to India and Burma, President Tito spoke in Rijeka as he boarded the training ship *Galeb*. He said one of the aims of his voyage was to make personal acquaintance with the statesmen of these countries and exchange ideas "about different international problems and especially about cooperation for the preservation of peace." He also pointed out that it was a visit to the countries "which are in many ways similar to our country in their internal efforts and developments, countries whose attitudes to the international problems and to the strengthening of peace are similar to ours and with which our cooperation can be extremely useful, not only for us and for them but also for that which men in the world want most today, and that is the strengthening of peace and international cooperation, that is, peaceful, active coexistence between states and nations having

---

[36] *Ibid.*, p. 99.

different systems, because we believe that it is the only way to avoid new wars and a catastrophe for mankind."[37]

The tour of Asia enlarged horizons and concretized views, and also contributed to a better acquaintance with the third world and its problems, without which a later cooperation would not be possible. "I must openly say that we did not know those countries as we should have. We did not know sufficiently either today's development or the efforts which they are making in that direction, and we knew them poorly in any case. For us this two month-long stay in these countries was something of a revelation...".[38] It is with these words that Tito spoke to the crowds which met him at Rijeka when he landed after his return from India.

Before the policy of nonalignment could be adopted as an active policy on the main world problems, it was necessary to overcome the pressures which had begun in March 1948, to get out of the isolation that followed, and to do away with the necessity of fighting for survival. It is therefore understandable that this policy cannot just begin to function at any given moment. Reference to President Tito's tour should therefore not be regarded as an attempt to date the beginning of that policy. This event had its pre-history as well as its direct consequences in the country's foreign policy. It took place at a time when Yugoslavia's position had become more stable and the general situation in the world had improved, and at a time when a lull occurred in the cold war after the achievement of a relative nuclear equilibrium between the U.S. and the U.S.S.R., as witnessed by the attitude of these countries in this United Nations and their decision to hold a summit meeting in Geneva in the summer of 1955.

This event had been preceded by many efforts by Yugoslavia to find her own place in the world. The first period of formation of a completely independent and autonomous policy was a sequel to dramatic conflicts and challenges, events which had taken place on the borders of Yugoslavia or which directly affected Yugoslavia. However, at that time and even a little before the movement

---

[37] *Ibid.*, pp. 7—8.
[38] *Ibid.*, p. 82.

213

of decolonization had started and gained in momentum. Thus the policy of nonalignment became the policy of the newly liberated countries.

Once she started to pay more attention to world problems, Yugoslavia became aware of two phenomena. First, there were the early beginnings of a zone of nonalignment in the areas which had previously been colonial empires. It was no longer India alone; it was India and Burma as well, and gradually the movement spread to some other countries, especially the Arab states. Second, there was the problem of the economically under-developed countries which had appeared on the international scene with their demands.

A large scale political action along the lines of nonalignment was not immediately possible. Although by 1951 the number of nonaligned countries had so increased that it was possible to move fairly important actions in the U. N. General Assembly on economic questions broad actions on political issues along the line of nonalignment were not yet possible. All the protagonists who subsequently helped to reaffirm the policy of nonalignment on the world scene were either not yet in existence or were not ready for action.

Results achieved on the world scene within the framework of nonalignment contributed to a greater sense of security and thus facilitated efforts in the internal development of Yugoslavia. All this helped to strengthen the new views as regards both internal socialist development and events in the world. The internal development of an independent, completely unique socialist society began to differ so much from that which was still developing in the Soviet Union and the countries of Eastern Europe that the Yugoslav society could no longer be identified with the social model and the foreign policy aims of the East European countries. This identification was broken in 1948 and the subsequent years and could no longer be reestablished. Identification with views concerning final goals could not have much effect on practical policies, because in international relations what matters is the government policy which evolves from day to day and not remote goals. Yugoslavia took up positions which channeled her actions along her own guidelines.

214

In the same way, Yugoslavia could not identify herself with the political goals of the Western countries either. Consequently, she was in a certain sense in a situation in which she could not accept the restriction of her own freedom on the basis of her identification with some broader tactical goals with either side. She opted for the policy of nonalignment for equally strong reasons as those for which this policy was also adopted by the newly liberated countries.

Yugoslavia was not one of them. She was a European country which, owing to a set of circumstances caused by the conflicts of 1948, lost contact with and estranged herself from her immediate political environment. She preserved her individuality through this hard, dramatic struggle in the most difficult moments of challenge from the great powers on both sides. Her policy was based on the fact that the reality was understood by the public, by the nation and by the political factors who guide her foreign policy. Her entire foreign policy effort during the ensuing years was channeled towards strengthening and inspiring collective actions of the nonaligned countries in the economic and political sphere. In that respect Yugoslavia achieved considerable results. In the formative period, in the period of ascent of the policy of nonalignment, she played a fairly important role.

Yugoslavia from then on appeared more clearly as a socialist country which had created for herself a position both in the nonaligned world and among the socialist countries and which was taking an increasingly active part in international politics as well as in world markets. It is quite certain that great strides forward were made between March 1948 and the end of the 1960s, and from total isolation Yugoslavia became closely linked with all the countries of the world. From the state of beleaguered independence with barricades on all the borders, she became a country which the citizens of most countries of the East and the West could enter without a visa.

This undoubtedly shows that her orientation, as hopeless as it might have seemed in 1948, did hold out some prospects. It was based on ethical values and the traditions of freedom and independence, but in this perhaps reckless courage there must have been a deeper wisdom which made the goal not only desirable but also attainable.

As a European country she was often elected into various international bodies on the quota of the countries of Africa or Asia. She often participated in Afro-Asian councils when the problems of development were discussed. She also wielded a very strong influence in Eastern Europe, while at the same time maintaining completely open economic, cultural, political and every other type of cooperation with the countries of the West. Indeed, a most unusual position for a country, especially if it is taken into consideration that it was a relatively small and still relatively poor country. Yugoslavia was something of a special case. She was not linked with very close ties to her neighbors, nor was she involved in border disputes or other issues as was the case with the majority of the nonaligned countries of Asia and Africa. Obviously, she could not have very developed neighbor relations within the group of the nonaligned, because she was cut off from all of them, being the only nonaligned country in the European continent.

Finally, she arrived at the policy of nonalignment having experienced extremely intensive conflicts in the early years of the cold war which were deeply imbued with fundamental ideological contents. She kept a distance from the two sides in the cold war and alienated herself from her own political environment, in a very concentrated and very harsh struggle for her bare survival, having to mobilize all her material and moral resources. Furthermore, that struggle did not leave Yugoslavia in any ambiguous position as regards her relations with either bloc. She was connected with the nonaligned countries of the third world only through the principle of nonalignment and nonidentification with sides in the cold war. Through the policy of nonalignment she could not hope to achieve anything other than her affirmation in a quite general sense of developing ties with countries with which she felt a kinship in their international status and views.

In the event of any problem of rivalry or intolerance within a region or subregion, Yugoslavia was able to play the role of disinterested friend that could help to bring back peace and reestablish unity. She could have no concrete goals other than the general success of nonalignment. Whereas all the other countries could count on certain quite concrete benefits from cooperation among the nonaligned, such concrete benefits could not exist for Yugoslavia. On the other hand she was far more intensively interested in the success of nonalignment as such and in cooperation within that circle. She moved towards nonalignment from isolation in her own continent and not from an environment where, like the other nonaligned countries, she could have developed natural ties and friendship within a relatively close neighborhood. An intensive feeling of attachment to nonalignment remained alive in Yugoslavia even when circumstances in the European continent improved to that extent that Yugoslavia developed very good relations with some of her neighbors and when prospects opened for her to find again her place within the circle of the European states that without having to chose between the two sides of the cold war nor to accept a subordination to the bloc discipline.

PART TWO
NONALIGNMENT IN ACTION

CHAPTER FOUR

THE PRINCIPAL LINES OF ACTIVITY IN THE YEARS OF THE COLD WAR

A. CHANGES IN WORLD PATTERNS AND INTERNATIONAL RELATIONS

SPECIFIC FORMS OF INTERNATIONAL COOPERATION OF THE NONALIGNED COUNTRIES

Not for a moment did the leaders of nonalignment wish to create an alliance or anything similar to it, and they made this clear on many occasions. Nehru used to say that the nonaligned wished to be nonaligned in relation to other nonaligned countries as well. A tentative suggestion that a kind of permanent secretariat be set up after the Belgrade Conference was rejected by an overwhelming majority of participants, even though the secretariat would have a very limited area of jurisdiction.[1] Not one attempt to coordinate foreign policy has been recorded, nor has there been any attempt to scrutinize the behavior of a nonaligned country on the basis of its obligations to others.

It is easy to understand why the nonaligned countries have consistently rejected any ideas of becoming a "third bloc", and

---

[1] Since there is very little published material on these matters, the author has used his own observations and facts collected in talks with Yugoslavs and others who took part in these activities

it is hardly necessary to try and explain this. No single country held such a dominant position as to be able to claim to be the center of the bloc, and it is difficult to imagine an organized bloc without a center similar to the central superpowers in the two existing alliances. Furthermore, a bloc is an organization based on power politics. It is unlikely that the nonaligned countries could impress the outside world with their material power, either military or economic, and so the creation of a military-political alliance based on material might would be entirely unconvincing.

Thus there were no real grounds for forming a bloc, even if these countries had wished to. The main question here should be the attitude of the nonaligned countries in regard to a partial renunciation of freedom of action in international affairs and in internal development. Willingness to make this renunciation arises from self-confidence and a feeling of security in regard to preservation of national identity. This does not include cases where a stronger power enforces its will and maintains a regional grouping on this basis, since this is not an alliance in the true sense of the word, in the sense of a community of interests.

Even regardless of such extreme cases where hegemony smothers the basic elements of sovereignty in weaker partners, the nonaligned countries are inclined to reject bloc alignment. Newly liberated or materially weak or poorly developed countries would not be at all enthusiastic about voluntarily renouncing freedom of action for fear of truncating their independence and their special identity, which in any case have not been sufficiently consolidated. Such an attitude is particularly in evidence where the process of national formation has not yet been completed. The feeling of insecurity is particularly strong in these cases, and so is disinclination to join any organization which could jeopardize the formation of a sovereign nation.

The seemingly contradictory situation in relations among the Arab countries can be explained by the fact that there are two theses which are still struggling for ascendancy: the conception of the Arab world as one nation still in the formative stage, and the thesis on the formation of separate nations in various Arab countries. Thus federations are made and unmade

222

with frequency, and trends towards a firm cohesion are offset by very fierce conflicts, including even wars. This, of course, can be no basis for the formation of a bloc in the true sense of the word. Finally, the blocs as military alliances require institutionally mature and stable countries and certain other indispensable conditions.

Of these necessary conditions, there are two that are pre-eminent. First there must be a common danger, or assumption that such a danger exists, and it must be of such a nature that it justifies the formation of a bloc and the corresponding restriction of individual freedom of action. Second, there must be a possibility of reaching a consensus on concrete actions in foreign affairs, so that the bloc organization could act effectively on day-to-day issues.

These conditions, of course, mean that quite remote countries could join together, but it is obvious that this would only be possible in exceptional cases and that alliances of territorially contiguous states are more typical. In other words, countries that are scattered about the entire globe rarely have common interests on concrete issues, and it is difficult to expect a coordinated action from them.

All examples of alliances among countries that are remote from one another have confirmed this in recent international practice, and alliances which are formed without the necessary proximity — as for instance the system of alliances connected with NATO — show a certain passivity or even signs of disintegration and shakiness. However, such alliances have been cemented together by the presence of a ubiquitous world power. The United States has shown the ability to make its presence felt materially and militarily in very distant parts of the world on a large scale and over a considerable number of years.

Obviously there is nothing similar to this in the case of the nonaligned countries, and a military-political alliance among them would be unrealistic. What is more, it would considerably restrict and weaken the political influence of these countries in the world and would bring no compensation of increased efficiency in their activities. For these reasons they coped with their position in the world in a completely different manner.

They certainly did consider themselves threatened, but it was a kind of threat that could not be removed by their association in a rigidly organized bloc. The fact that the nonaligned countries are scattered in distant parts of the world, that communications between them are poor, that the level of their economic development is very low and armies poorly equipped — undercuts the advantages of a military alliance. In fact, such a form of association would only be a burden for each member.

Furthermore the main concern of the nonaligned countries was not an open threat of military action by another country or group of countries. They feared more that their independence might be undermined by means which would take advantage of their internal troubles. A formal alliance would not be the best way of countering this threat. A military alliance would more likely diminish the value of what was to be protected, which is the maximum freedom of action in international affairs; in short, such an alliance would be more likely to achieve a negative and undesirable effect than to increase the feeling of security.

Finally, it would be difficult to achieve a consensus on the conduct of foreign policy which would justify the existence of an alliance. The nonaligned countries have already shown that they can agree on a policy on grand world problems, but that their policies on concrete issues which directly affect their national interests often differ and even conflict. This alone would make an alliance along the lines of a modern bloc organization impossible, even if no military organization were to be created. In other words, not even a purely political bloc is possible among the nonaligned countries.

For this reason, cooperation among the nonaligned countries has developed within the less formal framework of periodical meetings to discuss major international issues. One of the features of the summit meetings of nonaligned countries has been the superficial and evasive manner in which specific questions involving the interests of individual participants are treated. It is obvious that these issues were placed on the agenda and mentioned in the final declarations only at the insistence of the interested parties and in a watered down form in order to eschew taking a resolute stand on the policies and actions of the governments of these countries.[2]

The stands of the participants at the conference of nonaligned countries on specific questions — which are sometimes of vital importance, but always of direct interest for the countries placing them on the agenda — seem to be incompatible with an alliance. Without any doubt, these issues were not the motive for the calling of the conference. It could even be said that they were placed on the agenda only to produce a given effect in the initiators' countries or to impress opponents. The main reason for the convocation of the conference has always been to discuss the grand world issues placed on the agenda, but agreement on them was reached before the conference.

In contrast to his practice, military-political alliances hold meetings of their organs mainly to discuss current concrete problems and to define joint organized actions in connection with them. In bloc organizations, differences of opinion are sometimes allowed on matters which do not concern everyday political action. There is, of course, no uniform practice in this respect in all of the existing military-political alliances. No one would think that the unity of the North Atlantic Pact, for instance, was threatened because a NATO country might have taken a different stand on questions concerning aid to underdeveloped countries. However, differences on such questions among the nonaligned countries would present a serious problem.

There have been instances of differences in viewpoints on long-term problems closely connected with the military-political purpose of the alliance. We need only mention the disagreements on the formation of multilateral nuclear forces or, later, different interpretations of some basic provisions of the agreement on nonproliferation of nuclear weapons. All these differences within the Atlantic Pact were considered far less dangerous for NATO than differences in opinion which might develop on concrete

---

[2] See in the Appendix the formulation on various specific questions in the declarations from the conferences of the heads of nonaligned countries held in Belgrade in 1961 and in Cairo in 1964. Particular attention should be given to such questions as the situation in the Near East, military bases in Tunisia and Cuba.

issues, say, on the events in Czechoslovakia in 1968 and 1969.

At the meetings of statesmen of nonaligned countries there is an insistence on the uniformity of views on long-term and general world problems. What NATO would consider vital, i. e., current concrete situations, is given second place at the meetings of nonaligned and in a way is treated under miscellaneous problems. A joint formulation is, of course, reached in the end, but as a rule it excludes all contentious expressions and formulations, so the generalized texts are not as concrete as the interested countries would like them to be, and their political effect is very limited.

The nature of these problems and the manner in which they are treated at meetings of statesmen of nonaligned countries illustrate the character of these meetings and shed light on co-operation among the nonaligned countries. We have found that nonalignment is politically motivated by the need to defend national identity, but from the very outset certain positive aspirations in this policy have prevailed over purely defensive stands. International cooperation among the nonaligned countries has always been greatly inspired by a desire to promote these positive goals.

Not one of these goals (decolonization, advancement of the economy, recognition of equal rights for all nations) can be achieved by one state alone. Collective political action in the United Nations and elsewhere is necessary. The forms of organization are not identical with alliances of the bloc variety but rather resemble international trade union organizations in seeking to strengthen their negotiating powers or to exert political pressure to achieve collective goals by creating a common front of all the nonaligned countries which by themselves would have had insufficient strength.

This elastic form of cooperation is used to promote economic interests and to urge political solutions to the most important political problems of the modern world. This new form of co-operation did not follow a carefully prepared plan, but was rather a spontaneous outgrowth. The first meeting at which the new movement arose was the Bandung Conference of Asian and African countries. Its objective was to press for an accelerated

226

disintegration of colonial empires. However, the conference went further than that and became the first mass manifestation of a movement which was later to become the movement of nonaligned countries.

At that time, back in 1955, nonalignment was still not a finished political concept. The Bandung Conference was attended by countries which today are called nonaligned, but also by others which are aligned with the one or the other side.[3] The regional principle was paramount, which shows that the process of defining nonalignment had not made much progress by the middle of the 1950s. It was still hoped that anticolonialism would unite all the countries of Asia and Africa.

In a manner of speaking this did happen. The conference adopted relatively sharp and clearly expressed anti-colonial resolutions, although some of the participants visibly differed on other political questions. The Bandung Conference laid down the foundations of a movement which subsequently expanded the original program considerably, introducing into it a series of general policies which were not acceptable to the countries closely connected with either the Eastern or the Western political blocs. Thus the program was expanded, and the number of countries supporting it at first decreased, but subsequently increased as the newly emerged nonaligned countries multiplied.

Formally there was no direct and organic continuation to Bandung. The only attempt to convene a repeat performance of the Bandung Conference was in 1964, when Indonesia, in cooperation with the People's Republic of China, tried to convene one such conference that was to counterbalance the Cairo Conference of the heads of nonaligned countries scheduled for the same year. The leaders of the nonaligned countries, however, have always stressed their attachment to Bandung, and the movement of the nonaligned was regarded as the political continuation of the 1955 anti-colonial conference. This connection is significant because it stresses the importance of anti-colonialism in the years of the early movements to define nonalignment.

---

[3] See the Appendix for the list of participants at the Bandung Conference.

The first steps toward a summit meeting that would be determined by political motives and not according to the regional principle, were made a year after the Bandung Conference. In July 1956, Tito received two guests in his Brioni summer residence, Nehru and Nasser. This tripartite meeting was something more than just an accidental meeting of statesmen from three continents. It was the reflection of a definite policy which was more clearly defined than a year before. The meeting was preceded by a long series of bilateral encounters and a systematic cooperation among delegations in the United Nations, as well as by other kinds of cooperation and consultations.[4]

The next major step was made in 1960 at the United Nations General Assembly meeting in New York. Five heads of state of the nonaligned countries met to discuss joint actions in the United Nations and to send a direct appeal to the superpowers. These five were Nehru and Sukarno from Asia, Nasser and Nkrumah from Africa, and Tito, who was the host of the meeting held in the seat of the Yugoslav permanent mission to the United Nations in New York.[5] A year later the first conference of the heads of state of nonaligned countries was held in Belgrade, and the second three years later in Cairo. Furthermore, at the ministerial level, the representatives of these states met to discuss economic questions. That was in July 1962 in Cairo, and in the autumn of 1967 in Algiers.[6] Both of these meetings were convened with the purpose of coordinating the action of the underdeveloped countries at the two sessions of UNCTAD, which were held under the auspices of the United Nations.

One could object to the meetings of the underdeveloped countries being improperly mentioned together with the conferences of the nonaligned countries. This objection would not be reasonable, because the movement of nonalignment is not a formal organization with a definite membership, holding regular meetings. The Cairo economic conference and the idea to ask the United Nations to convene a U.N. conference on trade and development

---

4 See the Appendix for the communiqué on the meeting at Brioni in 1956.
5 See the Appendix for the communiqué on the meeting of the five leaders in New York in 1960.
6 See the Appendix for the final documents of these conferences.

228

were first mentioned at the Belgrade Conference of statesmen of the nonaligned countries.[7]

The flexibility in the movement's structure can also be seen in the fact that there was no formal tie even between two succeeding conferences of the heads of state, and that they were convened independently of each other and not as sessions of an established body. It is not even customary to identify them as the first and second conference; they are referred to by the name of the city where they were held and the year when they took place.

The number of participating countries also changed: there were more of them in Cairo than in Belgrade, but the question of who should be invited was never solved to the complete satisfaction of all the participants. At both conferences attempts were made to define the concept of nonalignment, but they did not produce any lasting accord, and the problem was always posed anew. It transpired, however, that there was some kind of agreement as to what should be understood under the concept of nonalignment, but it was never definitely established which countries did belong to the movement. No accurate definition was made which could be automatically applied to each and every case, and the view was accepted that it was better that there should be no formal and once-and-for-ever established and fully developed definition. Any rigid formula could only bring about political complications and would not be of much use.

The common denominator should be sought in another, less concrete sphere. There is a feeling of affinity for the movement, although it may be difficult to accurately state its definition and although it is open to different interpretations. Yet until now it has almost always been possible to formulate the generally accepted views in statements issued at the meetings of the heads of nonaligned states, and this has helped to maintain an exceptionally strong and lasting solidarity and a feeling of belonging to a common movement which inspires joint actions in the international scene. The intensity with which some of the countires identified themselves with the movement varied from one country to the next and from one period to another. It largely depended

---

[7] Paragraphs 21 and 22 in Chapter III of the Belgrade Declaration.

on internal developments, but also on the general situation in the world.

Nonalignment is not only an expression of specific views on some of the major questions from the field of international relations. It is also an expression of the feeling of belonging to a world which is different from the developed part of the world, whether East or West. Even when one of the third world countries did belong to a bloc, it could not identify itself with the bloc of the developed countries as much as the developed countries themselves do. The difference which divides the North from the South[8] in all the parts of the world is not merely the degree of economic development. The difference is considerably deeper and embraces all aspects of life as well as the form, substance and structure of society, to which we have already referred in Chapter Two of this book.

The loose character of cooperation among the nonaligned countries opened up important possibilities of achieving a broad unity, combined with a high degree of flexibility, but it also imposes some important restrictions. It was frequently pointed out that one could not expect the nonaligned countries being capable of undertaking urgent actions even when circumstances so demanded. This statement is correct. A movement which developed spontaneously cannot be compared with the rigorously planned mechanism of a military organization. It is better suited for long-range undertakings than for the overcoming of acute and current problems. Inability to comprehend this feature of the movement of nonalignment brought disillusionment to those statesmen of the nonaligned countries who were sometimes inclined to believe the nonaligned countries to constitute a third bloc, although they themselves would always be against it being described that way. This particularly applies to the instance when the nonaligned countries were expected to efficiently influence armed conflicts.[9]

---

[8] The terms North and South have become accepted in literature on this subject, and they are used here in spite of the fact that they are not sufficiently accurate, and sometimes not applicable, such as in the case of Australia and New Zealand on the one hand, and Mongolia on the other.

[9] Most of the actions by the nonaligned countries in the early stages of the war in Vietnam did not give the desired results, and in the case of some other conflicts not even any attempt was made to initiate a broad action, as e.g. in the case of Nigeria and Biafra or the Middle East war.

On the other hand, it was precisely because of its character, that the movement of nonalignment could so frequently rally a large number of countries and make them undertake joint efforts, although they did not have the material power of the great and the rich. The spontaneous character of nonalignment offered the movement greater chances of exercising political or, as some would say, moral or psychological influence in the international community.

This aspect should not be underestimated. Political or moral force has played a considerable role in the post-war period. It has played an important role in the ending of colonialism. Materially weaker forces of the national liberation movements were successful because moral force was on their side. Relatively small military forces were sufficient, in the politically less active past, to subject nations in overseas regions and to set up colonial empires, but even much greater forces were not able to keep them down in the middle of this century.

Voluntary maintenance of informal relations and organizational forms of cooperation among the nonaligned countries helps to overcome misunderstandings and disputes, and even armed conflicts, which from time to time appear in various places in the nonaligned part of the world. It should be constantly reemphasized that nonalignment does not mean nor has it ever meant the coordination of foreign policies. It could never stop the participating countries from freely forming their policies on questions which have a specific and direct bearing on them. It is quite certain that at no time had they felt the need to refrain from actions which they considered to be essential for their security or for important national interests. Nonalignment constitutes neither neutrality nor the application of nonviolence as a philosophical doctrine in international relations.

NONALIGNMENT AS A DEPOLARIZING FACTOR IN INTERNATIONAL RELATIONS

The emergence of nonalignment in the early postwar years contributed greatly to the development of the model of international relations for the coming decades. The area of nonalignment around the two blocs continued expanding and strengthening. The success marked by the anti-colonialist movement helped to increase the number of candidates for the group of nonaligned countries. This phenomenon was noted especially at the time when the wave of anti-colonialism overtook Africa, especially since the colonial empires in Africa consisted of a large number of small colonies, which gradually began to acquire independence.

Insisting on completing the decolonization processes as soon as possible, the nonaligned countries at the same time endeavored to extend the area of nonalignment in the world. As new states were admitted to the United Nations, a fundamental change occurred in the method of forming majorities and minorities in voting in the organs and bodies of the world organization. Various issues on the agenda were no longer resolved by an agreement between the two blocs, because there appeared a third, independent voting force which was constantly growing. There were cases where both the superpowers voted in the same manner, and yet were outvoted in the General Assembly.

This point is significant for the further development of international relations, especially for the development of relations between the two antagonistic groups of the East and West. It was no longer thought realistic to expect that the world would split up into two military camps. Furthermore, owing to the emergence of the nonaligned countries, a new situation was created in the world and for both blocs, while the presence of a voting force in the United Nations which could not be manipulated was bound to have far-reaching consequences for the work of the international bodies and conferences. In a bipolar political structure of the world a new element of a specific character appeared and paved its own way into the center of world events.

This new element not only contributed to the changing of the political structure but has also considerably upset the present structure of the world economy and introduced important changes in the functioning of the world market.[10] The problem of the under-

---

[10] For the effect of the expansion of the international community on stability and relations in the world, also see the book *International Stability: Military, Economic and Political Dimensions*, a collection of articles edited by Dale J. Hekhuis, Charles G. McClintock and Arthur L. Burns, John

developed countries could no longer be kept on the sidelines of general development, and thus the problem could no longer be expected to be resolved by limited efforts, including technical aid and development loans sent through existing channels to help finance the economies of the countries in trouble.

Already in the early days of the post-war period, and to a certain extent even before the end of the war, references were made to the division of the world into the East and the West. Gradually a new concept was introduced: that the world was divided into the North and South. At first it was thought that this was a division merely according to the levels of development, and that it was purely economic in character and effect. Soon, however, it was shown that this concept was not correct. The political aspect of the division which arose from the fundamentally different social structures and from different immediate needs and aspirations, could not be treated as an exclusively economic phenomenon.

Furthermore, the internal development of the underdeveloped countries could not unfold in conformity with the model of the political and general social development applicable to the countries of the North. Attempts at introducing patterns and elements of the political and economic organization of developed societies in these areas produced results which at best can be regarded as failures. These countries could not be politically absorbed into the existing blocs, nor could they be assimilated and turned into mere rubberstamps of the advanced countries. Efforts to achieve this by insisting or even by putting on pressure in fact only produced increased estrangement and distrust. There were cases on both sides in the cold war of such acts producing bitter disappointment.

The leaders of the policy of nonalignment represented countries which were burdened by extremely heavy and almost insoluble problems. Furthermore, they also had to face a growing instability in their own countries. Their views and policies in international relations were very largely overshadowed by their

---

Wiley & Sons, New York 1964. Of particular interest in connection with this problem is the article by Lucian W. Pye, "The Underdeveloped Areas as a Source of International Tensions through 1975", pp. 41—61.

specific internal problems. These problems were usually connected with other problems, sometimes even conflicts, with neighbors springing up from inherited and unresolved disputes and directly affecting these countries.

For this reason we should not be surprised that the growth of nonalignment and its increasing influence at the same time caused problems within the group itself. In the course of time specific problems, internal as well as those which arose from relationships with immediate neighbors, gained in momentum and exercised a decisive influence on the conduct of foreign affairs. This happened in a growing number of nonaligned countries. This development moved in two patterns: first, introduction of specific views and accents into the general platform of nonalignment, and second, withdrawal of some countries from global activities or a temporary weakening of efforts in that direction.

Sometimes internal problems, e. g., coups d'état and a momentary hesitation in regard to continuation of the overthrown regime's foreign policy, were responsible for this transient passivization, and sometimes conflicts in the immediate environment. Thus, for instance, the downfall of Sukarno and everything leading up to it and then the subsequent normalization in Indonesia weakened that country's involvement in world politics. The second point is best illustrated by Egypt's handicap as a result of the 1967 war in the Near East and the consequences of that war on the international situation and internal developments in that part of the world. India's conflicts first with China and then with Pakistan also caused a temporary weakening of its activity. It would be wrong, however, to explain the slackened activity of the nonaligned in the second half of the 1960s only as the result of such upheavals in individual countries.

How wrong this would be is shown by the fact that Egypt was absorbed by the war in 1956, too, without this affecting that country's activization within nonalignment immediately afterwards. In the same way, India's clash with China in the Himalayas did not cause so many disturbances as did the war with Pakistan in 1965.

In a way, success in winning over new adherents brought new problems and sometimes even critical situations. These difficul-

234

ties were caused not only by the greater number of participants and a growing internal instability, but also by the success and increased influence of the policy of nonalignment. What has always held the nonaligned countries close together is agreement on general goals. As their direct influence on world events increased, this platform no longer met their needs. The new situation demanded action for the solution of specific problems as well as constructive and well designed proposals.

In this new situation the nonaligned countries could not offer a palpable contribution to the solution of important current problems. They had been on the agendas of their earlier conferences, but had been discussed only in a very general way. The nonaligned countries praticipated in the bodies and organs of the United Nations in which these problems were discussed, but they could not efficiently contribute to the finding of specific solutions.

The mentioned tendencies and problems had already appeared in the debate at the 1964 summit conference of nonaligned nations in Cairo. This state of affairs was also reflected in their passive behavior during the crisis which broke out at the 19th session of the United Nations General Assembly[11] (where misunderstanding occurred concerning the financing of peace operations), as well as in their passivity in the disarmament committee in Geneva. The most obvious examples of weakened efforts by some of the most active protagonists of nonalignment were seen during the conflict between India and Pakistan and the war between Israel and the Arab countries in the Middle East.

The increasingly difficult problems of economic growth quite naturally shifted the main accent in the platform of the nonaligned countries from colonial problems to economic issues. The remaining colonies became less significant for the new states, because they could not be regarded as a threat in the sense of the renewal of colonialism. Nor could any new states which might emerge from the last colonial empires contribute very much to the strengthening of the third world's positions. This may explain the relative weakness of the attempts made in the mid-1960s to enforce the solution of this question. Prior to that, anti-colonialism had

---

[11] See the *Official records* of the 29th session of the U.N. General Assembly.

been not only an attitude of solidarity but also a means of increasing the number of combattants for the goals and interests of the third world. Anti-colonialism had also been encouraged by a strong feeling of insecurity because of the existence of powerful colonial empires which still resisted the growing demands for independence.

The significance of the liberation of the remaining colonies for the development, expansion and consequently the strengthening of nonalignment did not escape the attention of the heads of nonaligned states at the Belgrade Conference. In Chapter Three of the Belgrade Declaration this was clearly stated as follows: "The participants at the Conference are convinced that the emergence of newly-liberated countries will further assist in narrowing of the area of bloc antagonisms and thus encourage the tendencies aimed at strengthening peace and promoting peaceful cooperation among independent and equal nations."[12] This motive had been present throughout the history of the contemporary anti-colonial movement since the end of World War II. Colonialism was denounced not only as subjection and exploitation, but also as a means of preventing the nations of entire continents from being represented in the world and from being able to defend their own interests.

Economic problems were also no longer treated in the same generalized manner as before. Now there were two sides that could enter into a concrete and business-like dialogue. The North and the South had already more or less opened a global discussion, and problems were, roughly speaking, defined, or at least it was known what the demands of the underdeveloped part of the world meant. The developed countries of the North accepted the dialogue, and after a certain hesitation they admitted their responsibility to solve problems in order to ease the situation in the underdeveloped countries and permit an acceleration of their economic growth.

Many aspects of this complex problem remained unclarified, and in particular, practical steps towards reducing the existing tensions in economic relations were left undefined. Polemics

---

[12] See the Appendix for the text of the Declaration.

on this essential question are still going on. The nonaligned countries succeeded in their efforts to call up the United Nations Conference on Trade and Development (UNCTAD). Later on, UNCTAD set up permanent organs with the task of dealing with the problems of trade and development within the United Nations. The nonaligned countries were the moving force behind the efforts of the group of developing countries.

The rallying of the developing countries would have constituted a major difficulty had there been no nucleus to organize activities and formulate the platforms of the developing countries. However, this task was becoming increasingly complex. As the dialogue with the developed countries progressed, questions were increasingly acquiring a specific character and entering the sphere of practical solutions. The complexity and diversity of numerous developing countries were becoming an increasingly important factor.

It is relatively simple to determine the common denominator of the nonaligned countries or the ever broader category of the developing countries if we consider only their general demands or principles. It is practically impossible to define common denominators if we consider practical economic interests of different countries in the world market. The third world encompasses a wide range of different economies, from the most poorly developed to those having a budding or developing industry and trying to sell industrial goods in the markets of the developed countries. The third world also includes countries of different climes — those in the temperate zone and sub-tropical or tropical countries, — having very different possibilities for economic, social and political development. This diversity is the reason why the formulation of a common platform has always been a difficult job, but more trouble develops the moment discussion starts on practical steps. Precisely because of the complexity of this latter problem, the third world countries are today divided into the category of the least developed countries and the category of the developing countries which are at the medium degree of development. Sometimes the countries exporting oil are classified into a separate category.

These problems came to the surface immediately after the

end of the first session of the United Nations Conference on Trade and Development in Geneva in 1964. They considerably influenced the efforts to work out a platform for the second session. There was not much likelihood of defining measures that would simultaneously satisfy the interests of these two groups of underdeveloped countries. Some of them might succeed in accelerating the pace of their economic growth if they received loans at especially favorable terms and if their products were ensured a favorable treatment in the world markets, provided that technical aid granted them was well organized and included aid in the field of management and market research. Others again require massive aid in the form of grants and much more substantial assistance in various domains.

There is in addition the problem of how to organize internal efforts to reform or substitute institutions inherited from the past, eliminating also obsolete customs and social structures. It is essential to combine economic aid with efforts toward modernization, but this increases differences not only between the above-mentioned subcategories but also between individual countries. As the most active among the nonaligned countries tried to master the complicated task of coordinating the actions and policies of the numerous developing countries on controversial questions within the group or in dialogues with the developed countries, the gulf between the two worlds kept widening. In a certain sense this fact made it easier to maintain the unity of the developing countries, and enabled the most active among the nonaligned countries to retain their leading positions. But this unity was only maintained because there was a continuous need for the international forums to return to the consideration of the basic and general demands, in view of the deteriorated position of the underdeveloped countries throughout the world.

To put it in other terms, the nonaligned countries managed to make an effort to soften the hardships of the underdeveloped countries, but they did not succeed in effecting any substantial changes to prevent the gulf between the North and the South from widening. Hence, the initial period of the rallying and affirmation of the nonaligned countries was followed by stagnation and vacillation.

238

For as long as it was necessary to lay down overall objectives for the increasing number of new and nonaligned countries and move them into action, the initial form of activity was adequate. The nonaligned countries stormed into existence, bringing to surface a number of new problems and new views on the existing problems. Their emergence on the world scene was dramatic and full of impressive actions and declarations which echoed profoundly in the world. However, these actions only produced those results and effects which were possible under the conditions at that time. In other words, just as any other phenomenon, that of the nonaligned countries had its limitations in the first phase of its action. The time then came when action had to be adapted to those very changes which the movement of the nonaligned had helped to develop.

We must, therefore, make a special study of the activity of the nonaligned countries in that period which brought their international eminence. That was the period of their strongest influence, and we should closely scrutinize both their actions in the purely political field and those which were designed to improve their economic position.

B. ACTION FOR THE REALIZATION OF POLITICAL AIMS

PEACE AND INTERNATIONAL COOPERATION

Although the 1955 Bandung Conference of Afro-Asian countries was, according to Sukarno, the "first inter-continental conference of the so-called colored peoples in the history of mankind,"[13] it also dealt with questions related to general efforts for the maintenance of peace in the world. However, it approached those questions always conscious of its own composition and significance, as a conference of the so-called "colored nations".

---

[13] *Keesing's Contemporary Archives* 1955—1956, p. 14181.

This was felt in all the speeches and texts of resolutions and declarations which were passed at the conference. It was also evident in Nehru's final speech at the conference as he discussed world issues. "We want to be friends with Europe and America and co-operate with them," Nehru said, "but they are in the habit of thinking that their quarrels are world quarrels, and that therefore the world must follow them this way or that. Why should we be dragged into their quarrels and wars?" To this Nehru gave a resolute answer: "I hope we shall keep away."[14]

It would be exaggerated to say that Nehru fully and faithfully mirrored all the tendencies represented at the conference, but at a second look it seems that he did represent a much wider circle of political movements and nations than was obvious then. His words should be interpreted in the light of the situation in which the conference was held. It was an attempt to create a single front, or at least a coordinated action, of the countries of Asia and Africa, as Sukarno stressed in the mentioned inaugural speech.

The conference was held four months before the four-power conference in Geneva. A thaw in the cold war was already in the air. It was felt more strongly in Asia than in Europe and in America, and it was probably provoked by an intensive wish for the cold war to abate. At any rate, in a speech held on May 15, 1953, before the Indian parliament, Nehru thought that the intensity of the cold war was abating.[15] In these circumstances it seemed possible also to try and solve the outstanding issues in an atmosphere free from the bitterness of the cold war.

Thus on the last day of the conference the Chinese premier Chou En-lai expressed the hope and desire that "China and the United States should sit down and enter into negotiations to settle the question of relaxing tensions in the Formosa area," adding that "this should not affect in the slightest degree the sovereign rights of the people of China in liberating Formosa."[16] The presence of China and Pakistan, Turkey, Thailand and the Philippines

---

[14] *Ibid.*, p. 14183.

[15] "Spoljnopolitička dokumentacija", Institute of International Politics and Economics, Beograd 1953, No. 12, p. 472. At the very beginning of this speech, Nehru in fact underlines that no important problem had been solved, but that for the first time in many years a large number of people had begun to hope for a settlement.

[16] *Keesing's Contemporary Archives 1955—1956*, p. 14183.

reflected the general conviction of both the bloc-adhering and nonaligned countries that the cold war was nearing an end and that a joint action of the countries of Asia and Africa was also possible at the level of general political problems related to the question of peace and security in the world.

Chou En-lai's conciliatory gesture did not meet with a favorable response from the United States government. The initiative was rejected in a roundabout way. At first special, hardly acceptable conditions were set, and then it was explicitly emphasized that Washington would "insist on free China participating as an equal in any discussion concerning the area." Thailand, of course, refused to participate, and this whole episode, ended, provoking a denunciation of the U. S. attitude even from the pro-American delegates at the conference.[17]

The outcome of this initiative demonstrated how limited was the easing of tensions that truly did take place between the cold war adversaries, for it offered neither a solution nor prospects of a prompt solution for the open political or regional disputes and conflicts. This may have been partly influenced by the fact that the Prime Minister of Ceylon, Sir John Cotelawala, presented to the conference a plan on the final solution of the Taiwan question which provided the withdrawal of Chiang Kai-shek and a plebiscite after five years; this plan was very well received by the participants.[18]

Although the hopes were dashed and no constructive negotiations between China and the United States, nor the creation of a single political front of Afro-Asian countries, took place, the Bandung Conference holds a significant place in the history of the nonaligned countries. The most important protagonist of nonalignment and the statesman who most contributed to this role of the conference was undoubtedly Nehru, who already then enjoyed strong support from Sukarno and Nasser, as well as full backing from Ceylon and Burma.

The Bandung Conference, in contrast to the later Belgrade Conference of nonaligned countries, made provision for the con-

---

[17] *Ibid.*, p. 14185.
[18] *Ibid.*

vention of another Afro-Asian conference.[19] However, even in this respect the hopes of the statesmen gathered at the conference were not fulfilled. The holding of a new comprehensive regional conference became increasingly difficult and finally quite impossible as a result of developments in the world and in the area of Asia and Africa. One of the important developments was a considerable increase in the number of independent African countries and their organization into a regional African organization[20] (Organization of African Unity).

Bandung was the first, and at the same time fully successful, attempt at bringing together all the countries of two continents. Such a gathering was possible only in an exceptional situation which occurred briefly on the eve of the quadripartite summit conference. However, the newly arisen situation helped to make the Bandung conference the starting point for a new significant development, the scope of which the participants, and even the conveners, were then unable to foresee.

At any rate, the positions of the nonaligned countries in regard to peaceful coexistence were originally formulated not in Bandung but prior to that, within bilateral negotiations between India and China. Five points on peaceful cooperation, as well as the term coexistence, were presented in a joint statement by Nehru and Chou En-lai published after the end of their talks in New Delhi, June 25—28, 1954.[21] On that occasion the following five principles were formulated on which relations between the two countries should be based: 1) mutual respect for each other's territorial integrity and sovereignty, 2) nonaggression, 3) non-interference in each other's internal affairs, 4) equality and mutual benefit, and 5) peaceful co-existence.

The statement further pointed out that a general observance of these principles in international relations would contribute to the removal of the existing tensions and to the creation of conditions for cooperation. It was particularly emphasized that the existence of different social systems "should not come in the way of peace or create conflicts." These principles were formulated in

---

[19] See the last sentence in the Declaration on World Peace and Cooperation in the Appendix.
[20] Set up at the conference of the heads of African countries on May 25, 1963, in Addis Ababa.
[21] *Keesing's Contemporary Archives* 1952—1954, p. 13661.

242

connection with the agreement between the two countries made in April of the same year following the developments in Tibet. Not long after these principles were adopted, they were repudiated in connection with the same problem. As we know, it was precisely concerning India's border with Tibet that conflict arose between China and India in 1962, despite the existence of both the agreement and the mentioned principles.

However, the significance of this joint statement for the development of relations in Asia was very great in those years. The agreement between China and Indonesia of 1955 refers to these principles,[22] and they also inspired the resolution of the Bandung Conference. The list was extended to ten principles, included in the Declaration on World Peace and Cooperation.

The Declaration retained the first four points, although some of them were somewhat differently formulated. Coexistence in itself was not mentioned, but the additional points may be regarded as containing the elements of coexistence. The ten points of this declaration were subsequently often mentioned as the principles of coexistence of the Bandung Conference. However, the entire complex of international constructive cooperation began to be described as coexistence only later on, at the beginning of the 1960s.[23]

It is interesting that the ten points of the Bandung Declaration also stressed the principles of the equality of all races and nations, big and small, as well as the right to self-defense. This reemphasized the character of the gathering and underlined that it was not sufficient to denounce the interference of the stronger in the affairs of the weaker and the use or threat of force, but also that small and generally threatened countries should have a recognized right to defend themselves.[24]

The Bandung Conference thus laid down a system of principles and views which were subsequently elaborated and propa-

---

[22] *Keesing's Contemporary Archives 1955—1956*, p. 14184.

[23] The coexistence of countries with different social systems and their permanent cooperation can be found even earlier as a policy objective and a principle for the regulation of international relations. The attitude of Yugoslavia is illustrated in President Tito's response to a newsman on April 28, 1950, to the effect that conflicts between countries with different systems are not inevitable (Tito, *Govori i članci*, Vol. V, *op. cit.*, pp. 144—152).

[24] See the Appendix for the text of the declaration.

gated at the meetings of the nonaligned countries and in the forums of the United Nations. However, the later formulations also show the change in the composition and general orientation which took place as the nonaligned countries became a movement with a separate political orientation. The Bandung postulate about the observance of "justice and international obligations" does not appear again in the latter-day documents of the nonaligned countries.

This does not mean that the nonaligned countries hold that justice and international obligations should not be respected; the omission should be interpreted as an allowance for reality. What this means is that these precepts were often used as a weapon against changes, particularly against the abolition of colonialism. "Justice" in similar conditions applies not to the feeling of what is just but to the legal order, and "international obligations" often appear as imposed or forced agreements which concretize either purely colonial or otherwise unequitable relations. In Bandung this formulation was most probably a concession for the sake of the full representation of the two continents.

This can also be seen from the discussion at the Conference, which in addition to speeches which clearly set the tone for future meetings of the nonaligned (Nehru, Sukarno, Nasser, Kotelawala) also included anti-communist harangues — Romulo Carlos — or demagogic denunciations of "colonialism, Zionism and communism" — Mohammed Jamali. A characteristic speech in the general debate was that of the prime minister of Pakistan, Mohammed Ali, who proposed a list of seven principles, which for the most part tallied with the five points in the Nehru—Chou En-lai agreement and which were incorporated in the ten points of the declaration adopted at the end of the conference. This behavior was also indicative of the climate prevailing in those days.[25]

---

[25] The Bandung Conference was not homogeneous from the political standpoint. There were pro-Western countries: Ceylon, the Gold Coast (now Ghana), Iran, Iraq, Japan, Jordan, Lebanon, Liberia, Libya, Pakistan, the Philippines, Sudan, Thailand, Turkey, and South Vietnam. And there were communist and nonaligned countries: Afghanistan, Burma, Cambodia, China, Egypt, Ethiopia, India, Indonesia, Laos, Nepal, Saudi Arabia, Syria, North Vietnam and Yemen. This second group was more or less united at the conference. Immediately after the conference and in the years that followed there were significant changes in the orientation of these countries. They are classified here according to the stands they took at the conference.

The very constructive and conciliatory speech by the Chinese premier Chou En-lai was certainly accorded the greatest attention by participants at the conference and by the entire world. In the very beginning of his speech he stated that he had not come to sow dissension but rather to contribute to unity. He stated that Peking accepted the Soviet proposal for the Taiwan question to be discussed at an international conference, even though this was a "entirely the internal affair on the Chinese people". The conference, of course, would not deal with the final settlements of the essence of the question, i. e. the future of this island, but rather with questions of peace and security in this area.[26]

China's attendance and its behavior throughout the conference also gave rise to hopes that the foundations were being laid for a new constellation in international relations, and it was therefore necessary to adjust one's own behavior to the new general climate which was expected to promote the concept of a single Afro-Asian front. Finally, the behavior of the Japanese representative at the conference also suggested that the chances for such a new constellation were good.[27]

As we have already said, the conference did not succeed in endeavors to change the image of the world in regard to bloc grouping. A number of actions by bloc adherents dashed those hopes. At any rate, Nehru was right when he said in 1953, in the early mentioned speech before the Indian parliament, that no major problem was resolved yet. The gradual relaxation that influenced the events in Indochina (the 1954 Geneva Conference) and the Bandung Conference produced the summit meeting of the four great powers four months after Bandung. However, no major problem was resolved here either. The only thing that was achieved was recognition that the cold war should not escalate beyond the point of no return. This was, however, sign not of readiness for cooperation but rather of fear of possible effects in the event of a nuclear war.

The events which soon after the "spring" mood of 1955 spoiled the prospects of any follow-up of the Bandung action

---

[26] *Keesing's Contemporary Archives* 1955—1956, p. 14182.
[27] *Ibid.*

were the development in Vietnam following the Geneva Conference, and especially after the Bandung meeting, the events in Hungary and Poland in 1956, and the extremely hard line taken by the United States on China. All this affected mutual relations in Asia and Africa. In Asia there was again a rift between the countries outside the military blocs and those which adhered to blocs. Tension between India and Pakistan increased, contributing to the strengthening of bloc influences in Southeast Asia. The spirit of cooperation which prevailed in Bandung and temporarily suppressed controversies between individual participants was dissipating rapidly.

The Bandung Conference did therefore provide a solid basis for general policies governing the questions of peace and international security, but did not succeed in holding the participants together and in serving as a force of attraction that would make a lasting joint action possible.

After the Bandung Conference, a movement to continue with what was begun there, although in a different setting, became noticeable among the nonaligned statesmen. It became obvious that cooperation with the bloc aligned countries was no longer possible, and thus the Philippines, Thailand, Turkey and Pakistan on the one hand, as well as China on the other, were written off. Thus room for action in Asia was considerably reduced, but gradually Africa appeared more and more as an area where the ending of the colonial rule of the European powers was being prepared.

The lesson of Bandung was that under the circumstances it was not possible to act on the basis of a comprehensive and well-designed political platform within regional organizations or gatherings. To muster the broadest possible support for the new ideas of the Bandung Conference, it was necessary to get out of the narrow regional framework. As Yugoslavia at that time had appeared in the world in a new role and with new views which very largely coincided with the views of the nonaligned from Bandung, cooperation between them and Yugoslavia became possible and desirable.

The sounding out of each other's positions had been done already. This took place when President Tito visited India and

Burma in 1954, and during the first meeting and political contact with Nasser. The meeting of the three statesmen in June 1956 at Brioni was therefore not quite coincidental. Nehru's stopover in Yugoslavia on his return from London to India happily coincided with Nasser's visit to Yugoslavia, but had there been no earlier contacts and agreement on unity on the most important views, this meeting would hardly have had the importance which it acquired. It was the first meeting that was not on the basis of bilateral cooperation or on a regional basis.

A conference of the heads of nonaligned nations had since then been constantly discussed as a possibility and a need. The work started in Bandung had to be continued, but it was evident that the framework established there had become unsuitable. All the reasons which once prompted the calling up the Bandung Conference were still present, and the further development of the situation made it even more urgent to find a form in which another gathering of as many states as possible could take place.

At the Belgrade Conference in 1961 and later at the Cairo Conference in 1964, the elaboration of the ideas which made up the Bandung general political platform was continued. However, the construction was changed. It is therefore interesting to make a comparison of the general statements on peace and international cooperation at the two conferences. First of all, it is noticeable that in the later platforms the method of enumerating principles and formulations of brief and concise postulates was avoided. There were instead for the first time attempts at analyzing the current situation with much more subtly formulated conclusions. It could be said in a way that the declaration and resolution of Bandung were taken as theses from which to develop policies and assessments in Belgrade and Cairo.[28]

They introduced a very clear attitude of operative statesmanship to the general premises, although these remained generalized and related to the general lines of endeavors and aspirations of the participating countries.[29] However, much more significant

---

[28] See the Appendix for all these documents.

[29] In this respect the Bandung documents on peace and cooperation should be compared with the introduction and chapters I and II of the Belgrade Declaration and with the introduction and chapters IV, V, VI, VII and VIII of the Cairo Declaration.

than the differences in texts was the fact that the two latter conferences and the documents drafted at them really contributed to the joint action of a large number of countries. In fact, the number of those who participated in individual actions was larger than the number of countries represented at the conference of the heads of state. This more successful action was, of course, due to the fact that these conferences brought together the countries which had sufficiently consonant attitudes, so that a more concrete formulation was possible and the ensuing joint action had a sufficiently secure and firm basis. However, no less important was the fact that a movement thus formulated could rely on an increasing number of new participants. The newly liberated countries more and more frequently and wholeheartedly adopted the orientation of nonalignment in their international behavior.

Local and regional rivalries, especially in Africa, sometimes hindered a broad association of all the new countries, but this was overcome, and the eventually formed Organization of African Unity adopted the resolution to the effect that its policy was based on nonalignment. Thus also the material basis of nonalignment strengthened, and its influence in the United Nations increased. Furthermore, the general trend in international relations precipitated the association of the nonaligned in the belief that united they could influence the development of events in the world and ensure greater respect for their interests and views.

Another important spur comprised the economic problems and increasingly acute difficulties which the new countries faced, both in regard to accelerating their internal development and in regard to securing an equal position in the world market. Economic problems therefore became the basic political problems.

The new platform of 1961 was based on the fact that international relations had undergone a serious deterioration and that there was an increased threat to peace, and the second of 1964 on the fact that tensions had abated. Accents were placed differently, but both platforms reflected the same basic ideas and stands. Finally, both documents dealt with long-range and general tasks which were, or should be, faced by the international community.

In their efforts to strengthen peace and international co-operation, the nonaligned countries pursued two types of interests and tried to implement two objectives. First of all, they safeguarded their independence and integrity by efforts to create conditions which would offer a maximum guarantee of safety to the countries which do not have a military force comparable to that of the great powers. Next, they endeavored to remove the animosity between the great powers because of the danger that tensions and rivalries would be transferred to the areas of the nonaligned countries, or that they would be forced to toe the line and would thus lose their independence.

This distinction was more clearly reflected in later political platforms, when the tensions of the cold war diminished. Thus at the Cairo Conference differences arose because some countries felt relations between the great powers and the nonaligned countries to be more important than the confrontation between the great powers themselves. Nonalignment in any case meant insistence on international cooperation and on a better deal for the poorly armed countries. Action for the strengthening of peace and security therefore did not primarily arise as a reaction to the cold war, although in the early days the need to reduce tensions between the great powers was insisted on very strongly.

DISARMAMENT

Disarmament was one of the first issues that came up before the United Nations immediately after its foundation.[30] Before the Bandung Conference, and especially before the formal constitution of the nonaligned countries in 1961 at the Belgrade Conference, this question had already been widely discussed. These discussions were overshadowed by the international situation and were used as psychological and political weapons in the cold war between the two well-armed groups.

At first, the military strength of the West rested on the nuclear armament of the United States, and the strength of the

---

[30] See the *Yearbook of the United Nations* 1946—1947, pp. 64 and 139.

other side on the large and efficient conventional armament of the Soviet Union. As a result, any measure affecting a certain type of armament would have the effect of upsetting the balance. For instance, the U.S.S.R.'s insistence on immediate destruction and prohibition of nuclear armaments was inacceptable to the U.S.A., and by the same token, proposals which would leave untouched even a reduced nuclear force of the West were inacceptable to the U.S.S.R., especially since the latter would then be expected to reduce its own conventional forces.

Throughout this time both sides insisted on their adherence to the Charter's provision about disarmament,[31] and on a consistent implementation of the early resolution on disarmament, unanimously adopted at the first session of the U.N. General Assembly. The failure of the negotiations held in the period between 1946 and 1954 was due to the already mentioned differences in interest for one or another category of armament. The first unanimity after 1946 appeared in this matter again in 1954 at the ninth session of the General Assembly, when the resolution on the renewal of discussions in the London subcommittee was unanimously adopted, and then, also unanimously, the resolution about the essence of the question.[32] This renewed unanimity was achieved on the basis of a changed material ratio of strength when the Soviet Union developed its own nuclear armaments and simultaneously with the United States began to produce thermonuclear weapons.

The nonaligned countries, at their gatherings, in the United Nations and elsewhere, have always devoted attention to this question. However, in their joint action disarmament usually does not hold a very prominent place, nor have they shown much initiative on this question. In order to obtain an accurate idea about it we should first consider the evolution of attitudes in the United Nations in the years which preceded the nonaligned meetings in Bandung and then at the two conferences in Belgrade and Cairo. We shall not consider separately the attitudes of individual nonaligned countries because there were no great

---

[31] See in particular articles 11, 26 and 47.
[32] *Svetska konferencija o razoružanju* (The World Disarmament Conference), Institute of International Politics and Economics, Beograd, No. 7, 1969, p. 72.

differences between their chief protagonists, and because as a rule they were presented in the context of specialized discussions or in specific situations in the United Nations and do not provide a true picture about the significance that was given to that question.

The first United Nations resolution relating to the general problem of disarmament was the General Assembly resolution on founding the Atomic Energy Commission, that was unanimously adopted on January 24, 1946, at the first part of the First Session. It was drafted at a meeting of the foreign ministers of three great powers[33] in December 1945, and France and China joined later. The basic provisions in regard to the commission's terms of reference may by described in the following points:

1) Dissemination of scientific information for peaceful purposes among all countries;

2) Utilizations of atomic energy exclusively for peaceful purposes;

3) Elimination of atomic weapons from national armaments and also of any other weapon adaptable for mass destruction;

4) Inspection and control against violation or circumvention of the above provisions.[34]

In the second part of the same session, at a meeting held on December 14, 1946, the resolution on disarmament was adopted unanimously. In that resolution the Security Council was asked to immediately formulate measures for a "general regulation and reduction of armaments and armed forces and to assure that such regulation and reduction of armaments and armed forces will be generally observed by all participants and not unilaterally by only some of the participants." The Atomic Energy Commission was urged to fulfil its mandate in regard to "prohibiting and eliminating from national armament atomic and all other major weapons adaptable now or in the future to mass destruction." The resolution further called for the establishment of an efficient control of disarmament, for the convention of a special session of the General Assembly to review the disarmament plan, for the conclusion of a convention on this question, and for the creation

[33] The U.S.A., U.S.S.R. and Great Britain.
[34] *Yearbook of the United Nations* 1946—1947, p. 65.

of a special international control system, which in addition to supervision would also be concerned with the utilization of atomic energy for peaceful purposes. The resolution also called for the withdrawal of armed forces from foreign bases, except when they are there on the basis of "consent freely and publicly expressed." As regards former enemies, provision was made for a "progressive and balanced withdrawal, while taking into account the needs of the occupation, of their armed forces."[35]

These general attitudes and postulates had never been challenged by any side, and, what is more, they had been repeated and supplemented, and yet no agreement was achieved for reasons which have already been mentioned here. Thus after eight years of fruitless discussions and violent polemics, filled with charges and countercharges, policies were again unanimously formulated in the resolution adopted on October 27, 1954, at the ninth session of the General Assembly. In the meantime it was decided that both types of armament, conventional and nuclear, should be discussed in a single combined organ, the Commission for Disarmament.

The resolution of the ninth session contains the following basic provisions:

1) Conclusion of an international convention on general disarmament;

2) Regulation, limitation and major reduction of all armed forces and all conventional armaments;

3) Total prohibition of the use and manufacture of nuclear weapons and weapons of mass destruction of every type, and on the utilization of materials contained in the existing stocks of nuclear weapons for peaceful purposes;

4) Establishment of effective international control which would supervise peaceful application of nuclear energy;

5) No state should have cause to fear that its safety is threatened by this entire program.[36]

Even prior to this resolution, speaking on December 8, 1953, before the U.N. General Assembly, U.S. President Eisenhower

---

[35] *Ibid.*, p. 143.
[36] *Keesing's Contemporary Archives* 1955—1956, p. 13994. GAOR, 9th Session Suppl. No. 21 (A/2890) Resolution 808 (IX), p. 3.

proposed that all the nuclear powers should immediateiy start setting aside certain quantities of nuclear fuels from their arsenals and make them available to all the countries of the world through a special agency.[37] In the same speech he expressed readiness to support the dissemination of scientific information and training of cadres in the field of applied nuclear energy for peaceful purposes. This idea was later put into practice, and an agency, which has its seat in Vienna, is dealing with all these problems.

The action of the United Nations received a further boost when a world conference for the utilization of nuclear energy for peaceful purposes was called in the summer 1955. The chairman of that conference, which met in Geneva and worked from August 8 to 21, 1955, was the Indian physicist, Dr. Bhabha. The conference was convened following a unanimously adopted resolution at the ninth session of the U.N. General Assembly on December 4, 1954.[38]

Consequently, the Bandung Conference, and even more the subsequent conferences of the nonaligned nations, did not have to break new ground and to move new initiatives. The problem in connection with disarmament and especially in connection with nuclear energy did not call for a definition of general principles and final objectives; the question was how to implement them, how to overcome the political antagonism and political ambitions of the great powers, which stood as an obstacle to their implementation.

The agreement on disarmament between the U.S.A. and the U.S.S.R. which was attained at the end of 1954 led to the summit meeting in Geneva at which, between July 18 and 23, 1955, the highest representatives of the United States, the Soviet Union, Great Britain and France met.[39] However, this is where unanimity ended. Already at the meetings of the foreign ministers, who in the autumn of the same year (October 27 to November 16) continued the work of their chiefs in order to concretize conclusions, there arose some serious dissensions.[40]

---

[37] GAOR 8th Sess. Suppl. 470, Plenary meeting, pp. 450—453.
[38] GAOR, 9th Sess. Suppl. No. 21 (A/2890), Resolution 810 (IX), pp. 4—5.
[39] *Keesing's Contemporary Archives* 1955—1956, 14325.
[40] *Ibid.*, pp. 14537—14548.

Instead of an agreement being reached on an end to the armaments race, the race came into a new phase. Qualitatively new weapons with considerably increased destructive force and successful tests with long-range missiles gave rise to hopes that some advantage could yet be achieved over the rival great power. Furthermore, the weakness of the general agreements in Geneva was that no outstanding political question was resolved. The mere statement about the cataclysmic character of new weapons and the senselessness of war could not halt the armaments race and rivalry, although it had already contributed to a considerable extent to the taming of aggressive impulses and to the awareness that certain limits of tension should not be overstepped.

However, activity in Bandung, Belgrade and Cairo remained, as regards disarmament, at the level of general proclamations, bringing nothing new to the world discussions, which substantially differed from the earlier violent polemics of a generally propagandistic nature.

Although the Bandung Conference was held at the time when the most destructive weapon, the thermonuclear bomb, had already been fully developed, the question of disarmament did not receive a special place in the final acts of the conference. It was referred to in the resolution on world peace and cooperation as one of three points. The first point contained the demand to admit into the membership of the United Nations eight states of Asia and Africa; the second was for Asia and Africa to be given a seat in the Security Council, and the third refers to the relations between Yemen and Aden. The resolution on peace and cooperation was one of the five resolutions.[41]

Having in mind the horrors likely to be caused by the terrible destructive power of thermonuclear weapons, the participants at the conference "considered that disarmament and the prohibition of the production, experimentation and use of nuclear and thermonuclear weapons are imperative to save mankind from fear and prospect of wholesale destruction."[42] Supporting this ban, the participants at the conference demanded an effective international

---

[41] See the texts of the resolutions of the Bandung Conference in the Appendix.
[42] Paragraph 2 of the Resolution on World Peace and Cooperation.

control over its implementation. They further appealed to all interested powers to stop nuclear tests. The resolution also generally proclaims support for the ban on nuclear and thermonuclear weapons, but specifically demands only "the regulation, limitation, control and reduction of all armed forces and armaments, including the prohibition of the production, experimentation and use of all weapons of mass destruction," and the introduction of "effective international control to this end." This explicit demand was expected to help bring about "universal disarmament".

In one of the two declarations published at the conference, disarmament was also mentioned in a sentence in the preamble which was followed by the ten points, known as the "Bandung principles". The title of this declaration was the "Declaration on World Peace and Co-operation".[43] In this sentence all countries were called upon to effect through the United Nations "reduction of armaments and elimination of nuclear weapons under effective international control". Those demands were based on the conviction that peace would thus be safeguarded and the application of nuclear energy for peaceful purposes would be made possible.

In view of its composition, the Bandung Conference could hardly be more articulate than the U.N. General Assembly. In fact, the Bandung text was in a certain sense inferior to that which a few months earlier had been unanimously adopted in New York. Its only original contribution was the demand to stop nuclear tests, which was presented to the conference by Nehru.[44] The demand to use the savings from disarmament for increased aid to the underdeveloped countries was considered at the summer session of the Economic and Social Council in 1953, on the basis of proposals to that effect that were presented by the delegation of the United States, but which in fact served to suppress the proposal of the underdeveloped for the setting up of a special United Nations fund for financing development.

The policies adopted at the Bandung Conference consequently did not represent any new contribution but were repetitions of

[43] *Ibid.*
[44] *See Keesing's Contemporary Archives* 1955—1956, p. 14182.

the formulations which had been unanimously adopted earlier by the U.N. General Assembly. The conference therefore could not have a strong influence on the forthcoming summit meeting at Geneva within the framework of the scientific conference on atomic energy which met in the same summer also in Geneva.

As dissensions multiplied in the years that followed, neither the Afro-Asian countries nor any other forum of the third world or of nonalignment came forward with any initiatives. The participants at the Bandung Conference went along their several and politically opposing ways, and joined increasingly heated discussions about disarmament. In fact, the least active in these years in the field of disarmament were precisely the nonaligned countries which participated at the Bandung Conference. They were much more concerned with the problem of decolonization and improvement of the economic situation. This situation was also reflected in the work of the Belgrade Conference.

The participants at the Belgrade Conference met in a situation essentially different from that in which the Bandung Conference had been held. The international situation was burdened by considerably greater tensions between the Soviet Union and the United States. After the relaxation at the end of the 1950s, which culminated in the visit by the Soviet prime minister to the United States, relations again worsened after the shooting down of an American reconnaissance aircraft above the Central European regions of the Soviet Union on May Day 1960, and the Paris meeting of the four powers broke down at the very beginning.

The strained atmosphere, with no significant contacts made between the two superpowers, deteriorated even further when the Soviet Union announced the resumption of nuclear tests. This decision came immediately before the Belgrade Conference and three years after the unilateral decisions by both sides to stop tests. Thus the problem of nuclear weapons again came into the focus of attention of the entire world, and the absence of any talks between Moscow and Washington was highly ominous. The world situation and momentary deterioration were inevitably reflected in the work of the conference of the heads of state of nonaligned countries. The conference operated at two levels: at the level of urgent activity in connection with the situation of the moment, and at the level of long-range demands and interests of nonaligned countries.

During the preparations for the conference, an important task was to coordinate the activity of the nonaligned countries by direct understanding among leading statesmen. Then the need was stressed for the inauguration of a general platform which would lay down the essence and scope of a political programme of nonaligned countries. However, the newly arisen situation subordinated this activity to more urgent measures to bring about a relaxation of the cold war.

In addition to the voluminous declaration, the conference also published a special "Statement on the Danger of War and an Appeal for Peace" and sent identical letters to the President of the United States and the Prime Minister of the U.S.S.R.[45] In the two latter documents, the accent was on the urgent need for bilateral talks aimed at reducing the tensions of the cold war, and disarmament was only mentioned in the statement. It was hoped that these wide-range talks would lead to a "total disarmament and enduring peace."

The principal document of the conference discussed disarmament in separate points which made up the main part of the text of the third and last part of the Declaration. There were 27 points in all, and those numbered 15 to 20 were devoted to disarmament and allied problems. These six points contain the following demands:

1) Conclusion of a treaty on general, complete and strictly and internationally controlled disarmament within the framework of the United Nations, including the elimination of armed forces, foreign bases, manufacture of arms, and of institutions and installations for military training, except for the needs of internal security; complete prohibition of the production, possession and use of nuclear, thermonuclear, bacteriological and chemical weapons, and the elimination of equipment and installations for the launching, deployment and operative use of weapons for mass destruction on national territory;[46]

---

[45] See the texts of these documents in the Appendix.
[46] Paragraphs 15, 16 and 18.

2) Utilization of outer space for peaceful purposes and creation of an international agency for that purpose;[47]

3) Release of nuclear fuels for peaceful needs of all of mankind;[48]

4) Participation of nonaligned countries in all conferences on disarmament and especially in international supervision teams;[49]

5) An immediate halt to nuclear tests and the signing of an agreement to that effect, either within or outside the framework of the disarmament talks;[50]

6) Endorsement at the forthcoming U.N. General Assembly for the convention of a special session of the General Assembly or world conference on disarmament.[51]

Consequently, the Belgrade Conference did not substantially extend the framework of the jointly established general statements about disarmament. Since dissensions took place soon after the agreement was made at the end of 1954 and in the early part of 1955, the premises from the 1954/55 period were not further developed. This was only done following a renewed rapprochement of the two superpowers in 1958. However, even in this period of talks and relaxation, no significant steps forward were made in the field of disarmament, except that a moratorium on testing of nuclear weapons was unilaterally proclaimed. The break of the moratorium interrupted the short-lived thaw and disarmament talks came into an impasse. This was no wonder, because the race which had begun in the field of thermonuclear missiles received new impetus as powerful and highly accurate missiles were developed. The launching of the first Soviet artificial satellite around the earth in the autumn of 1957 opened a new stage in this race. Talks in this situation could lead to a reaffirmation of the need to keep hostilities under control, but could not put a stop to the race itself.

However, improvement in relations and considerable headway in armaments produced in the early 1960s the first agreements, even though they were peripheral to the problem of dis-

---

[47] Paragraph 17.
[48] Paragraph 18.
[49] Paragraph 18.
[50] Paragraph 19.
[51] Paragraph 20.

armament. Most important was the agreement on the utilization of outer space for peaceful purposes only, followed by the agreement on the discontinuation of nuclear tests except for underground tests. The atmosphere at the time of the second conference of nonaligned countries in Cairo between October 5 and 10, 1954, was altogether different from the one prevailing at the Belgrade Conference. This was reflected in the texts of the documents drafted there, which were infused with confidence in a further relaxation and in extended action of the nonaligned countries. Yet, even here disarmament failed to receive a place in or near the center of attention, although texts reflected what progress was made in this question.

In the fundamental Cairo document, *Program for Peace and International Cooperation*, as well as in the Belgrade Declaration, disarmament was referred to in a special part devoted to that issue, but was not mentioned anywhere in the preamble or general political sections of the document.[52] In addition to the preamble, the Program has 11 separate parts, of which the seventh is devoted to disarmament and allied question, and the eighth to the question of foreign bases. The document itself is much more extensive than those drafted in Bandung and Belgrade, and the texts are narrative and contain considerable description of past events.

The portion devoted to disarmament included the following demands related to this question:

1) Appeal to the great powers to urgently undertake steps for a general and total disarmament under a strict and efficient international control;

2) Invitation to all countries to join the agreement on nonproliferation of nuclear weapons and to undertake all necessary measures to prevent the spreading of these weapons in any way whatever;

3) Call to respective states to carry out preliminary measures in connection with disarmament;

4) Appeal for the conclusion of an agreement on the utilization of outer space for peaceful purposes and for the dissemination and publication of acquired knowledge and generally of

---

[52] See the texts in the Appendix.

knowledge about the utilization of nuclear energy for peaceful purposes;

5) Support for the declaration of the African states about the de-nuclearization of Africa and similar desires in Latin America, Europe and elsewhere;

6) Appeal to all countries to convene a disarmament conference.

In Cairo the need for disarmament was explained for the first time with the argument that the very existence of armaments creates a danger for peace. Whereas the main accent in the points on disarmament in the Belgrade Declaration was on the dimensions of the problem, i. e., the "present state of armament"[53] in Cairo disarmament is insisted upon because "weapons of mass destruction and their stockpiling threaten the world with armed conflict and annihilation".[54]

The new points included in the Cairo platform reproduce the results of the dialogue between the superpowers as, i. e., agreement on specific questions or at least an agreement to try to reach agreement on new questions. In this respect there is a noticeable tendency to accept everything that the superpowers had agreed upon or what they want to include in future agreements. Characteristic in that respect was a passage in the Cairo Program about the agreement on nonproliferation of nuclear arms. This agreement did not yet exist, so the appeal of the conference was in fact a *carte blanche* for a specific action in the field of disarmament based upon an agreement in principle of the superpowers.

When the text of the agreement on nonproliferation was published, the most active nonaligned countries found themselves joined with some of the developed countries in criticizing this agreement. This difference between behavior and action arises from the basic characteristic of the documents from the conferences of nonaligned nations; namely, from the fact that they dwell only on the most generalized formulations of an exhortative character, particularly in questions of disarmament. A similar attitude was usually taken also in connection with other questions

---

[53] Paragraph 15.
[54] Second paragraph in Chapter VII of the Program for Peace and International Cooperation.

which did not derive directly from the specific interests of the participating countries.

We get a better picture if we compare the Belgrade and Cairo texts with those which were written in the early months of the work of the United Nations. As was pointed out earlier, these texts contain almost all the demands and standpoints which we find in the platform of the nonaligned countries, except for some points connected with later developments, either technical or concerning repercussions which they had upon the international situation.

All the provisions and postulates in connection with disarmament in general, and with the prohibition of nuclear weapons, the utilization of nuclear energy for peaceful purposes, the conclusion of international agreements and the establishment of strict controls in particular — were contained in the early United Nations resolutions adopted in 1946. Only the formulations concerning conventional armament of 1946 were specific about its drastic reduction, whereas the later texts of the nonaligned countries are phrased in general terms. These formulations, however, differ from the earliest U. N. resolutions mainly because they set down the final, i. e., remote, goals in radical terms. Even in the text of the Belgrade Declaration, reference was made to the "radical solution of this problem,"[55] and a call was made for the "elimination of armed forces, armaments, foreign bases, manufacture of arms as well as elimination of institutions and installations for military training, except for purposes of internal security."[56]

Even the demand for the holding of a special meeting of the General Assembly, for the publication of scientific data and a number of other formulations were contained in the resolution adopted at the first session of the U. N. General Assembly. No reference was made as yet to a number of technical questions which appeared only later, such as outer space, nonproliferation, underground experiments, etc. However, the authors of these early texts did make provision for the development of science and technology; they introduced into the texts statements about weap-

---

[55] Paragraph 15.
[56] Paragraph 16.

ons "adaptable now or in the future to mass destruction."[57] The resolution passed at the first session provides for the setting up of an international organization that would help utilize nuclear energy for peaceful ends.

Some formulations from that time may today sound odd, such as the reference to the abolition of "national arsenals" of nuclear weapons. This conceals the implied hope that the United Nations might arrive at an agreement in the Security Council about the formation of international forces for the preservation of peace, which would also have nuclear weapons.

As we compare the texts of the Cairo Resolution with those of the resolutions adopted at the previous, Ninth Session of the General Assembly, we can also see that the Cairo Program departed very slightly, in the questions of disarmament, from the tone, content and even formulations of the U. N. resolutions. This attitude to the problems of disarmament was maintained even later, after the Cairo Conference. First of all, a contact is made between the superpowers; then the nonaligned support this initiative and call for immediate action to arrive at an operative agreement, and then either the superpowers agree in entirety or partially and the agreement is hailed, or, if it is not quite complete or perfect, these powers are requested to complete it. A typical example was the agreement on nonproliferation and the agreement on partial interruption of nuclear experiments. Even if allowances are made for the fact that the nonaligned countries could not have contributed very much more to disarmament, we find that they were less active in that field than in some other domains.

The nonaligned countries may well have been more interested in the act itself of agreement than in essentially contributing to the further development of the field of agreement on disarmament. Another motive which can be deducted from this behavior is their endeavor to reduce tensions, to achieve more favorable conditions for the accelerated development of the less developed countries, and to improve their political and economic position in the world. Characteristic in this respect is their very radical

---

[57] *Yearbook of the United Nations* 1946—1947, p. 143.

attitude on the abolition of all armed forces and military institutions, except as necessary for internal security.

The nonaligned countries have been more explicit and radical in regard to demands for the abolition of foreign bases.[58] What is more, in that part of their demands relating to concrete and current problems, this question is especially referred to, particularly the American base at Guantanamo in Cuba. It is mentioned in the Belgrade Declaration[59] and the Cairo Program.[60] This is understandable when we bear in mind that the nonaligned countries were frequently forced to withstand external pressures, certainly no less in the era of diminished international tension between the blocs.

Finally the great similarity between the texts of 1946 and later ones, whether made at the Bandung Conference or at the conferences of nonaligned countries, or in the United Nations, is due to the fact that it is very difficult to say anything substantially new within the framework of general statements. General formulations may be adapted to the requirements of the times, but they essentially remain identical or similar. If some words have been differently chosen or some postulates put down more radically or less, this cannot practically influence the real course of events.

It was at the Cairo Conference that for the first time the need was stressed for preliminary measures,[61] i. e., actions which do not even appertain to the actual matter of disarmament but rather serve to help create the necessary climate for taking up measures which are directly related to disarmament. It implied the desirability of passing from general formulations to something more concrete, to limited and pragmatically defined partial or even only preparatory measures.

At any rate, this road was opened by the superpowers, especially at the initiative of the United States. The earlier Soviet opposition to such measures stopped when the U. S. S. R. achieved nuclear equlibrium with America. As a result, the United Nations Disarmament Commission, the eighteen of Geneva, spent most

---

[58] Paragraph 11 of the Bandung Declaration and Chapter VIII of the Cairo "Program".
[59] Paragraph 12.
[60] Chapter VIII of the Cairo "Program".
[61] Chapter VII of the Cairo "Program".

of their time in discussing these particular and concrete steps. This, at any rate, was the reason for the nonaligned countries being relatively inactive at the sessions of the commissions and rather reticent about making proposals, and even taking part in discussions.

C. ACTION FOR THE ATTAINMENT OF ECONOMIC OBJECTIVES

INITIAL ACTIONS IN THE 1950s

The Second World War contributed to the dramatic development of natural sciences and technology, but this development was dearly paid for not only by unproductive activities and war casualties but also by an uneven rate of economic development and achievement in the social domain. The United States emerged from the war as the dominant power, both in regard to economic and military might. Even the contrast between the U. S. and the other most advanced countries in Western Europe became greater than ever before. This gulf was a little less wide in the case of those developed countries which kept themselves outside the war (Switzerland and Sweden), but even so the disparity was increased.

All the other developed countries were either completely wrecked or had obsolete and worn-out production plants. Furthermore, the war caused such deep upheavals and so thoroughly retarded further progress that there was danger of still further broadening this gap. The situation was such that it was in the economic interest of the United States to assist an efficient recovery of its allies across the Atlantic, as well as in the other areas of high development outside Europe (Japan, Australia, New Zealand).

Soon after the war, after U. N. R. R. A. was discontinued,[62]

---

[62] UNRRA (United Nations Relief and Rehabilitation Administration) stopped work by a decision taken at the conference of this organization in the summer of 1946. Of the activities carried on by UNRRA, only those for child care (UNICEF) and refugees (first the International Refugee Organization — IRO — and then the office of high commissioner for refugees) were continued.

economic aid to Europe was launched.[63] For the first time in history it was realized that the modern world was so tightly knit that in the cases of great upheavals it was necessary to apply new methods of economic intervention at an international scale in order to reestablish the upset equilibrium. The Marshall Plan, irrespective of all the political ingredients and the motivation which produced it, constituted a very significant innovation in international relations.

It was not important whether it was a matter of giving "grants in aid" or favorable credits, in other words, it was not essential whether this was "unselfish" assistance or a well conceived self-interest which coincided with the interests of others. In international relations there are hardly ever any "unselfish" actions, especially in the field of economic activity. If such actions are made, they are exceptional and usually granted in cases of emergencies and local disasters.

The developed countries, partly by making a good use of the very efficiently offered aid, partly by organizing their own resources skillfully and thoroughly, soon managed to stand on their own feet and create a basis for the further development of their economies and for gaining a better place in the world community. This phenomenon, which took place in the highly developed part of mankind, remained isolated and did not extend to the other parts of the world. It certainly did not extend to the underdeveloped countries, those that had just become liberated, the former colonies, nor to the countries which had been independent but remained on the margins of world development.

The creation of the Organization for European Cooperation (OEEC)[64] and the early results of this action encouraged some of the existing underdeveloped countries to raise the question of economic aid in their part of the world. They based themselves on the premise that this aid was in the interest of the economic development of the advanced countries themselves. They also

---

[63] The Marshall Plan of assistance to Europe was launched in 1947 in a speech by U.S. Secretary of State George Marshall at Harvard University on June 21, and was made official at a conference in Paris from July 12 to 15 of the same year. The countries of Eastern Europe were also invited to the conference, but they did not attend.

[64] This organization was set up to help in the implementation of the Marshall Plan. It was the forerunner of the present OECD.

265

overestimated the effect which foreign financial aid was likely to have on their development. It is difficult to tell how much of this was due to the overestimation of the role of foreign aid in the post-war development of Western Europe, and how much to the lack of comprehension of the importance of corresponding internal social and political conditions for accelerated economic development.

All we can say is that these hopes were not fulfilled and no world mechanism was created to play the role, at an extended scale which the OEEC played in relations between Europe and America during the post-war years.

After the war it was not possible to go back to the pre-war patterns of world economic cooperation. The post-war world breathed differently, and it became obvious from the very first days that it would be moving forward along completely new roads. The wave of anti-colonial struggle hinted at some very far-reaching changes. These early signs of a new age in relations among nations, the precedent of aid to Europe and the need to somehow continue U.N.R.R.A.'s action and extend it universally led to the dispensation of technical aid and, during the last phase of the formation of the United Nations, to the introduction of important innovations in the Charter.

During the post-war years, the problems of world trade and of economic development acquired new dimensions and became more complex than ever before in history. Activity in the international community regarding these problems increased considerably. The setting up of the Economic and Social Council within the United Nations shows that the authors of the U. N. Charter were aware of the forthcoming evolution. In fact, the proposal to set up the Economic and Social Council as a separate organ of the United Nations came up only in the last stage of the discussion on the creation of a new world organization at the end of the war.

There was no such specialized organ in the League of Nations, although activity in the economic field was already steadily increasing. It is therefore understandable that the initial concept of the United Nations was limited to the creation of a general council modeled on the pre-war structure of the League of Nations. However, the practice of the United Nations has shown that even the new major body, the Economic and Social Council, was not sufficient and so the number of international organizations around the United Nations in the field of economic relations steadily increased, and soon after the war regional economic commissions were established. The first among them was the Economic Commission for Europe.

It is interesting that not much had been done in the field of trade or in that of direct assistance to organize and develop such material and legal conditions as would promote international cooperation. The attempt to create an international organization for trade was not successful. Instead of the anticipated organization, the Havana Conference[65] produced only the General Agreement on Tariffs and Trade (GATT), formed as a provisional and temporary solution until the expected ratification of the Havana Charter of the International Trade Organization (ITO)[66]

An analysis into this initial failure would demand a study of the post-war problems far more thorough than is possible here.[67] It should be stated, however, that efforts of the international organization to deal with these problems were insufficient. For example, the activity of the Economic and Social Council and its auxiliary organs in that respect was always inadequate.

On the other hand, the problems of trade, with the emphasis on the question of tariffs, were handled within the limited scope of GATT, and, what is more, very unilaterally, in the interests of the highly advanced countries with a market economy. Concern is almost exclusively for the problems and interests deriving from the trade of the highly advanced industrial countries. The principles on which GATT was established were based on mutual economic relations between countries at a similar, high level of economic development.

Endeavors at an international level to obtain favorable con-

---

[65] From November 21, 1947, to March 24, 1948, the World Trade Organization met in Havana, Cuba. This conference was supposed to result in the establishment of the International Trade Organization (ITO). For a short review of this conference see *Keesing's Contemporary Archives* 1952 to 1954, p. 13388.

[66] *Ibid.*

[67] For more details on the Havana Conference and the Charter drawn up there, see Clair Wilcox, *A Charter for World Trade*, The Macmillan Company, New York 1949.

267

ditions for an accelerated economic development of the under-developed countries required the solution of a number of international political problems. There was also the need to set into motion the internal social processes in the developing countries. This applied not only to newly liberated countries, but also to the countries in which capitalist relationships had been established much earlier, as in Latin America. There is no doubt that social evolution in the newly liberated countries of Asia and Africa had given a strong impulse to these countries' efforts to free themselves from economic dependence, as well as to the development of the progressive forces on that continent in general.

New views about inter-governmental, and particularly about economic relations, which received material force through this evolution soon began to influence development in the world in general. As had been shown at the first session of the U. N. Conference on Trade and Development, the rigid attitude and frontal opposition to the fundamental revision of the existing principles in international economic relations was abandoned, especially in the domain of trade.[68]

It was within this framework that the developing countries tried to arouse international action to facilitate their economic development. This action was organized within the framework of the United Nations some fifteen years ago. In the first stage their efforts were concentrated on the demand for international aid through a United Nations fund for capital investments. They were, however, only partially successful. Although certain forms of international financing were created, they were not satisfactory, and what is more important, institutions formed for that purpose did not have the necessary resources.

This increased activity was concentrated primarily on the demands for a larger financial and technical aid through international organizations within the United Nations. Still in the first years after the war, the developing countries pointed out that the terms of trade in the world market were not favorable for them. However, their demands met with a poor response. In the

---

[68] See *Konferencija Ujedinjenih nacija za trgovinu i razvoj* (United Nations Conference on Trade and Development), Institute of International Politics and Economics, Beograd 1964.

years of the accelerated armaments race, especially following the Korean War, there was a temporary jump in the prices of some raw materials, which was used as an argument that the world market does not operate permanently and uncompromisingly against the interests of the underdeveloped countries — suppliers of raw materials.

In fact, this short-lived boom was soon followed by a catastrophic drop in prices and a deterioration in price ratios at the expense of the underdeveloped countries. The area of international trade at the same time constantly expanded. The increasing number of new countries made this disproportion even greater, and their stubborn demands gave this course of events the character of a serious world-wide ferment.

THE U.N. CONFERENCE ON TRADE AND DEVELOPMENT

The nonexistence of a universal international organization in the field of world trade and the absence of almost any effort to regulate the trends which were going more and more against the interests of the underdeveloped countries became a major problem of international relations. However, the attempt to fill this void during the 1960s was not and could not be just a mere repetition of the Havana failure.

The picture of the world in the meanwhile had so changed that it was necessary to give the entire question not only new dimensions, in view of the larger number of independent countries and increased volume of world trade, but also a new substance. This new substance derived not only from the greater significance of the trade of more developed countries with the underdeveloped countries, but also from the increased importance of trade for economic development in general. It arose from the ever faster development of natural sciences and the application of their results in technology and economic activities. An1, finally, it was conditioned by deep social changes resulting from the increased number of state trading socialist countries in the world, and from their greater participation in international life.

The growing disparity between the need to approach the question of world trade within a universal framework, in an organized and systematic method, and the unsatisfactory solutions provided by the U. N. and GATT, gave rise to demands for the convention of a U. N. conference on trade and development, and later to demands for the establishment of permanent, organized activity in the field of international economic relations and for certain corrections in trade relations which would tend to protect the underdeveloped countries.

This was the motive which triggered off the activity of the underdeveloped countries and of those nonaligned countries which assumed the initiative to press for the convention of the United Nations Conference on Trade and Development.[69]

In this action special attention was concentrated on the problems of trade. It was pointed out that theoretical premises about the unfavorable position of the underdeveloped countries in the world market were already sufficiently confirmed in practice, and that it was necessary for the international community to intervene in an organized manner in order to prevent a slowdown in the growth of these countries owing to the unfavorable influence of the new situation in international trade. Insistence on the creation of new relationships in trade between the developed and underdeveloped countries cannot, however, substitute for the transfer of larger resources into their countries. In other words, the need for international capital financing remained acute, but it was necessary to urgently correct market relationships in favor of the underdeveloped countries.

The action of the underdeveloped countries came into the center of attention of the international community as one of the most significant developments in international relations. It appeared on the world scene as a controversy in which the interested parties opposed each other at international conferences and outside them, and this dispute more and more affected the political constellation of the present-day world. On the other hand, the forcefulness of the problem of economic development greatly

---

[69] The need for a conference was mentioned for the first time at the Belgrade meeting of the heads of nonaligned countries, and later in the resolution of the U.N. General Assembly which met soon after the Belgrade Conference in 1961.

depends on political relations in the world. In other words, the problem of economic development and the demands of the underdeveloped countries took the form of a conflict between the rich and the poor countries.

However, this conflict did not have the character of an antagonism which is resolved by a social confrontation. The demands of the underdeveloped countries call for a joint and coordinated activity designed to promote the general interests of all countries, irrespective of the level of their economic development. The difference between the highly developed and the underdeveloped countries lies in the fact that the immediate as well as long-range interests of the latter coincide only with the long-range and not with the short-range interests of the developed countries.

Motivated by their immediate economic interests, as well as by certain socio-political considerations, the developed countries opposed internationally organized and coordinated efforts to overcome the existing differences in the levels of development. This subjective reaction, opposition based on narrowly understood short-range interests of the dominant social and political factors in the developed countries, gave this problem the character of a controversy, which in fact can be resolved only by establishing cooperation on the basis of common interests.

The problem of the underdeveloped countries cannot be solved by insistence on its conflict character, but rather by removal of the antagonisms based on narrowmindedness and bedazzlement by the benefits which the rich may momentarily have from inequality. However, the interests of the underdeveloped countries cannot be safeguarded if the conflict with the developed countries is aggravated, but only if the rich are brought around to actively participate in the general world action to accelerate the development of the underdeveloped countries. We should not be misled by the fact that the underdeveloped countries occasionally use methods of political pressure. It is not essential what methods are used, or even whether their efforts are being transferred to the political terrain. What is important is that the action is so conducted that it leads towards a solution, not through the defeat of the other side, through its downfall from the position it holds, but through agreement. Let us repeat, this is not a conflict of antagonistic social forces but rather a dispute between categories of countries having different immediate interests, but common long-range interests.

Characteristic in this respect was cooperation among all the underdeveloped countries at the U. N. Conference on Trade and Development. They formed themselves as a group, as a kind of association for the protection of their interests and for collective negotiation with the advanced countries. Their unanimity, despite economic differences and political and social disparity, showed that the pressure of the people in those countries had grown to such an extent that, at least as regards the underdeveloped countries, subjective factors and short-range interests had to give way before the permanent and general needs and requirements. This at any rate was the basis for cooperation among these countries at conferences on trade and development.

In the meantime, difficulties in the way of accelerated economic development of the underdeveloped countries ceaselessly grew and became more and more complicated. In order not to lag behind the developed countries, the underdeveloped countries had somehow to secure more resources to invest into their production and modernization. This was necessary not only in order to increase internal investment and final consumption but also in order to improve the structure of exports which would help to earn more foreign exchange to cover increased imports rendered necessary by economic growth.

Consequently, economic development requires more favorable terms of trade, and these on the other hand cannot be fully achieved without economic development and without export surpluses in those categories in which the price ratios in the market are most favorable. In other words, emphasis on trade does not exclude insistence on a speeded up economic development, but, on the contrary, cannot be realized without it. This brings us to the further conclusion that only by resolving the problem of trade can the basic problems of the underdeveloped countries be resolved.

This problem affects all the underdeveloped countries and areas in the world, but they have not all consciously and actively responded to these development tendencies. Only some countries were active, those which were able to raise an independent political action and at the same time were sufficiently resolute to make an independent approach and assume an energetic attitude in the defense of their interests. Those were the very same countries which paved the way for the policy of nonalignment.

As has already been mentioned earlier, the nonaligned countries insisted on actions which would improve their difficult economic position. From the very outset they were the politically active nucleus which rallied most of the third world countries in an endeavor to improve their economic position. They were the lodestar and the force of attraction which gave nonalignment resilience against erosion and undermining from outside.

The first idea which can be directly related to the Geneva Conference was mooted at the Belgrade Conference in September 1961, and the first opposition to that idea was manifested at the session of the United Nations General Assembly a few weeks later. The developed countries attempted to bloc the convening of the conference. The wide support which the nonaligned coun. tries received for their idea and the backing from a large number of underdeveloped countries forced the developed countries to postpone their decision.

The underdeveloped countries did not wish to force the issue although they had a large number of votes and also enjoyed the support of the COMECON socialist countries. They believed that for the success of the entire venture it was better that the developed countries should agree to the holding of the conference. Thus a compromise was achieved whereby the United Nations Secretary General would be asked to survey the opinion of the member countries and to communicate their replies to the U.N. Economic and Social Council during its session in the summer of 1962. Afterwards the matter was to be referred again to the General Assembly in the autumn of the same year.[70]

Soon afterwards the economic conference of the nonaligned countries was held in Cairo, immediately before the summer session of the Economic and Social Council. The number of replies which had by then reached the U.N. Secretary General was

---

[70] GAOR, 16th Sess. Suppl. No. 17 (A/5100), p. 14.

not large, and the position of the protagonists of the conference would have been rendered very difficult without the psychological impact of the Cairo Conference. The participants at the Cairo Conference, namely, acted unanimously in favor of a world economic conference and resolutely tried to influence the further course of events.[71] In this action the nonaligned countries have acted as a strong coordinating force for the underdeveloped world. At the U.N. Economic and Social Council session in the summer of 1962 in Geneva, the turning point was reached and the developed countries ended their opposition to the holding of the conference.[72]

This, of course, does not mean that they had given up being suspicious of that broad gathering at which fundamental international economic problems were to be considered. Agreement to the conference was only an overture to new controversies in connection with the agenda, basic character and goals of the conference, and later on, at the conference itself, in connection with the form and content of its final act. Throughout the preparations and during the conference itself, all these debates were exceptionally acrimonious, most of all in connection with the dialogue between the developed and the underdeveloped countries.

After the ruling of the Economic and Social Council in Geneva, the General Assembly's job was no longer difficult. However, the underdeveloped countries were not satisfied only with the decision to call the conference but immediately set about definiting its tasks. Thus in the year that followed, the platform of the 75 countries was formulated.[73] The declaration of the 75 underdeveloped countries served as the common point of departure in considering the fundamental questions and thus augured the unanimous stand of the underdeveloped countries at the forthcoming conference.

The declaration not only became a platform and starting position of all the underdeveloped countries, but also served

---

[71] For the text of the final act of the Cairo Economic Conference in 1962 see the Appendix.
[72] ESCOR, 34th Sess. Suppl. No. 1 (E/3671), p. 7.
[73] See the text in the Appendix as part of the U.N. General Assembly resolution on the convening of the Conference on Trade and Development, No. 1897, adopted on November 1, 1963.

274

as the base for the coordination of policies at the conference itself. The role of the New York meeting, at which the declaration of the 75 countries was passed, had become clear from the very first days of the Geneva Conference. The most active underdeveloped countries took up the initiative again, and so discussions started on how to implement the platform adopted at the New York meeting. Coordinating bodies for the plenary session of the conference and all its committees were agreed upon. They set up negotiating groups with other countries, with the developed Western countries and with the COMECON countries. These organizational measures assured a unity which had been already created on the basis of joint resolutions and declarations. Without these earlier common actions, there could have been no unity among the underdeveloped countries. However, it is equally clear that the problems which cropped up at the Geneva Conference were such as to demand a special effort to maintain this unity. It should be remembered that the underdeveloped countries include a large number of countries from different continents and from different climes, and that their per capita national income roughly varied between U.S. $ 50 and $ 500. These countries were at very different levels of economic as well as social development.

The significance of the close cooperation among the underdeveloped countries in Geneva should be assessed in the light of the fact that this cooperation was achieved by countries with totally different foreign policies. It is sufficient to name Cuba and South Vietnam as two extreme examples, both of which supported the action led by the nonaligned in Geneva. Consequently, cooperation among them was possible only on the basis of carefully formulated common interests, in fact vital interests which had to be recognized by the governments of these countries, irrespective of their orientations.

However, the concretization of general policies during discussions and negotiations at the conference set difficult tasks in regard to the maintenance of unity. There were special interests of some countries or groups of countries, which owing to geographical, climatic or other reasons had interests differing from those of other countries. This is, of course, where the degree of economic development and the structure of national economy and foreign trade mattered a great deal. These factors generally presented a much harder problem than political and social differences between some of the countries.

It was necessary to adhere strictly to democratic principles and parliamentarism within the coordination groups in order to find a common platform on each concrete question. This was all the more important as the developed countries had precisely reckoned that the underdeveloped countries would not be able to translate the general common policies from the platform of the 75 countries into the concrete language of demands and proposals for decisions. Coordinating efforts lasted almost throughout the conference, because new questions or new aspects of the questions under consideration constantly came up, especially in the phase of negotiations with other countries.[74]

The underdeveloped countries shaped their policies in separate committees,[75] their basic demand being to find ways and means of increasing the volume of their foreign trade and of increasing their income from that trade. For this purpose specific proposals were formulated about the freedom of access to the markets of the developed countries, about privileges and preferentials, about compensation for unfavorable price ratios, etc.

The developed countries did not come to the conference with prepared and coordinated policies. Even if some of the delegations did have some specific concepts, these were not formulated so as to be operatively considered, and in addition they were not coordinated with the policies of other countries on whose consent their application depended. This particularly applied to the conceptions of some West European countries, resulting in contradictory views among them and in a negative or passive

---

[74] Before and during the Geneva conference in 1964, there was a higher degree of regionalism than ever before among the underdeveloped countries. Each continent formed a caucus, and the entire group of "75" acted as an alliance of the continental groups of Asia, Africa and Latin America.

[75] The Conference had five plenary committees meeting simultaneously; their work was coordinated by the Conference Bureau headed by the president. The first committee studied trade in raw materials, the second — trade of manufactured goods, and the third — finances and invisible trade. The fourth committee considered organizational and institutional questions, and the fifth concerned itself with general principles. There were also a special committee within the third committee to study problems of maritime traffic, and a special committee for the problems of countries with no access to the sea which was formed within the fifth committee.

attitude to the initiatives put forward by the underdeveloped countries.

It was only towards the end of the conference, when it had become clear that the common front of the developing countries would not collapse, that the developed countries became disturbed about the possible consequences of the failure of the conference. Even then nothing much happened, which was understandable since they could not possibly work out a common platform within a matter of two to three weeks. Consequently, the only achievement was the promise that all these questions would be considered in more detail and more constructively after the conference.

It is interesting in this connection to read a passage from an article by André Philippe, head of the French delegation to the conference, published in the review *"Développement et civilisations"*:

"It would seem, therefore, that in the beginning the developed countries had no clear awareness of their worldwide responsibilities, nor willingness for a creative initiative. The majority of them came to a conference, which they did not want, with a general feeling of scepticism, with the conviction that the developing countries would spend their energy and come up with unrealizable demagogical demands that would produce no results. However, it may be said that one of the results of the conference was that the industrial countries during the debate took the developing countries more seriously and became more and more conscious of the importance of the problem. They did not yet come so far as to search for a political initiative. There is still, even with those who are taking some initiative, unwillingness for a real involvement; however, there is a beginning of disquiet, misgivings, of the feeling of a certain responsibility."[76]

Contempt for the conference was evident during the first two months in the behavior of the delegations of the developed countries in all the committees. It was obvious that short-term interests and short-sighted policies prevailed. What is more,

---

[76] "Développement et civilisations", Paris 1964, No. 19, p. 54.

insistence by the underdeveloped countries that the conference should at least concretize the agreement on principle achieved within GATT was taken as hostile pressure, and the developed Western countries responded by an uncompromising and often cynical attitude.

The underdeveloped countries also held talks during the conference with the East European member countries of COMECON, which were most frequently described as countries with a central system of planning or as countries with a monopoly in foreign trade. These distinctions were aimed at showing that there was no question of an ideological controversy but of distinction on the basis of differences in economic systems. The COMECON countries approached the idea of the conference predominantly from the standpoint of those problems which interested them most of all, primarily political discrimination in trade, which at that time was still applied against them by the Western countries. Gradually during the preparations in 1963 and before the conference in 1964, the COMECON countries and in particular the Soviet Union began to take a greater interest in the policies of the underdeveloped countries. During the conference, many initial policies were corrected, and negotiations with the underdeveloped countries soon produced agreed solutions. Naturally, the underdeveloped countries had to adjust some of their formulations and concrete demands which, with all the good will present, were inacceptable or inapplicable to the COMECON countries. Of all the COMECON countries, Rumania alone showed some independence and supported most of the basic policies of the underdeveloped countries. This difference did not bring about any modifications towards the end of the conference, because the underdeveloped countries and the COMECON countries arrived at a large measure of agreement.

The significance of the agreement between them does not only lie in the essence of the agreement but also in its political implications in regard to general international relations. There is no doubt that the favorable outcome of negotiations with the COMECON countries influenced the policies of the developed countries of the West. They were at first scornful about the importance of these talks and about the role of the COMECON

278

countries in the world economy in general, but at the same time they tried to convince the underdeveloped countries that it was not in their interest to hold talks with the COMECON countries. However, all their efforts were to no avail. All the underdeveloped countries, including those which otherwise follow an openly anti-Soviet policy, approved those talks and the agreements reached. However, later experience showed that the effect of these agreements for the development of economic relations between the underdeveloped countries and COMECON was very limited.

Besides direct talks there were also discussions at the public meetings of the committees and plenary meetings, and at the more or less public general meetings of the underdeveloped countries. These latter meetings became particularly important manifestations towards the end of the conference, at the time of the greatest crisis in the talks. This is when the members of the governments of the underdeveloped countries who were leading their delegations came together again, after having gone home following the general debate.

The discussions and final positions clearly showed the mood in different parts of the world. They showed that many underdeveloped countries in Africa and Asia believed that the critical point was arriving when either there would be a genuine change in the attitude of the developed countries or they would be forced to definitively state the impossibility of an agreement. Some ministers and prominent statesmen delivered very sharp speeches which betrayed no differences dividing their foreign policies. The same tone was used by the statesmen of the Philippines, Ethiopia and Tanzania, for instance.[77]

The conference on trade and development in Geneva was undoubtedly the most significant achievement of the nonaligned countries in their efforts to improve the economic situation of the underdeveloped countries. It had fully shown all the possibilities and breadth of action that can be realized when these countries activate themselves in the struggle for their basic and not unreasonable interests. Here their statesmen acted fully in accordance with the concepts of their peoples about their basic interests.

---

[77] There is no report on these meetings in the official records. The author here relies on his own observations made at the Conference.

It is precisely this action that should be especially mentioned, both as an achievement and as an example for the better understanding of the activity and potential of the nonaligned countries in world events.

The action was moved at a time when the economic difficulties of the underdeveloped countries were growing rapidly and when their international economic situation had become increasingly unfavorable. However, it also coincided with the time when the political movement of the nonaligned reached its peak and when the character of economic demands was so general that it easily united all the underdeveloped countries irrespective of the economic differences existing among them.

Furthermore, the character of the action, the convening of a world conference and the creation of institutions which would raise general questions, suited the needs of the underdeveloped countries and the position of the movement of nonalignment which at the same time had reaffirmed its standpoints at the Belgrade Conference and in the United Nations General Assembly. However, this character was a product of the moment, and the success of the action depended not only on its content but also on its timing.

Since general discussions were on the whole completed at the Geneva Conference in the spring of 1964 and then at the U.N. General Assembly in New York in the autumn of the same year, the continuation of the action could only be successful if results were achieved on the lines of the general policies which were more or less laid down in Geneva. There and at the United Nations meeting in the autumn of the same year the permanent organizational framework for further action was established. The U.N. Conference on Trade and Development became a new permanent and specialized institution within the framework of the United Nations.

What happened later is also characteristic, because a general world conference as an instrument for concrete decision-making was inadequate. Another conference at New Delhi, India, in 1968, proved to be a failure, precisely because it did not have anything to add to the general policies from Geneva, and was neither organizationally nor in regard to the content of the demands made a suitable forum for the achievement of concrete results.[78]

It was not easy to switch from a more or less parliamentary and principle-laying action in Geneva to the negotiating method of concrete dialogues between realistically grouped partners, in an atmosphere in which there was still a tendency for broad fronts to be created for general battles over questions of principle. It was necessary to preserve the political instrument of broad unity in order to safeguard the positions won in Geneva, which imposed the obligation of tabling the demands of all categories, and even of individual countries, from the group of the underdeveloped.

Finally, the state of relations was not ripe for altogether concrete and business-like talks, because there were certain still unresolved problems of a general character. Thus, for instance, it was necessary to see what tariff and other facilities could be allowed for the export of industrial products from the underdeveloped to the developed countries. This question was much too particular for consideration within a general world conference, but it could also not be resolved within the framework of a much too narrow group of negotiators on economic cooperation, because it affected the interests of a larger circle of countries and even the general regime of trade in the world.

The conference of the underdeveloped countries in Algiers in the autumn of 1967, which was prepared at New Delhi, foreshadowed the difficulties which really did occur at the world conference in New Delhi. The list of demands which was included in the "Algiers Charter"[79] was too large for concrete talks and did not suit such an approach at all, but it did reveal the differentiation among the underdeveloped countries. This document also showed that before concrete measures could be taken it was necessary to raise the question of the internal system and the efforts made by the underdeveloped countries themselves, as well as the question of their mutual cooperation as their own contribution to efforts to improve their position and accelerate their development.

---

[78] Vladimir Dragomanović, *Dileme UNCTAD-a* (Dilemmas of UNCTAD), Međunarodni problemi (International Problems), Beograd 1968, No. 3.

[79] See the Appendix for the text.

The conference was being held at an inauspicious time of acute difficulties in world finances and economic straits in a number of developed countries. This, of course, did not create a favorable background for discussions about concessions which the developed countries should make in order to ease the pressure on the underdeveloped countries. It should be borne in mind that the concessions in Geneva were very largely made because the developed countries knew from their political experience that the realization of principles in international relations is always more difficult than attainment of agreement in connection with a text. They did not agree to any concrete concessions in Geneva and thus interrupted the dialogue precisely at the transitory stage, a move which in advance hampered a clear definition of the next step which was to be made at New Delhi.

Regarded as a whole, the action of the nonaligned countries in the economic field had checkered fortunes. It started off with a relatively easy and certainly very important achievement of obtaining technical aid within the framework of the United Nations, followed by the formal setting up of a fund for financial aid after prolonged efforts in the U.N., which was, however, never set into operation. After that disappointment, there came another apparent success in the form of the conference on trade and development in Geneva, followed by the failure of the second conference at New Delhi.

As has already been pointed out, all the successes were of a general nature, and except for technical aid, were only formal and on paper, whereas failures came when realities were to be faced in connection with the concrete implementation of principles. In the case of technical aid, realization was simple and general principles could be implemented without any trouble, and the developed countries were quite prepared to do something. Later actions yielded essentially nothing more than what could be achieved by political pressure from a firmly united front. In brief, the action of the nonaligned in cooperation with the broadest circle of the underdeveloped countries was a very important case in international relations which showed the possibilities and limitations of political action in the economic field when it is not backed by real economic arguments, i. e., by pressure or by making use of the interests of one's own and the opposing sides. It is obvious that with a purely political arsenal one cannot win economic battles in the international arena, and political victories cannot be achieved in the economy if political, i. e., moral force, is not also backed by material strength.

D. ACTION AGAINST COLONIALISM AND NEOCOLONIALISM

The abolition of colonies and the struggle for the independence of colonial nations preceded the appearance of nonalignment in the world. As has been shown in the first chapter of this book, the liberation of the colonies was one of the prerequisites for the emergence of nonalignment. It is therefore quite understandable that this question has played a very important and specific role in the activity of the nonaligned nations, especially during the early years. First of all, it was the continuation of the same process which created the first protagonists of nonalignment, and it was the best, in fact practically the only way of increasing the number of adherents to nonalignment. The first international action which marked an independent political evolution in the third world, the Bandung Conference, devoted special attention to this question. It may even be said that it was mainly convened in connection with this question, which is what gave the conference the dimensions of an important international event.

Yet the struggle for the liberation of the colonies had begun long before the Bandung Conference. Its history began with resistance to the subjection by the colonial powers. After the loss of independence, almost everywhere in the colonies the struggle continued flickering and in some countries it was never extinguished at all. The series of mutinies in India marked the entire 19th century, and in the 20th century the modern anticolonial movement began. Similarly, in some of the colonies in North Africa, as well as in Central Africa, traditional resistance continued

283

almost right through to the period of the beginning of the modern anti-colonial movements.[80] The question therefore arises where the difference lies between these two categories of opposing the colonial powers.

It seems proper to describe as modern liberation movements those endeavors which are inspired not by the old order and the old, pre-colonial patterns, but rather by modern political concepts and aspirations. In other words, whereas in resisting colonization the old backward society was defending itself against outside intervention, occupation and subjugation, the modern movements are inspired by the achievements which had sprung up in Europe, and which refuse to go back to the old relationships but rather hope to create new institutions and a new society.

These movements, consequently, spring up from two sources: one from the people themselves and their struggle for emancipation, and the other from the contemporary social and political achievements, made mainly in Europe or under the influence of developments in Europe. Whereas desire for freedom partly relies upon the tradition of resistance to colonization, on the memories of the old society which inevitably tends to be idealized, it also partially springs up and grows under the influence of the changes which had taken place in society during colonialism. This second element is significant, although the metropolises were generally wary of allowing their colonies to develop social relationships and a sufficiently high level of education, in order to retain colonial power all the more easily.

Yet, the situation in some of the colonies was not the same as in others. In some places, education and development of modern social relationships were rapid and comprehensive; elsewhere they had only just begun to develop in the last years of colonial power.[81] However, we are not interested in history, but

---

[80] This refers in particular to the uprisings in North-West Africa and in the countries of the Maghreb and to resistance in some areas of Equatorial Africa, especially in the Ashanti region in the former Gold Coast colony (now Ghana). Armed struggles were still being carried on in the twentieth century.

[81] These differences were a product of the special conditions in each individual colony, but also of the time when the colony was liberated and of the nature of the interests which the colonizer had in a given colony. For instance, there is a great difference in the economic development in colonial times between Guinea and Ghana, even though they have similar traditions from the pre-colonial past and all other conditions are similar.

rather in the influence which this evolution has had upon the non-aligned countries in the years of their greatest activity in connection with the colonial question. We must therefore go back to the influence which was becoming gradually stronger and was penetrating into the colonies as a reflection of the socio-political development in Europe. We must bear in mind the revolutionary social and national movements which had so fundamentally changed the face of Europe since the French Revolution.

Nonaligned countries were able to rely in the majority of colonies on more or less widespread and more or less militant movements and organizations which were inspired by modern ideas. Some of these movements were under a very strong influence of the socialist revolutions in Russia and Eastern Europe, but others looked towards liberalistic and democratic ideas arisen in the highly developed countries of the West. The movements, therefore, were not unified, either in the colonies or in different regions, and not even within the regions themselves. However during the height of the struggles for liberation these dissensions usually did not come into the open in an acute form, and co-operation was usually possible.

This cooperation facilitated the joint action of the nonaligned countries, which even among themselves differed considerably from one another in the ideological sense. Furthermore, among them as well as in the colonies, there occurred gradual or sudden changes in ideological orientations. However, all this did not substantially affect their action. The nonaligned countries were also not able to substantially influence the orientation and profile of the liberation movements in various colonies. These movements generally had their ideological platform as soon as they appeared, and they appeared before the Bandung Conference and before nonalignment started influencing world events. This, of course, does not mean that these movements did not change. Changes were continual, especially after the achievement of independence, when these movements turned into ruling parties and their leaders were transformed from revolutionaries into statesmen.

Although the first wave of anti-colonial movements had started in Southeast Asia and embraced only a limited number of countries, it played a very important role, having encompassed an area inhibited by several hundred million people.[82] In Africa, independence-seeking movements and groups made their appearance from the very beginning of the operation of the United Nations. These early movements, relying exclusively upon the United Nations, were, of course, limited by the provisions of the Charter, which did not provide for independence or any form of emancipation of the colonies. Under the Charter the colonial governments were expected to very little more than render accounts about their administration of the colonies and to report on social and economic measures designed to improve the living conditions of the indigenous population.[83]

These were the circumstances in which the leaders of the emancipation movements in the colonies were to act. They were able to present before the committees of the United Nations the situation in their colonized countries. The support which these representatives of the so-called non-self-governing territories received in the United Nations grew from year to year, and it contributed to a certain measure to the strengthening of consciousness and mobilization of activists in some of the colonies, especially in Africa.

Even before the first collective and separate action of the third world countries, their cause received more and more support so that the idea of revising the policies in the Charter began to mature.[84] It is interesting to note that in the early discussions during the first post-war years it was customary to object that certain matters transcended the framework of the Charter whenever the questions of granting independence arose. In later years the representatives of the colonial powers used these arguments less and less, and by tacit agreement or by passive resignation the spirit of the chapter dealing with "non-self-governing territories" began to change.[85]

---

[82] India, Pakistan, Burma, Indochina and Indonesia were the first countries in which the anti-colonial movement gained strength and at that time these countries had close to 600 million inhabitants.

[83] See the U.N. Charter, articles 73 and 74.

[84] The question of colonies is discussed in the Charter in Chapter XI, which is entitled, "Declaration on Non-Self-Governing Territories".

[85] This is hard to document, because in the majority of these debates there are no verbatim transcripts of the proceedings. The author relies on his direct observations from this period in the United Nations.

This evolution took place during the first post-war decade, and the countries rallied in Bandung were already able to expect that no one would be prepared to defend the institutions of colonies as a matter of principle. The maintenance of the colonies was justified, if a formal justification was indeed attempted, with the claim that the people of a colony were not yet ripe for independence. The institution itself had been discredited and rejected during the first few years after the war. Merit for this mainly belongs to the liberation struggle of the peoples of Southeast Asia. Especially important was the long armed struggle of the Indonesian people, which mobilized not only the activists in other colonies but also progressive people in Europe and the other developed parts of the world.

The first United Nations action in connection with the colonial question was not directly relevant to the problem of the independence of colonies. It was the question of the status of Indians in South Africa. The question was raised by India during the second part of the first session of the General Assembly in the autumn of 1946.[86] It was the first delegation which represented independent India. The head of the delegation was Nehru's sister, Vijaya Lakshmi Pandit. The question was raised as a result of a racialist law in South Africa, which limited the right of citizens of Indian origin to purchase of land.

The question was further sharpened in the following year, when in addition to racial discrimination against citizens of Indian origin, the question of racial discrimination against the natives was also raised. Alongside this issue consideration was also given to the fate of South West Africa, which the Union of South Africa had decided to incorporate. These two questions, although no positive results had been reached in either of them, mobilized all the countries in the United Nations as well as the world public opinion in connection with the question of Africa.

When the Bandung Conference was held, these questions had been considered in the United Nations for several years without results, but in the meantime a broad and almost unanimous support crystallized for the resolution on racial discrimination

---

[86] GAOR, 1st Sess. Suppl. No. 136, 137, 138 (A/205 and A/205 Add. 1) pp. 1006—1062.

and the fate of the peoples in the colonies. The Bandung Conference continued and further encouraged developments in the existing world situation. A special resolution and a declaration[87] dedicated to this question were adopted at this conference. In the resolution two concrete questions were raised: support was given to Indonesia's demand for the inclusion of West Irian, and also to the struggle for the independence of Algeria, Morocco and Tunisia.

Far more significant was the declaration, in which the question of colonies was considered as a matter of principle. Colonialism was proclaimed as an evil which should be abolished. The provisions of the Charter about colonies were not at all mentioned, being unsatisfactory and contrary to this thesis, but the Charter provisions about the rights of man were emphasized. From these provisions the need for the abolition of colonialism was deduced. The participants at the conference proclaimed support for all those who fight for freedom and independence of the colonies, and the colonial powers were invited to endorse these demands.

In addition to these acts, the colonial question was indirectly raised in Bandung, too, in the declaration on peace and cooperation and in the resolution on the rights of man and on self-determination.[88] In the first of these two documents, a demand was made for the recognition of the sovereignty of "all the races and nations, big and small". This implicitly touched on the colonial question by reaffirming the right to sovereignty, while opposing the right, expressed in the Charter, for the colonial powers to govern the colonies. In the second document there were two points relevant to this problem. First of all the demand was made for the self-determination of "peoples and nations", which was included among the most important rights of man, and then again the question of racial discrimination in the Union of South Africa was separately raised.

As we can see from the above, Bandung gave a formal sanction to certain results of continuous endeavors in the United

---

[87] See the Appendix for the texts.
[88] See the Appendix for the texts.

288

Nations General Assembly. At the given moment it was difficult to go much further than that. It was still necessary to insist on the recognition of the basic demand, namely the rejection of colonialism as an acceptable relationship among peoples. The significance of the Bandung Conference in regard to the further development of this question was not so much in the presentation of new ideas or in the further development of concrete demands, but rather in the breadth of the political range at which discussions were conducted. Irrespective of pro-Western orientation, no Asian or African countries could turn a deaf ear to the invitation to struggle for the liquidation of colonialism.[89]

The Bandung Conference was being held at a moment when it seemed that the end had come to the violent period of the cold war and when the anti-colonial evolution in Africa was acquiring concrete aspects which were already hinting at the forthcoming decolonization of this continent. The subsequent actions in the United Nations and at separate gatherings of the nonaligned countries relied on the content and the breadth of the platform of this Afro-Asian conference. The colonial question had always received wide support in these circles, which contributed to the development of this idea in Europe, too.

How necessary this evolution was can best be seen from the fact that as early as 1946, at the second part of the first session of the General Assembly, a country as enlightened as Sweden took part in the endeavor to "de-politize" the question of racial discrimination in South Africa, suggesting, to the satisfaction of the colonial countries, that the question should be sent to the International Court of Justice.[90] Ten years later racial discrimination and colonialism became major international political issues, opposed by only a couple of countries, notably the Republic of South Africa and Portugal, with a few other countries, abstaining from voting.

---

[89] Political considerations and divisions were very much in evidence in discussions on general political questions, but the discussion of colonial problems was largely non-partisan.

[90] Whereas India advocated that this question should be handled as a political matter, the Western colonial powers insisted on referring it to the International Court of Justice in order to avoid a political discussion and bad feelings with South Africa. It is interesting that Sweden agreed to submit the resolution to the Court. *Keesing's Contemporary Archives* 1946—1948, p. 8325; *Yearbook of the United Nations* 1946—1947, p. 147.

A year before the first meeting of the heads of nonaligned countries, a joint move was made by the nonaligned countries at the fifteenth session of the United Nations General Assembly in regard to the colonial question. Here, at the proposal of the nonaligned countries, the resolution was voted on the colonial question[91] which in fact tacitly and in a roundabout way overruled the Charter premise on the colonial question. On this occasion, of course, no one even attempted to mention that the resolution was outside the framework of the Charter; in fact there was absolutely no open and frontal opposition. The resolution was adopted with 90 votes for and none against.[92]

The resolution of the nonaligned countries repeated the basic premises from Bandung about the rights of man and self-determination. However, it went considerably further than the position adopted in 1955. First of all, the argument that the natives were not yet "ripe" for independence and that they should first be "helped" to achieve an adequate political, educational, economic etc. level, was rejected out of hand. The resolution further called for the cessation of any armed or other reprisals against the liberation movements in the colonies, so as to enable them to develop freely and achieve their ends by peaceful methods. At the same time, the colonial powers were called upon to immediately take steps to hand over government to the indigenous population without any discrimination whatever. The resolution also expressed opposition to any attempt at breaking the national unity of the people in the colonies.

The resolution ended with a characteristic exhortation for the observance of this resolution parallel with the United Nations Charter and the Declaration on the Rights of Man. The aim was obviously to give this resolution the significance of a constitutional act. This was certainly out of the awareness that the Charter's provisions on this matter were inadequate. At any rate, while referring to the Charter, reference was made to the provisions on

---

[91] See the text of the resolution in the Appendix.

[92] In the voting in the General Assembly on November 28, 1960, the following delegations abstained: Australia, Belgium, the Dominican Republic, Great Britain, France, Portugal, the Republic of South Africa, Spain, and the U.S.A.

290

the rights of man in the Charter rather than to the chapter on colonies, which was not mentioned at all.

It is also significant that the resolution was adopted over a parallel resolution proposed by the Soviet Union. The Soviet draft resolution, which was rejected, asked for colonialism to be abolished by 1961 at the latest. The nonaligned countries were more realistic and did not set down such formalistic demands which would not have much of a chance of being implemented. The resolution was not treated as an operative act, but as an amendment to the conception of the United Nations. It was, the only possible wording, in fact, which was meaningful.

Having met in Belgrade, the heads of the nonaligned states were not able to say anything new in connection with the colonial question after the resolution that had been adopted the preceding year. The Belgrade Declaration[93] therefore reaffirmed its endorsement of that resolution. The participants at the conference "recommend the immediate unconditional, total and final abolition of colonialism and resolved to make a concerted effort to put an end to all types of new colonialism and imperialist domination in all its forms and manifestations."[94]

The first part of the Belgrade document established that "imperialism is weakening," and that "colonial empires and other forms of foreign oppression of the peoples in Asia, Africa and Latin America are gradually disappearing from the stage of history." This was a sign of optimism after successes achieved in all the three continents, as well as victories in the struggle for modern conceptions in the General Assembly the previous year. However, it was soon to become evident that the situation was not so rosy.

At the next meeting of the heads of the nonaligned countries the tone was already somewhat different. In the meantime a number of new conflicts arose or old conflicts flared up again. While referring to an improvement in the international situation (meaning the cold war), they found that the situation of the third world had deteriorated: "Imperialism, colonialism and neo-colo-

---

[93] See the text in the Appendix.
[94] Chapter III, paragraph 1.

nialism constitute a basic source of international tension and conflict because they endanger world peace and security." Instead of satisfaction with the achieved results of decolonization, in Cairo it is found with satisfaction "that the movements of national liberation are engaged in different regions of the world, in a heroic struggle against neo-colonialism, and the practice of apartheid and racial discrimination."[95]

Whereas in Belgrade the accent was on the achievement of independence, here it was rather on the threat to it. The abatement of the cold war did not bring peace to the third world but rather a worsening of the position of the newly liberated countries. This was also mentioned in some special points of the document, which relate to concrete cases. They were the Congo, the Portuguese colonies in Africa, Southern Rhodesia, the Palestinian problem, and racial discrimination in the Republic of South Africa.

In regard to the Congo, emphasis was placed on the foreign intervention and a call was made for unity and cooperation within the framework of the Organization of African Unity and for the settlement of disputes with neighboring countries. The toughest part was that relating to the Portuguese colonies. They reiterated the theses which had already been adopted in the Union Netions, but they went even further. Participants were invited to give the liberation movements all material aid, including financial and military; recognition and support was sought for the revolutionary government of Angola, as well as the application of very energetic measures against Portugal, such as the breaking off of all relations and an economic boycott, while the countries aiding Portugal were asked to stop doing so forthwith. Aid to the people of Southern Rhodesia followed the lines of the United Nations resolution, namely, to encourage the British government to intervene in Southern Rhodesia, establish a democratic order and abolish racial discrimination.

In the sections about Palestine and the Republic of South Africa, well-known attitudes were again taken. In regard to the situation in the Middle East, the Arabs succeeded in obtaining formulations which more faithfully reflected the Arab positions

---

[95] Chapter I of the Cairo "Program".

than had been done in Belgrade in 1961. In comparison with the earlier conference, more was said and more directly in Cairo than at any previous conference or gathering, in regard to concrete measures for an energetic action concerning colonial problems. However, this action did not ever take place. Soon after the Cairo Conference the activity of the nonaligned began to stagnate. In fact, the much less concrete conclusions from Belgrade had a greater reverberation in practice than the explicit and formally very energetic postulates from Cairo.

As can be concluded from this summary, the colonial question was in the focus of the nonaligned countries' attention form the beginning, and it remained there, but in rather different conditions. These changes derived both from the successes achieved in decolonization, which multiplied the number and increased the importance of the nonaligned countries, and from the new problems which appeared before the newly liberated countries.

CHAPTER FIVE

NEW TRENDS IN INTERNATIONAL
RELATIONS IN THE LATE 1960s

The easing of tensions between the great powers and blocs greatly influenced the general evolution in the world during the 1960s, especially in the second part of that decade. Although this tendency made itself strongly felt as early as the mid-1950s, it could not have a major bearing on international relations because of periodical relapses. The year 1955 indeed marked the beginning of relaxation, yet, just as after the shortest day in the middle of the winter, much time had to elapse before the spring thaw came.

This turning point was then hailed with great anticipation, but it was disappointed when a genuine relaxation did come about. Nonalignment aimed at the abolishment of the cold war and the rigid division into blocs as a prerequisite to the settlement of all the other problems of the third world. The new situation, therefore, had a very strong influence on the action and the behavior of the nonaligned countries. However, before we go into this matter, we should review the most important elements and characteristics of the easing of the cold war. It will make it easier for us to see how these changes influenced the nonaligned countries.

THE EASING OF TENSIONS WEAKENS
INTRA-BLOC COHESION

After the middle of the 1950s, or more exactly, after unanimity was reached on the disarmament resolutions at the ninth session of the United Nations General Assembly in 1954 and the four-power meeting in Geneva in the summer of 1955, the relations between the East and the West became much less strained. This timing has been accepted more or less by all the students of contemporary international relations, although momentary relaxations were occasionally followed by very severe deteriorations.[1]

It was, oddly enough, these deteriorations which showed that something essential did change in international relations. Whereas the crises in the early part of the 1950s, or still in the early years after the end of the Second World War, were used by both sides without any scruples or compunction to achieve maximum advantages in the psychological-political confrontation in order to retain or win over an ally, or in order to preserve or extend the area of influence — in the later crises the leading powers behaved with greater circumspection. Beside the desire to draw maximum benefit, there was an increasing awareness about the need to prevent the conflicts from degenerating into open and unrestrained strife between the leading world powers.[2]

Unanimity in the United Nations about disarmament and methods of achieving, it was based on a simultaneous realization of the implications for the world of the immensely increased destructive power of modern weapons.[3] The summit meeting of 1955 was the product of this consciousness which matured on both sides in the cold war at the same time. This meeting first of all

---

[1] There are as many different views on this question as there are studies. These differences in interpretation reflect frequently the influence of the momentary situation on the authors at the time they were making their analyses.

[2] This difference in behavior is brought into sharp focus if we compare the actions of each of the two superpowers in the Korean war in 1950 with their later behavior in regard to the war in Vietnam.

[3] There had been unanimity on only one other occasion — in 1946 at the first and second parts of the first session of the U.N. General Assembly.

served to openly endorse, in direct personal contacts between the most responsible statesmen, this general awareness and to indicate the steps that should be taken. In addition, the big four presented certain plans and agreed that foreign ministers, aided by experts, should start working out detailed plans which would transform this consciousness of the dangers arising from mutual conflicts into a permanent process of improvement in relations and stabilization of peace and security.[4]

The failure of the second part of the summer activity of the great powers was understandable, and it soon brought about a deterioration in relations. It was understandable because apart from awareness of the need to avoid a war at all costs, or the tension which might make war inevitable, nothing else substantially changed. The belief that international relations could be regulated by the influences of the governments of great powers proved to be naive and futile. This also meant that such subjective acts as conclusions and declarations or treaties and conventions cannot in themselves change political realities.

Consequently, deterioration immediately followed the first confrontation that came up as a result of essentially unchanged political relations between the protagonists of the cold war. The first great crisis appeared the very next year after the thaw of 1954 and 1955. Of the three events in the autumn of 1956, particularly significant was the crisis following the events in Hungary, because it produced a long deterioration in Soviet-American relations.[5] It was only in 1958 that a new thaw occurred, culminating in a visit to the United States by Soviet Premier Khrushchev.

And yet, the world did not go back to the old patterns nor to the renewal of tensions. The combination of the technical fact that armaments had become much too destructive to risk an open war, and of the political awareness on both sides that war must be avoided, created something new, something that never existed

---

[4] The four ministers of foreign affairs: John Foster Dulles, Harold Macmillan, V. M. Molotov and Antoine Pinnay met in Geneva from October 27 to November 16, 1955, but did not reach an agreement on any of the issues discussed. For the proceedings of the discussion, see *Keesing's Contemporary Archives 1955—1956*, p. 14537.

[5] That same autumn the well-known events in Poland took place, and there was an armed attack on Israel and the combined intervention of France and Great Britain in the area of the Suez Canal.

before, not even at times of relaxation, as, for example, during the efforts to put an end to the war in Korea.

The changed relations between the superpowers necessarily reflected on their relations with their allies. On the one hand, the danger of a war between the blocs was reduced, and thus the protective role of the bloc alliances lost much in urgency, whereas on the other hand, the credibility of the guarantees by the leading nuclear powers diminished because it was hard to believe that a superpower would fulfil its obligations to its allies at the price of a nuclear conflict with the other side.

This situation gave rise to doubts and gradually even to a weakening of faith in the defensive value of the alliance. At any rate, although in a different manner, the events in Poland and Hungary demonstrated reluctance to put up with a discipline which at the time of an acute danger was acceptable while the shield was plausible, that is to say, above any suspicion. Developments in Europe showed that the enforcement of bloc discipline in Hungary worsened the relations between the East and the West, whereas the agreement between Poland and the U. S. S. R. at the same time contributed to a lessening of tensions.[6]

Events in the Near East in the same year revealed to what extent relationships within the North Atlantic Pact had loosened. The crux of the matter was not that the United States openly acted against the undertaking of their allies in Suez zone, but that Great Britain and France had started an armed action in the region in which the United States professed to be vitally interested, without previously consulting with Washington. Placed before an accomplished fact, the U. S. government acted in accordance with its own interest to limit the conflict and to avoid the risk of a confrontation with the U. S. S. R. rather than to take sides or a neutral stand in regard to the action of its allies.[7]

---

[6] The Soviet intervention in Hungary provoked a strong reaction in the West, which was reflected in acrimonious debates at the U.N. General Assembly sessions in 1956, 1957 and 1958. The Polish events did not cause similar reactions, because the Soviet Union recognized the new leadership there.

[7] The Mediterranean Sea is included in the area of NATO operations. The United States keeps a powerful naval fleet there at all times. Since France and Great Britain justified their action as the protection of their vital interest, the U.S.A. felt that they should have consulted the United States within the NATO cooperation and consultation system.

Without any further analysis of subsequent crises in international relations or dispute and conflicts within one or the other alliances, let it suffice to say that, as tensions abated after 1954, some substantial changes did occur within the alliances. Intrabloc relationships were changed, and so was the general pattern of international relations. As the significance and the impact of the blocs in international relations diminished and the cold war receded into the background, more and more countries sought to act independently in the international scene.

This change was evident during occasional tensions, too, and not only in the periods of reduced tension. For example, the war in Vietnam did not produce a renewal of bloc cohesion in the West, nor did it bring about a relaxation between the Soviet Union and China. This, however, does not mean that the importance of the blocs can be completely written off. They remain, although in a considerably modified context, extremely important elements in the world constellation. Freedom of action varies from country to country and also depends on the general situation in international relations, as well as on special circumstances in special concrete cases.

There were many examples of these peculiarities in the events of the 1960s. Albania left the eastern alliance and France stepped out of the western military organization. The majority of European allies successfully opposed the creation of multilateral nuclear forces, Rumania reestablished diplomatic relations with the Federal Republic of Germany against the will of its allies, and on both sides the first draft agreement of the superpowers on non-proliferation of nuclear weapons met with opposition and criticism. The simple pattern based on a bipolar orientation of bloc aligned countries and the expansion of this structure to the outside world gave way to increased polycentrism and a much more complex pattern of relations within which, however, the old bloc scheme was still evident.

The new spirit spread to all the continents during the 1960s. Withdrawal from bloc organizations had however in some cases completely different political motives and consequences. The quitting of the Eastern bloc by China or Albania did not bring those countries around to the positions of the opposing bloc, nor to the positions of nonalignment or even neutrality. Although according to some attempts at categorization based on internal developments China and Albania have been described as similar to those countries which are organized in the Warsaw Pact, yet their foreign policy is seriously in conflict with the policies and actions of the U. S. S. R. and its allies.[8] What is more, there is considerable tension between them.

In the West, too, there are instances which reveal the same complexity that developed as a result of the abatement of tensions. Cuba fell away from the West, but during the 1960s she oscillated between the Soviet Union and China and the nonaligned countries. It would be very difficult, on the basis of Cuba's overall behavior, to determine her place within a pattern of structures dating back to the height of the cold war. However, similar problems also arose in connection with the countries which remained within their alliances or groups. We have again the example of Rumania, and there was also Pakistan, which remained formally attached to the western alliance, but which developed intensive ties (including the purchase of arms) with the Soviet Union and China.[9]

This state of fluidity in alignments revived a number of latent disputes, particularly in the regions of the former colonial empires. Some of these disputes were suppressed because of the priority of the liberation struggle and because of concentrated efforts to obtain independence. Later on some of them were held back again in order to consolidate the newly won independence. Owing to general uncertainty and strained international relations this situation maintained itself in some cases even over a lengthy period. Even when the dispute was so intensive that it could not be completely repressed, open large-scale military conflicts were avoided.

One of the most obvious examples of this behavior was the dispute between India and Pakistan over Kashmir. Although the dispute once led to open armed strife after the partition of former British India, a truce was more or less observed until the 1960s.

---

[8] Sonja Dapčević-Oreščanin, *Sovjetsko-kineski spor i problemi razvoja socijalizma* (The Soviet-Chinese Dispute and Problems of the Development of Socialism), Institute of International Politics and Economics, Beograd 1963, pp. 131—202.

[9] *See the SIPRI Yearbook of World Armaments and Disarmament 1968/69*, Stockholm, International Peace Research Institute 1969, p. 79.

It was only in 1965 that a violent military conflict broke out again, and in the course of just over three weeks produced heavy casualties and losses on both sides.[10] This conflict, of course, did not solve anything, and the problem remained unresolved even afterwards. It would be difficult to find a logical explanation for it other than inability of both the governments to repress friction with their own deliberate actions and prevent it from growing into something that cannot be controlled.

During the 1960s the number of clashes increased and old ones gained in intensity endangering peace. Armed conflicts and armed interventions by the great powers took place in all parts of the world. In addition to the escalation in Vietnam[11] and the revival of the war in the Middle East between the Arabs and Israel,[12] there were clashes, interventions, riots and coups d'état in other parts of the world as well. During the second half of the decade, serious riots broke out in the United States and in several European countries. Strong movements started in all societies in the world, not only conflicts based on racial or national differences, but also movements of workers and students in the developed countries.[13] There were also riots and ferment in socialist countries as well, especially in China.[14] If we add to this the coup d'état in Greece, we shall have covered range of violent movements which took place all over the world. There was no area in the world and no social system that was not affected.

All these problems, naturally, do not fall within the domain of international relations, but even those of a purely internal nature did affect relations among countries and whole areas. Although no direct confrontation occurred between the two blocs, the United Nations failed to act efficiently in the international conflicts of the 1960s and to be an instrument of peace and international cooperation as it should under the Charter. It is then understandable why, even after the relaxation of the cold war, no political or economic and social questions were resolved.

---

[10] *Keesing's Contemporary Archives* 1965—1966, p. 21103.

[11] *Vietnam — History, Documents and Opinions*, Editor Marvin E. Gettleman, Fawcett Publications, Greenwich, Conn. 1965, pp. 282—389.

[12] *Keesing's Contemporary Archives* 1967—1968, pp. 22063, 22075, 22099 and 22108.

[13] *The Student Revolt, The Activists Speak*, Panther Books Ltd., London 1968.

[14] *The Cultural Revolution in China*, Keesing's Research Report, Keesing's Publications Ltd.

Earlier suppositions and hopes that a relaxation of the cold war would be followed by an activization of the United Nations and by a considerable improvement in international relations were not fully realized. It is, though, true that the dissolution of the rigid bipolar alignment, as well as the new elements in relations between the great powers, made the debates in the world organization more business-like and more constructive. It did take the sting out of dissensions, but the difficulties impeding the solution of old problems, which awaited settlement for many years, remained. However, even when agreed solutions were achieved, they were usually not of such a nature as to substantially affect the basic course of international life.[15]

Improved relations between the superpowers and the consequent easing of inter-bloc conflict and weakening of intra-bloc discipline very largely removed the one source of danger for peace: a disastrous conflict between the two nuclear giants. Although the two world powers continued being opposed to one another, not only directly, as the strongest military powers in the world, but also indirectly, involved in all the outstanding disputes in various parts of the world, they succeeded to a considerable extent in preserving their relations from an exaggerated influence from those areas. It is most unlikely that any of those conflicts could escalate so far as to draw the two world powers into a direct war. This applies even to such major conflicts as the war in Vietnam and in the Middle East.

The danger of escalation into a world war was not an immediate one. The principal and more real danger was, and still is, the possibility that a local conflict would persist or worsen, leading to bipolarity and the reestablishment of cohesion within the bloc organizations. In such an event, the conflict might reach a dangerous level, because many of the appeasing factors present in today's polycentric constellation would cease to act or would largely lose their efficiency and credibility.

This danger was real, and such a development should not be excluded in the future, but we should also not lose sight

---

[15] Such agreements include those made in the 1960s on nuclear armaments. Not one of these agreements in any way restricted the armaments race, which in fact is the only concrete objective that could influence the course of international relations.

of those forces which act against such developments. First of all, there are the interests of the two world powers. They systematically avoid being brought to the point of no return in their mutual relations. This applies as well to questions which arise from their direct relationships as nuclear superpowers as to disputes in which they are only indirectly interested.[16]

EQUILIBRIUM IN NUCLEAR STRIKING FORCES OF THE SUPERPOWERS

Contacts in connection with disarmament, which again became business-like and constructive after the resumption of negotiations in 1955, were continued, although they were occasionally interrupted at moments of relapses as, for example, in the period between the shooting down of the American U-2 aircraft over the Soviet Union in May 1960, and the renewed improvement after the Soviet missile crisis in Cuba in the autumn of 1962.[17] In fact, after that period of marking time, there followed a series of agreements, and new topics began to be discussed with a view of restraining the armaments race. All these agreements were achieved on peripheral questions, and none of them entered the essence of the problem, i. e., the real slowdown if not the cessation of the race.

This is understandable, because an agreement that would go quite so far would need much more solid bases than simply a desire to avoid being drawn into a war. Until the end of 1969, agreements in the matter of disarmament were reached either with

---

[16] These considerations cover the period after 1955, when the cold war was on the wane. In the very next decade, the 1960s, however, China emerged as a contender for the rank of the third power in the world. In these years the chances for a return to the strictly bipolar power balance between the great powers were already diminishing.

[17] On May 1, 1960, an American U-2 reconnaissance plane on a mission to photograph and record the operations of military electronic installations was shot down near Sverdlovsk in the U.S.S.R. The pilot, Captain Francis Powers, parachuted to safety and was arrested and tried by Soviet authorities. This incident led to the canceling of the planned four-power summit meeting scheduled to begin on May 17 in Paris. See *Keesing's Contemporary Archives* 1959—1960, pp. 17425 and 17437.

the intent of restricting other powers wanting to develop nuclear weapons, or when such a restriction was in the interest of, or insignificant for, the superpowers themselves. This applies to the ban on nuclear tests, to the utilization of space and the seabed as well as to other less important agreements.

During the discussions about these problems in the various bodies of the United Nations, and particularly at the sessions of the General Assembly during the period 1963—1969, there was increasing evidence of opposition against the armament of the superpowers and against the creation of a frozen hierarchy of powers in the world.[18] As a result, the two mightiest powers stood out as a separate category of powers which, albeit in a latent conflict or at least in a state of intensive rivalry and competition, stood by themselves above the normal course of international relations. Polycentrism thus acquired a new feature; as strict bipolarity was thrust aside, in addition to the division into the East and the West and the increasingly pronounced division into the North and South, there was now another division into real nuclear powers and those which do not have atomic weapons, the powers with a limited nuclear potential having a special status and belonging to neither camp.

This trend of development after the end of 1967 gradually began to acquire a new and much more clearly defined significance. It came as the result of new technical achievements and opportunities created on this basis. However, the first important strides were made after the armaments race, based on existing weapons systems and verified technology, came to the end of an important stage in the period 1967—1968. At that time, namely, the United States ended its program of deployment of a more or less complete offensive missile system capable of surviving a first or surprise nuclear missile attack and of annihilating with retaliatory weapons the civilian population or any opponent believed to be the cause of the first strike or any accomplices.

---

[18] The U.S.-Soviet draft Agreement on the non-proliferation of nuclear armament is of particular importance. On the basis of this agreement, only countries not already possessing nuclear armaments are subject to restriction, while the nuclear powers undertake no concrete limitations. A special conference of non-nuclear powers was held under the auspices of the United Nations from August 29 to September 28, 1968, in Geneva. See *Keesing's Contemporary Archives 1969—1970*, p. 23113.

It is interesting that the U.S. government subsequently slowed down the pace of building this striking power and thus permitted the Soviet Union to complete this phase in the building up of the nuclear powers during 1968—1969. Whereas military spending in the United States showed a slight drop in the period 1966—1969, except for disbursements for the war in Vietnam, this expenditure was considerably increased in the Soviet Union, as can be seen from the table below.[19]

Annual Growth of Military Expenditure in Percentages

	1966	1967	1968	1969
U. S. A.	2.8	—5.0	4.1	—5.7
U. S. S. R.	4.7	8.0	15.5	5.9

Percentages have been calculated on the basis of fixed prices in 1961 for the U.S.A., and in 1960 for the U.S.S.R. In the case of the U.S.A., the cost of the war in Vietnam has been deducted in order to obtain comparable expenditures. Figures for 1969 were based on budget estimates.

This trend in military expenditure coincided with the estimated development of the basic strategical armaments of the two superpowers during the same years. According to figures published by the Institute of Strategic Studies in London, the number of intercontinental ballistic missiles grew very unevenly during those years:[20]

Number of Intercontinental Ballistic Missiles

	1965	1966	1967	1968	1969
U. S. A.	854	904	1,054	1,054	1,054
U. S. S. R.	270	300	460	800	1,050

This publication also showed the increase in the number of nuclear submarines able to launch nuclear missiles. It revealed that in recent years the U.S.S.R. has considerably increased its strength, although according to the Institute it has a considerably smaller number of long-range submarine-based missiles.[21]

---

[19] *SIPRI Yearbook of World Armaments and Disarmament 1968/69*, Stockholm, International Peace Research Institute 1969, pp. 20 and 30.

[20] *The Military Balance 1969—1970*, The Institute of Strategic Studies, London 1969, p. 55.

[21] *Ibid.*

However, the same publication alleged that the U.S.S.R. developed mobile medium-range land-based missiles, which may be considered protected from a surprise attack almost like those missiles in the submarines.[22]

The general conclusion from these figures could be that a phase had been reached in the development of strategic armament that constituted the end of a stage in the race. It was obvious that a simple increase in the number of the existing weapons or the increase in their striking force was not justified by any advantage comparable to the expenditure that it would require. Consequently, once again a constructive cooperation between the two nuclear powers became possible and necessary. However, this time there was no question of a precarious equilibrium as in 1946, when an enormous conventional army challenged the still poorly developed nuclear power of the U.S.A. Similarly, the present situation cannot be compared with that of 1954, when both sides switched from the fission nuclear bombs to the thermonuclear megaton bomb and started testing long-range missiles. This time a much more critical point in the race was attained. To stop the race in 1954 would have meant to renounce thermonuclear missile weapons, and that could not be supervised. However, a secret violation of a possible agreement could then very quickly upset the equilibrium and bring the violator a decisive advantage.

In the newly arisen situation, agreement was much more realistic, because it sought restrictions that could be verified. This was the meaning of the SALT talks which were started on November 17, 1969 in Helsinki, between the representatives of the U.S.A. and the U.S.S.R. These talks were designed to examine the possibility of restraining the further race or preventing the beginning of a new stage.[23]

The entire armaments race in nuclear weapons had been limited before 1968 to competition in perfecting and mass producing offensive weapons. This denomination is used here as a technical description of the weapons, regardless of the character

---

[22] *Ibid.*, p. 6.
[23] These negotiations were continued in Vienna in 1970.

of war or military operation in which they would be used. They are offensive in the sense in which a bomber is offensive and anti-aircraft artillery defensive, irrespective of whether they form part of the armed forces which are defending themselves or which are attacking.

In other words, from a nuclear strike carried by missiles, the other side protected itself by threatening retaliation from its own similar weapons ensured against destruction in fortified silos or auxiliary launching pads on the land or in naval craft. The cities and populations of the opponent were a kind of hostage to deter the opponent from attempts to win a war by a surprise attack. This was basically so also at the time when the airforce was still the main carrier of nuclear weapons, and the ability of striking back was based on the concealment of the nuclear bomb carriers in a mass bomber attack and on the great destructive potential of each nuclear bomber.[24]

During the 1960s, none of the superpowers possessed the means capable of protecting either their civilian population or their own strategical striking forces from an opponent's attack; in other words, there was no possibility of stopping, intercepting or destroying in flight missiles with nuclear warheads. The armaments race consequently went on between the producers of offensive missiles in order to increase their number, striking force, and accuracy, while at the same time protecting the same missiles while they are still on the ground, or kept in readiness to be used for a first strike or retaliatory strike.

It is quite natural that such a race had to end up in a deadlock with both sides having a striking force able to survive the first strike and capable to carry out retaliation, and thus bring the war to its only possible conclusion — destruction of both sides. The answer to the threat by one side was the equivalent threat by the other side, and the major war deterrent was the threat of mutual destruction.

---

[24] Whereas in the Second World War the destruction of some of the planes attacking a city could reduce bombing destruction, in the era of nuclear bombers it would be enough for one plane to penetrate defenses to destroy an entire city. For more on the problems of nuclear strategy in the 1950s, see Henry A. Kissinger, *Nuclear Weapons and Foreign Policy*, Council on Foreign Relations, New York 1957, pp. 65—85 and P.M.S. Blackett, *Atomic Weapons and East-West Relations*, Cambridge University Press 1956, pp. 48—49.

Quantity played a role only inasmuch as it was necessary to provide for a sufficient retaliatory striking force.[25] This problem gradually became increasingly complex in view of the accuracy of the instruments by which it was possible to establish the location of the fortified missile launching sites on the ground, namely, the reconnaissance satellites which, launched by both sides, are ceaselessly circling the earth.[26] However, since it is exceedingly difficult to destroy the very strongly fortified silos with launching ramps what was needed was a considerable preponderance in the number of missiles designed for this purpose. This number of missiles should be supplemented by the strength of the reserve of missiles which must remain intact after the opponent's strike and be capable of an efficient second strike.

Yet, even this race, which theoretically could go on forever, started slowing down as missiles, whose location could not be established, started being developed and manufactured in numbers. These were mainly the missiles in nuclear powered submarines, which can remain under water for increasingly long periods of time. Furthermore, they also include mobile launching pads and missiles on surface ships.

As these fairly safe reserves were created, all the remaining missiles in fact mutually canceled each other out, and in the last analysis they represented an enormous capital senselessly frozen. Since there was not much point in using these safe and mobile reserves to destroy the opponent's missiles, they were designed for the destruction of cities and populations, and their upper limit was fixed. What is more, as their reliability, destructive power and accuracy increased, their number could even be reduced without altering the effect of the ultimate distinction, which would remain total.

It is hardly necessary to argue that a second retaliatory strike cannot and must not be directed against the opponent's missile forces, but rather against the cities and other life centers. It is, however, also obvious that the development of a large number

---

[25] Henry Kissinger, *op. cit.*, pp. 93—94.

[26] Although President Eisenhower's "open-skies plan", that is an exchange of air reconnaissance, was rejected by the Soviet Union in 1955, such inspection was carried out by both sides in the 1960s by satellite.

of highly accurate and powerful missiles fortified in silos achieves nothing, even if *all* the fortified missiles of the other side were to be destroyed, because the mobile ramps which threaten cities and vital centers with their protected missiles, would be left intact. The hope that one side could destroy the opponent's striking force and threaten his cities if he does not surrender, while at the same time having his own civilian population protected, became unreal. The remaining reserves of mobile missiles, which are sufficiently accurate for the destruction of large targets, remain as a threat or as a retaliatory force.

Thus the armament race in strategical weapons began to stabilize around 1968—1969 at a very advanced level. At this level, the two superpowers found themselves equal and in a stalemate. Any increase in existing armaments became meaningless.

After two decades of competition in perfecting and producing increasingly powerful and accurate types of simple missiles with thermonuclear warheads, a new component appeared: the development of antiballistic missile defense systems.[27] In other words, on the eve of the 1970s, the two superpowers found themselves in an exceptional situation in which the continuation of the race of the past decades in the deployment of technically offensive missiles had become meaningless. The increased efficiency of the missiles, by arming them with multiple separately guided thermonuclear warheads, is also justified only as a method of enhancing the penetration of the opponent's defensive system armed with antiballistic missiles. Consequently, everything is reduced to the one dilemma whether a reasonably reliable antiballistic missile defense system should be built. The answer to this question also contain the answer to the question about the continuation of the armaments race in strategical weapons.

The invention and perfection of antiballistic missiles set off a new race recalling the classical race between the arrow and the shield, the bullet and armor, aircraft and ack-ack. An antiballistic

---

[27] These defense systems are composed of three basic parts: radar equipment for detecting and tracking enemy missiles; electronic computer centers for calculating the trajectory of the enemy missile and that of the missile sent to destroy it; antiballistic missiles designed to intercept the enemy missile and destroy it by exploding in its vicinity. For a more detailed discussion, see *ABM — An Evaluation of the Decision to Deploy an Antiballistic Missile System*, Ed. Abram Chayes and Jerome B. Wiesner, The New American Library, New York 1969, pp. 30—60.

missile is not yet an ABM system, but if one of the two super-powers achieved a reliable ABM system, it would be freed of the fear that its population would be destroyed through retaliation. Thus it would have an advantage, because it could carry out an attack against the opponent with impunity. In other words, the power having that advantage could impose its will upon the other, as well as on any other country. Until such ascendancy is achieved, the mortally wounded opponent is always capable of levelling a devastating blow against the attacker if, having withstood the first strike, it succeeded in preserving sufficient retaliatory resources. Both the U.S.A. and the U.S.S.R. had the capability of withstanding the initial blow and striking back to destroy the attacker by the end of the 1960s.

Thus a seductive although still elusive desire arose to upset the equilibrium and enter a new stage in the race, in the hope that one side might achieve a total advantage and thereby absolute military domination. It would substantially differ from the first stage precisely because it would be concentrated on perfecting and deploying a reliable antiballistic defense system.[28] The first stage of the race, as we have already said, was the race in the production of technically offensive weapons. However, this would not be the only difference, because the antiballistic systems are incomparable more complex[29] and far more expensive[30] than the offensive missiles. There is another and very important reason against such a race, which is that there is no prospect of making a completely reliable defense system.[31] In addition to analyses by the most eminent experts, this was also shown by experience with all the earlier defense systems, such as for example, the system of defense from air attacks. The percentage of effectiveness had always been fairly modest, although the problem of intercepting and destroying aircraft was much simpler.

With long-range missiles armed with thermonuclear war-heads, the problems are much more complex, particularly as re-

---

[28] A general survey of innovations in antimissile defense is given in *ABM — An Evaluation, op. cit.*, pp. 3—60 and especially p. 54.

[29] *Ibid.*, pp. 4—9.

[30] *Ibid.*, pp. 9—10, 23 and 54.

[31] *Ibid.*, pp. 10—17, 107—118, and particularly 130—143.

310

gards the efficiency of the human element, in view of the exceedingly short time available for action. Even in the most automated system decisions must be taken by man, a man holding a high post in the hierarchy of command. Furthermore, even a minute, mathematically insignificant percentage of penetration of the protective belt could be sufficient to cause a total or at least a definitely unacceptable amount of destruction of the country.

We have already said that besides competition between the two powers there was also competition between the efficiency of strike and that of defense. In this field, too, the first steps have already been made. The two sides are perfecting a new type of missile with multiple thermonuclear warheads. All these warheads can at a selected moment in the trajectory separate from the carrier missile and continue moving along different, and for the enemy unexpected, paths towards selected targets.[32] These systems may not yet be sufficiently perfected in regard to the accuracy of the paths of different warheads, but there is no doubt that accuracy can be relatively easily achieved.[33] The change of trajectory and of the speed of different warheads, once they have been perfected, will place some insurmountable difficulties before the ABM defense systems. This, of course, is not the only way of breaking through the defenses, nor is it the last word of technology in making ABM systems ineffective. What is essential, however, is that the race in the second stage could not give greater security but, on the contrary, security on both sides would be impaired, while political relations would become more tense, which in itself would increase the feeling of insecurity.[34]

If an agreement were reached not to do this, the perfection of multi-warhead missiles, the MIRV-s, would have lesser significance. The agreement would mainly be designed to put a stop to the development of ABM systems and to slow down the armaments race in strategical weapons. The two sides should then have a sufficiently reliable system of observation to test compliance with the agreement by the other side. According to Ameri-

---

[32] *Ibid.*, pp. 52—53.
[33] *The Military Balance 1969—1970, op. cit.*, pp. 2—3 and 6.
[34] *ABM — An Evaluation, op. cit.*, p. 60.

can estimates, the U.S.S.R. has such a system. There is a conviction in the U.S.A. that the Soviet ability of observation is on a par with the American, in other words, quite adequate.[35] This may be concluded on the basis of Soviet photographs of the moon taken in conditions which are even more difficult than those for observation on the earth.[36]

However, neither side could know reliably what the other side was doing and in what ways it was endeavoring to perfect its war machine in an attempt to achieve a strategical advantage. It is interesting in this connection to note a statement by President Nixon, made at the end of December 1969, about the elimination of biological weapons, which met with an immediate warm welcome in the Soviet press.[37] Here again, the professional circles know more or less what can be achieved in this field, and it may be expected that competition has arrived at a stage in which the attainment of a strategical advantage is no longer a reasonable proposition.

This is first of all suggested by the notorious fact that there is no efficient protection against sophisticated chemical and biological weapons, and that the possible number of variants of chemical composition of poisons or various strains of bacteria is so great that protection is unfeasible in the present state of science. Mutual intimidation with these methods is therefore not effective.[38] Threats are equally uncertain and terrifying, and it may be assumed that by themselves they act as a deterrent against even the thought of using these methods. Any weapon that would provide a real strategical advantage would have to create a one-sided situation in which the threat by one side would be credible, whereas a counter-strike and protection against the first strike by the other side would be impossible or highly not credible, taking into consideration any mass destruction weapon of the opponent.

---

[35] *Ibid.*, pp. 193—198.

[36] The first photographs of the "dark" side of the moon were sent to earth by the Soviet spaceship *Lunik III* on October 4, 1959. These photos appeared in "Pravda" and "Izvestiia" on October 26.

[37] *The New York Times* and *International Herald Tribune*, November 26, 1969, published the statement made by President Nixon on November 25.

[38] For the latest developments in chemical and biological warfare, see the *SIPRI Yearbook of World Armaments and Disarmament 1968/69, op. cit.*, pp. 112—134.

Finally, the development of a new weapon is only an addition to the existing arsenal and each side, whenever it felt itself vitally menaced, would be tempted to reach out for any weapon. Consequently, both the threat of a first surprise strike and the possibility of retaliation must always be calculated against the assumption of such a variegation of methods of warfare. The armaments race in strategical weapons if continued would most probably remain in the domain of nuclear weapons and missiles. As regards the armaments race in nuclear weapons, the behavior of the superpowers was not inhibited by the development of chemical and biological weapons. It may be supposed that even in a foreseeable future they will not essentially influence their mutual relations in view of the inherent qualities of these weapons.

Preponderance in nuclear armament has always been seen as the ability to deliver a strike without risking a counter-strike, thus forcing a decision by a brief effort.[39] In this event, as distinct from the application of chemical or bacteriological methods, the strike can be unexpected, crushing and instant, and the consequences disastrous. In other words, a retaliation by chemical and bacteriological methods would hardly be possible or effective. On the other hand, the effects of chemical and biological methods can be neither momentary nor overwhelming, but can at best cause a relatively slow action, while the defence of selected nuclear units and installations for retaliation are relatively simple.[40] In this case there is always sufficient time to react with the available nuclear weapons for a total destruction of the attacking country. Only nuclear weapons can satisfy the craving for supremacy, because chemical and biological weapons cannot prevent retaliation, either by the same method or by nuclear weapons.

Distinction should be made between a strike aimed at annihilating the opponent's striking ability from a strike aiming at total destruction.[41] Whereas the former would be directed against launching pads and other military installations (com-

---

[39] Compare: Henry A. Kissinger, *Nuclear Weapons, op. cit.*, pp. 92—94 and P.M.S. Blackett, *Atomic Weapons, op. cit.*, pp. 59—60, as well as General Beaufre, *Interduction a la strategie*, Arman Collin, Paris 1963, pp. 76 and 89.

[40] *SIPRI Yearbook, op. cit.*

[41] For a concise description of this problem, see Morton H. Halperin *Contemporary Military Strategy*, Little, Brown & Company, Boston 1967, pp. 23—32.

mand centers, etc.), the latter would be aimed against cities and civilian populations and the country as a whole. The former would be concentrated, and could not be achieved today by any methods other than nuclear weapons carried by long-range missiles. The latter strike could possibly be carried out by chemical and biological methods, but with the already described limitations.[42]

Since there is no possibility of protecting the civilian population, the utilization of modern strategical weapons is becoming senseless in a conflict between superpowers. A total strike cannot prevent the possibility of retaliation. Any further development of defense systems and the carrying of the race into a new stage would increase expenditure without providing security. If this race were to be harnessed, it is highly possible that it would produce some completely new relationships, because in other aspects of the race relaxation would have to occur.

There is, consequently, a possibility for the talks between the U.S.A. and the U.S.S.R., begun in November 1969, to yield some real results in regard to the easing of the armaments race in strategical weapons. In this event, the reciprocity of interests of the two superpowers would be very much enhanced. It would be an unusual combination of confrontation and community of interests, which would be dominated more than ever before by the awareness that a conflict is something to be avoided at all costs. However, it will most probably be necessary to progress beyond what we had mutual relations in the second half of the 1960s, and certainly very much beyond the situation prevailing in the first half of that decade.

It would no longer be just a matter of avoiding an open war or a situation leading to a war. Steps would have to be taken to ensure an intimate contact and dialogue as an additional measure of protection, for the sake of maintaining the achieved agreement. The vital necessity of preserving the agreement, notwithstanding the existence of political rivalry and pressure, would require the maintenance of a considerably high amount of minimum contact and working relations. In other words, the

---

[42] *SIPRI Yearbook, op. cit.*

agreement would demand considerable restraint in mutual relations. This restraint, if maintained over a sufficiently long period of time, would have an easing effect upon mutual antagonisms, at least in the political and military realms.

TRIANGULAR RELATIONS:
U.S.S.R.—U.S.A.—CHINA

In addition to the two superpowers, China appeared on the world scene in the 1960s as a claimant to the role of a superpower. As we have already pointed out, in the first half of that decade China undertook a broadly conceived and intensive and dynamic international action, in the second half she concentrated on her own internal problems.[43] China's future role cannot be judged only on the basis of her momentary position on the international scene, nor would it be correct to extrapolate on the basis of the events of just a few past years. In order to obtain a complete picture about her evolution and increasing influence on world events, we must begin from the situation which China was in at the time of the breaking out of the first Chinese revolution in 1911, and follow her development through the vicissitudes of the 1920s, '30s, and especially in the years following World War II.[44]

If we look back upon these sixty years of China's history, we shall see an ascending line marking highly important new successes in regard to her assertion as a great and finally a world power. For brevity's sake, let us dwell only on China's role in international relations. From a state of complete impotence just prior to the revolution of 1911, China became the only country

---

[43] See *The Cultural Revolution in China*, Keesing's Research Report, Keesing's Publications Ltd., pp. 15—38.

[44] Compare the copiously documented book by Heinrich Bechtold, *Chinas Revolutionsstrategie*, Deutscher Taschenbuch Verlag, München 1969. The author comes to the conclusion that at the 9th Congress of the Communist Party of China in April 1969, the foundations were laid for a transition from an inward-looking to an outward-looking policy after the upheaval of the "cultural revolution" (p. 34). Also see pp. 300—301 on the development of Chinese nuclear weapons.

which openly defied both superpowers and which wielded a significant influence along a broad front, withstanding the pressures from both the superpowers. She has a plan of global action and openly challenges both the Soviet Union and the United States.[45]

It might be argued that China does not have the thermonuclear and missile potential necessary to rank as a military power on a par with the other two world powers. This may be true only inasfar as China has no offensive potential that would be equal to that of the other two powers. However, China stands her ground despite hostility, because she relies on the mobilization of the third world nations and on her own defensive force.[46] If she is not able to hold her own in offensive power, she has a practically unlimited defensive potential in the present military and political setup in the world.

The war in Vietnam, an incomparably smaller country than China, testifies to the impotence of modern armies in such warfare. The reason why nuclear weapons have not been used can be ascribed to the moral-political situation in the world and to internal resistance within the superpower itself. China's resilience is consequently due to the combination of an exceedingly great ability to absorb blows levelled by any weapon, and of reliance on the political impossibility of applying modern strategical weapons on a scale that could break down internal cohesion and will for resistance in China.

Experience from the war in Vietnam has done much to increase the awareness about this combined military-political defensive strength of China. At the same time, a strange triangular constellation has developed of China and the two superpowers. Once China's special position as an independent factor in the world was recognized, relationships between the superpowers became considerably complicated. The basic logic of this special relationship consists in the endeavor by each of the three powers to keep the other two as far apart as possible and then to involve them in a mutual confrontation, so that the third power would

---

[45] *Ibid.*, p. 353.

[46] See the quotations from the speech by Lin Piao at the 9th Congress of the Chinese Communist Party, *ibid.*, pp. 352—355.

achieve a maximum advantage vis-à-vis either side, and generally an increased freedom of action in the world.

A parallel action by all the three powers should consequently create such a state of equilibrium that would approximately equalize the degree of tension or cooperation on all the three lines of bilateral relations among them. Such an ideal situation is, of course, not possible, and therefore it is here discussed as an ideal case based on the assumption that all the three powers have a similar or identical ability of influencing developments. This in reality does not exist, but there are obviously limits to which differences in relations among these three bilateral combinations can develop. In safeguarding its own interests, each power has a choice between two methods of action: by positive steps designed to ease tensions, it may endeavor to counter the unfavorable trend in the world through a rapprochement with one or both the other powers; or, on the other hand, it may use negative influence by exerting pressure upon one or both other powers, pushing them into a sharpening of their differences.

This interpretation may be subjected to criticism, just as any other in its place. However, the fact is that the moment the U. S. realized that China may become an important world power, it established an ever so tenuous but enduring contact through the ambassadors of the two powers in Warsaw. China accepted this initiative and kept this channel open in all situations and developments in its relations both with the U. S. A. and with the U. S. S. R.[47]

Links between the U. S. A. and the U. S. S. R. had existed from before, and a very subtle game developed within the triangle. This question cannot be considered in detail here. Still, for the sake of illustration we should point to some moves which confirm the hypotheses. Early in the 1960s, especially after the thaw following the Cuban missile crisis, China tried very hard to prevent a Soviet understanding with the U. S. A. The attempt was conducted through propaganda about "serving the objectives of American imperialism", as well as in various areas of the world in

---

[47] Up to the end of 1969, 134 meetings had been held between ambassadors of the two powers. The meetings began after the Bandung Conference in 1955 and were held in Geneva until 1958, when they were transferred to Warsaw.

which the Soviet Union was very much interested, particularly in Cuba itself, where the Soviet decision to withdraw before the American pressure was used to the hilt, but also in a number of countries in Asia and Africa. The armed conflict on the Indian border was another opportunity to charge the U. S. S. R. with "betrayal of the communist movement and solidarity" by helping India.[48]

At that time the attacks against the Soviet Union were more frequent and intensive than the attacks against the United States, which was only denounced inasfar as it was necessary to charge the U. S. S. R. with collusion with American imperialism.[49] However, the situation began to change as the war in Vietnam escalated. The Soviet Union opposed the American intervention, and China stepped up its offensive against the United States in order to create a maximum of tension over the Vietnam war, and still more upset the development of relations between Washington and Moscow. The transport of Soviet arms through China was impeded, and the Soviet Union was forced to use much longer and more expensive supply lines which, besides, crossed areas in which the U. S. navy and airforce operated, thus creating the possibilities of incidents between those two powers.[50]

At the end of 1969, China agreed, and even herself gave the initiative, to renew contacts between ambassadors, which had been continued during 1968 and 1969, and the U. S. took up this initiative. However, as developments, unpleasant for Moscow, began to take place in the European countries allied to the U.S.S.R., China strained her relations with the Soviet Union. Border incidents took place.[51] This took place in a situation when it

---

[48] Compare the capsulized account of relations among the three powers: China—U.S.A.—U.S.S.R. in *Chinas Revolutionsstrategie, op. cit.*, pp. 78—79.

[49] *Ibid.*, pp. 78—94.

[50] In a letter sent to other communist parties in the first half of February 1966, the Central Committee of the C.P.S.U. accuses China of not allowing "Soviet transport airplanes with weapons to fly over the People's Republic of China". The letter goes on to say that "Chinese personages also obstructed the transport of war material by train to Vietnam". The text of the letter, which was not denied, was published in *Die Welt* in Hamburg, March 22, 1966. This letter is also expressly mentioned in the letter sent by the Central Committee of the Chinese Communist Party to the Central Committee of the C.P.S.U. informing them about the decision not to send a delegation to the 23rd Congress of the C.P.S.U. The Chinese letter was published on March 23, 1966. Quotations are from *Keesing's Contemporary Archives* 1965—1966, pp. 21464 and 21633.

[51] The most important was the incident on the Ussuri river on March 2 and 15, 1969 (*Keesing's Contemporary Archives* 1969—1970, p. 23313).

318

seemed that a deep and permanent deterioration was taking place between the U. S. S. R. and the U. S. A.

As soon as the situation began to clarify, China invited Kosygin to visit Peking,[52] and soon afterwards agreed to open negotiations about the settlement of border problems.[53] It is not quite clear who had made the first move. We assume here that it was Peking. However, nothing changes the logic of things if it is assumed that the initiative had come from Moscow, because in fact the interests of both sides were involved. The U. S. S. R. was interested in starting negotiations with China at the time when a positive answer was given to the U. S. A. and when it was expected that negotiations about the restriction of strategical armaments between these two superpowers were imminent.[54] In both cases the action was designed to prevent the situation within the triangle from becoming upset.

Consequently, if we attempt to make an assessment of future developments, we may expect the outcome of the negotiations between the U. S. S. R. and the U. S. A. to affect the constellation inside the triangle and consequently China's influence on those relations and on the general situation in the world. However, there is also no doubt that the development of Soviet-American relations will strongly influence the relations of either power with China.

INTERNAL AND REGIONAL PROBLEMS
AND CONFLICTS

As these macro-cosmic changes took place, another process was under way which could be described as a process of the emancipation of man's personality from the fetters which contemporary society has imposed upon him. They were becoming

---

[52] Kosygin had a talk with Chou En-lai on September 11, 1969.

[53] Negotiations began on October 20, 1969.

[54] Negotiations between the United States and the U.S.S.R. began on October 17, 1969, in Helsinki.

all the more difficult to bear as relationships and the material base of society were changing and calling for adjustments, which frequently transcended the possibilities and inclinations of men formed in different circumstances. This process had been appearing in different forms, different times and different intensities in all societies, developed as well as underdeveloped.

This "rebellion" of the "ordinary" man was taking place in the form of broad movements within national societies just as outside pressures caused by the cold war abated. It enhanced the existing tendencies, somewhat suppressed during the cold war, toward further and faster changes in all societies, whether involving revivals of "forgotten" nationality problems, as with the Scots, Welsh and Irish in Great Britain or with the Bretons in France, or resistance against the inequality of Negroes in the U. S. A.

There is no doubt that changes were taking place and that the pace was "suddenly" accelerated in the developed countries of the West, where beside partial demands of different groups, also demands of a general significance were raised, such as participation in the economic and political decision-making outside and beyond the classical parliamentary framework. In the countries of Eastern Europe, economic reforms were launched in order to effect far-reaching changes in social relationships which occasionally caused conflicts within individual countries as well as in relations among the countries of that region.

All these trends helped to speed up the process of abating the intensity of the cold war. Thus the world quickly and, if it may be said so, unprepared, entered the new stage of decreased tension which revealed the possibility of a complete eclipse of the cold war as a dominant influence in international relations.

However, the speed of political evolution created problems which hindered this very same evolution. Namely, every sudden change demands an adjustment in the existing social structures and the relationships within and among the different structures. The ability to adjust is limited and rapid changes may cause instability, both in national and multi-national societies, or in relations among countries or groups of countries.

The stability of a social structure or system is nothing more than the ability of absorbing innovations and change. The peak

320

of stability, which Morton Kaplan described as "ultra-stability", consists in the ability of absorbing the innovation and change and using them for the strengthening of the system.[55] In other words, fast and thorough changes demand maximum ability of adaptation, which in reality can exist only exceptionally and may apply only to certain categories of destabilizing influences. Understandably enough, as this political movement gained in impetus, crises developed within different societies and within the system of international alliances and in international relations in general.

The example of such an effect of the political development in Europe was the outbreak of conflicts due to the relaxation of intra-bloc discipline caused by the easing of the cold war tensions. The most drastic example of such an evolution was the case of Czechoslovakia. She had begun to develop new forms of international relationships which were viewed with disapproval by the leading forces in the alliance in which she was a member. The international crisis which developed as a consequence is sufficiently well known, as are the outcome and the repercussions of the military intervention in Czechoslovakia on the relations between the East and the West. Here we have an instance of the negative influence of the feedback effect of the internal development on the international détente which set in motion the internal evolution in Czechoslovakia.[56]

Less complex were the examples of conflicts in the third world, e. g. the armed border clashes between Morocco and Algeria, or the war between India and Pakistan. They showed how the cessation of the cold war or of an armed liberation struggle helped to sharpen internal controversies. However, in addition to a large number of international disputes, particularly among neighbors and mostly in connection with border questions, the third world also experienced developments within society and the existing political systems. After the rift in India's Congress Party in the autumn of 1969, it can be said that practically in all the countries in the third world, accelerated social and political de-

---

[55] Morton A. Kaplan, *Macropolitics*, Aldine Publishing Co., Chicago 1969, pp. 61—70.

[56] See Živorad Jevtić, *Čehoslovačka 1968* (Czechoslovakia 1968) (mss), Institute of International Politics and Economics, Beograd 1970.

velopment after independence and stresses in foreign relations significantly strained the basic political systems.

The first shock for those countries was the actual achievement of independence. Later events put their stability again and again to test, and these societies underwent chronic crises. Their destructive influence was, however, considerably checked by the feeling of threat from outside. As this threat diminished, centrifugal and destructive tendencies increased. The feeling of security increased, either because a permanently strained atmosphere, began to be regarded as normal, or because outside pressure really did decrease as the cold war abated, sometimes also because internal development within countries reduced the probability of a conflict.

However, internal political problems and increased internal instability were almost invariably the cause of deteriorated international relations. Thus in this domain, too, the easing of international tensions increased tendencies toward internal crises and local or regional disputes. According to the data collected by the Stockholm International Peace Research Institute, in the years 1945—1953 there had been a total of 27 conflicts, and in the period 1954—1967 no less than 67 conflicts either internal or international, or a combination.[57] Their frequency increased to about 4.8 per annum in comparison with 3 from the period of the cold war.[58] However summary these figures might be, they nevertheless reveal the existing tendency of instability in the third world.

This situation necessarily increased concentration, firstly, on internal problems and settlement of local conflicts, and secondly, on efforts to improve the internal economic situation and increase stability. At the same time it marked a decline in interest in general political problems and a reduced concern for the problems of colonialism.

---

[57] *SIPRI Yearbook, op. cit.*
[58] Calculated from data contained in the *SIPRI Yearbook, op. cit.*

322

DIFFICULTY IN SECURING CONSENSUS
OF NONALIGNED COUNTRIES

At that same time there appeared on the international scene another political tendency, the action of China, particularly between the beginning of the 1960s and the cultural revolution. During the first half of the 1960s, China developed very intensive international activity after her attempts to improve relations with the U.S.A. at the Bandung Conference were rejected and after the conflict had broken out between China and the U.S.S.R. Without entering into the motives which had brought about this turn of events, it seems obvious that China's intent was to rally the poor countries of the third world and to oppose on this broad front the developed countries of Eastern and Western Europe and North America.

China obviously understood the internal and international difficulties of the third world countries and their great internal instability. She was thus able to conduct her action along two outwardly contradictory tracks. On the one hand, she tried to rally those countries, including the existing governments, and at the same time to encourage and assist those forces there which wanted to bring down the existing governments. This action did not meet with much success, partly because the conference of the African and Asian countries, which was to meet in 1965, could not take place as a result of the coup d'état in Algeria.[59] It was postponed for November, but in the meantime a military coup took place in Indonesia, and the conference was postponed *sine die*.[60] The coup in Indonesia took away one of China's main supports in Asia. No other country except Indonesia in the last years of Sukarno's government left the United Nations to create a crisis in this organization and helping to set up a rival organization of "the New Emerging Forces".[61]

---

[59] The Conference was slated for June 29, 1965, and the coup d état was carried out on June 19. See *Keesing's Contemporary Archives* 1965—1966, p. 20983 (on the Afro-Asian conference), p. 20965 (on the coup in Algeria).

[60] *Ibid.*, p. 21039.

[61] *Ibid.*, p. 20579.

The peak of China's activity and influence was in 1964, when preparations were being made for the convention of an Afro-Asian conference and when UNCTAD was subjected to a very strong extremist pressure which created considerable difficulties within the "group of 75 countries". At the end of that year, Indonesia left the United Nations. Soon thereafter trouble started, so that finally, towards the end of 1965, China began to turn inward and then, in the following year, all her energy became concentraded on the international struggles within the cultural revolution.[62]

This brief review of China's activities should help to explain more clearly the political climate in the world during the years following the Cairo Conference of nonaligned countries. As bipolar bloc division of the world faded away and polycentrism developed among the countries which did not aim at creating a new world center of alignment, another force appeared with precisely those ambitions. Although China did not succeeded in creating a major center of alignment and in rallying a large number of countries, rapprochement with China was one of the possible options for the less developed and nonaligned countries. Some of them really began to orient their policies in that direction. The discussions at the Cairo Conference also reflected those tendencies.

It is therefore understandable why in these years it was not easy to move the nonaligned countries into joint actions. It was not accidental that although the second conference of the heads of nonaligned countries took place only three years after the first, but there was no other meeting until the end of the decade, and that attempts between 1967 and 1969 to call up such a meeting met with very great difficulties. Another symptom of the situation was the inactivity of the nonaligned countries at the 19th session of the United Nations General Assembly. Attempts to move the nonaligned countries into an action to end the war in Vietnam were feeble, and also characteristic was the slight activity of these countries in the United Nations Disarmament Commission in Geneva.

---

[62] *The Cultural Revolution in China*, Keesing's Research Report, pp. 9—14.

Whereas it seemed in the years of the intensive cold war that once the global conflict weakened all the basic political and economic problems of the third world would be resolved, experience showed that in the era of the thaw events took a reverse trend. Not only were tranquility and stabilization not achieved, but the political situation became worse, and the economic problems remained unresolved.

What is more, the developed countries themselves were swept by economic troubles, particularly in regard to liquidity and international monetary problems in general. The eve of the second session of the Conference on Trade and Development was a period of serious crises and upheavals which threatened the international status of the British Pound and even menaced the U.S. Dollar. These events created among the ranks of the nonaligned countries a feeling of dissatisfaction and brought on endeavors to combat the passivity of countries concerning international issues outside the framework of their immediate interest, and to revive international cooperation in earlier frameworks. One of the attempts in that direction was the consultative meeting in Belgrade.[63]

Thus we reach the last problem before us, which is a look into the future, an assessment of the prospects of nonalignment in the 1970s, and a review of the situation as the world and the nonaligned countries enter this certainly very important decade of modern history.

---

[63] The meeting was held from July 8 to 12, 1969, in Belgrade. The text of the communiqué is given in the Appendix.

CHAPTER SIX

FUTURE DEVELOPMENT
OF NONALIGNMENT

To consider possible trends of development does not mean devising the future or proposing any defined political, tactical or strategical positions. The object of this analysis is therefore only to try and draw some general conclusions suggested by the given facts, and then to test them against the existing trends in international relations. The value of this consideration will very much depend on the accuracy of assumptions about how general relationships will develop in the world, that is to say, within what framework and in what kind of environment the nonaligned countries will act in the future.

Only within the general context of current events can we deal with specific issues — possible forms and possible contents of activity in the field of nonalignment — and answer the question of what value and significance the policy of nonalignment will have in a foreseeable and possibly even in a long-range future. This answer, obviously, cannot be precise and specific, but it must give the key features which would better enable us to understand the character, possibilities and limitations of this important movement in the contemporary world.

In politics, and possibly more so in international relations, the well-known rule applies that the most reliable forecasts are those which are so generalized that their practical value is highly limited. This is why forecasts in this domain belong more to the sphere of the intuition of politicians than to the sphere of a strictly rational and methodical consideration by a researcher. At times it is unavoidable to step over into the domain of predictions, because no one can discuss international relations as a researcher and at the same time resist the understandable desire to let his intuition roam free.

A scientific approach in such endeavors is always uncertain and subject to errors. We should bear in mind the wise saying that "a series of judgements, revised without ceasing, goes to make up the incontestable progress of Science. We must believe in this progress, but we must never accord more than a limited amount of confidence to the forms in which it is successively vested".[1]

A. THE TENDENCY OF MAINTENANCE OF EQUILIBRIUM AMONG THE GREAT POWERS

LIMITS TO TENSION AND RELAXATION

The known behavior of both the superpowers in their mutual relations does not provide sufficient grounds for predicting the possible course and character of further evolution. In fact, their behavior so far has produced contradictory indications in this respect.[2] At any rate, experience is all too short to permit extrapolations and forecasts of developments in a far-off future. There is no doubt that at short-term intervals it was possible for these relations to develop even at a rather high level of cooperation.

However, it is much safer to take a longer period for the purpose of extrapolation and to base assumptions about the future on changes which took place in the past. A comparison of

---

[1] E. Duclaux, quoted in Arnold J. Toynbee, *A Study of History*, Vol. I, Oxford University Press, p. 50.

[2] Since the first relaxation of tensions, 1954—1955, there have been sharp confrontations alternating with periods of detente, when there was even cooperation. The main conflicts were in 1956 over Hungary, 1960 after the U-2 incident, and 1962 over the Soviet missiles on Cuba.

the state of relations in the years 1948—1950[3] with that of 1968 to 1969[4] would provide a convenient yardstick. During that interval some fundamental changes took place on both sides. They had to adjust themselves to the new situation arising from an altered balance of forces and character of military power owing to the development and mass production of new weapons and equipment. Since in an imaginary future we shall again deal with a fundamentally new and possibly again symetrical change on both sides, it is permissible to use this comparison from the past. The difference between the two situations is, of course, very significant, but it suggests that the same factors will in the future act more strongly and at a higher level, and consequently close relationships will be even more probable and more lasting and intensive than was the case at the end of the 1950's.

The basic difference between the situations at the end of the 1960s and that about the middle of the 1950s is that there the armaments race had began with a new category of weapons, and late in the 1960s we saw the end of that race and a new one has not yet begun.[5] At that time it was not possible to agree on ending the race, because the development of the new weapons as the inevitable next step in the technical development of the armed forces of both sides; it was, at any rate, a new contest that had already opened. Hence the new situation was pregnant with uncertainties and antagonisms attendant to any race of that kind which is run on an unfamiliar ground. The agreed *modus vivendi* was only the introduction into a possible genuine and lasting

---

[3] These years were marked by the following important events: the coup in Czechoslovakia, the beginning of the cold war of the U.S.S.R. and other Cominform countries against Yugoslavia, the Berlin crisis, formation of the North Atlantic Treaty Organization, the United States' refusal to recognize China, and the outbreak of war in Korea. In this period the United States had at its disposal nuclear fission bombs carried by long-range bombers. The U.S.S.R. had superior land forces armed with conventional weapons.

[4] These years saw the nuclear test ban (except for underground tests) and the prohibition on using space for war aims, as well as other important agreements and conventions. Agreements were concluded on restricting the use of the seabed for purposes of war, and on the non-proliferation of nuclear armaments. Negotiations were also begun on limiting the arms race in strategical weapons. Although in these years the wars in Vietnam and the Middle East were still being fought, the two powers tried hard to keep this form interfering with their mutual relations; they used the "hot line" for communication between the White House and the Kremlin and agreed on pacifying situations. At this time both powers were practically equal in the domain of strategical weapons, and each had a large number of long-range missiles.

[5] Abram Chayes and Jerome Wiesner, *ABM — An Evaluation, op. cit.*, p. 50.

agreement which could only be attained in the event that both sides end up the race more or less level with each other. When finally, at the end of the 1960s, the end of this race came in sight, a formerly unattainable permanent agreement became possible provided a further race was regarded to be senseless. The alternative was not the continuation of the old race, but the beginning of a completely new stage in which besides a race between the two powers there is also a contest between offensive and defensive armaments.[6] As we have shown earlier, such an armaments race necessarily brings about a quantitative and qualitative escalation on an unforeseeable scale.

If we assume the achievement of a truly meaningful and reliable agreement between the superpowers, we obtain an entirely new model of international relations. The superpowers are immobilized on their reciprocal positions and are compelled to give up competition, rivalry and expansion based on the might of arms. What is more, they would be highly restricted in the use of their military power, even within the narrow confines of their own spheres of interest, if it was liable to have broader repercussions. The only exception would be agreed intervention, with explicit or tacit consent for each case separately, on the basis of reciprocity.

It would be wrong to conclude that their military and political influence on local and regional conflicts would grow to that extent that they could prevent them. The immobilization in the relations between the superpowers that would hinder their action in regional disputes. Firstly, it is difficult to believe that their rival interests could become so reconciled that they would be able to act in unison, even when a dispute moves into the critical phase of an open conflict. Such cooperation is, of course, possible in exceptional cases, as has been shown during the attack of Israel, France and Great Britain against Egypt in 1956, but in the majority of cases the action would most probably only reach the stage of attempts at appeasement, as in connection with the June war in the Middle East in 1967 and after the conclusion of the armistice.

---

[6] *Ibid.*, p. 27.

Secondly, a general easing of tensions would most probably encourage the outbreaks of local and regional conflicts as it had already happened after the relaxation in the mid-1950s. In fact, the political influence of the superpowers might well have the same fate as their weapons, a considerably increased potential may hinder its efficient application and operative use.

This theoretical model should be regarded as one possible and fully developed variant of further developments. However, we must also reckon with different possibilities. A reverse situation would occur if attempts to prevent a new stage in the race failed, or if an agreement were to be canceled after it had been concluded. In such an event we should expect a rapid increase of expenditures for armaments, and a continuous instability and tension arising out of increased insecurity, which in fact would be made use of in order to justify the sacrifices demanded of the population.

Naturally, this tension would still have to be restricted lest it should move into the dangerous zone from which it might not be possible to get out without a war. The rivalry between the two superpowers would become very bitter in the sense that periods of relaxation would not last as long as they did during the 1960s or at the end of the 1950s. Oscillations in tensions would continue, with the upper limit of tension being more or less unchanged, and the bottom limit of relaxation situated at a higher degree of tension. This means that the oscillation of tensions and relaxation would continue with the general resultant of this movement being at a higher level of tensions than in the first model.

Thus the entire international picture would find itself in a state of fluidity even more pronounced than in the earlier race. Agreements on interventions and in particular to nip emerging conflicts in the bud, would be less likely, and each unilateral action by one of the superpowers would immediately cause suspicion and provoke a reaction from the other side. This situation, of course, would not exclude occasional agreements which would be necessary to keep the tension under control.

Increase in general tension between the superpowers would not automatically bring back rigidity in the bloc alliances and the strengthening of cohesion in them. On the contrary, those elements which in the previous stage in the race during the 1960s had helped to decrease cohesion would continue operating, perhaps even more intensively.[7] The superpowers would be even less likely to fulfil their obligations to their bloc partners, while the allies of both sides, by staying outside the race, would be less involved in direct controversies between the superpowers. At the same time, the allies would also feel the economic burden of the race in their economic relations within the alliance. However, we should not lose sight of the renewed atmosphere of general insecurity which would be felt in intra-European relations, although they could develop more favorably than the relations between the U.S.A. and the U.S.S.R., as had frequently been the case during the 1960s.

Both of these models have been presented as extreme and "pure" solutions which are rare in practice. They should, as far as it is possible, provide rationally foreseeable limits of future developments. It would be imaginable to make from a detailed analysis of the development of relations between the superpowers between the war and the end of the 1960s an extrapolation that would show the likelihood of developments approaching the first variant, i. e. the agreement on slowing down the armaments race in strategical weapons. This analysis does not fall within the terms of reference of this discussion, and we should content ourselves with a brief survey of its main elements.[8]

---

[7] Charles de Gaulle was the first statesman to recognize this problem, and he made his opinions on it clear at a press conference on January 14, 1963: "In these conditions no one in the world, and especially in America, could say if, where, when, how and in what measure, American nuclear weapons would be used to defend Europe." *Keesing's Contemporary Archives* 1963—1964, p. 19198.

[8] The reader can find analyses and authoritative assessments of developments in the relations between the two superpowers in a large number of works and in a number of published documents. A few sources and places of special interest are given below:

1) *Mezhdunarodnye otnosheniia posle pervoi mirovoi voiny*, Vol. 3, Izdatel'stvo politicheskoi literatury, Moskva 1965. In this comprehensive work prepared by Institute of the Academy of Sciences of the U.S.S.R. for World Economics and Foreign Relations, the passage on pages 60 and 61 is especially significant: "Nevertheless, the change in objective conditions in world politics, in which there is no longer today any room for imperialistic absolutism or for its free choice in starting a war, cannot help, of course, but affect in a certain way the subjective policy of imperialism, by restricting its possibilities and laying down firm historical boundaries for it."

Further on the text mentions the existence of two contradictory tendencies — "adventuristic" and "realistic" — in the countries of the West. The ascendance of realism and political coexistence "merely indicates a certain realism in their thinking, their more or less correct evaluation of the strength of the world socialist system, of the total world revolutionary process, of the practical balance of forces in the modern world..." (page 60). From the foregoing a conclusion is drawn on the possibility of avoiding war.

The general conviction on both sides that all-out war must be avoided at all costs, reliance on a sophisticated and powerful striking force which was matched by a similar force on the other side, and endeavors to whittle down one's own striking force without weakening its deterrence and efficiency, all this led in the past to limited agreements in the sphere of armaments. What was not possible to achieve was an agreement on the reduction of the existing armaments, when it was not just a matter of replacing one type of weapons with a better and more advanced one (e. g. missiles instead of aircraft, etc.).

Agreements were made only when there was no danger of circumventing them even without the existence of on-the-spot inspection by authorized experts. An important instance was the agreement not to extend the race to new areas, as for example space and the seabed. In other words, the domain of competition has been limited to familiar ground, in which all major changes can be directly observed from satellites, both sides having an adequate and sufficiently protected striking force which *in any case* can serve as a deterrent should the need arise to carry out a total retaliation to a surprise attack.

Finally, the confrontation of the two superpowers in concrete regionally confined conflicts has shown that even harsh confrontations with the maximum permissible deterioration of

"The lessons of history in one way or another are reflected in the consciousness of the ruling groups of imperialism, no matter how hard they resist accepting these lessons. Undoubtedly they have been reflected in the development of more realistic political thinking in certain circles of American monopolistic capital." (page 61).

2) In the West there is much more literature on foreign affairs. One interesting passage can be found in the analysis prepared by the U.S. Council on Foreign Relations with the collaboration of outstanding scientists, politicians and diplomats. This analysis was submitted to the U.S. Senate and was published by the government as Report No. 7, November 25, 1959.

After summing up the course of foreign policy, the text states: "Whatever the reasons, the tendency of the United States up to now has been to treat foreign relations as a series of crises, of moves and countermoves in the cold war, with which the United States has attempted to combine firmness in holding the line against Communist expansion with measures to build up defensive strength in the Free World and with a willingness to negotiate on outstanding issues. This will not be sufficient for the future... Present conditions are as favorable to initiatives on the part of free nations as they are to those of the Soviet Union or Communist China. Opportunities to create conditions conducive to the growth of freedom in the world and to the establishment of a durable peace are these. The question is whether the United States will have the will and ability to seize them." *Quoted from American Strategy for the Nuclear Age*, edited by Walter F. Hahn and John C. Neff, Doubleday, New York 1960, p. 15.

Also of interest is a shorter study by Marshall D. Shulman, *Beyond the Cold War*, Yale University Press, New Haven 1966.

relations were usually followed by a denouement, and therefore over the years a noticeable tendency has developed of avoiding such crises. This experience, which can be traced over a period of twenty-five years, may be much too short for definitive conclusions, but it is sufficiently reliable for relatively short-range forecasts, for speculations about the future relating to a shorter period than the one that had been studied in the past.

From the above it would seem reasonable to accept that relations between the two greatest powers would be developing closer to the first variant rather than the second one, i. e., that they would tend to agree on matters arising from their direct relationship, especially in limiting a further armaments race in strategical weapons. This, of course, is valid for a foreseeable, relatively near future, in which presumably there will be no unexpected changes that would fundamentally alter that situation. In a distant future, and certainly at the turn of the next century, some unanticipated new moments may arise which may very thoroughly alter the present tendencies. Understanding between the superpowers would, however, run parallel with their rivalry, which would continually put a strain on their relations.

THE EFFECT OF GENERAL TRENDS IN THE WORLD ON THE BEHAVIOR OF THE GREAT POWERS

The successful outcome of negotiations and the gradually achieved more or less formally presented and publicized agreements between the two superpowers are bound to bring about a further relaxation of tensions and cooperation between the East and the West in Europe. The basic course and development of relations need not be subject to any major changes as a result of China's presence. This does not lessen China's influence on world events, but it is assumed that her claim to the status of a superpower may strengthen the already existing tendencies governing U.S.-Soviet relations. This tendency may then influence China's behavior as a feed-back. In other words, agreement between the U.S.A. and the U.S.S.R. may hinder China's maneuvering ability, and any strain or conflict between them is bound to extend and strengthen China's influence and to increase tensions all round.

This is neither a completely new nor a completely unexpected situation. International relations brought on a similar dilemma immediately after the war, or even before the end of the war. This was when a confrontation took place between two great powers, the U.S.A. and the U.S.S.R. and their allies in Europe and North America. This aggravation of differences between the two camps produced developments and phenomena which in turn tended to aggravate the original differences in a feed-back process.

In this manner a precarious balance was created. Once the scales were tipped, they continued to move under their own momentum. In the given case this momentum led straight towards a complete deterioration and might even have resulted in open and all-out conflict. This conflict did not take place only because some other factors intervened, independently of the spiralling escalation of acridities. These other factors produced a situation in which any conflict would become senseless and without a future for either side.[9]

The unstable equilibrium of that time cost the world many sacrifices and losses and was responsible for a durable instability in international relations. Thus, of course, peace and international cooperation were neither assured nor in fact possible. The result was the cold war and all its consequences in the world, political as well as economic.

However, the character and importance of relationships between the superpowers in the new conditions cannot be likened to those of the early years after the war. Account must be taken of the new atmosphere in the world as a result of the profound revolutionary changes in all the continents. A directorium, such as conceived in Yalta[10] and in Potsdam[11] at the end of the war, was no longer possible. The relations between the superpowers,

---

[9] Compare the very clear and cogent presentation of this problem in the study by Charles O. Lerche, Jr., *The Cold War ... and after*, Prentice-Hall, 1965; see especially pp. 30—34.

[10] The Yalta conference of the leaders of the U.S.A., the U.S.S.R. and Great Britain was held from February 4 to 11, 1945. A concise summary can be found in *Keesing's Contemporary Archives* 1943—1945, p. 6991 *et seq.*

[11] The Potsdam conference was held from July 7 to August 1, 1945, and an account is given in *Keesing's Contemporary Archives* 1943—1945, p. 7361 *et seq.*

also, could hardly serve as the basis for a harmonious cooperation. The most probable model of relations will be the traditional one, with certain modifications. This means that we should expect the great powers to act more on their own and less within the framework of blocs. This "traditional" method of action was forecast by Lerche in his book, *The Cold War ... and after*.[12] It is not a replica of pre-war relations between the great powers, but the development of a rationalized relationship among the great powers acting independently in a new setting, given the presence of modern armaments and a new atmosphere in the world. "It is crucial, however, to remind ourselves that the restructuring of Soviet-American relations in a world freed from the intellectual dominance of the cold war would transform both the practical and the conceptual bases of the conflicts between the two states".[13] Lerche also points out that even at the height of the controversy in past years both sides were careful not to go too far, and that conflicts in reality were not fought as hard as one could be led to expect from policy proclamations.[14]

It is highly improbable that the behavior of any other great power or of other bloc partners could have influenced the above trends in superpower relations. European relations might have altered under the influence of increased freedom of the West European countries vis-à-vis the United States and NATO, but this freedom was considerably restricted and intra-European relations could not differ too much from the relations between the U.S.S.R. and the U.S.A. Some autonomy of intra-European relations did exist exactly at the time of relaxation between the two superpowers, as the cold war thawed, and the West European states returned to their traditional political orientations and behavior. Even so they remained close to the U.S.A. Intra-European development was also inhibited owing to the fact that both Western Europe and the U.S.A. have the same partner on the other side, the Soviet Union, and the latter's behavoir towards Western Europe cannot differ too much from that toward the United States.

---

12 Charles O. Lerche Jr., *The Cold War*, *op. cit.*, p. 131.

13 *Ibid.*, p. 132.

14 *Ibid.*, p. 133.

336

Of the developed countries and potential military factors outside Europe we should only mention Japan. Her opportunities are great and they will increase as Japan joins the ranks of the economically most advanced countries.[15] However, it is unlikely that Japan might try, and even less that it could manage, to join the superpowers as a military power and change the situation in the highest ranks of military power in the world.[16] However, Japan certainly will not and cannot relinquish her role as an economically great power maintaining close economic ties with all the countries of the world. Yet in this way Japan cannot influence appreciably the behavior of the main world powers. But it is most unlikely that she will give up her independent policy. A deep involvement with any one of the three world political powers would, in the event of a deterioration, seriously impair her economic position, interests and prospects.

In summing up, we may be permitted to conclude that in the relationship between the superpowers change will probably be very gradually and that this change will not substantially alter the basis on which their relationship as founded in the past. This basis consists in their tremendous supremacy in armaments over all the other powers, and in the comparability of their respective striking forces commending a tacit respect of their reciprocal capability of levelling a devastating blow.

An understanding about the new stage in the armaments race might give rise to more unanimity on the basis of recognized mutual interests notwithstanding their continued rivalry. However, irrespective of what consensus might be achieved, their mutual relations will continue slanting toward a controlled confrontation with varying degrees of tension, frequency and violence.

China's presence in the triumvirate of major powers may operate more than heretofore as a catalyst in the behavior of the

---

[15] In 1967 Japan outstripped the Federal Republic of Germany in the total value of industrial output, and in 1968 in the value of the total national product. Japan has firmly established itself in the third place as a world economic power. *Godišnjak* (Yearbook) *1968*. Institute of International Politics and Economics, Beograd, 1969, p. 626.

[16] In 1969 the Japanese armed forces did not markedly differ from those of Indonesia in the number of soldiers and units and in the amount of equipment in all three branches of the armed services, even though the quality of Japan's equipment was far better. Japan's military budget is estimated at 1,344 million dollars, whereas the German Federal Republic spends 5,301 million dollars. See *The Military Balance 1969—1970*, Institute of Strategic Studies, London 1969, p. 23 and 44—45.

two other superpowers. In fact, all three powers may try to maintain a symmetry in their mutual relations and act as rivals in spreading and strengthening their influence in the third world. This may create new problems for the nonaligned countries, which may, more than ever before, have to defend themselves from external attacks or influence. What is more, they may have to strengthen their cooperation and act in unison in all the fields of activity of nonalignment.

B. ROLE AND STATUS OF THE NONALIGNED IN A CHANGING WORLD

CHANGES IN THE POLITICAL SITUATION OF THE NONALIGNED COUNTRIES

Already in the period of relaxation in the mid-1960s the nonaligned countries became victims of increasingly frequent outside interventions, and so as early as 1964 in Cairo, their policies emphasized the increased danger from "imperialism" and "neocolonialism". Irrespective of whether tensions heightened or abated, the countries of the third world were bound to be exposed to pressures and interventions. The three-cornered contest among the superpowers, subject to China's eventually becoming active during the 1970s, reduces the probability of a deterioration in their relations to a degree dangerous for peace. Hence the role of the nonaligned countries will be to protect the interests of the third world and improve international relations rather than to mediate among the great powers.

The superpowers and other great powers will undoubtedly try, by means of their economic power and other methods of influence, to strengthen their role in the world. Their endeavors will be principally directed, as before, at the underdeveloped and economically weak countries of the third world. It is, therefore, necessary to examine the resources available to the nonaligned countries and the third world countries in general for resisting the continuation of that policy which may become even more dangerous as confrontation between the greatest powers slackens.

They obviously can oppose external influences by relying on their special position and special interests, which enables them to act in agreement. Precisely because they are not overtly tied to the superpowers, they can act more autonomously than any other power or group of powers. This faculty gives them a limited measure of potential influence on the behavior of the superpowers.

This influence depends, firstly, on how important their behavior is from the viewpoint of the superpowers and, secondly, on how willing and capable they are to act autonomously and in a concerted endeavor in matters which are relevant for the behavior of the superpowers. In order to examine what prospects there are in that respect, we must first of all devote some attention to those two factors.

The activity of the nonaligned countries and their influence on the behavior of the superpowers may be significant only when very important and fundamental questions are at stake. This is due, firstly, to the fact that the nonaligned countries are effective only when they mobilize world public opinion, and secondly, because moral-political influence, in order to be efficient, must be clearly and simply formulated. It is hard to swing public opinion especially against the basic policy of a great power, except on issues which are easily understandable and of major significance. This is valid even more with regard to world public opinion, which means the opinion in a number of countries including great powers and superpowers. Hence the significance of the second argument, namely that a clear and convincing formulation of political action and goals is indispensable. Success in that direction is possible only with fundamental issues which are topical over a long period of time, highly important and easily comprehensible.

The second factor, namely the ability and readiness of the nonaligned countries to act in coordination, is also possible only when some really important matters are at stake which are of permanent value, and at the same time really understood as vital interests of the nonaligned countries as a whole. These criteria for successful action of the nonaligned countries have proved to be valid in the light of these countries' performance during the 1960s, as well as in earlier actions.

Whereas in the course of the 1960s the nonaligned countries found it difficult to undertake systematic action whenever a practical and concrete elaboration of specific problems was involved, they have always shown efficiency in undertakings of a general nature. At any rate, their method of action, which mainly involves policy declarations and long-term programs, is suitable only for such undertakings. Large gatherings, which as a rule have been favored by the group of the most active nonaligned countries, have called for this method of action. All attempts at those gatherings to isolate individual problems and establish priorities ended with the inclusion on the agenda of a very long list of practically all the problems that might have been proposed by any participant.

It is less likely that within a foreseeable future, especially during the 1970s, they will need to make demands for the elimination of conflicts between the superpowers and try to reestablish relations between them. Such situations, which did happen at one time and to which the nonaligned countries reacted energetically on several occasions, may only arise in the event of a new deterioration of relations between Moscow and Washington. Difficulties may also occur in the course of the Soviet-American talks on the limitation of strategical armaments, and they could cause breakdowns or occasional misunderstandings. However, it will be difficult for the countries outside the talks to express their opinions or influence the course of the talks. Most probably very little will be known about concrete problems, and they will be mainly formulated in a technical jargon and will refer to differences in views which will be very difficult to interpret objectively. The nonaligned could raise only the principle of the need for an agreement, and such an action can only be effective if it is very broad. They would need cooperation from a wide circle of countries, including those outside the usual circle of the nonaligned.

The nonaligned countries may feel an intensive need, perhaps even a desire, to move actions in order to protect the interests of threatened countries of the third world. This implies regional or local situations, as for instance the war in Vietnam. However, these actions will be more delicate and complicated as direct co-

340

operation develops between the superpowers or as they try to avoid trouble between themselves.

When we say that such actions would become more complex, we do not refer only to the complexity of relations among participating countries, but also to the fact that in such situations it would be increas¦ngly difficult to organize a broad cooperation. In this connection we could quote the example of the nonaligned attitude to the civil war in Nigeria and the war in the Near East. As direct confrontation of the superpowers eases and polarization dissolves into a pluralist system of relations, it is not always possible to rally a large number of nonaligned countries to a clearly defined platform necessary to move even a sufficiently impressive declaratory action to exert pressure on the main protagonists and world public opinion. With the emergence and greater activization of China, such problems will inevitably become still more difficult.

The nonaligned countries have participated in the shaping of relations in the world including the relations between the superpowers. The subsequent easing of tensions has then been felt in the whole world including the regions outside the blocs. The nonaligned countries even played a significant role in various crises which followed occasional increases in tensions. Sometimes they have helped in the finding of solutions in international councils. There may be different opinions about their role in some of the crises and tense situations, but it is difficult to deny that they have contributed to the easing of the cold war by the very fact of their existence and of their increasing numbers.

The most publicized aim of the nonaligned countries was their steadfast determination to keep outside the cold war and to help ease it. The reduction of tensions in the early 1960s and the weakening of cohesion within the blocs was hailed by the nonaligned countries as the attainment of at least one of the positive aims of their movement in the realm of general international relations.[17] This success came after the success of the anti-colonial movement[18]

---

[17] See the assessment of the international situation in the introductory part of the Program adopted at the Cairo Conference in 1964, given in the Appendix.

[18] At the end of the 1960s, the only sizable colonies left were Angola and Mozambique in Africa and East Irian in the Pacific. All the other colonies are of small size and population and represent only a very small remnant of earlier colonial empires.

and would have given them good reason for satisfaction had it not been for some other problems that arose at the same time. In fact, the relaxation did open some new horizons and brought to surface some new problems which had been obscured by the confrontation of the two blocs.

It is obvious that the breakup of the large colonial empires and the easing of tensions cannot be regarded simply as victories of the nonaligned countries. The first of these phenomena, decolonization, preceded and subsequently contributed to the full development of nonalignment and made it a very wide-spread movement in world politics. Although the nonaligned countries took an active part in this process, they cannot ascribe the success of the anti-colonial movement exclusively to their own policies. The breakup of the colonial empires was principally the result of the determination of the colonial people to win their independence and freedom, and of the view the colonial powers took toward those aspirations. It is the product of a comprehensive world-wide movement for emancipation, which appeared after the Second World War in the form of anti-colonialism, renewed nationalism and anti-racialism, but also as a demand for greater independence and for a greater integrity of the human personality in all contemporary societies. It is also the result of the evolution within the colonial powers caused by the technical and social progress during the twentieth century.

In consequence of this progress, direct economic benefits from the colonies became less and less important to the highly developed countries. As a result, and because of an increased resistance of the colonial population, the colonial powers were reluctant to let themselves into a hard struggle to keep the colonies. This applies particularly to the developed colonial powers, and not so much to the less developed, as Portugal. We should also take into consideration the diminished strategical value of the colonies and a considerably decreased interest in them from the military point of view. These are, of course, additional elements, but they have some significance in a comprehensive analysis of the breakup of colonial empires.

Nonalignment is also a product of this general course of events but we must not completely discard its role in the process of decolonization. The nonaligned countries have always believed that the struggle being waged by the peoples in the colonies was a component part of their movement. They considered themselves directly and vitally interested in the question of decolonization, but, in contrast to this, their efforts to contribute to the lessening of tensions between the blocs were those of an interested but nevertheless a third party acting from outside.

They acted from the sidelines of the conflict and did not develop the immediacy of involvement as it was the case with the anticolonial movement, because they neither could nor would identify themselves with either side. Such an uncommitted position was possible in a strictly bipolar system of international relations, for as long as this bipolarity was sufficiently pronounced and dominant in the totality of relationships in the world. A disagreement with bipolarity could in those circumstances be a fairly clearly defined as a distinct third position.

In other words, for as long as the cold war imposed its logic and interests on events in the world, any noninvolvement led either towards nonalignment or towards neutrality which, at least in political questions connected with the cold war, had been very close to the position of the nonaligned countries. The general changes in relations in the world during the 1960s provoked some deep changes also in the status of the nonaligned countries. They were less and less able to play the role of mediator and catalyst in the dispute, since they were preoccupied with defending themselves as they increasingly became a target of attacks and pressures from outside. In a series of interventions (as for example in the Dominican Republic) the nonaligned countries were brought into the position of opposing (only politically, of course) the actions of the superpowers. Two kinds of conflicts broke out in succession: first, conflicts between the forces which aspire to emancipation and the forces of intervention, and second, strife between the countries of the third world themselves (as for example the war between India and Pakistan in 1965).

In both cases the nonaligned countries were directly involved. If we expect the war in Vietnam, and possibly also the war in the Middle East, the main protagonists in the conflict were never the

343

two superpowers.[19] Conflicts arose either between the countries of the third world, or between one of them and one great power. This was a new element in comparison with the years of the intensive cold war, when all the conflicts had generally taken place either within the framework or at least under the shadow of the East-West conflict. At the same time, looser cohesion in the blocs created new possibilities for cooperation with the bloc-adhering countries. The area of cooperation enlarged, and the fact that a country did not belong to any bloc lost much of its previous significance. Cooperation with members of a bloc became possible even on such questions as the criticism of the original text of the draft agreement on the nonproliferation of nuclear armaments. As tension eased between the blocs, a much more fluid model of international relations became possible, and the customary anti-bloc stand of the nonaligned countries necessarily underwent great change.

This fact was recognized by some of the leading statesmen of the nonaligned countries already at the beginning of the 1960s. Thus President Tito, alluding to the changes in the international constellation, stated before the UN General Assembly on October 22, 1963:

"The question of non-alignment is posed today in a far broader sense, in view of the growing number of States and peoples that are participating in the active struggle for peace. The polarization of the forces of peace, on the one hand, and of the forces of cold war on the other, is taking place at an accelerated pace, practically in all the countries of the world, with the forces of peace in ascendancy. Non-alignment is thus changing, both in quantitative and in qualitative terms, and is transforming itself into a general movement for peace and for the finding of peaceful and constructive means for the settlement of various problems among nations. Active "non-alignment" is thus becoming an increasingly broad and active participation in the struggle for the

---

[19] Just how much the conflict in the Middle East is conditioned by the antagonism arising from the local situation is shown by the difficulties that both superpowers have met with in their attempts to influence one or the other side in the conflict. The situation there exists regardless of the fact that the grounds for the conflict were created by an action outside the region, when it was decided by a resolution of the United Nations to create the state of Israel.

triumph of the principles of the United Nations Charter, as was so powerfully expressed by the Heads of State or Government of twenty-five countries at the Belgrade Conference in September 1961. These principles are endorsed by the overwhelming majority of nations. That is understandable, because we all bear a responsibility for the fate of the international community. The participation of all peace-loving forces in this process should be constructive and realistic and be inspired by a desire to find a solution to existing problems.

"We stand at historical cross-roads, branching out towards new and more constructive and more humane international relations. This should make it possible for mankind to live without fear — for its fate to develop and to harness towards peaceful ends all the human mind has so far achieved."[20]

During the preparations for a new meeting of the heads of nonaligned countries in 1968, it was proposed to extend the term of nonalignment again and to include "likeminded" countries. Thus the conference would have been enlarged and would have included nonaligned and likeminded countries. This means that the political platform championing the struggle against military alliances — which tend to divide the world into two antagonistic camps — has today lost much of its significance as a deciding factor in the formulation of the policies of nonalignment. In other words, nonalignment ceased to be non-commitment. Essentially, it had never been just that, yet not belonging to a bloc and opposing blocs had been an important characteristic of the movement since its beginning.

A long road had been covered from Nehru's statement of 1946 to Tito's of 1963, although the two statements were divided by a span of a little less than one score years. The outlook which gave a name to this policy has been rendered obsolete by the course of events, and if nonalignment continues to act under the same label, it is probably because of the habit which takes long to die. This is not so unusual, because the same thing happened with many other political movements in the past. In any case, the term nonalignment has never been fully adequate. It must be

---

[20] GAOR, 18th Session, 1251 Plenary Meeting, p. 3 (22 October 1963).

remembered that Nehru's statement of 1946 expressed much more than a simple desire to stand aloof from the bloc policies.

Since the mentioned changes in the world of the 1960s had taken place, the activity of the nonaligned countries may be divided into two categories: firstly, cooperation with all the nations throughout the world which have the same or similar conceptions about the problems concerning peace and war; secondly, organization and coordination of efforts of the countries of the third world to improve their position in international relations and preserve, strengthen and promote independence of the underdeveloped countries in general.

In view of the fundamental change in the status and aims of the nonaligned countries, cooperation with countries having similar views on bloc policies and not belonging to the "third world" had to undergo important changes. They joined with the nonaligned countries of the third world whenever problems of peace and security were at stake, as for example in the elaboration of the texts on the agreement on nonproliferation of nuclear weapons. This cooperation, however, has become practically impossible, in such specific situation in which the countries of the third world have to stand up for their specific interests, political or economic.

It is therefore understandable that the concept of likeminded nations remained fairly nebulous and vaguely defined. The neutral highly advanced countries of Western Europe found a common language with the nonaligned countries when they acted on behalf of the broader and permanent interests of the international community opposing the cold war and armaments race. In their relations with the nonaligned countries they found themselves in a much more difficult position whenever these countries became involved in disputes with neighboring countries. The developed neutrals opposed the blocs only because of bloc policies, while the nonaligned countries based their separate political identity and activity on altogether different interests, which were specifically their own, on their position and belonging to the third world, which is above all the world of the less developed countries, economically and politically threatened by the rich and powerful countries.

The Geneva Conference of the countries having no nuclear weapons, called under the aegis of the United Nations, constitutes a good example of possibilities for cooperation among the nations of the North and South and for broadening the political activities of nonaligned countries. But there remains still the task of resolving the entire complex of special problems affecting the countries of the South, which inspires a special and close relationship and cooperation among the nonaligned countries as the most politically active underdeveloped countries. The world in a certain sense is shrinking, and all the countries in the world are coming closer to each other, but at the same time the world is becoming more and more divided into two parts — the developed and the under-developed.

ANTI-COLONIALISM IN NEW CIRCUMSTANCES

A major lever in the struggle against colonialism is the already achieved success of decolonization. The rulers of the large colonial empires offered in places strong and stubborn resistance to more or less intensive and militant liberation movements; elsewhere, they gave in without much fight, even in the absence of strong pressure from the liberation movements, thus reckoning that they would better preserve their positions after the liberation of the colonies in question. However, the colonial rule has held out longest in the Portuguese colonies of Angola and Mozambique, if we consider colonies with large areas and numerous population only.

This apparently paradoxical situation can be understood if we take two important facts into consideration. First of all, it is only towards the end of the 1960s that in these colonies appeared a large scale anti-colonial movement. Even then this movement lacked the breadth and intensity necessary to force the colonial rule to withdraw. Furthermore, the colonial ruler, in this case Portugal, was not interested in making a peaceful withdrawal in order to retain its positions, because it was highly improbable that she could retain them. Whereas the highly developed and economically powerful colonial countries hoped to keep the well-

347

run-in channels of economic activities in their own hands, even after their former wards achieved independence, Portugal could not count on such a contingency. If she were to lose administrative and military control, she could not expect to be economically capable of standing up to the much stronger competition of the more developed and more powerful states. Even in the possession of a complete monopoly of power she was not able to create such economic positions and connections which would be acceptable and attractive in the event of the colony's ability to chose its own economic partners.

It is difficult to suppose that the position of the nonaligned countries could substantially change in a foreseeable future in regard to the remaining major colonies. The movements in those colonies will continue receiving verbal support from the nonaligned countries, but it is unlikely that this support would rise to a scale that could really effect the course of events, unless a considerably more intensive and large-scale liberation struggle is undertaken in those colonies. This also applies to the situation in Southern Rhodesia which, although no longer a British colony, holds out no prospect of liberation for as long as the racialist regime of the white minority remains in power.

However, the policy of the nonaligned countries in regard to Southern Rhodesia lacks the punch needed to influence the course of events in that colony. Their ceaseless appeals to Great Britain to intervene are difficult to reconcile with consequent anti-colonial stand.[21] An intervention by Great Britain on behalf of the black majority of the population would benefit their immediate interests, but on the other hand it would bring British troops there, creating again a very unnatural situation.

These unusual appeals, which acknowledge the right of Great Britain to intervene in Rhodesia, were made because there was no anti-colonial movement in Southern Rhodesia strong

---

[21] The nonaligned countries proposed a resolution on Southern Rhodesia to the U.N. General Assembly, which was adopted on November 17, 1966, with 86 votes in favor, 2 against (Portugal and South Africa) and 17 abstentions. The eighth paragraph of the resolution states that the U.N. "calls once again upon the Government of the United Kingdom to take all the necessary measures, including in particular the use of force, in the exercise of its powers as the administering Power, to put an end to the illegal racist minority régime..." General Assembly — 21st Session, 1468 Plenary Meeting, p. 69, 17 November 1966.

enough to threaten the present regime, and the neighboring emancipated countries do not wish to take the risk of helping such a movement from their territories, as had been done earlier for the movements in Algeria and the Congo (Kinshasa). All the efforts by the countries of Black Africa to provide collective material assistance for the remaining liberation movements in Africa have failed to produce any outstanding results.

Aside from these large territories, there are still a considerable number of small and even miniscule territories under colonial rule. In some cases these are small islands or archipelagos scattered about the oceans. In many such cases, the independent existence and development of these colonies is scarcely feasible. So far no proposal has been made on the future of these territories which would hold out the promise of a lasting solution.

The relatively scant interest of the nonaligned countries in these territories and their populations may be attributed to two reasons. First, solutions would have to be found including these territories into larger and sufficiently developed economic systems so that their survival and development would be ensured. In many cases, however, such a solution would involve very delicate political questions. Second, the movement of the nonaligned countries would not gain strength by the independence of these territories, but on the contrary would be burdened by a moral and political obligation. The demand for full independence and sovereignty as a general principle would, namely, involve an obligation to provide assistance to these miniscule countries to preserve their independence, and there are no real possibilities for the nonaligned countries to do this. There is even less hope that the United Nations could solve this problem satisfactorily. The unsuccessful efforts of the Conference on Trade and Development made it quite clear that not even the large and politically important underdeveloped countries could solve their economic problems in an even remotely acceptable manner.

In a way, the only possible solution in given circumstances would be to leave these countries or territories to their fate and restrict the campaign for their final status to declarations which would keep the anti-colonial principle alive, even though they would not make any concrete contribution to the settlement of their problems. In some cases, particularly in the Caribbean possessions of Great Britain, tiny island countries have appeared, to which London has awarded independence, but which are not able to make this independence a reality.

The question of the so-called "mini states" has already been raised in the United Nations, and it has posed a very delicate problem for the nonaligned countries. The very existence of these countries imposes the need for something to be done in regard to their real international status. Obviously it would be very difficult to imagine that a country with just a few thousand inhabitants could meet the obligations that the United Nations Charter imposes on its members, and it is also very unlikely that they could meet even formal obligations in an acceptable manner. It is difficult to find a way out of this situation if unqualified insistence is made on the principle that every country, regardless of its size, should have equal rights and a full deciding vote in international forums.

Abandonment of these principles could also have very dangerous implications for the future, and for this reason action to liberate the "mini colonies" has been soft-pedalled so that the number of "mini states" would not multiply.

It would appear, then, that the issue which at the very beginning had top priority with the nonaligned countries has lost its impetus. Since this decline in activity is the result of successes in decolonization, there is little chance that there will be a revival of these activities. It is a certainty that this question will not be central in the future international activities of the nonaligned countries. Liberation is of course often mentioned in connection with neo-colonialism, but this in fact is just a play on words. Neo-colonialism can mean nothing other than outside interference in internal, primarily economic, affairs of an independent country. The issues at stake are the preservation and strengthening of independence and freedom of internal development and the autonomy of foreign policy of states which have already been acknowledged as independent. This question, therefore, belongs to the category either of political relations or of the economic conditions of development of the countries of the third world.

PROTECTION OF THE ECONOMIC INTERESTS OF THE UNDERDEVELOPED COUNTRIES

The question of economic development and relations in the world market was always a major domain of activity of the nonaligned countries. This activity has a long history. The economic issue was more or less outlined early in the 'fifties, i. e., very soon after the beginning of the anti-colonial drive. But, in contrast to the colonial question, the dimensions of this problem have been constantly growing. Every newly liberated country is automatically categorized as an underdeveloped country. In the 1970s and after, there will be only a few insignificant additions to their ranks. It is, therefore, the magnified dimensions of their economic problems that will constitute the principal issue. Firstly, the underdeveloped areas are lagging behind the development of the highly advanced countries more and more, and they will not be able to catch up for a long time to come. Secondly, the number of inhabitants in these areas is growing very rapidly, and there is little chance that this population growth could be curbed in a foreseeable future.

The effects of increased population growth and lagging behind the advanced countries are often interconnected. The rapid growth of population cancels out a large proportion of increased production, and in some places over-population in respect to the level of economic development itself becomes an acute problem. It is, therefore, reasonable to expect a continued activity by the nonaligned countries in economic and social question. These issues have always been on the agenda, and there is no reason to suppose that they can be pushed into the background. The problem rather involves the manner in which these issues have been handled and their prospects for the future.

To assess these prospects, we must first examine the general extent of the problem and consider future economic relations between the advanced and the underdeveloped countries. As has been already shown, and this is almost always emphasized in discussions on these problems, the developed countries are developing much more intensive economic relations among themselves than with the underdeveloped countries. This trend seems to be stable, and there are no grounds to suppose that it will change in the foreseeable future.

This phenomenon is of great significance for the general development of relations, including the outlook for assistance to underdeveloped countries. Since it is not based on political considerations but rather on economic expediency, it indicates that the developed world can develop further even if its economic ties with the underdeveloped countries diminish.

The often repeated assertion that the developed countries would enjoy greater benefits if they helped the more rapid development of the underdeveloped countries can be neither proven nor disproven. It may prove itself only in a rather remote future.[22] Insistence on it can, however, be understood, since it is one of the ways in which the underdeveloped countries hope to create an atmosphere conducive to a change in the current attitude of the developed countries, which act according to what they see to be their interests.

The highly developed countries enjoyed a very rapid development in the 1950s and 1960s, while the third world remained behind. Furthermore, statistics show that trade among the developed countries grew far more rapidly than trade between them and the underdeveloped countries. However, the period from the war to the end of the 1960s is perhaps not long enough, and we should consider the period of development from the time when today's underdeveloped countries were colonies of the advanced world. Even then the initial and later accelerated development of the developed countries failed to lead to a comparable growth of the underdeveloped regions. It is also inconclusive to point out the benefits that the colonial powers had drawn from the colonies, even when they were considerable, since they do not explain the growth of such countries as Sweden and Switzerland, or the United States and Japan.

These latter countries benefited from colonies only through

---

[22] Vladimir Dragomanović in his article "Dileme UNCTAD-a", which has already been cited, on page 22 mentions this problem: "Instead of the traditional trade principles of reciprocity and *quid pro quo*, in the confrontation between these two groups there is most often only the undefined long-term interest of the advanced countries, in spite of the demands of the underdeveloped for concrete concessions on the basis of non-reciprocity".

the mechanism of the world market, and this indicates that the production of raw materials in the underdeveloped regions is insufficient for the accumulation of the capital necessary for economic development. After their liberation, these countries sometimes considerably speeded up their development. However, neither the dependent and colonial relationship, nor the somewhat better conditions after liberation, influenced essentially the economic development of the developed countries. If the loss of colonies did have any effect on the economies of the colonial powers, it was not decisive for their further growth and prosperity, while the economic growth of the countries which did not have colonies in any case did not depend on the fate of the underdeveloped countries in the past.

The activity in the economic sphere has been and will continue to be of a predominantly political nature. This political activity will be distinguished from other political activities by its special aim of creating more favorable conditions for national economic development. No means other than political can wrest any concessions, owing to the fact that the developed countries do not depend on the underdeveloped countries economically.

The fact that the developed countries utilize various important and at present irreplaceable raw materials or sources of energy from the underdeveloped countries still does not create a state of real dependence. It is very wrong to think that the need for a product of some other country makes a country automatically dependent on it. Dependency is the product of a much more complex inter-relationship and represents the final result when all relevant factors are taken into consideration. In this instance it should be realized that the sales of raw materials by underdeveloped countries are not a concession to the developed countries, but rather an operation which is often overdone in order to fulfil the urgent need for the money needed for imports. Sometimes it is simply a matter of ensuring the livelihood of that sector of the population engaged in the production of a raw material, which usually has a very limited domestic use.

The underdeveloped countries are increasingly required to supply their primary products, whereas in the advanced countries there is a trend towards stagnation or even decline in the consumption of these products. This explains why the trade between complementary economies, of primary producers and industrial states, as in the early period of industrialization, has given way since the Second World War to a particularly rapid development of trade between countries on a similar level of development, i. e., among highly advanced countries.

In fact, all economic conferences dealing with problems of development have been political assemblies, whether held among the nonaligned or underdeveloped countries or within the United Nations. Their objective was to achieve multilateral agreements which, by the enforcement of national authority on national territory or regulation of international relations, would provide facilities for the development of the underdeveloped countries. Behind all the economic arguments there was a tangle of political factors and interests. The advanced countries were not impressed by the interpretation of their economic interests by the representatives of the underdeveloped countries. They could only be impressed by possible political consequences if current trends continued in the third world. But they obviously were not sufficiently impressed in order to satisfy any of the basic demands of the underdeveloped countries in practice. The adoption of certain premises has so far not produced any tangible results.

Future developments, therefore, can only be along the lines of implementation of agreements and compromises.[23] This means that concrete problems must be studied, and they differ considerably from country to country. They are particularly disparate in countries at the bottom of the ladder of development and those which have already entered the process of industrialization. The nonaligned countries had to face this reality in the 1960s.

Their activities followed two lines: on the one hand the need was stressed for differentiation which was defined in the Algiers Charter, but on the other hand, insistence was made on collective action within as broad a circle of underdeveloped countries as possible. This bent for broad and general actions is understandable in light of the fact that their action is political. They worked

---

[23] This thesis is included in the *Algiers Charter*, see the Appendix, and also in the declaration of the Cairo meeting of the leaders of nonaligned countries in 1964; see the Appendix.

on the assumption that any action by a large number of countries was bound to exert a stronger influence. Any partial agreements by small groups of countries were frowned on and rejected, since it was believed that they would weaken the force of the under-developed partners in such collective negotiations. In addition, it was thought that negotiations in small groups would neglect the demands of some of the most underdeveloped countries.

Such views are unfounded and not based on real facts. First of all, it would be hard to believe that a developed country would be pressured into making practical concessions or into complying with U.N. resolutions just because they may have been passed by a large number of votes. This is even more unlikely in view of the nature of concessions that are sought, which are financial assistance either directly or in the form of facilities or benefits in prices or fiscal concessions. After all, for the country giving the concession it would mean reduced revenue either to the state directly or to the economy. Under the second category of concessions they would be expected to amend their internal legislations or legally regulated practices in relations with the outside world.

No success, however, has been forthcoming so far as a result of pressure by a large number of countries supporting resolutions with similar demands in international forums. The course of post-war international relations gives ample proof of this. Yet, on the other hand, such steps, particularly grants in aid and even of large gifts, were often made. But in each case they were restricted to individual countries and made not under the pressure of a large number of votes, but rather on the basis of a judicious assessment of an advanced country's interest in granting aid to a beneficiary. This of course does not mean that these countries in every case had to meet certain requirements imposed by the aid granting countries. There were such cases, indeed, but it should be recalled that Yugoslavia and India, countries which preserved their independence and the autonomy of their internal development, also received assistance. This phenomenon is not new in international affairs — in the years after the end of the First World War, the United States provided large assistance to hunger victims in the Soviet Union, and after the end of the Second World War, such organizations as UNRRA helped the distressed areas in the

Soviet Union, even though the relations between them were strained.

Finally, a broad collective action of all the underdeveloped countries by no means guarantees that the demands of all those countries would be met. The underdeveloped countries had to accept this when they tried at the second session of the Conference on Trade and Development in New Delhi to obtain a preferential fiscal treatment for exports of industrial products from the underdeveloped countries to the markets of the advanced countries.[24] This measure, although defined in very general terms, would benefit only a limited number of underdeveloped countries having sizable industrial exports. This benefit would be insignificant or nil for the other countries.

It seems that further actions concerning economic matters are probable, but it is obvious that they must be aimed at solving concrete questions. The drafting of general principles and declarations at large meetings will contribute very little to what has already been achieved. By expecting the developed countries to be politically interested, various groups of underdeveloped countries may try to obtain solutions of their concrete problems. Internal measures must also be taken to ensure the most advantageous utilization of assistance which would foster the modernization of the economy and a rapid economic development. Another possibility is to try and enlarge their market through integration or other forms of association or cooperation among the underdeveloped countries to create better conditions for the development of their economies.

However, it is essential that economic objectives should be fixed with due regard for realities and the inevitable course of modern economic trends. It is very problematical whether the underdeveloped countries will manage to keep up the level of interest and dynamics of action by going back to the earlier goal of catching up with the advanced countries and closing the gap dividing them. The gap is obviously widening, and it is also obvious that it will continue to do so. This conclusion is based on the fact that even a comparatively rapid development of a poor country

---

24 Vladimir Dragomanović, "Dileme UNCTAD-a", *op. cit.*, p. 11.

still only makes an insignificant contribution to the absolute amount which is annually added to the national income, and particularly to the income per head of population.

In other words, strategical objectives must be brought into line with reality, and this means that the primary task is not to achieve as rapid a growth as possible in order to overtake the developed countries, so the conception of catching up is wrong. Instead, it is essential to concentrate on an intensive modernization of society, which will create the basis for a gradual acceleration of the rate of development. Modernization should include both the general development of social relations and structures and education of citizens to take part in modern trends in the economy and in society. It should also include all measures which will help to reduce internal tensions and therefore increase as much as possible flexibility in regard to outside and internal tensions and pressures resulting from modernization and social development.

Such objectives must also include the acceleration of economic growth, not as an end in itself, but rather as a means of improving the social system and creating a base for a lasting rapid growth. The problem of catching up with the advanced countries can only be dealt with at a much higher level of development. Today it is difficult to say what chances there are in this respect for the most underdeveloped countries. The future will be determined by changes which in the course of time will undoubtedly take place in economic trends, both in the developed and in the underdeveloped countries. The most important thing is to take national needs and attainable goals as a basis for the strategy of development rather than the concept of a race at any cost.

Finally, activity in this field is closely connected, and will probably remain so, with the development of general political relations in the world. The appearance of an active China in international affairs is particularly important here. There is no doubt that the cold war and rivalry between the great powers was one of the reasons for giving aid in the years immediately after the end of the Second World War. This rivalry may weaken if a lasting and close cooperation between the U.S.S.R. and the U.S.A. is reached, but continued rivalry also will be of little use if the arms race continues. So far they have shown to be less interested in granting economic aid to the third world countries at the time when they were developing ultra-modern and very expensive long-range weapons.[25]

They may become more interested as China becomes more active in world affairs. Although towards the end of the 1960s China's world activity considerably diminished, it might intensify again.[26] Dissatisfaction with the increasing economic problems and China's rise to the status of a superpower, which she may attain in a foreseeable future, may revive the interest of the powerful developed countries in the situation and stability in the third world.[27] On several significant occasions the Soviet Union displayed its interest in the stability of the existing relations and situations in various areas of the third world. Since the end of the war the U. S. A. has been doing all it can to preserve the favorable status quo, so China's ambition to change the existing state of affairs could lead to increased U. S. interest in the fate and prosperity of the third world, in order to counter her influence. China again apparently is counting on a further deterioration of the situation in the underdeveloped countries. All this provides a much more realistic basis for hope in the success of the economic demands of the third world than the passing of resolutions and declarations which so far have not produced concrete results, and which are even less likely to be effective in the situation which is taking shape in the relations between the two greatest powers. This holds true whether relations between them improve or deteriorate.

However, it would be wrong to underestimate the importance of the political efforts being made by the underdeveloped countries in the United Nations, in the forums of the United Nations Con-

---

25 It is difficult to establish a direct link between the change in strategical conceptions, arising from the development of military techniques, and that in attitudes towards countries of the third world. Nevertheless, the fact remains that the share of grants in aid to the underdeveloped countries dropped from 88% in 1960 to 60% in 1966, according to OECD data, quoted in the study by Djordje Ladjević, "Spoljno finansiranje privrednog razvoja zemalja u razvoju" (Foreign Financing of the Economic Development of Developing Countries), published in *Položaj zemalja u razvoju* (The Position of the Developing Countries), II, Institute of International Politics and Economics, Beograd 1968, p. 146 (mimeographed).

26 In the course of 1969, China entered talks with a certain number of countries in Europe and outside Europe on the establishment or normalization of diplomatic ties. This action, according to unofficial reports, was favorably received in these countries.

27 The launching of the first Chinese earth satellite on April 24, 1970, contributed much in this direction.

ference on Trade and Development, and at other meetings. They are justified because they promote understanding among the underdeveloped countries and lead to selective political actions in accordance with a given situation. Experience has shown that the possible effects of political actions aiming at economic goals are limited in, even when they can be backed with administrative measures, i. e., when there is state power behind the political will. The scope of such international political activities of the under-developed countries is still more limited because they have no real power to put behind them, and they must rely mostly on the world public opinion as a background against which they could throw into sharper relief the political and economic problems of the present-day world.

C. CONCLUSIONS

A general conclusion that can be drawn is that in any case the activities of the nonaligned countries must undergo certain changes in their further development. First of all, it is undeniable that activities in connection with the colonial question are being pushed more and more into the background and that they will not loom large in their future activities. However, the nonaligned countries must become more active in the political sphere along two lines: in regard to relations between the two greatest world powers, where the most urgent question is to halt the race in producing new categories of modern strategical weapons, and in regard to the protection of the interests of the countries of the third world from pressures and intervention.

They will also have to continue energetically promoting their economic interests through political activities in the United Nations and elsewhere, but more and more they will have to work within limited circles of countries with similar economic problems, and entertain at the same time a dialogue on concrete problems with the developed countries. These actions will have to be very concrete and specific. Their arguments and political logic can be based only on the actual political interest of the two negotiating sides, i. e., the developed and the underdeveloped countries.

This means that the forms of action of the nonaligned countries may be declarative only in regard to very general issues, e. g. to influence the superpowers into making greater efforts to find an agreed settlement in their mutual relations. In other questions concerning concrete problems, such declarative actions are pointless and cannot give positive results. This is particularly true for putting the adopted principles into practice.

Activities in fostering economic interests concerning concrete problems should be conducted jointly with similar and directly interested countries only, and with the aim of strengthening their cooperation and of obtaining assistance and concessions from others. However, political actions should be conducted on as broad a front as possible. The larger the number of countries taking an active part in them, the better their chances of exerting moral and political pressure. It would be wrong to exclude from such joint actions those countries which are formally linked by a military-political treaty with a superpower, as long as they are willing to take part in a given action.

Before such a broad political action can succeed, it is necessary to create a general mood in the world and politically involve as many countries as possible, regardless of political alignment, if they are willing to work together. As the U.S.-Soviet dialogue proceeds this action will unfold and take on quite concrete aspects and will have to concentrate on definite questions which at this time are hard to foresee. It is essential that it should not become enclosed within artificial circles, and its emphasis should be calculated to produce the maximum effect. The best effect would be made by a broad and well-timed action which could truly arouse public opinion in the world and in the superpowers themselves. There can be no doubt that this is possible. However, such actions largely transcend the customary limits of the nonaligned countries, which have tended towards exclusiveness and working within a closed circle of countries irrespective of the various fields of action.

Such methods were abandoned only in actions concerning

trade and development, particularly in the creation of the group of 77 countries. However, whenever political questions were at stake, or whenever a new political conference was called, a certain exclusiveness reappeared and frustrated all attempts of taking a broader and more flexible approach. This exclusiveness is not accidental, nor is it a unique phenomenon in international relations. In a way it mirrors the exclusiveness of the blocs. Not wishing to create a bloc for themselves, the protagonists of nonalignment nevertheless find it difficult to resist the temptation of creating a precisely defined cooperation or association of countries. Admission to the group then necessarily becomes one of the prerogatives and indispensable attributes of this grouping. There is also parallel tendency visible to coordinate the overall foreign policy and to treat the nonaligned countries as a group whose members have identical views on all questions. This could also be described as an attempt to ideologize nonalignment, which could jeopardize a broad cooperation in the ever more complicated international constellation.

Although the resolve taken in 1961, that there could be no question of creating a new international organization, has not been contradicted by any act or statement, nevertheless the lasting cooperation has imperceptibly and inexorably imposed a certain feeling of belonging, of membership in an association. This was evident at the consultative conference in Belgrade in 1969. After a lengthy discussion, attendance at earlier conferences was acknowledged as the only title to admission except in the case of a special decision or invitation.[28]

This practice may prove to be a very serious obstacle to truly broad and flexible activity in the 1970s. It is not likely that the economic problems of countries at different levels of development (or rather underdevelopment) can be settled by cooperation

---

[28] The final sentence in the communiqué from this meeting, which was held in Belgrade from July 8 to 12, 1969, reads as follows: "The desire was expressed at the Consultative Meeting that those interested countries that proclaim their adherence to the policy of nonalignment and particularly those who had won their independence after the Cairo Conference and all member countries of the Organization of African Unity should also be invited to the future gatherings of the nonaligned countries in accordance with the principles and criteria observed at the Belgrade and Cairo Conferences". *Review of International Affairs*, Beograd vol. XX, issue 464—465, from August 1—16, 1969, Special Supplement, p. 28.

within the present circle of the nonaligned, which is too broad for it. At the same time, the circle of participations is not sufficiently broad and flexible to produce the necessary effect and to arouse public opinion where general political demands are made.

In addition to general conferences of the statesmen of nonaligned countries, whose direct influence on world events is bound to decrease through repetition, and special *ad hoc* political meetings, cooperation could be carried out in various specialized meetings of countries interested in special, particularly economic, problems. But this proposition should be taken more as an illustration than a concrete proposal. It stresses the undeniable need for a break in the routine approach and a rigid pattern of cooperation, and for a far more flexible approach to problems in international affairs at a time when all problems, even the most general ones, come up as concrete questions, and cannot be solved by generalized postulates and principles.

Our remaining task is to try to give an answer to the question of the general outlook for nonalignment. But in answering this question, we must immediately point out the difference between the role of nonalignment as a behavior and activity in world politics, and the role of those countries which have been championing this activity. In other words, the future of nonalignment and the future of the nonaligned countries are not the same thing. For this reason it is necessary first to say something about the nonaligned countries, i. e., those which consider themselves to be nonaligned and which have been the supporters of nonalignment during its first twenty years.

The nonaligned countries, which are identified more according to their position in the international community than according to their concrete and specific foreign policies, undeniably remain an exceptionally important element of any possible constellation in the world. They comprise an enormous portion of mankind, indeed that part which is understandably dissatisfied with its status and position in the international community. Therefore, no matter how these countries behave and how they conduct their foreign policies, either in cooperation or individually, they will be a very important factor in the future as well. If they do not succeed in exerting a positive influence on international events, they will still play an important role either through their defensive action or their instability and weakness.

The success and positive influence of the nonaligned countries will very largely depend on the ability of its most active protagonists to reorient the other countries from the old positions of appealing to the conscience of mankind as a third factor outside the blocs to a positive action in resolving the main world problems. It will also depend on their ability to defend themselves from foreign intervention in a number of disputes or defensive actions, which it will not always be easy to combine into a large united front, but which will appear more as individual conflicts or defensive actions of small and materially weak countries desiring to preserve their independence.

The question of the further development of nonalignment should be viewed in the light of these possibilities, and defined as a question of the policy and behavior of the nonaligned countries in changed world conditions. In other words, the weight and impact of their active and positive involvement will depend on their ability to adjust their behavior and attitudes to the changes which do not always depend on their will, but in which they often participate and which are even sometimes the result of their own actions.

In the second half of the 1960s they did not show very great flexibility in this respect. The very significant assertion that "in this new phase of international relations the conditions in which the policy of nonalignment originated are changing", as stated by President Tito in 1963 before the General Assembly of the United Nations,[29] did not meet with the expected response. It did not essentially affect the forthcoming meeting of statesmen of nonaligned countries in Cairo in 1964. Also without an effect was the premise drawn from the above statement in the same speech: "Having in view the changed international situation, we can say that the term nonalignment has been rendered somewhat obsolete by new positive trends in international relations".[30]

If it was true that at that time, in 1963, the world was at a

---

[29] GAOR, 18th Session, *op. cit.*
[30] *Ibid.*

"historical crossroads", then this fact is even more obvious at the end of the decade than ever before. Whether the impact of the deep and important changes will move the nonaligned countries, or whether they will show insufficient flexibility, this cannot be foreseen by methods of research of international relations. Nevertheless, the behavior of the nonaligned countries so far, both in their internal affairs as well as in respect to their reactions to international events, does not indicate a great proclivity for spontaneous adjustment. This can only lead to the conclusion that their future activity will depend on the energy, capability and mainly purposefulness of the actions of those most dynamic actors and most influential protagonists which have always directed their activities.

POSTSCRIPT

Since the publication of this book in the original Serbo-Croat version the nonaligned statesmen met again in Lusaka at the third nonaligned conference 8—10 September 1970. The number of participants in this conference exceeded both the Belgrade and the Cairo Conference. There were 54 full participants and 10 observers. The Conference passed two Declarations — *Lusaka Declaration on Peace, Independence, Development, Co-operation and Democratization of International Relations* and *Lusaka Declaration on Non-alignment and Economic Progress.*[1] Besides these two main documents the conference passed also 15 more documents covering different subjects.[2]

The participation of so many statesmen from nonaligned countries demonstrated the vitality of the movement of the nonaligned and also the constancy of the members of the group. Absences of participants from earlier conferences were few and did not indicate the desertion of those who did not show at Lusaka. It is more significant that the level of representation came down considerably in comparison with the Belgrade Conference

---

[1] See the text of the two Declarations in the Appendix.

[2] The other final documents are: Resolution on Apartheid and Racial Discrimination; Resolution on the Portuguese Colonies (Angola, Mozambique and Guinea Bissau); Resolution on Zimbabwe; Resolution on Indo-China; General Resolution on Decolonization; Resolution on the Middle East; Resolution on the Question of the Illegal Arrest and Detention of Two Algerian Citizens by Israel Authorities; Declaration on Disarmament; Statement on the Seabed; Statement on the United Nations; Resolution on the Strengthening of the Role of the Non-Aligned Countries; Resolution on Cyprus; Revised Draft Resolution on Namibia; Resolution on Israel Aggression on Liban; Expression of Thanks to the Host Government.

and even the Cairo Conference. With only 41% of the participating countries represented by heads of state or government (Belgrade 85% and Cairo 72%) this was hardly a real summit conference.[3] The anticipated devolution from summit to the level of intergovernmental conference has already set in.[4]

The conference debated mainly the topics contained in the final documents, but it was visible that some of the participants whose countries were at that time under stress in international relations or believed to be directly threatened emphasized the danger of colonialism and imperialism more than others. The conference as a whole, as well as the majority of the discussants, underlined the need for better conditions for economic development. This apparently reflected the internal needs as well as the desire to become stronger and better equipped to resist external pressures.

The platform of the conference could be summarized in the following two points: (1) political equality, independence, preservation of the peace in the world and the completion of the decolonization and (2) economic development. As already mentioned some participants concentraded more on the first, others on the second point. In spite of differences in emphasis and even, in some cases of polemical confrontations, these two points were finally accepted by all participants and all documents were passed unanimously.

The conference discussed for the first time also proposals of establishing some permanent form of organization. The final document on future cooperation, however, did not go much beyond the existing practice. Kaunda, the president of the host country, was only requested to take steps to assure further contacts and cooperation.

In sum, the nonaligned countries remained within traditional

---

[3] More about the composition, as well as on the debates in Lusaka can be found in Leo Mates, *The Issues at the Conference in Lusaka*, International Problems 1971.

[4] Compare Chapter Six — Conclusions, pp. 359.

[5] More about the role of the nonaligned countries in international affairs see in Leo Mates: *Can the Nonaligned Act as a Pressure Group*, Pacific Community, Tokyo, April 1971.

forms of acting and the conference addressed the world with another series of declarations and exhortations.[5] If anything, the established circle of participants and the strict observation of qualifications for admission were strengthened. It remains to be seen whether the planned special meetings after Lusaka will introduce more flexibility in seeking cooperation and joint actions with countries outside the circle of participants of Lusaka.

APPENDIX

FINAL COMMUNIQUE
OF THE ASIAN-AFRICAN CONFERENCE

HELD AT BANDUNG FROM 18th TO 24th APRIL, 1955.

The Asian-African Conference, convened upon the invitation of the Prime Ministers of Burma, Ceylon, India, Indonesia and Pakistan met in Bandung from the 18th to the 24th April, 1955. In addition to the sponsoring countries the following 24 countries participated in the Conference:

1. Afghanistan	13. Liberia
2. Cambodia	14. Libya
3. People's Republic of China	15. Nepal
4. Egypt	16. Philippines
5. Ethiopia	17. Saudi Arabia
6. Gold Coast	18. Sudan
7. Iran	19. Syria
8. Iraq	20. Thailand
9. Japan	21. Turkey
10. Jordan	22. Democratic Republic of Vietnam
11. Laos	23. State of Vietnam
12. Lebanon	24. Yemen

The Asian-African Conference considered problems of common interest and concern to countries of Asia and Africa and discussed ways and means by which their people could achieve fuller economic, cultural and political cooperation.

A. ECONOMIC COOPERATION

1. The Asian-African Conference recognized the urgency of promoting economic development in the Asian-African region. There was general desire for economic cooperation among the participating countries on the basis of mutual interest and respect for national sovereignty. The proposals with regard to economic cooperation within the participating countries do not preclude either the desirability or the need for cooperation with countries outside the region, including the investment of foreign capital. It was further recognized that the assistance being received

by certain participating countries from outside the region, through international or under bilateral arrangements, had made a valuable contribution to the implementation of their development programmes.

2. The participating countries agreed to provide technical assistance to one another, to the maximum extent practicable, in the form of: experts, trainees, pilot projects and equipment for demonstration purposes; exchange of know-how and establishment of national, and where possible, regional training and research institutes for importing technical knowledge and skills in cooperation with the existing international agencies.

3. The Asian-African Conference recommended: the early establishment of the Special United Nations Fund for Economic Development; the allocation by the International Bank for Reconstruction and Development of a greater part of its resources to Asian-African countries; the early establishment of the International Finance Corporation which should include in its activities the undertaking of equity investment; and encouragement to the promotion of joint ventures among Asian-African countries in so far as this will promote their common interest.

4. The Asian-African Conference recognised the vital need for stabilizing commodity trade in the region. The principle of enlarging the scope of multilateral trade and payments was accepted. However, it was recognised that some countries would have to take recourse to bilateral trade arrangements in view of their prevailing economic conditions.

5. The Asian-African Conference recommended that collective action be taken by participating countries for stabilizing the international prices of and demand for primary commodities through bilateral and multilateral arrangements, and that as far as practicable and desirable, they should adopt a unified approach on the subject in the United Nations Permanent Advisory Commission on International Commodity Trade and other international forums.

6. The Asian-African Conference further recommended that: Asian-African countries should diversify their export trade by processing their raw material, wherever economically feasible, before export; intra-regional trade fairs should be promoted and encouragement given to the exchange of trade delegations and groups of businessmen; exchange of information and of samples should be encouraged with a view to promoting intra-regional trade; and normal facilities should be provided for transit trade of land-locked countries.

7. The Asian-African Conference attached considerable importance to Shipping and expressed concern that shipping lines reviewed from time to time their freight rates, often to the detriment of participating countries. It recommended a study of this problem, and collective action thereafter, to induce the shipping lines to adopt a more reasonable attitude. It was suggested that a study of railway freight of transit trade may be made.

8. The Asian-African Conference agreed that encouragement should be given to the establishment of national and regional banks and insurance companies.

9. The Asian-African Conference felt that exchange of information on matters relating to oil, such as remittance of profits and taxation, might eventually lead to the formulation of common policies.

10. The Asian-African Conference emphasized the particular significance of the development of nuclear energy for peaceful purposes, for the Asian-African countries. The Conference welcomed the initiative of the Powers principally concerned in offering to make available information regarding the use of atomic energy for peaceful purposes; urged the speedy establishment of the International Atomic Energy Agency which should provide for adequate representation of the Asian-African countries on the executive authority of the Agency; and recommended to the Asian and African Governments to take full advantage of the training and other facilities in the peaceful uses of atomic energy offered by the countries sponsoring such programmes.

11. The Asian-African Conference agreed to the appointment of Liason Officers in participating countries, to be nominated by their respective national Governments, for the exchange of information and ideas on matters of mutual interest. It recommended that fuller use should be made of the existing international organisations, and participating countries who were not members of such international organisations, but were eligible, should secure membership.

12. The Asian-African Conference recommended that there should be prior consultation of participating countries in international forums with a view, as far as possible, to furthering their mutual economic interest. It is, however, not intended to form a regional bloc.

B. CULTURAL COOPERATION

1. The Asian-African Conference was convinced that among the most powerful means of promoting understanding among nations is the development of cultural cooperation. Asia and Africa have been the cradle of great religions and civilisations while themselves being enriched in the process. Thus the cultures of Asia and Africa are based on spiritual and universal foundations. Unfortunately contacts among Asian and African countries were interrupted during the past centuries. The peoples of Asia and Africa are now animated by a keen and sincere desire to renew their old cultural contacts and develop new ones in the context of the modern world. All participating governments at the Conference reiterated their determination to work for closer cultural cooperation.

2. The Asian-African Conference took note of the fact that the existence of colonialism in many parts of Asia and Africa in whatever form it may be not only prevents cultural cooperation but also suppresses the national cultures of the people. Some colonial powers have denied to their dependent peoples basic rights in the sphere of education and culture which hampers the development of their personality and also prevents cultural intercourse with other Asian and African peoples. This is particularly true in the case of Tunisia, Algeria and Morocco, where the basic right of the people to study their own language and culture has been suppressed. Similar discrimination has been practised against African and coloured people in some parts of the Continent of Africa. The Conference felt that these policies amount to a denial of the fundamental rights of man, impede cultural advancement in this region and also hamper cultural cooperation on the wider international

plane. The Conference condemned such a denial of fundamental rights in the sphere of education and culture in some parts of Asia and Africa by this and other forms of cultural suppression.

In particular, the Conference condemned racialism as a means of cultural suppression.

3. It was not from any sense of exclusiveness or rivalry with other groups of nations and other civilisations and cultures that the Conference viewed the development of cultural cooperation among Asian and African countries. True to the age-old tradition of tolerance and universality, the Conference believed that Asian and African cultural cooperation should be developed in the larger context of world cooperation.

Side by side with the development of Asian-African cultural cooperation the countries of Asia and Africa desire to develop cultural contacts with others. This would enrich their own culture and would also help in the promotion of world peace and understanding.

4. There are many countries in Asia and Africa which have not yet been able to develop their educational, scientific and technical institutions. The Conference recommended that countries in Asia and Africa which are more fortunately placed in this respect should give facilities for the admission of students and trainees from such countries to their institutions. Such facilities should also be made available to the Asian and African people in Africa to whom opportunities for acquiring higher education are at present denied.

5. The Asian-African Conference felt that the promotion of cultural cooperation among countries of Asia and Africa should be directed towards:

(I) the acquisition of knowledge of each others' country;

(II) mutual cultural exchange, and

(III) exchange of information.

6. The Asian-African Conference was of opinion that at this stage the best results in cultural cooperation would be achieved by pursuing bilateral arrangements to implement its recommendations and by each country taking action on its own, wherever possible and feasible.

C. HUMAN RIGHTS AND SELF DETERMINATION

1. The Asian-African Conference declared its full support of the fundamental principles of Human Rights as set forth in the Charter of the United Nations and took note of the Universal Declaration of Human Rights as a common standard of achievement for all peoples and all nations.

The Conference declared its full support of the principle of self-determination of peoples and nations as set forth in the Charter of the United Nations and took note of the United Nations resolutions on the rights of peoples and nations to self-determination, which is a pre-requisite of the full enjoyment of all fundamental Human Rights.

2. The Asian-African Conference deplored the policies and practices of racial segregation and discrimination which form the basis of government and human

374

relations in large regions of Africa and in other parts of the world. Such conduct is not only a gross violation of human rights, but also a denial of the fundamental values of civilisation and the dignity of man.

The Conference extended its warm sympathy and support for the courageous stand taken by the victims of racial discrimination, especially by the peoples of African and Indian and Pakistani origin in South Africa; applauded all those who sustain their cause; re-affirmed the determination of Asian-African peoples to eradicate every trace of racialism that might exist in their own countries; and pledged to use its full moral influence to guard against the danger of falling victims to the same evil in their struggle to eradicate it.

D. PROBLEMS OF DEPENDENT PEOPLES

1. The Asian-African Conference discussed the problems of dependent peoples and colonialism and the evils arising from the subjection of peoples to alien subjugation, domination and exploitation.

The Conference is agreed:

(a) in declaring that colonialism in all its manifestations is an evil which should speedily be brought to an end;

(b) in affirming that the subjection of peoples to alien subjugation, domination and exploitation constitutes a denial of fundamental human rights, is contrary to the Charter of the United Nations and is an impediment to the promotion of world peace and co-operation;

(c) in declaring its support of the cause of freedom and independence for all such peoples, and

(d) in calling upon the powers concerned to grant freedom and independence to such peoples.

2. In view of the unsettled situation in North Africa and of the persisting denial to the peoples of North Africa of their right to self-determination, the Asian-African Conference declared its support of the rights of the people of Algeria, Morocco and Tunisia to self-determination and independence and urged the French Government to bring about a peaceful settlement of the issue without delay.

E. OTHER PROBLEMS

1. In view of the existing tension in the Middle East, caused by the situation in Palestine and of the danger of that tension to world peace, the Asian-African Conference declared its support of the rights of the Arab people of Palestine and called for the implementation of the United Nations Resolutions on Palestine and the achievement of the peaceful settlement of the Palestine question.

2. The Asian-African Conference, in the context of its expressed attitude on the abolition of colonialism, supported the position of Indonesia in the case of West Irian based on the relevant agreements between Indonesia and the Netherlands.

The Asian-African Conference urged the Netherlands Government to reopen negotiations as soon as possible, to implement their obligations under the above-mentioned agreements and expressed the earnest hope that the United Nations would assist the parties concerned in finding a peaceful solution to the dispute.

3. The Asian-African Conference supported the position of Yemen in the case of Aden and the Southern parts of Yemen known as the Protectorates and urged the parties concerned to arrive at a peaceful settlement of the dispute.

F. PROMOTION OF WORLD PEACE AND COOPERATION

1. The Asian-African Conference, taking note of the fact that several States have still not been admitted to the United Nations, considered that for effective cooperation for world peace, membership in the United Nations should be universal, called on the Security Council to support the admission of all those States which are qualified for membership in terms of the Charter. In the opinion of the Asian-African Conference, the following among participating countries, viz.: Cambodia, Ceylon, Japan Jordan, Libya, Nepal, a unified Vietnam were so qualified.

The Conference considered that the representation of the countries of the Asian-African region on the Security Council, in relation to the principle of equitable geographical distribution, was inadequate. It expressed the view that as regards the distribution of the non-permanent seats, the Asian-African countries which, under the arrangement arrived at in London in 1946, are precluded from being elected, should be enabled to serve on the Security Council, so that they might take a more effective contribution to the maintenance of international peace and security.

2. The Asian-African Conference having considered the dangerous situation of international tension existing and the risks confronting the whole human race from the outbreak of global war in which the destructive power of all types of armaments, including nuclear and thermo-nuclear weapons, would be employed, invited the attention of all nations to the terrible consequences that would follow if such a war were to break out.

The Conference considered that disarmament and the prohibition of the production, experimentation and use of nuclear and thermo-nuclear weapons of war are imperative to save mankind and civilisation from the fear and prospect of wholesale destruction. It considered that the nations of Asia and Africa assembled here have a duty towards humanity and civilisation to proclaim their support for disarmament and for the prohibition of these weapons and to appeal to nations principally concerned and to world opinion, to bring about such disarmament and prohibition.

The Conference considered that effective international control should be established and maintained to implement such disarmament and prohibition and that speedy and determined efforts should be made to this end.

Pending the total prohibition of the manufacture of nuclear and thermo-nuclear weapons, this Conference appealed to all the powers concerned to reach agreement to suspend experiments with such weapons.

The Conference declared that universal disarmament is an absolute necessity for the preservation of peace and requested the United Nations to continue its efforts and appealed to all concerned speedily to bring about the regulation, limitation, control and reduction of all armed forces and armaments, including the prohibition of the production, experimentation and use of all weapons of mass destruction, and to establish effective international control to this end.

G. DECLARATION ON THE PROMOTION OF WORLD PEACE AND COOPERATION

The Asian-African Conference gave anxious thought to the question of world peace and cooperation. It viewed with deep concern the present state of international tension with its danger of an atomic world war. The problem of peace is correlative with the problem of international security. In this connection, all States should cooperate, especially through the United Nations, in bringing about the reduction of armaments and the elimination of nuclear weapons under effective international control. In this way, international peace can be promoted and nuclear energy may be used exclusively for peaceful purposes. This would help answer the needs particularly of Asia and Africa, for what they urgently require are social progress and better standards of life in larger freedom. Freedom and peace are independent. The right of self-determination must be enjoyed by all peoples, and freedom and independence must be granted, with the least possible delay, to those who are still dependent peoples. Indeed, all nations should have the right freely to choose their own political and economic systems and their own way of life, in conformity with the purposes and principles of the Charter of the United Nations.

Free from mistrust and fear, and with confidence and goodwill towards each other, 'nations should practise tolerance and live together in peace with one another as good neighbours and develop friendly cooperation on the basis of the following principles:

1. Respect for fundamental human rights and for the purposes and principles of the Charter of the United Nations.

2. Respect for the sovereignty and territorial integrity of all nations.

3. Recognition of the equality of all races and of the equality of all nations large and small.

4. Abstention from intervention or interference in the internal affairs of another country.

5. Respect for the right of each nation to defend itself singly or collectively, in conformity with the Charter of the United Nations.

6. (a) Abstention from the use of arra.igements of collective defence to serve the particular interests of any of the big powers.

(b) Abstention by any country from exerting pressures on other countries.

7. Refraining from acts or threats of aggression or the use of force against the territorial integrity or political independence of any country.

8. Settlement of all international disputes by peaceful means, such as negotiation, conciliation, arbitration or judicial settlement as well as other peaceful means of the parties' own choice, in conformity with the Charter of the United Nations.

9. Promotion of mutual interests and cooperation.

10. Respect for justice and international obligations.

The Asian and African Conference declares its conviction that friendly cooperation in accordance with these principles would effectively contribute to the maintenance and promotion of international peace and security, while cooperation in the economic, social and cultural fields would help bring about the common prosperity and well-being of all.

The Asian-African Conference recommended that the five sponsoring countries consider the convening of the next meeting of the Conference, in consultation with the participating countries.

Bandung, 24 April, 1955.

THE BRIONI DOCUMENT

JOINT COMMUNIQUE BY PRESIDENT TITO, PRESIDENT NASSER
AND PREMIER NEHRU

1) During the course of the visit to Yugoslavia of the President of the Republic of Egypt, Gamal Abdel Nasser, and the Prime Minister of India, Jawaharlal Nehru, talks took place at Brioni on July 18 and 19, 1956, between President Tito, President Nasser and Premier Nehru.

2) The three chiefs of government reviewed developments which had taken place in the international sphere after their separate meetings twelve months earlier. The similarity of their approach to international questions has led to close cooperation between them, and they noted with satisfaction that the policies pursued by their countries had, to a certain extent, contributed towards the lessening of international tension and to the development of equal relations between nations.

3) Latest developments and contacts and talks between the leaders of different countries which pursue different policies have contributed to a better understanding of one another's views and to a growing affirmation of the principles of peaceful and active coexistence. The three chiefs of government consider that such contacts and exchanges of opinions should continue and be given every encouragement.

4) Last year's conference in Bandung laid down certain principles by which all should be governed in international relations. The three chiefs of government affirm these ten principles which they have always supported. They are aware that conflicts and tension existing in the world today lead to fears and apprehensions for the present and for the future. As long as these fears and apprehensions dominate the world, no firm basis for peace can be established. At the same time, it is difficult to remove quickly these fears and apprehensions, and gradual steps will have to be taken for their elimination. Every such step helps in lessening tension and is therefore to be welcomed.

5) The division of the present-day world into powerful blocs of states tends to perpetuate these fears. Peace cannot be achieved through division, but by working for collective security on the world scale and by expanding the region of freedom, as well as by terminating the domination of one country over another.

6) Progress towards disarmament is essential in order to lessen fear and conflicts. This progress must, in the first place, be made within the United Nations, and it should include both atomic and thermonuclear weapons and conventional armaments, together with adequate control of concluded agreements. Explosions

379

of weapons mass-destruction, even for experimental purposes, should be stopped, because they violate international morality and contain possible dangers to humanity — the pollution of the atmosphere which affects other countries and large peaceloving areas regardless of frontiers. Fissionable material should in the future be used only for peaceful purposes and its further use for military purposes should be prohibited. The three chiefs of government are deeply interested in full and equal international cooperation in the field of the peace-time uses of atomic energy. Such cooperation should be organized within the United Nations and all countries should be represented in the proposed international agencies.

7) The intensification of efforts to speed-up the development of underdeveloped regions in the world constitutes one of the chief tasks in establishing a permanent and stable peace among nations. In this connection the three chiefs of government recognize the importance of international economic and financial cooperation and consider that it is necessary and desirable that the proposed United Nations special fund for economic development be constituted and made capable of acting effectively.

8) During their talks the three chiefs of government emphasized the great importance of removing embargoes and obstacles to the normal flow and expansion of international trade.

9) The three chief areas of tension and possible conflicts are Central Europe, the Far East of Asia and the Middle East region between Europe and Asia. The problems of the Far East cannot be solved in a satisfactory way without full cooperation of the People's Republic of China. The three chiefs of government express their belief that the People's Republic of China should be represented in the United Nations. They also consider that all those countries which applied for membership and are qualified under the Charter should be admitted to the Unit d Nations.

10) The problems of Central Europe are closely linked with the problem of Germany. This important question must be settled in conformity with the desires of the German people through agreement to be reached by peaceful negotiations.

11) In the Middle East the conflicting interests of the great powers make the situation more difficult. These problems should be considered on their merits, taking into account the legitimate economic interests but basing solutions on the freedom of the peoples concerned. The freedom and goodwill of the peoples of these areas are essential not only for peace but also to safeguard legitimate economic interests. The situation caused by the problem of Palestine represents a particular danger to world peace. In this respect the three chiefs of government support the resolutions of the Bandung conference.

12) The three chiefs of government considered the situation in Algeria, which is, in their opinion, of great importance and which requires immediate attention, both from the viewpoint of the basic rights of the people of Algeria and from the viewpoint of consolidating peace in that part of the world. Being convinced that colonial domination is completely undesirable and unworthy of both those who rule and those who are ruled, the three chiefs of government express their sympathy for the desire of the people of Algeria for freedom. They are aware that there are in Algeria a considerable number of people of European descent whose interests should be protected, but this should not be the reason to refuse recognition of the

legitimate rights of the Algerians. They warmly support all efforts directed towards finding a just and peaceful settlement, and especially towards ending the violent conflicts in this area and towards negotiations. A cease fire and negotiations between the parties concerned should lead to a peaceful settlement of the problem.

The three chiefs of government are aware that the problems of the world cannot be settled all at once, and that it is necessary to persevere, with patience and goodwill, in the attempts to reach solutions. However, it is essential to exert efforts to create an atmosphere of peace and to act in conformity with the fundamental principles of the Charter of the United Nations.

COMMUNIQUÉ ON THE VISIT OF PRESIDENT GAMAL ABDEL NASSER TO YUGOSLAVIA

BRIONI, JULY 18, 1956

Gamal Abdel Nasser, President of the Republic of Egypt, and his associates visited the Federal People's Republic of Yugoslavia from July 12 to July 19, 1956, at the invitation of Josip Broz Tito, President of the FPRY.

During this visit, cordial and open talks were held on all questions concerning the international relations of the two countries and the further advancement of Egyptian-Yugoslav cooperation, and there was a friendly exchange of views on the main world problems and the general development of the international situation.

In addition to President Nasser, on the Egyptian side there were the following participants in the talks: Abdel-Latif Mahmoud el Bogdadi, Minister of Communal Affairs and Planning, Dr. Mahmoud Fawzi, Minister of Foreign Affairs, Ali Sabri, Chief of the Cabinet of the President of the Republic, Hussein Ruzhdi, ambassador extraordinary and plenipotentiary in Belgrade, and Abdel Gawad Ali Tobalah, Minister Plenipotentiary.

Participants in the talks on the Yugoslav side, in addition to President Tito, were: Edvard Kardelj, Vice-President of the Federal Executive Council, Koča Popović, State Secretary for Foreign Affairs, Mijalko Todorović, member of the Federal Executive Council, Josip Đerđa, ambassador extraordinary and plenipotentiary in Cairo, Dr. Joža Vilfan, General Secretary to the President of the Republic, and Dr. Antun Vratuša, Assistant State Secretary in the Federal Executive Council.

The visit and talks took place in an atmosphere of complete mutual trust and sincere friendship, which characterize relations between the governments and peoples of the two countries.

In the course of the talks, President Nasser and President Tito found a great similarity in their views on the main problems of the modern-day world, which both countries approach guided by the principles of peaceful and active coexistence and non-adherence to blocs.

They agreed that the positive development of the international situation was continuing toward a reduction in tensions in the world, thanks to the general, increased efforts for the expansion of international cooperation and for the strengthening of trust among peoples through the increasingly successful use of the method of negotiations in settling matters under dispute.

The two presidents discussed the situation in the Middle and Near East. They reaffirmed their support for the resolutions of the Bandung Conference concerning these areas.

The two presidents ascertained with satisfaction that relations between the two countries developing successfully on the principles set forth in the joint declaration of January 5, 1956, and that the implementation of these principles, both in the sphere of relations between the two countries and in t1e sphere of international affairs, had already proved to be a considerable contribution to the cause of consolidating peace and international cooperation in the world.

The two presidents felt that direct exchanges of opinions and personal contacts at the highest level have proved to be mutually very advantageous. They accordingly decided to continue this useful practice and to hold mutual consultations at regular intervals in the future.

The talks held during this visit showed that there were broad possibilities for the expansion of mutual economic cooperation and trade, and for this purpose it was decided that in the months to come more concrete negotiations should be held between specialists and competent institutions.

The comprehensive, informative talks held during this visit proved to be of considerable mutual benefit, and the two presidents agreed that such contacts should be continued, especially in the form of exchanges of experience and information in the field of economic policy, planning, etc., and for this purpose periodical visits of planners, economic leaders, experts, etc. will be organized.

On the assumption that an all-round mutual acquaintance between the peoples of the two countries is one of the essential conditions for the building of a lasting friendship and cooperation, it was decided that measures should be taken for the promotion and expansion of the existing cultural cooperation in general and in particular for the conclusion of a cultural convention in the near future.

Special attention was given to the problem of general mutual cooperation and assistance in the technical sphere and in the sphere of the use of atomic energy for peaceful purposes. The two presidents agreed that in this area there are also considerable possibilities for cooperation, assistance and the exchange of mutual information, and the corresponding measures will be taken in this respect.

1514 (XV). DECLARATION ON THE GRANTING OF INDEPENDENCE TO COLONIAL COUNTRIES AND PEOPLES

The General Assembly,

Mindful of the determination proclaimed by the peoples of the world in the Charter of the United Nations to reaffirm faith in fundamental human rights, in the dignity and worth of the human person, in the equal rights of men and women and of nations large and small and to promote social progress and better standards of life in larger freedom,

Conscious of the need for the creation of conditions of stability and well-being and peaceful and friendly relations based on respect for the principles of equal rights and self-determination of all peoples, and of universal respect for, and observance of, human rights and fundamental freedoms for all without distinction as to race, sex, language or religion.

Recognizing the passionate yearning for freedom in all dependent peoples and the decisive role of such peoples in the attainment of their independence,

Aware of the increasing conflicts resulting from the denial of or impediments in the way of the freedom of such peoples, which constitute a serious threat to world peace,

Considering the important role of the United Nations in assisting the movement for independence in Trust and Non-Self-Governing Territories,

Recognizing that the peoples of the world ardently desire the end of colonialism in all its manifestations,

Convinced that the continued existence of colonialism prevents the development of international economic co-operation, impedes the social, cultural and economic development of dependent peoples and militates against the United Nations ideal of universal peace,

Affirming that peoples may, for their own ends, freely dispose of their natural wealth and resources without prejudice to any obligations arising out of international economic co-operation, based upon the principle of mutual benefit, and international law,

Believing that the process of liberation is irresistible and irreversible and that, in order to avoid serious crises, an end must be put to colonialism and all practices of segregation and discrimination associated therewith,

Welcoming the emergence in recent years of a large number of dependent territories into freedom and independence, and recognizing the increasingly powerful trends towards freedom in such territories which have not yet attained independence,

Convinced that all peoples have an inalienable right to complete freedom, the exercise of their sovereignty and the integrity of their national territory,

Solemnly proclaims the necessity of bringing to a speedy and unconditional end colonialism in all its forms and manifestations;

And to this end

Declares that:

1. The subjection of peoples to alien subjugation, domination and exploitation constitutes a denial of fundamental human rights, is contrary to the Charter of the United Nations and is an impediment to the promotion of world peace and co-operation.

2. All peoples have the right to self-determination; by virtue of that right they freely determine their political status and freely pursue their economic, social and cultural development.

3. Inadequacy of political, economic, social or educational preparedness should never serve as a pretext for delaying independence.

4. All armed action or repressive measures of all kinds directed against dependent peoples shall cease in order to enable them to exercise peacefully and freely their right to complete independence, and the integrity of their national territory shall be respected.

5. Immediate steps shall be taken, in Trust and Non-Self-Governing Territories or all other territories which have not yet attained independence, to transfer all powers to the peoples of those territories, without any conditions or reservations, in accordance with their freely expressed will and desire, without any distinction as to race, creed or colour, in order to enable them to enjoy complete independence and freedom.

6. Any attempt aimed at the partial or total disruption of the national unity and the territorial integrity of a country is incompatible with the purposes and principles of the Charter of the United Nations.

7. All States shall observe faithfully and strictly the provisions of the Charter of the United Nations, the Universal Declaration of Human Rights and the present Declaration on the basis of equality, non-interference in the internal affairs of all States, and respect for the sovereign rights of all peoples and their territorial integrity.

497th plenary meeting,
14 December 1960.

DOCUMENTS OF THE BELGRADE CONFERENCE OF THE HEADS OF STATE OR GOVERNMENT OF NON-ALIGNED COUNTRIES

1. DANGER OF WAR AND APPEAL FOR PEACE
BELGRADE, SEPTEMBER 6, 1961

This Conference of the Heads of State or Government of Non-Aligned Countries is deeply concerned that even apart from already existing tension the grave and critical situation which, as never before, threatens the world with the imminent and ominous prospect of conflict would almost certainly later develop into a World War. In this age of nuclear weapons and the accumulation of the power of mass destruction, such conflict and war would inevitably lead to devastation on a scale hitherto unknown, if not to world annihilation.

2. This Conference considers that this calamity must be avoided, and it is therefore urgent and imperative that the parties concerned, and more particularly the United States of America and the U.S.S.R. should immediately suspend their recent war preparations and approaches, take no steps that would aggravate or contribute to further deteriorations in the situations, and resume negotiation for a peaceful settlement of any outstanding differences between them with due regard to the principles of the United Nations Charter and continue negotiating until both they and the rest of the world achieve total disarmament and enduring peace.

3. While decisions leading to war or peace at present rest with these great powers, the consequences affect the entire world. All nations and peoples have, therefore, an abiding concern and interest that the approaches and actions of the great powers should be such as to enable mankind to move forward to peace and prosperity and not to the doom of extinction. In the certain knowledge that they seek peace, this Conference appeals to the President of the United States of America and the Chairman of the Council of Ministers of the U.S.S.R. to make most immediate and direct approaches to each other to avert the imminent conflict and establish peace.

4. This Conference expresses the earnest hope that all nations not represented here, conscious of the extreme gravity of the situation will make a similar appeal to the leaders of the Powers concerned thereby proclaiming and promoting the desire and determination of all mankind to see the achievement of lasting peace and security for all nations.

2. DECLARATION OF THE HEADS OF STATE OR GOVERNMENT OF NON-ALIGNED COUNTRIES

The Conference of Heads of State or Government of the following non-aligned countries: 1. Afghanistan, 2. Algeria, 3. Burma, 4. Cambodia, 5. Ceylon, 6. Congo 7. Cuba, 8. Cyprus, 9. Ethiopia, 10. Ghana, 11. Guinea, 12. India, 13. Indonesia 14. Iraq, 15. Lebanon, 16. Mali, 17. Morocco, 18. Nepal, 19. Saudi Arabia, 20. Somalia, 21. Sudan, 22. Tunisia, 23. United Arab Republic, 24. Yemen, 25. Yugoslavia and of the following countries represented by observers:

1. Bolivia, 2. Brazil, 3. Ecuador

was held in Belgrade from September 1 to 6, 1961, for the purpose of exchanging views on international problems with a view to contributing more effectively to world peace and security and peaceful co-operation among peoples.

The Heads of State or Government of the aforementioned countries have met at a moment when international events have taken a turn for the worst and when world peace is seriously threatened. Deeply concerned for the future of peace, voicing the aspirations of the vast majority of people of the world, aware that, in our time, no people and no government can or should abandon its responsibilities in regard to the safeguarding of world peace, the participating countries — having examined in detail, in an atmosphere of equality, sincerity and mutual confidence, the current state of international relations and trends prevailing in the present-day world — make the following decision:

The Heads of State or Government of Non-Aligned Countries noting that there are crises that lead towards a world conflict in the transition from an old order based on domination to a new order based on cooperation between nations, founded on freedom, equality and social justice for the promotion of prosperity; considering that the dynamic processes and forms of social change often result in or represent a conflict between the old established and the new emerging nationalist forces; considering that a lasting peace can be achieved only if this confrontation leads to a world where the domination of colonialism-imperialism and neo-colonialism in all their manifestations is radically eliminated;

That acute emergencies threatening world peace now exist in this period of conflict in Africa, Asia, Europe and Latin America and big power rivalry likely to result in world conflagration cannot be excluded; that to eradicate basically the source of conflict is to eradicate colonialism in all its manifestations and to accept and practice a policy of peaceful co-existence in the world;

that guided by these principles the period of transition and conflict can lay a firm foundation of cooperation and brotherhood between nations, state the following:

I

War has never threatened mankind with graver consequences than today. On the other hand, never before has mankind had at its disposal stronger forces for eliminating war as an instrument of policy in international relations.

Imperialism is weakening. Colonial empires and other forms of foreign oppression of peoples in Asia, Africa and Latin America are gradually disappearing from the stage of history. Great successes have been achieved in the struggle of many peoples for national independence and equality. In the same way, the peoples of Latin America are continuing to make an increasingly effective contribution to the improvement of international relations. Great social changes in the world are further promoting such a development. All this not only accelerates the end of the epoch of foreign oppression of peoples, but also makes peaceful cooperation among peoples, based on the principles of independence and equal rights, an essential condition for their freedom and progress.

Tremendous progress has been achieved in the development of science, techniques and in the means of economic development.

Prompted by such developments in the world, the vast majority of people are becoming increasingly conscious of the fact that war between peoples constitutes not only an anachronism but also a crime against humanity. This awareness of peoples is becoming a great moral force, capable of exercising a vital influence on the development of international relations.

Relying on this and on the will of their peoples, the Governments of countries participating in the Conference resolutely reject the view that war, including the "cold war", is inevitable, as this view reflects a sense both of helplessness and is contrary to the progress of the world. They affirm their unwavering faith that the international community is able to organize its life without resorting to means which actually belong to a past epoch of human history.

However, the existing military blocs, which are growing into more and more powerful military, economic and political groupings, which, by the logic and nature of their mutual relations, necessarily provoke periodical aggravations of international relations.

The cold war and the constant and acute danger of its being transformed into actual war have become a part of the situation prevailing in international relations.

For all these reasons, the Heads of State and Representatives of Government of non-aligned countries wish, in this way, to draw the attention of the world community to the existing situation and to the necessity that all peoples should exert efforts to find a sure road towards the stabilization of peace.

II

The present-day world is characterized by the existence of different social systems. The participating countries do not consider that these differences constitute an insurmountable obstacle for the stabilization of peace, provided attempts at domination and interference in the internal development of other peoples and nations are ruled out.

All peoples and nations have to solve the problems of their own political, economic, social and cultural systems in accordance with their own conditions, needs and potentialities.

Furthermore, any attempt at imposing upon peoples one social or political system or another by force and from outside is a direct threat to world peace. The participating countries consider that under such conditions the principles of peaceful coexistence are the only alternative to the "cold war" and to a possible general nuclear catastrophe. Therefore, these principles — which include the right of peoples to self-determination, to independence and to the free determination of the forms and methods of economic, social and cultural development — must be the only basis of all international relations.

Active international cooperation in the fields of material and cultural exchanges among peoples is an essential means for the strengthening of confidence in the possibility of peaceful coexistence among States with different social systems.

The participants in the Conference emphasize, in this connexion, that the policy of coexistence amounts to an active effort towards the elimination of historical injustices and the liquidation of national oppression, guaranteeing, at the same time, to every people their independent development.

Aware that ideological differences are necessarily a part of the growth of the human society, the participating countries consider that peoples and Governments shall refrain from any use of ideologies for the purpose of waging cold war, exercising pressure, or imposing their will.

III

The Heads of State or Government of non-aligned countries participating in the Conference are not making concrete proposals for the solution of all international disputes, and particularly disputes between the two blocs. They wish, above all, to draw attention to those acute problems of our time which must be solved rapidly, so that they should not lead to irreparable consequences.

In this respect, they particularly emphasize the need for a great sense of responsibility and realism when undertaking the solution of various problems resulting from differences in social systems.

The non-aligned countries represented at this Conference do not wish to form a new bloc and cannot be a bloc. They sincerely desire to cooperate with any Government which seeks to contribute to the strengthening of confidence and peace in the world. The non-aligned countries wish to proceed in this manner all the more so as they are aware that peace and stability in the world depend, to a considerable extent, on the mutual relations of the Great Powers;

Aware of this, the participants in the Conference consider it a matter of principle that the Great Powers take more determined action for the solving of various problems by means of negotiations, displaying at the same time the necessary constructive approach and readiness for reaching solutions which will be mutually acceptable and useful for world peace.

The participants in the Conference consider that, under present conditions, the existence and the activities of non-aligned countries in the interests of peace are one of the more important factors for safeguarding world peace.

The participants in the Conference consider it essential that the non-aligned countries should participate in solving outstanding international issues concerning peace and security in the world as none of them can remain unaffected by or indifferent to these issues.

They consider that the further extension of the non-committed area of the world constitutes the only possible and indispensable alternative to the policy of total division of the world into blocs, and intensification of cold war policies. The non-aligned countries provide encouragement and support to all peoples fighting for their independence and equality. The participants in the Conference are convinced that the emergence of newly-liberated countries will further assist in narrowing of the area of bloc antagonisms and thus encourage all tendencies aimed at strengthening peace and promoting peaceful cooperation among independent and equal nations.

1. The participants in the Conference solemnly reaffirm their support to the "Declaration on the Granting of Independence to Colonial Countries and Peoples", adopted at the 15th Session of the General Assembly of the United Nations and recommend the immediate unconditional, total and final abolition of colonialism and resolved to make a concerted effort to put an end to all types of new colonialism and imperialist domination in all its forms and manifestations.

2. The participants in the Conference demand that an immediate stop be put to armed action and repressive measures of any kind directed against dependent peoples to enable them to exercise peacefully and freely their right to complete independence and that the integrity of their national territory should be respected. Any aid given by any country to a colonial power in such suppression is contrary to the Charter of the United Nations.

The participating countries respecting scrupulously the territorial integrity of all states oppose by all means any aims of annexation by other nations.

3. The participating countries consider the struggle of the people of Algeria for freedom, self-determination and independence, and for the integrity of its national territory including the Sahara, to be just and necessary and are therefore, determined to extend to the people of Algeria all the possible support and aid. The Heads of State or Government are particularly gratified that Algeria is represented at this Conference by its rightful representative, the Prime Minister of the Provisional Government of Algeria.

4. The participating countries drew attention with great concern to the developments in Angola and to the intolerable measures of repression taken by the Portuguese colonial authorities against the people of Angola and demand that an immediate end should be put to any further shedding of blood of the Angolan people, and the people of Angola should be assisted by all peace-loving countries, particularly member states of the United Nations, to establish their free and independent state without delay.

5. The participants in the Conference demand the immediate termination of all colonial occupation and the restoration of the territorial integrity to the rightful people in countries in which it has been violated in Asia, Africa and Latin America as well as the withdrawal of foreign forces from their national soil.

6. The participating countries demand the immediate evacuation of French

armed forces from the whole of the Tunisian territory in accordance with the legitimate right of Tunisia to the exercise of its full national sovereignty.

7. The participating countries demand that the tragic events in the Congo must not be repeated and they feel that it is the duty of the world community to continue to do everything in its power in order to erase the consequences and to prevent any further foreign intervention in this young African state, and to enable the Congo to embark freely upon the road of its independent development based on respect for its sovereignty, unity and its territorial integrity.

8. The participants in the Conference resolutely condemn the policy of apartheid practised by the Union of South Africa and demand the immediate abandonment of this policy. They further state that the policy of racial discrimination anywhere in the world constitutes a grave violation of the Charter of the United Nations and the Universal Declaration of Human Rights.

9. The participating countries declare solemnly the absolute respect of the rights of ethnic or religious minorities to be protected in particular against crimes of genocide or any other violation of their fundamental human rights.

10. The participants in the Conference condemn the imperialist policies pursued in the Middle East, and declare their support for the full restoration of all the rights of the Arab people of Palestine in conformity with the Charter and resolutions of the United Nations.

11. The participating countries consider the establishment and maintenance of foreign military bases in the territories of other countries, particularly against their express will, a gross violation of the sovereignty of such States. They declare their full support to countries who are endeavouring to secure the vacation of these bases. They call upon those countries maintaining foreign bases to consider seriously their abolition as a contribution to world peace.

12. They also acknowledge that the North American military base at Guantanamo, Cuba, to the permanence of which the Government and people of Cuba have expressed their opposition, affects the sovereignty and territorial integrity of that country.

13. The participants in the Conference reaffirm their conviction that:

(a) All nations have the right of unity, self-determination, and independence by virtue of which right they can determine their political status and freely pursue their economic, social and cultural development without intimidation or hindrance.

(b) All peoples may, for their own ends, freely dispose of their natural wealth and resources without prejudice to any obligations arising out of international economic co-operation, based upon the principle of mutual benefit, and international law. In no case may a people be deprived of its own means of subsistence.

The participating countries believe that the right of Cuba as that of any other nation to freely choose their political and social systems in accordance with their own conditions, needs and possibilities should be respected.

14. The participating countries express their determination that no intimidation, interference or intervention should be brought to bear in the exercise of right of self-determination of peoples, including their right to pursue constructive and independent policies for the attainment and preservation of their sovereignty.

391

15. The participants in the Conference consider that disarmament is an imperative need and the most urgent task of mankind. A radical solution of this problem, which has become an urgent necessity in the present state of armaments, in the unanimous view of participating countries, can be achieved only by means of a general, complete and strictly and internationally controlled disarmament.

16. The Heads of State or Government point out that general and complete disarmament should include the elimination of armed forces, armaments, foreign bases, manufacture of arms as well as elimination of institutions and installations for military training, except for purposes of internal security; and the total prohibition of the production, possession and utilization of nuclear and thermo-nuclear arms, bacteriological and chemical weapons as well as the elimination of equipment and installations for the delivery and placement and operational use of weapons of mass destruction on national territories.

17. The participating countries call upon all States in general, and States exploring outer space at present in particular, to undertake to use outer space exclusively for peaceful purposes. They expressed the hope that the international community will, through collective action, establish an international agency with a view to promote and coordinate the human actions in the field of international cooperation in the peaceful uses of outer space.

18. The participants in the Conference urge the Great Powers to sign without further delay a treaty for general and complete disarmament in order to save mankind from the scourge of war and to release energy and resources now being spent on armaments to be used for the peaceful economic and social development of all mankind. The participating countries also consider that:

(a) The non-aligned Nations should be represented at all future world conferences on disarmament;

(b) All discussions on disarmament should be held under the auspices of the United Nations;

(c) General and complete disarmament should be guaranteed by an effective system of inspection and control, the teams of which should include members of non-aligned Nations.

19. The participants in the Conference consider it essential that an agreement on the prohibition of all nuclear and thermo-nuclear tests should be urgently concluded. With this aim in view, it is necessary that negotiations be immediately resumed, separately or as part of the negotiations on general disarmament. Meanwhile, the moratorium on the testing of all nuclear weapons should be resumed and observed by all countries.

20. The participants in the Conference recommend that the General Assembly of the United Nations should, at its forthcoming session, adopt a decision on the convening either of a special session of the General Assembly of the United Nations devoted to discussion of disarmament or on the convening of a world disarmament conference under the auspices of the United Nations with a view to setting in motion the process of general disarmament.

21. The participants in the Conference consider that efforts should be made to remove economic inbalance inherited from colonialism and imperialism. They

consider it necessary to close, through accelerated economic, industrial and agricultural development, the ever-widening gap in the standards of living between the few economically advanced countries and the many economically less-developed countries. The participants in the Conference recommend the immediate establishment and operation of a United Nations Capital Development Fund. They further agree to demand a just terms of trade for the economically less-developed countries and, in particular, constructive efforts to eliminate the excessive fluctuations in primary commodity trade and the restrictive measures and practices which adversely affect the trade and revenues of the newly-developing countries. In general to demand that the fruits of the scientific and technological revolution be applied in all fields of economic development to hasten the achievement of international social justice.

22. The participating countries invite all the countries in the course of development to co-operate effectively in the economic and commercial fields so as to face the policies of pressure in the economic sphere, as well as the harmful results which may be created by the economic blocs of the industrial countries. They invite all the countries concerned to consider to convene, as soon as possible an international conference to discuss their common problems and to reach an agreement on the ways and means of repelling all damage which may hinder their development; and to discuss and agree upon the most effective measures to ensure the realization of their economic and social development.

23. The countries participating in the Conference declare that the recipient countries must be free to determine the use of the economic and technical assistance which they receive, and to draw up their own plans and assign priorities in accordance with their needs.

24. The participating countries consider it essential that the General Assembly of the United Nations should, through the revision of the Charter, find a solution to the question of expanding the membership of the Security Council and of the Economic and Social Council in order to bring the composition and work of these two most important organs of the General Assembly into harmony with the needs of the Organisation and with the expanded membership of the United Nations.

25. The unity of the world Organisation and the assuring of the efficiency of its work make it absolutely necessary to evolve a more appropriate structure for the Secretariat of the United Nations, bearing in mind equitable regional distribution.

26. Those of the countries participating in the Conference who recognize the Government of the People's Republic of China recommend that the General Assembly in its forthcoming Session should accept the representatives of the Government of the People's Republic of China as the only legitimate representatives of that country in the United Nations.

27. The countries participating in the Conference consider that the German problem is not merely a regional problem put liable to exercise a decisive influence on the course of future developments in international relations.

Concerned at the developments which have led to the present acute aggravation of the situation in regard to Germany and Berlin, the participating countries call upon all parties concerned not to resort to or threaten the use of force to solve the German question or the problem of Berlin, in accordance with the appeal made by the Heads of State or Governments on 5 September, 1961.

The Heads of State or Government of non-aligned countries resolve that this Declaration should be forwarded to the United Nations and brought to the attention of all the Member States of the world Organization. The present Declaration will be also forwarded to all the other States.

MESSAGE TO PRESIDENT KENNEDY AND PREMIER KHRUSHCHEV

"Your Excellency,

We, the Heads of State or Government of the countries which took part in the Belgrade Conference held from September 1 to 6, 1961, are taking the liberty of sending you a message treating a question of vital and direct interest to all of us and to the whole of mankind. We are not taking this step in our own name only, but also in the name of the Conference and our peoples — as an expression of their unanimous wishes.

We are deeply concerned over the present deterioration of the international situation and a possible war which threatens mankind. Your Excellency has often pointed out the horrors of a modern war and the use of nuclear weapons, which might destroy the human race, and has often appealed for the preservation of world peace.

At present, we find ourselves on the brink of this danger threatening the world and humanity. We are completely aware of the fact that Your Excellency, like all of us, wishes to prevent such an unfortunate development of the international situation which may not only destroy the hopes for prosperity of our peoples, but also endanger the very existence of mankind. It is our deep conviction that Your Excellency will do all that can be done in order to prevent a catastrophe.

Bearing in mind the gravity of the present crisis which threatens the world and the imperative need to avoid developments which may accelerate this crisis, however, we are taking the liberty of appealing to the Great Powers to renew their negotiations, so as to remove the danger of war in the world and enable mankind to embark upon the road of peace.

In the first place, we are asking for direct negotiations between Your Excellency and the President of the United States, Mr. John Kennedy (in the message to President Kennedy this reads: "... between Your Excellency and the President of the Ministerial Council of the Soviet Union, Mr. Nikita Khrushchev..."), as representatives of the two most powerful nations of our day, in whose hands lies the key to peace and war. Owing to the fact that both of you are devoted to the cause of world peace, we are convinced that your efforts, channeled through constant negotiations, will lead mankind out of the present blind alley, and will enable it to live and create in peace and prosperity.

It is our belief that Your Excellency will understand that, in sending this message, we have been guided by pure love for peace and fear of war, and by an irresistable desire to find solutions to the outstanding problems before mankind finds itself faced with disaster."

394

CAIRO DECLARATION OF DEVELOPING COUNTRIES

A Conference on the Problems of Economic Development was held in Cairo from 9—18 July, 1962 and was sponsored by the following Countries: 1. Ceylon, 2. Ethiopia, 3. Ghana, 4. Guinea 5. India, 6. Indonesia, 7. Libya, 8. Mali, 9. Sudan 10. United Arab Rebublic, 11. Yugoslavia.

In addition to Sponsoring Countries, the following countries participated in the Conference as full members: 12. Afghanistan, 13. Algeria, 14. Bolivia, 15. Brazil, 16. Burma, 17. Cambodia, 18. Congo (Leopoldville), 19. Cuba, 20. Cyprus, 21. Federation of Malaya, 22. Kuwait, 23. Lebanon, 24. Mexico, 25. Morocco, 26. Pakistan, 27. Saudi Arabia, 28. Somalia, 29. Tanganyika, 30. Tunisia, 31. Yemen.

The following countries were represented by observers: 32. Chile, 33. Ecuador, 34. Singapore, 35. Uruguay, 36. Venezuela.

The following international organizations sent observers: United Nations, Food and Agriculture Organization of the United Nations, The International Monetary Fund, The International Bank for Reconstruction and Development, The League of Arab States, Organization of Afro-Asian Economic Co-operation.

After ten days of deliberations, in the course of which the Conference heard the statement of the Heads of Delegations dealing with the problems on the Agenda, the Conference decided to make the following declaration:

PREAMBLE

1. The Conference views with concern the growing disparity in the standards of living prevailing in different parts of the world.

2. The Conference notes that despite universal acknowledgement of the necessity to accelerate the pace of development in less developed countries, adequate means of a concrete and positive nature have not been adopted to enable the developing countries to attain a reasonable rate of growth.

3. The Conference observes that the terms of trade continue to operate to the disadvantage of the developing countries, thus accentuating their unfavourable balance of payment position.

4. The Conference recognises that in order to ensure lasting peace and progress in the World, the developing countries must have the maximum opportunities and facilities to take the fullest advantage of their resources.

The developing countries have made progress in their economic development, in spite of unfavourable factors mainly inherited from a colonial past, relying primarily on their own resources, whilst making full use of such external assistance as has been made available to them, which assistance needs to be substantially increased.

5. The Conference acknowledges that as a result of the progress made by developing countries, new opportunities for international co-operation amongst the developing countries have been created and maximum advantage should be taken of these opportunities to formulate and implement joint programmes and projects in the fields of education, research, technical assistance, trade, industry, transport and communication.

The Conference affirms that joint action by the developing countries themselves can solve many of their problems and will promote more rapid progress on a wider international basis.

6. The Conference recognises the importance of maximum mobilization of internal resources of the developing countries including the establishment of suitable institutions for this purpose.

7. The Conference recognises that the economic development of developing countries is meeting with increasing difficulties due partly to some international factors beyond their control and to tendencies which might have the result of perpetuating past structures of international economic relations.

8. The Conference recalling the United Nations Declaration on granting independence to dependent countries, urges complete decolonisation as being necessary for the economic development of the dependent peoples and the exercise of sovereign rights over their national resources.

9. The Conference affirms that the economic and social problems of developing countries could be solved effectively within a reasonably short period of time through common endeavour on the national and international planes and within the framework of United Nations Charter and of international cooperation and assistance.

INTERNAL PROBLEMS OF DEVELOPMENT

10. The Conference recognises that there are internal problems of economic development facing the developing countries, including the mobilization of human, material and financial resources.

11. The Conference recognises that rapidly increasing per capita income through accelerated economic development should be the cardinal aim of developing countries.

12. The Conference recommends the drawing up and implementation of appropriate national development plans, as effective instruments of rapid economic growth.

13. Countries that suffer from the pressure of population on resources available should accelerate their rate of economic development and in the meantime take appropriate legitimate measures to deal with their population problems.

14. The Conference recognises the need for developing countries to take appropriate measures of agricultural reforms for raising agricultural productivity.

15. The Conference stresses the importance of diversification and of industrialization in broadening the basis of the national economy, increasing the national income as well as in creating new job opportunities.

16. In order that this diversification and industrialization bear fruit in the internal, inter-regional and international field, developing countries should improve the means of transportation and communication among them.

17. The Conference recognises that a deficiency, common to developing countries is the lack of adequate skilled manpower and of technically and scientifically trained personnel. It is therefore vital that all developing countries should launch more intensified programmes for imparting technical and scientific training to a much larger proportion of their population.

18. The Conference stresses the importance of the maintenance of financial and monetary stability, the encouragement of savings and the mobilisation of resources for economic development.

19. Public and institutional savings should be developed as major sources of domestic financing of development. In this respect, care should be taken to co-ordinate domestic sources of financing with the foreign resources available.

20. The mobilization of savings and formation of capital through proper utilization of human resources, in particular by community development techniques, should be given special care by the developing countries.

21. The experience gained by developing countries in their internal development is increasing continuously and it is of the greatest value for cooperation both among themselves and as between them and the developed countries.

CO-OPERATION AMONG DEVELOPING COUNTRIES

22. The Conference considers that expansion of trade between developing countries, particularly on a regional basis, can make a useful contribution to economic development and recommends that appropriate measures be taken to promote this objective.

23. The Conference calls upon the developing countries to undertake initiative for the promotion of mutual, bilateral and broader relations in the fields of trade, payments, financing, technical and scientific co-operation, industrial co-operation, transport and communications.

24. The furtherance of trade and co-operation between the developing countries necessitates the establishment of suitable means of transport and communications, between them in addition to the traditional trade routes and the provision of administrative and transit facilities.

25. The Conference took note of the concern expressed by certain landlocked countries regarding transit facilities, including access to the sea and recommends that appropriate facilities of access to the sea, the use of ports, transport and transit facilities should be extended to and from ports in the littoral countries.

26. The Conference is agreed that close co-operation should be established

amongst developing countries producing primary commodities with a view to coping with marketing problems including improvement of quality, as well as other matters relating to the exchange of goods and services. Joint action should be taken to promote the study and forecasting of world market trends including fluctuation of prices, production stocks and consumption of raw materials.

27. The Conference recommends to the governments of participating countries to promote co-operation amongst themselves in all problems of common interest such as the implementation of projects of geological surveys, land reclamation, training centres as well as in the preparation of investment projects and study of possibilities for financing them through national or international means.

28. The Conference particularly draws attention to the need of a more intensive study of problems relating to mutual trade of developing countries.

PROBLEMS OF INTERNATIONAL TRADE

29. The Conference notes that a rapid expansion in the export earnings of the developing countries is vital to their economic development.

30. The Conference is aware that the problems facing the developing countries in the field of international trade require continued action and mutual consultation on the part of developing countries and recommends the governments of participating countries, as well as the governments of other developing countries to continue consultations in order to:

— Exchange information and views between them on questions regarding economic relations with industrial countries,

— Concert mutually the attitudes to be adopted by them with regard to economic questions examined by international organizations,

— Exchange views and prepare the ground for concerted action in connection with any negative effects of integration policies of industrial countries.

31. The Conference invites the industrial countries to adopt as a matter of urgency, a programme of measures for the abolition of tariff and non-tariff and of all other discriminatory economic barriers adversely affecting the exports of developing countries.

32. The Conference urges, in the interest of producer and consumer countries alike that concrete and resolute steps be taken within the framework of the United Nations Organization for the purpose of stabilising international primary commodity markets in short term as well as in the long run, on a fair and remunerative basis and taking into consideration the trend of prices of manufactured goods.

33. The Conference urges the Governments of the participating countries to continue studying the problems with a view to initiating regional or world-wide programmes of stabilisation. To this end the Conference urges the industrially advanced countries to operate their stock disposal programmes without jeopardising the interests of primary commodity producing countries.

34. The Conference recommends the immediate and energetic implementation of the programme of action adopted by GATT with a view to improving the prospects of the exports of developing countries.

35. The Conference invites the participating Governments to co-operate effectively within the framework of GATT for the purpose of protecting their common interests.

36. At the same time, the Conference considers the establishment of an international compensatory financing system, a matter of great urgency and invites the International Monetary Fund to examine the undertaking of measures for a more effective balancing of payments of developing countries.

REGIONAL ECONOMIC GROUPINGS

37. The Conference expresses its apprehension that regional economic groupings of industrialised countries will adversely affect the interests of the developing economies, if conceived and operated in a restrictive or discriminatory manner.

38. The Conference considers that international trade should expand on the basis of equality and non-discrimination and that actions should be taken to minimise the consequences of the various economic communities and associations of the industrialised countries on the economies of the developing countries as well as on world trade.

39. Such action should take form of the industrialised countries adopting positive and continued measures to ensure that exports of developing countries to their markets are enabled to expand steadily on a non discriminatory basis, with a view to enable the developing countries to rectify their balance of payments position.

40. The Conference urges that where any revised tariff arrangement and non-tariff barriers adversely affect the interests of any of the developing countries, measures should be adopted in which would counteract such adverse effect.

41. The Conference considered the possible impacts of economic grouping on the economy of developing countries and agreed than in formulating their policy of economic relations with the industrial economic groupings, the developing countries should take into consideration the effects of such relations on their programme of industrialization and on their trade structure.

ECONOMIC AID FOR DEVELOPMENT

42. The Conference affirms its support for international aid based on mutual respect and common benefit, and recognises the usefulness to developing countries of all aid given on this basis.

43. The Conference notes that the present volume of international aid, although it has contributed to the development of developing countries, is not sufficient and its forms and methods are not satisfactory. This results in widening the gap between developed and developing countries, and by diminishing the quantum of trade, affects adversely world economic activity and progress. Consequently, the demand for imports from industrialized countries and level of economic activity are adversely affected.

44. The distribution of international aid has also tended in the past to be uneven and the Conference urges that steps be taken to correct this situation.

45. The Conference particularly draws attention to the necessity of ensuring the continuity of international assistance as well as the necessity of integrating international assistance with national economic development plans and programmes.

46. The Conference emphasises that international financing in the form of low-interests, long-term credits and social development and economic emancipation of developing countries, which can be best achieved through public financing in the form of low interest, long-term credits and other forms that do not burden unduly the balances of payments of developing countries.

47. The Conference urges that the financing of projects through IBRD and IDA and other international institutions be further expanded.

48. The Conference appeals that the recommendation of the General Assembly concerning the allocation of 1% of the combined national incomes of the economically advanced countries for the economic development of developing countries be implemented as a matter of urgency.

49. The Conference stresses that the general tasks of international financing can be achieved in the most adequate way through channeling of such assistance to a greater extent through the United Nations and urges, therefore, that SUNFED should start its work without delay in accordance with Resolution 1521/XV of the General Assembly of the United Nations.

50. The Conference appeals to the economically developed countries to increase, in accordance with the recommendations of the General Assembly of the United Nations, the volume of international financial aid for development and to implement as soon as possible the solemn Declaration embodied in the United Nations General Assembly Resolution 724 A (VIII) on the allocation of a portion of any savings resulting from disarmament to a fund for the economic development of developing countries.

INTERNATIONAL TECHNICAL ASSISTANCE

51. The Conference recognises that the lack of adequate skilled manpower and trained personnel is one of the major obstacles to economic growth in the developing countries. Thus, all measures intended to develop scientific, technological and human resources in such countries become of vital importance.

52. In this respect, the programme of international technical co-operation conducted by the United Nations and other mutual programmes of technical assistance have been and should continue to be of great value and help to developing countries.

53. Technical, professional and managerial training in developing countries must be carried on at a rate far exceeding what would be justified by their own financial resources. The Conference urges therefore a substantial increase in the funds provided by the United Nations and advanced countries for training activities.

54. Increasing efforts should be made to adapt scientific research and technol-

400

ogical developments to the specific conditions and requirements of the developing countries.

55. Conference recommends that measures be taken to increase the exchange of experts and technicians between the developing countries on the one hand and among the developing and developed countries on the other hand.

UNITED NATIONS DEVELOPMENT ACTIVITIES

56. The Conference invites the participating countries to co-operate closely in the United Nations and other international bodies with a view to ensuring economic progress and strengthening peace among all nations.

57. In this sense, the Conference recommends to the governments of participating countries to strengthen the economic and social activities of the United Nations.

58. The Conference welcomes the initiative of the United Nations expressed in the General Assembly Resolution 1707/XVI entitled "International trade as a primary instrument for economic development".

59. The Conference declares itself resolutely in favour of the holding of an international economic Conference within the framework of the United Nations, and calls upon developing countries to work for the convening of this Conference at an early date, in 1963.

60. The Conference recommends that the agenda of the international economic conference should include all vital questions relating to international trade, primary commodity trade, economic relations between developing and developed countries.

61. The Conference welcomes the aims of the "United Nations Development Decade" and urges the taking of adequate measures for the implementation of these aims, considering that the activities of the Economic and Social Council of the United Nations should be particularly intensified in this respect, and recommends the participating countries to co-operate effectively towards the achievement of the targets set.

62. The Conference recommends that the participating countries take full advantage of the forthcoming Conference of the United Nations on the application of Science and Technology for the benefit of the developing countries, including the possibility of establishing an agency for science and technology for the promotion of the technological advancement and the building up of the scientific structure in the developing countries.

63. The Conference recommends to the United Nations that the Executive Secretaries of the regional economic commissions, meet periodically to discuss matters of common interest with a view to promoting economic co-operation between the Regions and to make available periodical reports about the same.

RECOMMENDATIONS FOR FURTHER CO-OPERATION

64. The Conference requests its Chairman to transmit its Declaration formally to the Governments of participating and other interested countries and to the Sec-

retary-General of the United Nations so as to be included in the agenda of the Seventeenth Session of the General Assembly of the United Nations as a separate item.

65. The Conference urges the participating countries to keep continuously in touch with each other on all matters relevant to the implementation of the conclusions of the Conference.

66. In particular consultations should be established whenever appropriate, to ensure co-operation between the participating countries in the presentation of the conclusions reached in Cairo both in the meetings of the United Nations General Assembly and of other international agencies.

67. In order to ensure the effective continuity of their economic efforts, the participating countries agreed to call meetings, seminars, expert groups and Conferences that will further the development aims of developing countries as well as the cause of a just and equitable economic co-operation among all Nations.

68. In view of the proposed United Nations World Trade Conference, mutual consultations and studies should be initiated to ensure the proper presentation of the points of view of the developing countries in the Conference.

69. The Conference invites the developing countries to co-operate closely with a view to ensuring economic progress and strengthening Peace among Nations.

*
*   *

The Conference wishes to express its warmest thanks and sincere gratitude to His Excellency President Gamal Abdel Nasser for his inspiring inaugural address and for the interest that he has shown for the work and success of the Conference.

The Conference wishes to express its appreciation to the Government and people of the United Arab Republic for the warm hospitality and welcome that have been extended to it during the period of its deliberations.

The Conference wishes likewise to express sincere gratitude to His Excellency Dr. Abdel Moneim El Kaissouny for his able and wise Chairmanship of the Conference.

1897 (XVIII). UNITED NATIONS CONFERENCE ON TRADE AND DEVELOPMENT

The General Assembly,

Recalling its resolution 1785 (XVII) of 8 December 1962, as well as Economic and Social Council resolutions 917 (XXXIV) of 3 August 1962, 944 (XXXV) of 18 April 1963 and 963 (XXXVI) of 18 July 1963.

Having considered the part of the report of the Economic and Social Council pertaining to the United Nations Conference on Trade and Development.[1]

Noting with satisfaction that the purposes of the forthcoming United Nations Conference on Trade and Development are gaining strong support, which has been reflected during the eighteenth session of the Assembly in a general recognition of the need for thorough preparations for the Conference in order to ensure its full success,

Believing that the joint statement by representatives of the developing countries, contained in the report on the second session of the Preparatory Committee of the United Nations Conference on Trade and Development,[2] summarizing the views, needs and aspirations of those countries with regard to the Conference, represents a well-considered basis for the examination of the problems of developing countries at the Conference and an important contribution to its deliberations,

1. *Notes with appreciation* the work already done by the Preparatory Committee of the United Nations Conference on Trade and Development at its first and second sessions and by the Secretary-General of the Conference;

2. *Welcomes* the Joint Declaration of the Developing Countries with regard to the United Nations Conference on Trade and Development, which was made at the eighteenth session of the General Assembly and which is annexed to the present resolution;

3. *Invites* the States which will participate in the United Nations Conference on Trade and Development, in dealing with the various items on the agenda and with documents and proposals contributing to the lofty aims of the Conference, to give serious consideration to the Joint Declaration of the Developing countries.

1256th plenary meeting
11 November 1963.

---

[1] *Official Records of the General Assembly, Eighteenth Session, Supplement No. 3* (A/5503), chapter III, section II.

[2] *Official Records of the Economic and Social Council, Thirty-sixth Session, Annexes*, agenda item 5, part III, document E/3799, para 186

Joint Declaration of the Developing Countries made at the eighteenth session of the General Assembly by the representatives of the following States: Afghanistan, Algeria, Argentina, Bolivia, Brazil, Burma, Burundi, Cambodia, Cameroon, Central African Republic, Ceylon, Chad, Chile, Colombia, Congo (Brazzaville), Congo (Leopoldville), Costa Rica, Cyprus, Dahomey, Dominican Republic, Ecuador, El Salvador, Ethiopia, Gabon, Ghana, Guatemala, Guinea, Haiti, Honduras, India, Indonesia, Iran, Iraq, Jamaica, Jordan, Kuwait, Laos, Lebanon, Liberia, Libya, Madagascar, Malaysia, Mali, Mauritania, Mexico, Morocco, Nepal, New Zealand, Nicaragua, Niger, Nigeria, Pakistan, Panama, Paraguay, Peru, Philippines, Rwanda, Saudi Arabia, Senegal, Sierra Leone, Somalia, Sudan, Syria, Tanganyika, Thailand, Togo, Trinidad and Tobago, Tunisia, Uganda, United Arab Republic, Upper Volta, Uruguay, Venezuela, Yemen and Yugoslavia.

I

1. The developing countries consider that the United Nations Conference on Trade and Development should represent an outstanding event in international co-operation conducive to the development of their economies and to the integrated growth of the world economy as a whole. They believe that the full attainment of even the modest targets of the United Nations Development Decade will depend on the concrete decisions taken at this Conference and on their effective implementation. The developing countries are already making, and are determined to continue to make, great efforts for their economic and social advancement through full mobilization of domestic resources, agricultural development, industrialization and diversification of their production and trade. However, this task can be accomplished only if these domestic efforts are supplemented and assisted by adequate international action. The developing countries look to the Conference to help them reach the stage of self-sustaining growth.

II

2. International trade could become a more powerful instrument and vehicle of economic development not only through the expansion of the traditional exports of the developing countries, but also through the development of markets for their new products and a general increase in their share of world exports under improved terms of trade. For this purpose, a new international division of labour, with new patterns of production and trade, is necessary. Only in this way will the economic independence of the developing countries be strengthened and a truly interdependent and integrated world economy emerge. The development of production and the increase in productivity and purchasing power of the developing countries will contribute to the economic growth of the industrialized countries as well, and thus become a means to world-wide prosperity.

3. The existing principles and patterns of world trade still mainly favour the advanced parts of the world. Instead of helping the developing countries to promote the development and diversification of their economies, the present tendencies in world trade frustrate their efforts to attain more rapid growth. These trends

must be reversed. The volume of trade of the developing countries should be increased and its composition diversified; the prices of their exports should be stabilized at fair and remunerative levels, and international transfers of capital should be made more favourable to those countries so as to enable them to obtain through trade more of the means needed for their economic development.

4. To achieve these objectives, a dynamic international trade policy is required. This policy should be based on the need for providing special assistance and protection for the less developed parts of the world economy. The removal of obstacles to the trade of the developing countries is important, but the accelarated development of the parts of the world which are lagging behind requires more than the unconditional application of the most-favoured-nation principle and the mere reduction of tariffs. More positive measures aimed at achieving a new international division of labour are essential to bring about the necessary increase in productivity and diversification of economic activity in the developing countries. The measures taken by developed countries to promote the development of the relatively backward areas within their national boundaries provide a guide for the purposeful and dynamic action which needs to be taken in the field of international economic co-operation.

III

5. The fundamental trade problems of developing countries are well identified. What the world lacks today is, therefore, not the awareness of the problem, but the readiness to act. Many constructive proposals were advanced during the second session of the Preparatory Committee of the United Nations Conference on Trade and Development. The representatives of developing countries making the present Declaration recommend to all Members of the United Nations that they give earnest consideration to these proposals and that they explore, before the beginning of the Conference, all practical means for their implementation, so as to make it possible to reach at the Conference basic agreement on a new international trade and development policy. This policy, in accordance with General Assembly resolution 1785 (XVII) of 8 December 1962, should lead to the adoption by the Conference of concrete measures to achieve, *inter alia*, the following:

(a) Creation of conditions for the expansion of trade between countries at a similar level of development, at different stages of development or having different systems of social and economic organization;

(b) Progressive reduction and early elimination of all barriers and restrictions impeding the exports of the developing countries, without reciprocal concessions on their part;

(c) Increase in the volume of exports of the developing countries in primary products, both raw and processed, to the industrialized countries, and stabilization of prices at fair and remunerative levels;

(d) Expansion of the markets for exports of manufactured and semi-manufactured goods from the developing countries;

(e) Provision of more adequate financial resources at favourable terms so as to enable the developing countries to increase their imports of capital goods and ndustrial raw materials essential for their economic development, and better co-ordination of trade and aid policies;

(f) Improvement of the invisible trade of the developing countries, particularly by reducing their payments for freight and insurance and the burden of their debt charges;

(g) improvement of institutional arrangements, including, if necessary, the establishment of new machinery and methods for implementing the decisions of the Conference.

IV

6. The developing countries are looking to more stable and healthy international economic relations in which they can increasingly find from their own resources the means required for self-sustaining growth. The developing countries are confident that the United Nations Conference on Trade and Development will not only be able to contribute to the acceleration of their economic development, but will also be an important instrument for promoting stability and security in the world.

7. The developing countries expect that the Conference will offer an opportunity for the manifestation, in the field of trade and development, of the same political will that was responsible for the Charter of the United Nations signed at San Francisco and the creation of the Organization. They are confident that, in this spirit, the decisions of the Conference will bring about fuller international co-operation and that greater progress can be made towards the attainment of collective economic security. International trade will thus become a strong guarantee of world peace and the Conference will be a landmark in the fulfilment of the Charter.

UNITED NATIONS CONFERENCE ON TRADE AND DEVELOPMENT

GENEVA, 23 MARCH—16 JUNE 1964

FINAL ACT
FIRST PART — PREAMBLE

The United Nations Conference on Trade and Development has adopted this Final Act.

Section I

BACKGROUND

1. The States participating in the Conference are determined to achieve the high purposes embodied in the United Nations Charter "to promote social progress and better standards of life in larger freedom"[1]; to seek a better and more effective system of international economic co-operation, whereby the division of the world into areas of poverty and plenty may be banished and prosperity achieved by all; and to find ways by which the human and material resources of the world may be harnessed for the abolition of poverty everywhere. In an age when scientific progress has put unprecedented abundance within man's reach, it is essential that the flows of world trade should help to eliminate the wide economic disparities among nations. The international community must combine its efforts to ensure that all countries — regardless of size, of wealth, of economic and social system — enjoy the benefits of international trade for their economic development and social progress.

2. Recognizing that universal peace and prosperity are closely linked and that the economic growth of the developing countries will also contribute to the economic growth of the developed countries, realizing the dangers of a widening gulf in living standards between peoples, and convinced of the benefits of international co-operation with a view to helping the developing countries to reach a higher standard of life, the States signatories of this Final Act are resolved, in a

---

[1] Preamble to the Charter of the United Nations.

sense of human solidarity, "to employ international machinery for the promotion of the economic and social advancement of all peoples".[2]

3. In endorsing the decision to convene the United Nations Conference on Trade and Development, the General Assembly of the United Nations was motivated by certain basic considerations. Economic and social progress throughout the world depends in large measure on a steady expansion in international trade. The extensive development of equitable and mutually advantageous international trade creates a good basis for the establishment of neighbourly relations between States, help to strengthen peace and an atmosphere of mutual confidence and understanding among nations, and promotes higher living standards and more rapid economic progress in all countries of the world. Finally, the accelerated economic development of the developing countries depends largely on a substantial increase in their share in international trade.

4. The task of development, which implies a complex of structural changes in the economic and social environment in which men live, is for the benefit of the people as a whole. The developing countries are already engaged in a determined attempt to achieve, by their own efforts, a breakthrough into self-sustaining economic growth which furthers social progress. These efforts must continue and be enlarged. Economic and social progress should go together. If privilege, extremes of wealth and poverty, and social injustice persist, then the goal of development is lost. If the social and cultural dimension of development is ignored, economic advance alone can bring no abiding benefit.

5. The developing countries recognize that they have the primary responsibility to raise the living standards of their peoples; but their national exertions to this end will be greatly impaired if not supplemented and strengthened by constructive international action based on respect for national so vereignty. An essential element of such action is that international policies in the field of trade and development should result in a modified international division of labour, which is more rationai and equitable and is accompanied by the necessary adjustments in world production and trade. The resultant increase in productivity and purchasing power of the developing countries will contribute to the economic growth of the industrialized countries as well, and thus become a means to world-wide prosperity.

6. The issues before the Conference have been at once challenging and urgent. While there are varying degrees of development, the joint income of the developing countries with two-thirds of the world's population, is not much more than one-tenth of that of the industrialized countries. Moreover, the dramatic increase in the population of the developing countries multiplies the difficulties they face in assuring to their peoples even the simplest elements of a decent human life. The aim must be to create, jointly, new trade and new wealth, so as to share a common prosperity, and thereby avoid the waste and other unfavourable consequences of closed paths to development. The international community is called upon to join in a constructive and universal policy of co-operation for trade and development which will further economic progress throughout the world.

7. The designation of the nineteen-sixties as the United Nations Development

---

[2] Preamble to the Charter of the United Nations.

Decade was a recognition of deep world-wide concern with the urgent necessity of raising the standard of living of the developing countries and an earnest of the resolve of the United Nations, working together, to accomplish this task. Wide concern has been expressed regarding the inadequacy of the Decade's objective of a minimum rate of growth of aggregate national income of 5 per cent per annum by 1970. To attain even this rate of growth it is essential that measures and action be taken by both the developing and the developed countries, including measures to raise the level and accelerate the rate of growth of earnings of the developing countries from trade, as a means of helping them to overcome their persistent external imbalance.

8. The United Nations Conference on Trade and Development was convened in order to provide, by means of international co-operation, appropriate solutions to the problems of world trade in the interest of all peoples and particularly to the urgent trade and development problems of the developing countries. In a period when their need for imports of development goods and for technical knowledge has been increasing, developing countries have been faced with a situation in which their export earnings and capacity to import goods and services have been inadequate. The growth in import requirements has not been matched by a commensurate expansion in export earnings. The resultant trade gap, which gold and foreign exchange reserves have been inadequate to bridge, has had to be filled very largely by capital imports. This, in itself, cannot provide a complete or permanent solution, and indeed, the servicing of external debts and the outgoings on other "invisible" items themselves present severe burdens for developing countries. Moreover, the terms of trade have operated to the disadvantage of the developing countries. In recent years many developing countries have been faced with declining prices for their exports of primary commodities, at a time when prices of their imports of manufactured goods, particularly capital equipment, have increased. This, together with the heavy dependence of individual developing countries on primary commodity exports has reduced their capacity to import. Unless these and other unfavourable trends are changed in the near future, the efforts of the developing countries to develop, diversify and industrialize their economies will be seriously hampered.

9. Deeply conscious of the urgency of the problems with which the Conference has dealt, the States participating in this Conference, taking note of the recommendations of the Conference, are determined to do their utmost to lay the foundations of a better world economic order.

Section II

CONSTITUTION AND PROCEEDINGS

10. When, in the third week of December 1961, the General Assembly of the United Nations designated the current decade as "the United Nations Development Decade", it also asked the Secretary-General to consult members on the advisability of convening an international conference on international trade problems. Both resolutions (1707 /XVI/ and 1710 /XVI/) sprang from the growing conviction that

the economic aims of the Charter would best be furthered by a bold new programme of international economic co-operation; and it was in this conviction that the United Nations Conference on Trade and Development had its origin.

11. The Cairo Conference on the Problems of Economic Development, held in July 1962, issued a Declaration (which was later welcomed by the United Nations General Assembly in resolution 1820 /XVII/) strongly recommending the early convening of an international conference on trade and development. The idea of such a conference having gained ground, the General Assembly of the United Nations endorsed, on 8 December 1962 (resolution 1785 /XVII/), the decision taken in August 1962 by the Economic and Social Council (resolution 917 /XXXIV/) whereby the Council resolved to convene this Conference and to establish a Preparatory Committee to consider its agenda. The Secretary-General was requested to invite all States Membres of the United Nations and members of the specialized agencies and of the International Atomic Energy Agency to take part in the Conference. The deliberation of the Preparatory Committee's three sessions[3] were fruitful: a detailed provisional agenda for the Conference was drawn up, and a report was prepared defining the problems to be examined and suggesting the directions in which possible solutions might be sought. At the Committee's request the secretariats of the United Nations family of organizations prepared many studies of the issues involved. The Secretary-General of the Conference sought the advice of Governments and scholars, and prepared his report entitled *Towards a New Trade Policy for Development* (see Vol. II). Member States, individually and in groups, also submitted useful proposals and suggestions to the Conference.

12. On 18 July 1963, the Economic and Social Council decided that the United Nations Conference on Trade and Development should be held in Geneva, beginning on 23 March 1964 and continuing until 15 June 1964, and approved the provisional agenda drawn up by the Preparatory Commitee (Economic and Social Council resolution 963 /XXXVI/). By its resolution of 11 November 1963 the General Assembly (resolution 1897 /XVIII/) noted the work of the Preparatory Committee and of the Secretary-General of the Conference, welcomed the Joint Declaration of the Developing Countries,[4] and invited States to give serious consideration to it. The regional economic commissions and other regional organizations considered questions of trade and development and adopted important resolutions and declarations.[5] Meanwhile, as the practical arrangements for the Conference went forward, the General Assembly and the Economic and Social Council were the principal forum for debates expressing the high hopes vested by the peoples of the United

---

[3] The first session of the Preparatory Committee took place at United Nations Headquarters from 22 January to 5 February 1963; the second was held at the European Office of the United Nations, in Geneva, from 21 May to 29 June 1963; and the third session was at United Nations Headquarters from 3 to 15 February 1964. At its third session, the Committee decided that informal closed meetings should be held prior to the opening of the Conference. These pre-Conference meetings were held in Geneva from 18 to 23 March 1964.

[4] The Joint Declaration of the Developing Countries was adopted at the same time as, and forms an annex to, the General Assembly resolution in question.

[5] See the reports relating to the Brasilia meeting convened by the Economic Commission for Latin America and the Alta Gracia Charter approved by the Special Latin American Co-ordinating Committee of the Organization of American States, the resolutions adopted by the Economic Commission for Africa and by the Economic and Social Commission of the Organization of African Unity at Naimey, the resolution of the Economic Commission for Europe and the Teheran resolutions of the Economic Commission for Asia and the Far East (for all these reports see Vols. VI and VII).

Nations in the Conference as a potential turning point in international co-operation in the field of trade and development.

13. Aware of these high hopes, the representatives of the following one hundred and twenty[6] States gathered in Geneva from 23 March to 16 June 1964 to take part in the United Nations Conference on Trade and Development:

Afghanistan, Albania, Algeria, Argentina, Australia, Austria, Belgium, Bolivia, Brazil, Bulgaria, Burma, Burundi, Byelorussian Soviet Socialist Republic, Cambodia, Cameroon, Canada, Central African Republic, Ceylon, Chad, Chile, China, Colombia, Congo (Brazzaville), Congo (Leopoldville), Costa Rica, Cuba, Cyprus, Czechoslovakia, Dahomey, Denmark, Dominican Republic, Ecuador, El Salvador, Ethiopia, Federal Republic of Germany, Finland, France, Gabon, Ghana, Greece, Guatemala, Guinea, Haiti, Holy See, Honduras, Hungary, Iceland, India, Indonesia, Iran, Iraq, Ireland, Israel, Italy, Ivory Coast, Jamaica, Japan, Jordan, Kenya, Kuwait, Laos, Lebanon, Liberia, Libya, Liechtenstein, Luxembourg, Madagascar, Malaysia, Mali, Mauritania, Mexico, Monaco, Mongolia, Morocco, Nepal, Netherlands, New Zealand, Nicaragua, Niger, Nigeria, Norway, Pakistan, Panama, Paraguay, Peru, Philippines, Poland, Portugal, Republic of Korea, Republic of Viet-Nam, Romania, Rwanda, San Marino, Saudi Arabia, Senegal, Sierra Leone, South Africa, Spain, Sudan, Sweden, Switzerland, Syria Tanganyika,[7] Thailand, Togo, Trinidad and Tobago, Tunisia, Turkey, Uganda, Ukrainian Soviet Socialist Republic, Union of Soviet Socialist Republics, United Arab Republic, United Kingdom of Great Britain and Northern Ireland, United States of America, Upper Volta, Uruguay, Venezuela, Yemen, Yugoslavia, Zanzibar.[7]

14. The inaugural address was delivered by the President of the Swiss Confederation; the Secretary-General of the United Nations also addressed the Conference; and messages of goodwill and good wishes for success were received from numerous Heads of State. After adopting its agenda and electing its officers — a President, twenty-seven Vice-Presidents, and a Rapporteur — the Conference was addressed by its President and heard, over a period of twelve days, an address by its Secretary-General and a series of policy statements by heads of delegations, most of whom were Cabinet ministers, and by representatives of a number of inter-governmental economic organizations. Five Committees of the whole were established for detailed study of the items of the agenda. The General Committee of the Conference comprised the President, the Vice-Presidents, the Rapporteur, and the Chairman of the five Committees. The Conference also established a Drafting Committee for the Final Act.

15. With a view to reaching agreement on the issues before the Conference, many informal meetings were held and important consultations conducted among groups of delegations. A notable feature of the Conference was the fact that the delegations of the States signatories of the Joint Declaration of the Developing Countries co-ordinated their work with a view to enhancing general co-operation among all delegations.

---

[6] Somalia and Western Samoa were invited, but did not attend the Conference.
[7] On 27 May 1964, as a result of the formation of the United Republic of Tanganyika and Zanzibar, the delegations of Tanganyika and Zanzibar were reconstituted as a unified delegation.

Section III

FINDINGS

The Conference has been guided by the following findings:

16. World trade has expanded substantially in reçent years: the value of world exports has more than doubled since 1950. The principal impulse for this growth has been provided by the over-all expansion of the world economy, aided by national and international action as well as enormous scientific and technical progress and the social and economic changes in the world.

17. The countries of the world did not share proportionately in this expansion of international trade. While exports of developing countries rose from $ 19,200 million to $ 28,900 million between 1950 and 1962, that is by 50 per cent, the expansion of exports from these countries proceeded at an appreciably lower rate than that of the developed countries. As a result, the share of the developing countries in world exports declined steadily from nearly one-third in 1950 to only slightly more than one-fifth in 1962. Concurrently, the developed market economies increased their share from three-fifths to two-thirds, and the centrally planned economies from 8 per cent to 13 per cent. One of the reasons for the decline in the rate of expansion of world exports from 8.4 per cent per annum in the early fifties to rather less than 5 per cent in the early sixties is the inability of the developing countries to attain a higher rate of export expansion.

18. The difficulties experienced by developing countries in increasing the sale of their products at remunerative prices in the markets of most of the highly industrialized countries have placed a limit on the extent to which they can purchase capital goods and machinery from the developed countries, which in turn has contributed to a slower rate of expansion of world trade than would have been the case if the developing countries had been enabled to increase their exports at a faster rate. Further, measures having discriminatory or protectionist effects applied by certain developed countries have hampered the development of the trade of developing countries and of world trade in general.

19. The difficulties of the developing countries were aggravated by a deterioration in their terms of trade during the period 1950—1962. The slower growth in the quantity of exports of the developing countries and the adverse movement of their terms of trade were largely the reflexion of the present commodity composition of their trade, consisting, as it does, predominantly of the exchange of primary product exports for manufactured imports whose relative positions in world markets have undergone significant changes. World trade in manufactures has been increasing at an annual rate more than twice that of trade in primary products. Factors contributing to the sluggishness of primary product exports include the low response of consumer demand for food to increases in income of consumers in the advanced countries where incomes and food consumption are already high, the widespread use of substitutes and synthetics, and the increasing output of primary products in advanced countries which has been the result both of domestic policies, in many cases reinforced by protective barriers, as well as a general increase in productivity stemming from technological progress. These long-term

412

trends have been accentuated by short-term fluctuations in export earnings caused by economic recessions and other factors.

20. The deterioration in terms of trade and the sluggish expansion of the export quantum of the developing countries occurred at a time when their need for imported supplies to speed up the pace of their economic development sharply increased. There is a close link between the rate of economic growth and the available supply of investment goods. The developing countries require a specific increase in the supply of investment goods in order to achieve the Development Decade target. Since their domestic capacity to produce these goods is limited, a substantial amount of such goods has to be imported. Imports have to be financed through export receipts and inflows of capital from abroad. Thus, the resources required for a higher rate of growth would obviously have to be sought in additional export earnings and an increase in the net inflow of long-term public and private funds.

21. The developing countries' surplus of exports over imports in 1950 became a deficit in 1962 of $ 2,300 million, while their net payments for investment income and other invisibles were about $ 3,300 million around 1960. This deficit was covered by the provision of aid and other capital flows. However, the gap between the import requirements of developing countries and their export earnings has been widening. According to United Nations Secretariat estimates, this gap could be of the order of $ 20,000 million a year in 1970, on the basis of a 5 per cent per annum rate of growth set as the target for the United Nations Development Decade, assuming no change in the trends of the fifties upon which these estimates were based.

22. In recent years, the developing countries have been turning increasingly to economic and social planning as the most effective means for accelerating their growth. Their plans, policies and institutions are designed to achieve the transformation of their economic and social structures and to provide for maximum saving, investment and output to a predetermined order of priorities for a targeted rate of growth. However realistic the plans drawn up by the developing countries may be, their achievement is hindered by the instability of international markets for primary products and by conditions restricting the access of primary commodities and semi-manufactures and manufactures to the markets of the developed countries. The continued dependence on the export of a single product or a few commodities whose prices have been declining in the past has made the carrying out of the development plans all the more difficult. The achievement of the economic and social development plans of the developing countries necessitates an appropriate change in the present structure of international trade in such a way as to afford them the opportunity of earning adequate and stable supplies of foreign exchange.

23. An overwhelming proportion — over two-thirds — of the import and export trade of developing countries is with the developed market economies. Between 1950 and 1962 the total exports of the developed market economies to the developing countries increased by 98 per cent, rising from $ 10,650 million to $ 21,060 million. This contrasted with the exports of the developing countries to the developed market countries which increased by 56 per cent, rising from $ 13,220 million to $ 20,660 million.

413

24. The reason for the failure of exports of the developing countries to the developed market economies to expand at a faster rate can be attributed to a number of factors. Reference has already been made in the foregoing passages to contributory factors of a general character. Specific policies include price-support programmes, customs duties and internal taxes and fiscal charges imposed on the consumption of tropical products, export subsidies on commodities of interest to developing countries, and higher levels of tariffs imposed on processed products relative to those applied to such products when exported in their natural form. These factors have contributed to the sluggishness of the demand for the products of developing countries and in the case of some commodities to the accumulation of surpluses which have tended to exercise a depressing effect on world commodity prices. There is need for the elimination of these obstacles by national and international action designed to improve access and expand market opportunities for the exports of primary products, semi-manufactures and manufactures of the developing countries in order to increase their export earnings.

25. Owing to its relatively recent origin, trade between developing countries and the centrally planned economies is so far limited to a relatively small number of countries and constitutes a small part of the trade turnover of developing countries as a whole. In 1962, $ 1,630 million, or 5.6 per cent of the total exports of the developing countries went to the centrally planned economies, while imports from the latter into the former totalled $ 2,150 million and formed 7.3 per cent of total imports. This trade has, however, shown a tendency to increase rapidly in recent years. Thus, in terms of value, the exports of the countries with centrally planned economies to developing countries increased from $ 405 million to $ 2,150 million, or by 430 per cent, between 1950 and 1962, while exports from the developing countries to the countries with centrally planned economies showed an expansion from $ 610 million to $ 1,630 million, or by 167 per cent, over the same period.

26. The expansion in trade has been secured mainly through medium and long-term bilateral trade agreements which stipulate the quantity and/or the value of goods to be exchanged. In spite of the rapidity of growth in trade between the two groups of countries, there is still considerable scope for expansion, which can be secured through the removal of certain obstacles which prevent a faster rate of growth and by further positive measures taken by the interested countries. The major obstacles arise from the fact that trade relations have not yet been established between many developing countries and centrally planned economies; the need, in some cases, due to the bilateral trade system for individual developing countries to balance their trade with individual centrally planned economies; and the paucity of knowledge among public and private organizations of trade partners in some developing countries, about the products and the trade policies and practices of the centrally planned economies.

27. These problems can be solved and trade between countries of the two groups expanded at a more rapid rate through the establishment of normal trade relations between centrally planned economies and a larger number of developing countries; through the granting by countries with centrally planned economies to developing countries, within the framework of the former's foreign trade system, of special

414

advantages conductive to the promotion of such trade; through the adoption by the centrally planned economies, within the framework of their long-term plans, of appropriate measures to secure the diversification and a proportionately increasing growth of their imports of primary, semi-manufactured and manufactured products from developing countries; and through increased utilization by centrally planned economies, in addition to bilateral arrangements, of multilateral trade and payment methods, when these are considered to be of mutual advantage to all partners in the trade. Developing countries for their part should accord the countries with centrally planned economies conditions for trade not inferior to those granted normally to the developed market economy countries.

28. Trade between the centrally planned countries and the developed market economies has grown rapidly in recent years. The full potentiality of this trade, however, has not been realized because of administrative, economic and trade policy obstacles. Efforts to discover means to solve these problems and increase trade, to the mutual benefit of all partners concerned, and thus achieve levels of trade commensurate with the apparent possibilities, have shown increasing progress in recent years.

29. Continuation of such efforts in whatever available forums, including within the framework of the future institutional arrangements recommended by the Conference, should result in progressively. greater levels of trade between countries having different economic and social systems. It is recognized that such a development would be in the interest of world trade as a whole.

30. While trade between developed countries is increasing and while the share of such exchanges in total world trade is also rising, the level of trade between developing countries is very low and its importance in world trade has been decreasing. The expansion of inter-regional and intra-regional trade is important to developing countries in so far as it provides them with wider markets for their products and enables them to further diversify their trade and to save on scarce foreign exchange. Hence, the establishment of closer and broader trade ties between developing countries is necessary.

Section IV

REASONS AND CONSIDERATIONS

In drawing up its recommendations, the Conference has been guided by the following essential reasons and considerations:

31. The development of equitable and mutually advantageous trade can promote higher standards of living, full employment and rapid economic progress in all countries of the world.

32. The fundamental problems of developing countries are well identified and what is now required is a universal readiness to act and generally to adopt practical measures aimed at increasing exports and export earnings of developing countries and accelerating their economic development.

33. At the root of the foreign trade difficulties facing the developing coun-

415

tries and other countries highly dependent on a narrow range of primary commodities are the slow rate of growth of demand for their exports of primary commodities, accounting for 90 per cent of their exports, the increasing participation of developed countries in world trade in primary commodities, and the deterioration in the terms of trade of developing countries from 1950 to 1962.

34. During the period of structural readjustments of their economies, the developing countries will remain heavily dependent on commodity exports to meet growing import needs involved in the process of industrialization and diversification.

35. Because of the outstanding importance of commodity trade for economic development, particularly of the developing countries, and the special difficulties affecting trade in primary commodities, it is important and urgent that action be taken over a wide front and on dynamic and comprehensive lines so as to conduct a concerted attack on international commodity problems.

36. There is accordingly a need for a deliberate effort on the part of all industrialized countries to remedy the adverse tendencies in question.

37. This comprehensive action should include international commodity arrangements as one of the means of stimulating a dynamic and steady growth of the real export earnings of the developing countries so as to provide them with expanding resources for their economic and social development and of securing over-all stabilization in primary commodity markets. It is also necessary to accelerate the removal of existing obstacles and to forestall the creation of new obstacles to commodity trade.

38. Compensatory financing is an appropriate solution to meet the serious residual problems caused by short-term fluctuations in the prices of and earnings from primary commodity exports. For residual long-term problems, financial solutions should be sought.

39. The developing countries should not rely merely on the expansion of traditional exports of primary products and raw materials. Promotion of industries with an export potential in developing countries is essential. Diversification and expansion of exports of manufactured and semi-manufactured goods are among the important means to assist the developing countries to achieve, in time, a balance in their external accounts.

40. The establishment and expansion, in developing countries, of industries with an export potential call for a whole series of interrelated measures and action on the part of the developing countries within the framework of over-all planning, as well as by developed countries and appropriate international organizations.

41. The role of the public sector in the economic development of the developing countries is recognized, as well as the role of private capital, domestic and foreign.

42. Developing countries face obstacles and difficulties in marketing their manufactures and semi-manufactures in the developed countries. In order to facilitate the industrial exports of developing countries, their products should have freer access, particularly to the markets of the developed countries, but also to the markets of other developing countries.

43. Easier access to markets should be provided, not only for existing and

416

traditional exports of manufactures and semi-manufactures, but also for a wider range of products in order to improve the opportunities for the establishment, in the developing countries, of a wider range of industries more technically evolved and producing industrial goods of higher degrees of complexity.

44. Substantial imports of manufactures and semi-manufactures may involve some readjustment in the industrial structures of the developed countries.

45. A lowering of trade barriers would improve the competitive position of the developing countries relative to that of domestic producers in the market of each developed country, but it would not improve their competitive position in that market in relation to exports from other developed countries. Special measures in favour of exports from the developing countries would be needed to bring about the required expansion of such exports.

46. In addition to the expansion of exports of manufactures to developed countries, the expansion of such trade among the developing countries themselves would contribute towards solving the dilemma posed by the economic and technological requirements of modern industry, on the one hand, and the limited domestic markets of individual countries on the other. Because of the many forms which economic co-operation might have in various cases and the problems which they might cause, it is considered that a certain flexibility is needed.

47. The Conference has considered the general targets on which the international community might focus in dealing with the problems of development through trade and international cooperation. A number of principles and criteria, aimed at providing constructive guidelines for policies in the various areas of international financial and technical co-operation, have been formulated. The major questions identified are as follows:

(a) The need for higher growth rates for developing countries; measures to be taken by developed and developing countries, including measures to increase foreign exchange availabilities.

(b) Guidelines for international financial and technical co-operation; terms and conditions of aid, and the relation of trade and aid to maintain the continuity of sound development plans or programmes.

(c) External debt problems.

(d) The need and means for increasing the flow of financial resources to the developing countries.

(e) Compensatory finance; supplementary financial measures.

(f) Aspects of shipping and all other invisible items.

(g) The need for periodic reviews.

48. There is wide recognition of the importance and gravity of the problem posed by the financing of development, in all its many complex aspects, and this recognition should form the basis for continuing reviews and action in this field.

49. There is also recognition of the need for greater and more systematic efforts by all parties involved, with a fair division of responsibilities among developed and developing countries, in order to engender the necessary co-operative efforts at the national, regional and international levels.

50. More specifically, there is wide agreement in some key areas which,

through necessarily limited in scope, constituted forward steps. These areas include measures for accelerated growht in developing countries and increase in foreign exchange availabilities; guidelines for international financial and technical co-operation, compensatory financing and supplementary financial measures, and for dealing with external debt problems; and some aspects of shipping in relation to the trade of developing countries.

51. Finally, in some other areas, there is also agreement that specific measures, which have been proposed, should be given further consideration or should be studied by the appropriate international organizations.

52. In approaching the problem of institutional arrangements, the Conference has taken into account the fact that sustained efforts are necessary to raise standards of living in all countries and to accelerate the economic growth of developing countries, and that international trade is an important instrument for economic development. The Conference has provided a unique opportunity to make a com-prehensive review of the problems of trade and of trade in relation to economic development, particularly those problems affecting the developing countries. It has recognized that adequate and effectively functioning organizational arrangements are essential if the full contribution of international trade to the accelerated growth of the developing countries is to be successfully achieved through the formulation and implementation of the necessary policies.

53. To this end, the Conference has examined the operation of existing international institutions and has recognized both their contributions and their limitations in dealing with all the problems of trade and related problems of develop-ment. It believes that participating Governments should make the most effective use of institutions and arrangements to which they are or may become parties, and is convinced, at the same time, that there should be a further review of both the present and the proposed institutional arrangements, in the light of the experi-ence of their work and activities. The Conference has further taken note of the widespread desire among developing countries for a comprehensive trade organiza-tion, and has recognized that further institutional arrangements are necessary in order to continue the work initiated by this Conference and to implement its recommendations and conclusions.

SECOND PART — A CONSOLIDATION OF THE RECOMMENDATIONS OF THE CONFERENCE[8]

Section I

PRINCIPLES

54. The Conference has recommended the following General Principles to govern international trade relations and trade policies conducive to development: (see Annex A. I. 1).

---

[8] The results of the voting on the Principles and Recommendations adopted by the Confe-rence appear in Annex A. Observations and reservations appear in Annex B.

General Principle One

Economic relations between countries, including trade relations, shall be based on respect for the principle of sovereign equality of States, self-determination of peoples, and non-interference in the internal affairs of other countries.

General Principle Two

There shall be no discrimination on the basis of differences in socio-economic systems. Adaptation of trading methods shall be consistent with this principle.

General Principle Three

Every country has the sovereign right freely to trade with other countries, and freely to dispose of its natural resources in the interest of the economic development and well-being of its own people.

General Principle Four

Economic development and social progress should be the common concern of the whole international community and should, by increasing economic prosperity and well-being, help strengthen peaceful relations and co-operation among nations. Accordingly, all countries pledge themselves to pursue internal and external economic policies designed to accelerate economic growth throughout the world, and in particular to help promote, in developing countries, a rate of growth consistent with the need to bring about a substantial and steady increase in average income, in order to narrow the gap between the standard of living in developing countries and that in the developed countries.

General Principle Five

National and international economic policies should be directed towards the attainment of an international division of labour in harmony with the needs and interests of developing countries in particular, and of the world as a whole. Developed countries should assist the developing countries in their efforts to speed up their economic and social progress, should co-operate in measures taken by developing countries for diversifying their economies, and should encourage appropriate adjustments in their own economies to this end.

General Principle Six

International trade is one of the most important factors in economic development. It should be governed by such rules as are consistent with the attainment of economic and social progress and should not be hampered by measures incompatible therewith. All countries should co-operate in creating conditions of international trade conducive, in particular, to the achievement of a rapid increase in the export earnings of developing countries and, in general, to the promotion of an expansion and diversification of trade between all countries, whether at similar levels of development, at different levels of development, or having different economic and social systems.

General Principle Seven

The expansion and diversification of international trade depends upon increasing access to markets, and upon remunerative prices for the exports of primary products. Developed countries shall progressively reduce and eliminate barriers and other restrictions that hinder trade and consumption of products from developing countries and take positive measures such as will create and increase markets for the exports of developing countries. All countries should co-operate through suitable international arrangements, on an orderly basis, in implementing measures designed to increase and stabilize primary commodity export earnings, particularly of developing countries, at equitable and remunerative prices and to maintain a mutually acceptable relationship between the prices of manufactured goods and those of primary products.

General Principle Eight

International trade should be conducted to mutual advantage on the basis of the most-favoured-nation treatment and should be free from measures detrimental to the trading interests of other countries. However, developed countries should grant concessions to all developing countries and extend to developing countries all concessions they grant to one another and should not, in granting these or other concessions, require any concessions in return from developing countries. New preferential concessions, both tariff and non-tariff, should be made to developing countries as a whole and such preferences should not be extended to developed countries. Developing countries need not extend to developed countries preferential treatment in operation amongst them. Special preferences at present enjoyed by certain developing countries in certain developed countries should be regarded as transitional and subject to progressive reduction. They should be eliminated as and when effective international measures guaranteeing at least equivalent advantages to the countries concerned come into operation.

General Principle Nine

Developed countries participating in regional economic groupings should do their utmost to ensure that their economic integration does not cause injury to, or

420

otherwise adversely affect, the expansion of their imports from third countries, and, in particular, from developing countries, either individually or collectively.

General Principle Ten

Regional economic groupings, integration or other forms of economic co-operation should be promoted among developing countries as a means of expanding their intra-regional and extra-regional trade and encouraging their economic growth and their industrial and agricultural diversification, with due regard to the special features of development of the various countries concerned, as well as their economic and social systems. It will be necessary to ensure that such co-operation makes an effective contribution to the economic development of these countries, and does not inhibit the economic development of other developing countries outside such groupings.

General Principle Eleven

International institutions and developed countries should provide an increasing net flow of international financial, technical and economic assistance to support and reinforce, by supplementing the export earnings of developing countries, the efforts made by them to accelerate their economic growth through diversification, industrialization and increase of productivity, on the basis of their national policies, plans and programmes of economic development. Such assistance should not be subject to any political or military conditions. This assistance, whatever its form and from whatever source, including foreign public and private loans and capital, should flow to developing countries on terms fully in keeping with their trade and development needs. International financial and monetary policies should be designed to take full account of the trade and development needs of developing countries.

General Principle Twelve

All countries recognize that a significant portion of resources released in successive stages as a result of the conclusion of an agreement on general and complete disarmament under effective international control should be allocated to the promotion of economic development in developing countries.

General Principle Thirteen

The Conference decided to include, as a separate part of the Principles adopted by the Conference, the Principles relating to the transit trade of land-locked countries set forth in Annex A. I. 2 below.

General Principle Fourteen

Complete decolonization in compliance with the United Nations Declaration on the Granting of Independence to Colonial Countries and Peoples and the liquidation of the remnants of colonialism in all its forms, is a necessary condition for economic development and the exercise of sovereign rights over natural resources.

General Principle Fifteen

The adoption of international policies and measures for the economic development of the developing countries shall take into account the individual characteristics and different stages of development of the developing countries, special attention being paid to the less developed among them, as an effective means of ensuring sustained growth with equitable opportunity for each developing country.

55. The Conference has recommended a number of Special Principles to govern international trade relations and trade policies conducive to development (see Annex A. I. 1.)

56. The Conference has adopted the following recommendation on Principles relating to the transit trade of land-locked countries (see Annex A. I. 2).

The Conference,

Having regard to the various aspects of the problem of transit trade of land-locked States,

Considering that, for the promotion of the economic development of the land-locked States, it is essential to provide facilities to enable them to overcome the effects of their land-locked position on their trade,

Adopts the following principles together with the Interpretative Note:

Principle I

The recognition of the right of each land-locked State of free access to the sea is an essential principle for the expansion of international trade and economic development.

Principle II

In territorial and on internal waters, vessels flying the flag of land-locked countries should have identical rights, and enjoy treatment identical to that enjoyed by vessels flying the flag of coastal States other than the territorial State.

Principle III

In order to enjoy the freedom of the seas on equal terms with coastal States, States having no sea coast should have free access to the sea. To this end States situated between the sea and a State having no sea coast shall, by common agreement with the latter, and in conformity with existing international conventions, accord to ships flying the flag of that State treatment equal to that accorded to their own ships or to the ships of any other State as regards access to sea ports and the use of such ports.

Principle IV

In order to promote fully the economic development of the land-locked countries, the said countries should be afforded by all States, on the basis of reciprocity, free and unrestricted transit, in such a manner that they have free access to regional and international trade in all circumstances and for every type of goods.

Goods in transit should not be subject to any customs duty.

Means of transport in transit should not be subject to special taxes or charges higher than those levied for the use of means of transport of the transit country.

Principle V

The State of transit, while maintaining full sovereignty over its territory, shall have the right to take all indispensable measures to ensure that the exercise of the right of free and unrestricted transit shall in no way infringe its legitimate interests of any kind.

Principle VI

In order to accelerate the evolution of a universal approach to the solution of the special and particular problems of trade and development of land-locked countries in the different geographical areas, the conclusion of regional and other international agreements in this regard should be encouraged by all States.

Principle VII

The facilities and special rights accorded to land-locked countries in view of their special geographical position are excluded from the operation of the most-favoured-nation clause.

Principle VIII

The principles which govern the right of free access to the sea of the land-locked State shall in no way abrogate existing agreements between two or more contracting parties concerning the problems, nor shall they raise an obstacle as regards the conclusion of such agreements in the future, provided that the latter do not establish a régime which is less favourable than or opposed to the above-mentioned provisions.

423

These Principles are interrelated and each Principle should be construed in the context of the other Principles.

*

*   *

57. In the light of its adoption of principles governing international trade relations and trade policies conducive to development, the Conference has recognized the necessity of achieving the broadest possible measure of agreement at the earliest possible moment on a set of Principles, and has recommended that the institutional machinery proposed by the Conference should continue efforts to that end (see Annex A. I. 3.).

Section II
INTERNATIONAL COMMODITY PROBLEMS

58. In order to deal with the problems facing the primary commodity trade of developing countries, the Conference has recommended that the provisions outlined below should be considered as means of increasing the export earnings of the developing countries by general measures as well as by specific measures related to individual commodities and, that, to this end, practical steps should be taken by Governments concerned to implement, at the earliest possible date, those of the following provisions which are applicable in the light of certain considerations (see Annex A. II. 1), as solutions of the urgent problems of developing countries.

(a) Provisions for international commodity arrangements, with a basic objective of stimulating a dynamic and steady growth and ensuring reasonable predictability in the real export earnings of the developing countries so as to provide them with expanding resources for their economic and social development, while taking into account the interests of consumers in importing countries, through remunerative, equitable and stable prices for primary commodities, having due regard to their import purchasing power, assured satisfactory access and increased imports and consumption, as well as co-ordination of production and marketing policies (see Annexes A. II. 1 and A. II. 2);

(b) Provisions for a programme of measures and actions for the removal of obstacles (tariff, non-tariff and other) and discriminatory practices and for expansion of market opportunities for primary commodity exports and for increases in their consumption and imports in developed countries (see Annexes A. II. 1 and A. II. 2).

The Conference has given general approval to the establishment of a Commission on Commodity Arrangements and Policies within the framework of the continuing institutional machinery which will be established following the United

424

Nations Conference on Trade and Development. The Conference has also generally formulated terms of reference for the new commission and requested that they be given prompt and favourable consideration by the continuing institutional machinery (see Annex A. II. 1).

60. The Conference has also adopted recommendations for active measures to promote market opportunities for primary commodity exports and for increases in consumption and imports in both developed and developing countries. It has expressed the belief that food aid should become an integral and continuing part of international aid under the United Nations and the Food and Agriculture Organization of the United Nations. It has also recommended special action, both national and international, to deal with cases where natural products exported by developing countries face competition from synthetics and other substitutes. It has also recommended, *inter alia*, the study and preparation of a programme of action for the organization of commodity trade (see Annexes A. II. 3, A. II. 4, A. II. 5, A. II. 6, A. II. 7 and A. II. 8).

61. The Conference has noted the heavy dependence of some developing countries on foreign exchange earnings from the export of minerals and fuels, and has recommended that the developed countries should effectively reduce and/or eliminate barriers and discrimination against the trade and consumption of those products, particularly internal taxation, with a view to increasing the real income of the developing countries from these exports. It has also recommended action to provide the developing countries producing minerals and fuels with an appreciable increase in the revenues which accrue to them as a result of the export of these natural resources (see Annex A. II. 9).

Section III

TRADE IN MANUFACTURES AND SEMI-MANUFACTURES

62. The Conference recognizes the urgent need for the diversification and expansion of the export trade of developing countries in manufactures and semi-manufactures, as a means of accelerating their economic development and raising their standards of living. It considers that individual and joint action by both developed and developing countries is necessary to enable the latter to obtain increased participation, commensurate with the needs of their development, in the growth of international trade in manufactured and semi-manufactured products.

63. The Conference has adopted a series of recommendations designed to help in the promotion of industries with an export potential and in the expansion of their export trade in manufactures and semi-manufactures. These recommendations deal with the following questions:

(a) Industrial development (see Annex A. III. 1), dealing with the creation of a specialized agency for industrial development;

(b) Industrial branch agreements on partial division of labour (see Annex A. III. 2);

(c) The establishment and expansion of industries with an export potential (see Annex A. III. 3.).

64. The Conference has recommended the adoption by Governments participating in the Conference of certain guidelines in their foreign trade and assistance policies and programmes providing for increased access, in the largest possible measure, to markets for manufactured and semi-manufactured products of interest to developing countries, so as to enable these countries to increase and diversify their exports of these products on a stable and lasting basis. These guidelines also include appropriate provision by developing and developed countries for co-operation between Governments and private groups to build up export production in developing countries (see Annexes A. III. 4, and A. III. 6).

65. The Conference has noted both the agreement, signified by all developing countries and a great majority of the developed countries, with the principle of assisting the industrial development of developing countries, by the extension of preferences in their favour, and the opposition to this principle expressed by some developed countries. The Conference has recommended that the Secretary-General of the United Nations establish a committee of governmental representatives to consider the matter with view to working out the best method of implementing such preferences on the basis of non-reciprocity from the developing countries, as well as to discuss further the differences on principle involved (see Annex A. III. 5.)

66. The Conference has adopted a recommendation based on the readiness of the centrally planned economies to take action with a view to increasing through appropriate measures, the import of manufactures and semi-manufactures from the developing countries (see Annex A. III. 7).

67. The Conference has adopted a recommendation outlining practical measures for the promotion of trade in manufactures and semi-manufactures among developing countries (see Annex A. III. 8).

68. The Conference has also adopted a recommendation calling on developed countries to take certain measures, *inter alia* on import promotion and industrial adjustment (see Annex A. III. 6).

Section IV

FINANCING FOR AN EXPANSION OF INTERNATIONAL TRADE
AND IMPROVEMENT OF THE INVISIBLE TRADE
OF DEVELOPING COUNTRIES

69. On the main issues before the Conference on the financing of development, trade and invisible transactions, a large consensus of agreement was reached, though complete agreement was not always achieved.

70. The Conference recognizes the wide concern expressed regarding the inadequacy of the growth target of 5 per cent per annum set for the United Nations Development Decade. The Conference acknowledges the need for steps to be taken, by both developing and developed countries, to mobilize domestic and international resources for accelerated growth in developing countries at rates even higher than

that envisaged for the Development Decade where feasible; and that the economic situations, policies and plans of individual developing countries be examined for this purpose with the consent of the country concerned. The Conference also recognizes in this connexion, that the import capacity of developing countries, resulting from the combined total of export proceeds, invisible earnings and capital inflow, and taking into account the evolution of prices, should rise sufficiently, and the measures taken by the developing countries themselves should be adequate, so as to enable these higher rates of growth to be achieved; and that all countries, developed and developing, should undertake, individually and in co-operation, such measures as may be necessary to ensure this. The Conference has also recommended that each economically advanced country should endeavour to supply, in the light of principles set forth in Annex A. IV. 1, financial resources to the developing countries of a minimum net amount approaching as nearly as possible to 1 per cent of its national income, having regard, however, to the special position of certain countries which are net importers of capital (see Annex A. IV. 2). The Conference has also adopted a recommendation providing, *inter alia*, that the rate of interest on government loans to the developing countries should not normally exceed 3 per cent (see Annex A. IV. 3).

71. The Conference has adopted recommendations concerning terms and conditions of financial and technical cooperation provided by industrialized countries through bilateral and multilateral programmes of assistance to developing countries (see Annexes A. IV. 1, A. IV. 3 and A. IV. 4).

72. The Conference has proposed certain measures to deal with the increasing burden of accumulated debt and service payments in developing countries, with the objective of facilitating, whenever warranted and under appropriate conditions, the re-scheduling or consolidation of debts, with appropriate periods of grace and amortization, and reasonable rates of interest (see Annexes A. IV. 1 and A. IV. 5). It has also approved the possibility of deliveries on credit of industrial equipment reimbursable in goods (see Annex A. IV. 6).

73. The Conference has adopted the following recommendations proposing measures and studies concerning an increase in the volume or an improvement in the terms of financing for developing countries:

(a) Recommendations concerning a United Nations Capital Development Fund (see Annex A. IV. 7), and the gradual transformation of the United Nations Special Fund (see Annex A. IV. 8);

(b) The provision of aid for development on a regional basis (see Annexes A. IV. 9 and A. IV. 10);

(c) The promotion of the flow of public and private capital both to the public and private sectors in developing countries (see Annexes A. IV. 11, A. IV. 12 and A. IV. 13);

(d) Review of the use and terms of credit, export financing and marketing, and credit insurance (see Annexes A. IV. 14, A. IV. 15 and A. IV. 16).

74. The Conference has recognized, further, that adverse movements in the export proceeds of developing countries can be disruptive of development. The Conference has, therefore, recommended that, as regards payments difficulties

caused by temporary export shortfalls, members of the International Monetary Fund should study certain measures with a view to liberalizing the terms of the compensatory credit system operated by the Fund since February 1963 (see Annex A. IV. 17). As regards longer-term problems, the Conference has recommended (see Annex A. IV. 18):

(a) That the International Bank for Reconstruction and Development be invited to study the feasibility of a scheme that would provide supplementary financial resources to developing countries experiencing shortfalls in export proceeds from reasonable expectations. The relevant economic circumstances for consideration would include the adverse effects of significant increases in import prices.

(b) That the continuing machinery recommended by this Conference be invited to study and organize further discussion of concepts and proposals for compensatory financing put forward by the delegations of developing countries at the Conference, taking into account the effect of shortfalls in export earnings and adverse movements in the terms of trade.

75. The Conference has also recommended a study of the international monetary issues relating to problems of trade and development with special reference to the objectives and decisions of this Conference (see Annex A. IV. 19). It has also approved a recommendation on the participation of nationals of developing countries in the process of policy formulation in international financial and monetary agencies (see Annex A. IV. 20).

76. The Conference has agreed on a draft text containing a Common Measure of Understanding on shipping question, and has recommended that appropriate intergovernmental procedures, including any committee that might be deemed necessary, be established to promote understanding and co-operation in the field of shipping, and to study and report on its economic aspects (see Annexes A. IV. 21 and A. IV. 22).

77. The Conference has also considered and recommended measures on insurance, tourism, technical assistance and transfer of technology, taking into account the need to improve the invisible trade of developing countries (see Annexes A. IV. 23, A. IV. 24, A. IV. 25 and A. IV. 26).

Section V

INSTITUTIONAL ARRANGEMENTS

78. The Conference has recommended to the United Nations General Assembly that it adopt, at its nineteenth session, the following provisions, *inter alia:*

(a) The present United Nations Conference on Trade and Development should be established as an organ of the General Assembly to be convened at intervals of not more than three years and with a membership comprising those States which are members of the United Nations, the specialized agencies, or the International Atomic Energy Agency.

(b) The principal functions of the Conference shall be:

(i) To promote international trade, especially with a view to accelerating economic development, particularly trade between countries at different stages of development, between developing countries and between countries with different systems of economic and social organization, taking into account the functions performed by existing international organizations;

(ii) To formulate principles and policies on international trade and related problems of economic development;

(iii) To make proposals for putting the said principles and policies into effect and to take such other steps within its competence as may be relevant to this end, having regard to differences in economic systems and stages of development;

(iv) Generally, to review and facilitate the co-ordination of activities of other institutions within the United Nations system in the field of international trade and related problems of economic development, and in this regard to co-operate with the General Assembly and the Economic and Social Council in respect to the performance of their Charter responsibilities for co-ordination;

(v) To initiate action, where appropriate, in co-operation with the competent organs of the United Nations for the negotiation and adoption of multilateral legal instruments in the field of trade, with due regard to the adequacy of existing organs of negotiation and without duplication of their activities;

(vi) To be available as a centre for harmonizing the trade and related development policies of Governments and regional economic groupings in pursuance of article 1 of the United Nations Charter; and

(vii) To deal with any other matters within the scope of its competence.

(c) A permanent organ of the Conference, to be known as the Trade and Development Board, should be established as part of the United Nations machinery in the economic field, consisting of fifty-five members elected by the Conference from among its membership, with full regard for both equitable geographical distribution and the desirability of continuing representation for the principal trading States.

(d) For the effective discharge of its functions, the Board should establish such subsidiary organs as may be necessary, and in particular three committees — on commodities, manufactures, and invisibles and financing related to trade.

(e) Each State represented at the Conference should have one vote. Subject to provisions to be determined by the General Assembly at its nineteenth session after consideration by it of a report and proposals to be made by a Special Committee to be appointed by the Secretary-General of the United Nations, decisions of the Conference on matters of substance should be taken by a two-thirds majority of the representatives present and voting, and decisions of the Board by simple majority. The task of the Special Committee shall be to prepare proposals for procedures, within the continuing machinery, designed to establish a process of conciliation to take place before voting, and to provide an adequate basis for the adoption of recommendations with regard to proposals of a specific nature for action substantially affecting the economic or financial interests of particular countries.

(f) Arrangements should be made, in accordance with Article 101 of the Charter, for the immediate establishment of an adequate, permanent and full-time secretariat within the United Nations Secretariat for the proper servicing of the Conference, the Board and its subsidiary bodies.

(g) The Conference should review, in the light of experience, the effectiveness and further evolution of institutional arrangements with a view to recommending such changes and improvements as might be necessary. To this end it should study all relevant subjects including matters relating to the establishment of a comprehensive organization based on the entire membership of the United Nations system of organizations to deal with trade and with trade in relation to development (see Annex A. V. 1).

79. The Conference has also recommended action concerning interim institutional arrangements, and the terms of reference of subsidiary organs of the Trade and Development Board (see Annexes A. V. 2 and A. V. 3).

Section VI
SPECIAL PROBLEMS

80. The Conference has requested the Secretary-General of the United Nations to appoint a committee of twenty-four members, representing land-locked, transit and other interested States as governmental experts and on the basis of equitable geographical distribution. The said committee is to be convened during 1964 to prepare a new draft convention dealing with the transit trade of land-locked countries. The Conference has recommended that the new draft convention be submitted for consideration and adoption by a conference of plenipotentiaries to be convened by the United Nations in the middle of 1965 (see Annex A. VI. 1).

81. The Conference has recommended that international organizations set up by the developing countries which are the principal exporters of non-renewable natural products be recognized and encouraged to enable them to defend their interests (see Annex A. VI. 2).

82. The Conference has also adopted a recommendation concerning expanded utilization of long-term trade agreements (see Annex A. VI. 3).

83. The Conference has recommended non-discrimination in dealing with governmental trading organizations in foreign trade (see Annex A. VI. 4).

Section VII
PROGRAMME OF WORK

84. In addition to the Programme of Work implied in the recommendations referred to above, the Conference has recommended the following:

(1) A study of the feasibility of rates of growth higher than those which have been experienced by most countries individually during the past decade, and even higher than those envisaged for the United Nations Development Decade, and of measures for developing and developed countries to take to achieve them (see Annex A. IV. 2);

430

(2) An over-all economic and social survey of the depressed areas of the developing world and of special measures to make possible immediate action to secure a substantial improvement in the living standards of the populations of these areas (see Annex A. VI. 5);

(3) A programme of work for the Commission on Commodity Arrangements and Policies, or any equivalent body that may be established within the continuing machinery, for the development of appropriate guidelines and procedures for commodity arrangements and, in respect of commodities to which certain conditions apply, for commodity negotiations and export studies (see Annexes A. II. 1 and A. II. 3);

(4) Further studies in the commodity field regarding promotion and marketing arrangements, and measures to deal with problems of substitution and various types of research aiming at an expansion of market opportunities for exports of primary commodities from developing countries (see Annexes A. II. 4, A. II. 5, A. II. 7 and A. II. 8);

(5) Work related to the provision of economic and technical assistance with a view to expanding the export earnings of developing countries from primary commodities, semi-manufactures and finished manufactures (see Annexes A. II. 5, A. II. 7, A. III. 2, A. III. 3, A. III. 4, A. III. 6, A. III. 7, A. III. 8, A. IV. 1, A. IV. 3, A. IV. 4, A. IV. 12 and A. IV. 25);

(6) A study of methods of payment that would assist in promoting trade among developing countries (see Annexes A. II. 5. and A. IV. 19);

(7) The necessary economic and statistical studies of world trade, with special reference to the problems of developing countries (see Annex A. VI. 6);

(8) The transmittal to the continuing United Nations trade machinery which it is proposed to establish, for further consideration and action, a draft recommendation submitted by Czechoslovakia on measures for expansion of trade between countries having different economic and social systems (see Annex A. VI. 7);

(9) The transmittal to the continuing trade machinery, for further consideration and action, of draft recommendations on the policies and practices of regional economic groupings among developed countries and on the promotion of regional economic groupings among developing countries, submitted by a number of developing countries (see Annex A. VI. 8);

(10) The transmittal to one of the organs to be set up by the Conference for further study of part III of the proposal concerning the use of subsidies for improving the competitive position of manufactures and semi-manufactures of developing countries (see report of the Conference, Annex E, para. 24);

(11) The elaboration of trade aspects of an economic programme of disarmament (see Annex A. VI. 10).

SECOND CONFERENCE OF NON-ALIGNED COUNTRIES

CAIRO, OCTOBER 5 TO 10, 1964

FINAL DOCUMENT

THE PROGRAMME FOR PEACE AND INTERNATIONAL CO-OPERATION

On October 11 was published in Cairo the official text of the Declaration adopted by the Second Conference of Heads of State or Government of Non-aligned Countries. The text of the Declaration which bears the title "Programme for peace and international cooperation" reads as follows:

The Second Conference of Heads of State or Government of the following non-aligned countries:

Afghanistan, Algeria, Angola, Burma, Burundi, Cambodia, Cameroon, Central African Republic, Ceylon, Chad, Congo (Brazzaville), Cuba, Cyprus, Dahomey, Ethiopia, Ghana, Guinea, India, Indonesia, Iraq, Islamic Republic of Mauritania, Jordan, Kenya, Kuwait, Laos, Lebanon, Liberia, Libya, Malawi, Mali, Morocco, Nepal, Nigeria, Saudi Arabia, Senegal, Sierra Leone, Somalia, Sudan, Syria, Togo, Tunisia, Uganda, United Arab Republic, United Republic of Tanganyika and Zanzibar, Yemen, Yugoslavia and Zambia was held in Cairo from October 5 to 10 1964.

The following countries:

Argentina, Bolivia, Brazil, Chile, Finland, Jamaica, Mexico, Trinidad and Tobago, Uruguay and Venezuela were represented by observers.

The Secretary-General of the Organization of African Unity and the Secretary-General of the League of Arab States were present as observers.

The Conference undertook an analysis of the international situation with a view to making an effective contribution to the solution of the major problems which are of concern to mankind in view of their effects on peace and security in the world.

To this end, and on the basis of the principles embodied in the Belgrade Declaration of September 1961, the Heads of State or Government of the above-mentioned countries proceeded, in an amicable, frank and fraternal atmosphere,

432

to hold detailed discussions and an exchange of views on the present state of international relations and the predominant trends in the modern world. The Heads of State or Government of the participating countries note with satisfaction that nearly half of the independent countries of the world have participated in this Second non-aligned conference.

The Conference also notes with satisfaction the growing interest and confidence displayed by peoples still under foreign domination, and by those whose rights and sovereignty are being violated by imperialism and neo-colonialism, in the highly positive role which the non-aligned countries are called upon to play in the settlement of international problems or disputes.

The Conference expresses satisfaction at the favourable reaction throughout the world to this second meeting of nonaligned countries. This emphasises the rightness, efficacy and vigour of the policy of nonalignment, and its constructive role in the maintenance and consolidation of international peace and security.

The principle of nonalignment, thanks to the confidence they inspire in the world, are becoming an increasingly dynamic and powerful force for the promotion of peace and the welfare of mankind.

The participating Heads of State or Government note with satisfaction that, thanks to the combined efforts of the forces of freedom, peace and progress, this second Non-Aligned Conference is being held at a time when the international situation has improved as compared with that which existed between the two power blocs at the time of the historic Belgrade Conference. The Heads of State or Government of the Non-Aligned Countries are well aware, however, that, despite the present improvement in international relations, and notwithstanding the conclusion and signature of the Treaty of Moscow, sources of tension still exist in many parts of the world.

This situation shows that the forces of imperialism are still powerful and that they do not hesitate to resort to the use of force to defend their interests and maintain their privileges.

This policy, if not firmly resisted by the forces of freedom and peace, is likely to jeopardise the improvement in the international situation and the lessening of tension which has occurred, and to constitute a threat to world peace.

The policy of active peaceful co-existence is an indivisible whole. It cannot be applied partially, in accordance with special interests and criteria.

Important changes have also taken place within the Eastern and Western blocs, and this new phenomenon should be taken into account in the objective assessment of the current international situation.

The Conference notes with satisfaction that the movements of national liberation are engaged, in different regions of the world, in a heroic struggle against neo-colonialism, and the practices of apartheid and racial discrimination. This struggle forms part of the common striving towards freedom, justice and peace.

The Conference reaffirms that interference by economically developed foreign States in the internal affairs of newly independent, developing countries and the existence of territories which are still dependent constitute a standing threat to peace and security.

The Heads of State or Government of the non-aligned countries, while appreciative of the efforts which resulted in the holding of the United Nations Conference on Trade and Development, and mindful of the results of that Conference, nevertheless note that much ground still remains to be covered to eliminate existing inequalities in the relationship between industrialized and developing countries.

The Heads of State or Government of the non-aligned countries, while declaring their determination to contribute towards the establishment of just and lasting peace in the world, affirm that the preservation of peace and the promotion of the well-being of peoples are a collective responsibility deriving from the natural aspirations of mankind to live in a better world.

The Heads of State or Government have arrived in their deliberations at a common understanding of the various problems with which the world is now faced, and a common approach to them. Reaffirming the basic principles of the Declaration of Belgrade, they express their agreement upon the following points:

I

CONCERTED ACTION FOR THE LIBERATION OF THE COUNTRIES STILL DEPENDENT; ELIMINATION OF COLONIALISM, NEO-COLONIALISM AND IMPERIALISM

The Heads of State or Government of the Non-Aligned Countries declare that lasting world peace cannot be realized so long as unjust conditions prevail and peoples under foreign domination continue to be deprived of their fundamental right to freedom, independence and self-determination.

Imperialism, colonialism and neo-colonialism constitute a basic source of international tension and conflict because they endanger world peace and security. The participants in the Conference deplore that the Declaration of the United Nations on the granting of independence to colonial countries and peoples has not been implemented everywhere and call for the unconditional, complete and final abolition of colonialism now.

At present a particular cause of concern is the military or other assistance extended to certain countries to enable them to perpetuate by force colonialist and neo-colonialist situations which are contrary to the spirit of the Charter of the United Nations.

The exploitation by colonialist forces of the difficulties and problems of recently liberated or developing countries, interference in the internal affairs of these States, and colonialist attempts to maintain unequal relationships, particularly in the economic field, constitute serious dangers to these young countries. Colonialism and neo-colonialism have many forms and manifestations.

Imperialism uses many devices to impose its will on independent nations. Economic pressure and domination, interference, racial discrimination, subversion, intervention and the threat of force are neo-colonialist devices against which the newly independent nations have to defend themselves. The Conference condemns

434

all colonialist, neo-colonialist and imperialist policies applied in various parts of the world.

Deeply concerned at the rapidly deteriorating situation in the Congo, the participants:

(1) support all the efforts being made by the Organisation of African Unity to bring peace and harmony speedily to that country;

(2) urge the Ad Hoc commission of the Organisation of African Unity to shirk no effort in the attempt to achieve national reconciliation in the Congo, and to eliminate the existing tension between that country and the Republic of Congo (Brazzaville) and the Kingdom of Burundi;

(3) appeal to the Congolese Government and to all combatants to cease hostilities immediately and to seek, with the help of the Organisation of African Unity, a solution permitting national reconciliation and the restoration of order and peace;

(4) urgently appeal to all foreign powers at present interfering in the internal affairs of the Democratic Republic of the Congo, particularly those engaged in military intervention in that country, to cease such interference, which infringes the interests and sovereignty of the Congolese people and constitutes a threat to neighbouring countries;

(5) affirm their full support for the efforts being made to this end by the Organisation of African Unity's Ad Hoc Commission of good offices in the Congo;

(6) call upon the Government of the Democratic Republic of the Congo to discontinue the recruitment of mercenaries immediately and to expel all mercenaries, of whatever origin who are already in the Congo, in order to facilitate an African solution.

The newly independent countries have, like all other countries, the right of sovereign disposal in regard to their natural resources, and the right to utilise these resources as they deem appropriate in the interest of their peoples, without outside interference.

The process of liberation is irresistible and irreversible. Colonized peoples may legitimately resort to arms to secure the full exercise of their right to self-determination and independence if the colonial powers persist in opposing their natural aspirations.

The participants in the Conference undertake to work unremittingly to eradicate all vestiges of colonialism, and to combine all their efforts to render all necessary aid and support, whether moral, political or material, to the peoples struggling against colonialism and neo-colonialism. The participating countries recognize the nationalist movements of the peoples which are struggling to free themselves from colonial domination as being authentic representatives of the colonial peoples, and urgently call upon the colonial powers to negotiate with their leaders.

Portugal continues to hold in bondage by repression, persecution and force, in Angola, Mozambique, so-called Portuguese Guinea and the other Portuguese colonies in Africa and Asia, millions of people who have been suffering far too long under the foreign yoke. The Conference declares its determination to ensure that the peoples of these territories accede immediately to independence without any conditions or reservations.

The Conference condemns the government of Portugal for its obstinate refusal to recognize the inalienable right of the peoples of those territories to self-determination and independence in accordance with the Charter of the United Nations and the Declaration on the granting of independence to colonial countries and peoples.

The Conference:

(1) urges the participating countries to afford all necessary material support — financial and military — to the Freedom Fighters in the territories under Portuguese colonial rule;

(2) takes the view that support should be given to the Revolutionary Government of Angola in exile and to the nationalist movements struggling for the independence of the Portuguese colonies and assistance to the Special Bureau set up by the OAU in regard to the application of sanctions against Portugal;

(3) calls upon all participating States to break off diplomatic and consular relations with the government of Portugal and to take effective measures to suspend all trade and economic relations with Portugal;

(4) calls upon the participating countries to take all measures to compel Portugal to carry out the decisions of the General Assembly of the United Nations;

(5) addresses an urgent appeal to the Powers which are extending military aid and assistance to Portugal to withdraw such aid and assistance.

The countries participating in the Conference condemn the policy of the racist minority regime in Southern Rhodesia, which continues to defy the Charter and the Resolutions of the United Nations in that it denies fundamental freedoms to the people by acts of repression and terror.

The participating countries urge all States not to recognize the independence of Southern Rhodesia if proclaimed under the rule of the racist minority, and instead to give favourable consideration to according recognition to an African nationalist government in exile, should such a government be set up. To this effect, the Conference states its opposition to the sham consultation through tribal chiefs envisaged by the present Minority Government of Southern Rhodesia.

The Conference deplores the British Government's failure to implement the various resolutions of the United Nations relating to Southern Rhodesia and calls upon the United Kingdom to convene immediately a Constitutional Conference, to which all political groups in Southern Rhodesia would be invited, for the purpose of preparing a new constitution based on the "one man, one vote" principle, instituting universal suffrage, and ensuring majority rule.

The Conference urges the Government of the United Kingdom to call for the immediate release of all political prisoners and detainees in Southern Rhodesia.

The Conference reaffirms the inalienable right of the people of South West Africa to self-determination and independence and condemns the Government of South Africa for its persistent refusal to co-operate with the United Nations in the implementation of the pertinent resolutions of the General Assembly.

It urges all States to refrain from supplying in any manner or form any arms or military equipment or petroleum products to South Africa, and to implement the Resolutions of the United Nations.

The Conference recommends that the United Nations should guarantee the territorial integrity for their speedy accession to independence and for the subsequent safeguarding of their sovereignty.

The participants in the Conference call upon the French Government to take the necessary steps to enable French Somaliland to become free and independent in accordance with paragraph 5 of Resolution 1514 (XV) of the United Nations.

The Conference appeals to all participating countries to lend support and assistance to the Liberation Committee of the Organization of African Unity.

The Conference condemns the imperialistic policy pursued in the Middle East and, in conformity with the Charter of the United Nations, decides to:

(1) endorse the full restoration of all the rights of the Arab people of Palestine to their homeland, and their inalienable right to self-determination;

(2) declare their full support to the Arab people of Palestine in their struggle for liberation from colonialism and racism.

The Conference condemns the continued refusal of the United Kingdom Government to implement the United Nations Resolutions on Aden and the Protectorates, providing for the free exercise by the peoples of the territory of their right to self-determination and calling for the liquidation of the British military base in Aden and the withdrawal of British troops from the territory.

The Conference fully supports the struggle of the people of Aden and the Protectorates and *urges* the immediate implementation of the Resolutions of the United Nations which are based on the expressed wishes of the people of the territory.

The countries participating in the Conference condemn the continued armed action waged by British colonialism against the people of Oman who are fighting to attain their freedom.

The Conference recommends that all necessary political, moral and material assistance be rendered to the liberation movements of these territories in their struggle against colonial rule.

The Conference condemns the manifestations of colonialism and neo-colonialism in Latin America and declares itself in favour of the implementation in that region of the right of peoples to self-determination and independence.

Basing itself on this principle, the Conference deplores the delay in granting full independence to British Guiana and requests the United Kingdom to grant independence speedily to that country. It notes with regret that Martinique, Guadoloupe and other Caribbean Islands are still not self-governing. It draws the attention of the ad hoc Decolonization Commission of the United Nations to the case of Puerto Rico and calls upon that commission to consider the situation of these territories in the light of Resolution 1514 (XV) of the United Nations.

RESPECT FOR THE RIGHT OF PEOPLES TO SELF-DETERMINATION AND CONDEMNATION OF THE USE OF FORCE AGAINST THE EXERCISE OF THIS RIGHT

The Conference solemnly reaffirms the right of peoples to self-determination and to make their own destiny.

It stresses that this right constitutes one of the essential principles of the United Nations Charter, that it was laid down also in the Charter of the Organisation of African Unity, and that the Conference of Bandung and Belgrade demanded that it should be respected, and in particular insisted that it should be effectively exercised.

The Conference notes that this right is still violated or its exercise denied in many regions of the world and results in a continued increase of tension and the extension of the areas of war.

The Conference denounces the attitude of those Powers which oppose the exercise of the right of peoples to self-determination.

It condemns the use of force, and all forms of intimidation, interference and intervention which are aimed at preventing the exercise of this right.

III

RACIAL DISCRIMINATION AND THE POLICY OF APARTHEID

The Heads of State or Government declare that racial discrimination — and particularly its most odious manifestations, *apartheid* — constitutes a violation of the Universal Declaration of Human Rights and of the principle of the equality of peoples. Accordingly, all governments still persisting in the practice of racial discrimination should be completely ostracized until they have abandoned their unjust and inhuman policies. In particular the governments and peoples represented at this Conference have decided that they will not tolerate much longer the presence of the Republic of South Africa in the community of Nations. The inhuman racial policies of South Africa constitute a threat to international peace and security. All countries interested in peace must therefore do everything in their power to ensure that liberty and fundamental freedoms are secured to the people of South Africa.

The Heads of State or Government solemnly affirm their absolute respect for the right of ethnic or religious minorities to protection in particular against the crimes of genocide or any other violation of a fundamental human right.

Sanctions against the Republic of South Africa

(1) The Conference regrets to note that the Pretoria Government's obstinacy in defying the conscience of mankind has been strengthened by the refusal of its

438

friends and allies, particularly some major powers, to implement United Nations resolutions concerning sanctions against South Africa.

(2) The Conference therefore:

(a) calls upon all States to boycott all South African goods and to refrain exporting goods, especially arms, ammunition, oil and minerals to South Africa;

(b) calls upon all States which have not yet done so to break off diplomatic, consular and other relations with South Africa;

(c) requests the Government represented at this conference to deny airport and overflying facilities to aircraft and port facilities to ships proceeding to and from South Africa, and to discontinue all road or railway traffic with that country;

(d) demands the release of all persons imprisoned, interned or subjected to other restrictions on account of their opposition to the policy of apartheid;

(e) invites all countries to give their support to the special bureau set up by the Organization of African Unity for the application of sanctions against South Africa.

IV

PEACEFUL CO-EXISTENCE AND THE CODIFICATION OF ITS PRINCIPLES BY THE UNITED NATIONS

Considering the principles proclaimed at Bandung in 1955, Resolution 1514 (XV) adopted by the United Nations in 1960, the Declaration of the Belgrade Conference, the Charter of the Organisation of African Unity, and numerous joint declarations by Heads of State or Government on peaceful co-existence;

Reaffirming their deep conviction that, in present circumstances, mankind must regard peaceful co-existence as the only way to strengthen world peace, which must be based on freedom, equality and justice between peoples within a new framework of peaceful and harmonious relations between the States and nations of the world;

Considering the fact that the principle of peaceful co-existence is based on the right of all peoples to be free and to choose their own political, economic and social systems according to their own national identity and their ideals, and is opposed to any form of foreign domination;

Convinced also that peaceful co-existence cannot be fully achieved throughout the world without the abolition of imperialism, colonialism and neo-colonialism;

Deeply convinced that the absolute prohibition of the threat or use of force, direct or disguised, the renunciation of all forms of coercion in international relations, the abolition of relations of inequality and the promotion of international cooperation with a view to accelerating economic, social and cultural development, are necessary conditions for safeguarding peace and achieving the general advancement of mankind.

The Heads of State or Government solemnly proclaim the following fundamental principles of peaceful co-existence;

439

1. The right to complete independence, which is an inalienable right, must be recognized immediately and unconditionally as pertaining to all peoples, in conformity with the Charter and resolutions of the United Nations General Assembly; it is incumbent upon all states to respect this right and facilitate its exercise.

2. The right to self-determination, which is an inalienable right, must be recognized as pertaining to all peoples, accordingly, all nations and peoples have the right to determine their political status and freely pursue their economic, social and cultural development without intimidation or hindrance.

3. Peaceful co-existence between States with differing social and political systems is both possible and necessary; it favours the creation of good-neighbourly relations between States with a view to the establishment of lasting peace and general well-being, free from domination and exploitation.

4. The sovereign equality of States must be recognised and respected. It includes the right of all peoples to the free exploitation of their natural resources.

5. States must abstain from all use of threat or force directed against the territorial integrity and political independence of other States; a situation brought about by the threat or use of force shall not be recognised, and in particular the established frontiers of States shall be inviolable. Accordingly, every State must abstain from interfering in the affairs of other States, whether openly, or insidiously, or by means of subversion and the various forms of political, economic and military pressure.

Frontier disputes shall be settled by peaceful means.

6. All States respect the fundamental rights and freedoms of the human person and the equality of all nations and races.

7. All international conflicts must be settled by peaceful means, in a spirit of mutual understanding and on the basis of equality and sovereignty, in such a manner that justice and legitimate rights are not impaired, all States must apply themselves to promoting and strengthening measures designed to diminish international tension and achieve general and complete disarmament.

8. All States must co-operate with a view to accelerating economic development in the world, and particularly in the developing countries. This co-operation, which must be aimed at narrowing the gap, at present widening, between the levels of living in the developing and developed countries respectively, is essential to the maintenance of a lasting peace.

9. States shall meet their international obligations in good faith in conformity with the principles and purposes of the United Nations.

The Conference recommends to the General Assembly of the United Nations to adopt, on the occasion of its twentieth anniversary, a declaration on the principles of peaceful co-existence. This declaration will constitute an important step towards the codification of these principles.

440

RESPECT FOR THE SOVEREIGNTY OF STATES
AND THEIR TERRITORIAL INTEGRITY:
PROBLEMS OF DIVIDED NATIONS

(1) The Conference of Heads of State or Government proclaims its full adherence to the fundamental principle of international relations, in accordance with which the sovereignty and territorial integrity of all States, great and small, are inviolable and must be respected.

(2) The countries participating in the Conference, having for the most part achieved their national independence after years of struggle, reaffirm their determination to oppose by every means in their power any attempt to compromise their sovereignty or violate their territorial integrity. They pledge themselves to respect frontiers as they existed when the States gained independence; nevertheless, parts of territories taken away by occupying powers or converted into autonomous bases for their own benefit at the time of independence must be given back to the country concerned.

(3) The Conference solemnly reaffirms the right of all peoples to adopt the form of government they consider best suited to their development.

(4) The Conference considers that one of the causes of international tension lies in the problem of divided nations. It expresses its entire sympathy with the peoples of such countries and upholds their desire to achieve unity. It exhorts the countries concerned to seek a just and lasting solution in order to achieve the unification of their territories by peaceful methods without outside interference or pressure. It considers that the resort to threat or force can lead to no satisfactory settlement, cannot do otherwise than jeopardize international security.

Concerned by the situation existing with regard to Cyprus, the Conference calls upon all States in conformity with their obligations under the Charter of the United Nations, and in particular under Article 2, paragraph 4, to respect the sovereignty, unity, independence and territorial integrity of Cyprus and to refrain from any threat or use of force or intervention directed against Cyprus and from any efforts to impose upon Cyprus unjust solution unacceptable to the people of Cyprus.

Cyprus, as an equal member of the United Nations, is entitled to and should enjoy unrestricted and unfettered sovereignty and independence, and allowing its people to determine freely, and without any foreign intervention or interference, the political future of the country, in accordance with the Charter of the United Nations.

The Conference, considering that foreign pressure and intervention to impose changes in the political, economic and social system chosen by a country are contrary to the principles of international law and peaceful co-existence, requests the Government of United States of America to lift the commercial and economic blockade applied against Cuba.

The Conference takes note of the readiness of the Cuban Government to settle its differences with the United States on an equal footing, and invites these two

Governments to enter into negotiations to this end and in conformity with the principles of peaceful co-existence and international co-operation.

Taking into account the principles set forth above and with a view to restoring peace and stability in the Indo-China Peninsula, the Conference appeals to the Powers which participated in the Geneva Conference of 1954 and 1962:

(1) to abstain from any action likely to aggravate the situation which is already tense in the Peninsula;

(2) to terminate all foreign interference in the *internal* affairs of the countries of that region;

(3) to convene urgently a new Geneva Conference on Indo-China with a view to seeking a satisfactory political solution for the peaceful settlement of the problems arising in that part of the world, namely:

a) ensuring the strict application of the 1962 agreements on Laos;

b) recognizing and guaranteeing the neutrality and territorial integrity of Cambodia;

c) ensuring the strict application of the 1954 Geneva Agreement on Vietnam, and finding a political solution to the problem in accordance with the legitimate aspirations of the Vietnamese people to freedom, peace and independence.

VI

SETTLEMENT OF DISPUTES WITHOUT THREAT OR USE OF FORCE IN ACCORDANCE WITH THE PRINCIPLES OF THE UNITED NATIONS CHARTER

(1) As the use of force may take a number of forms, military, political and economic, the participating countries deem it essential to reaffirm the principles that all States shall refrain in their international relations from the threat or use of force against the territorial integrity or political independence of any State, or in any other manner inconsistent with the purposes of the Charter of the United Nations.

(2) They consider that disputes between States should be settled by peaceful means in accordance with the Charter on the bases of sovereign equality and justice.

(3) The participating countries are convinced of the necessity of exerting all international efforts to find solutions to all situations which threaten international peace or impair friendly relations among nations.

(4) The participating countries gave special attention to the problems of frontiers which may threaten international peace or disturb friendly relations among States, and are convinced that in order to settle such problems, all States should resort to negotiation, mediation or arbitration or other peaceful means set forth in the United Nations Charter in conformity with the legitimate rights of all peoples.

(5) The Conference considers that disputes between neighbouring States must be settled peacefully in a spirit of mutual understanding, without foreign intervention or interference.

GENERAL AND COMPLETE DISARMAMENT; PEACEFUL USE OF ATOMIC ENERGY, PROHIBITION OF ALL NUCLEAR WEAPON TESTS, ESTABLISHMENT OF NUCLEAR-FREE ZONES, PREVENTION OF DISSEMINATION OF NUCLEAR WEAPONS AND ABOLITION OF ALL NUCLEAR WEAPONS

The Conference emphasises the paramount importance of disarmament as one of the basic problems of the contemporary world, and stresses the necessity of reaching immediate and practical solutions which would free mankind from the danger of war and from a sense of insecurity.

The Conference notes with concern that the continuing arms race and the tremendous advances that have been made in the production of weapons of mass destruction and their stockpiling threaten the world with armed conflict and annihilation. The Conference urges the great Powers to take new and urgent steps toward achieving general and complete disarmament under strict and effective international control.

The Conference regrets that despite the efforts of the members of the 18-Nation Committee on Disarmament, and in particular those of the non-aligned countries, the results have not been satisfactory. It urges the great Powers, in collaboration with the other members of that Committee, to renew their efforts with determination with a view to the rapid conclusion of an agreement on general and complete disarmament.

The Conference calls upon all States to accede to the Moscow treaty partially banning the testing of nuclear weapons, and to abide by its provisions in the interests of peace and the welfare of humanity.

The Conference urges the extension of the Moscow Treaty so as to include underground tests, and the discontinuance of such tests pending the extension of the agreement.

The Conference urges the speedy conclusion of agreements on various other partial and collateral measures of disarmament proposed by the members of the 18-Nation Committee on Disarmament.

The Conference appeals to the Great Powers to take the lead in giving effect to decisive and immediate measures which would make possible substantial reductions in their military budgets.

The Conference requests the Great Powers to abstain from all policies conducive to the dissemination of nuclear weapons and their by-products among those States which do not at present possess them. It underlines the great danger in the dissemination of nuclear weapons and urges all States, particularly those possessing nuclear weapons, to conclude non-dissemination agreements and to agree on measures providing for the gradual liquidation of the existing stockpiles of nuclear weapons.

As part of these efforts, the Heads of State or Government declare their own readiness not to produce, acquire or test any nuclear weapons, and call on all countries including those who have not subscribed to the Moscow Treaty to enter into a similar undertaking and to take the necessary steps to prevent their territories, ports and airfields from being used by nuclear powers for the deployment or disposition of nuclear weapons. This undertaking should be the subject of a treaty to be concluded in an international Conference convened under the auspices of the United Nations and open to accession by all States. The Conference further calls upon all nuclear Powers to observe the spirit of this declaration.

The Conference welcomes the agreement of the Great Powers not to orbit in outer space nuclear or other weapons of mass destruction and expresses its conviction that it is necessary to conclude an international treaty prohibiting the utilisation of outer space for military purposes. The Conference urges full international cooperation in the peaceful uses of outer space.

The Conference requests those States which have succeeded in exploring outer space, to exchange and disseminate information related to the research they have carried out in this field, so that scientific progress for the peaceful utilization of outer space be of common benefit to all. The Conference is of the view that for this purpose an international conference should be convened at an appropriate time.

The Conference considers that the declaration by African States regarding the denuclearization of Africa, the aspirations of the Latin American countries to denuclearize their continent and the various proposals pertaining to the denuclearization of areas in Europe and Asia are steps in the right direction because they assist in consolidating international peace and security and lessening international tensions.

The Conference recommends the establishment of denuclearized zones covering these and other areas and the oceans of the world, particularly those which have been hitherto free from nuclear weapons, in accordance with the desires expressed by the States and peoples concerned.

The Conference also requests the nuclear Powers to respect these denuclearized zones.

The Conference is convinced that the convening of a world disarmament conference under the auspices of the United Nations to which all countries would be invited, would provide powerful support to the efforts which are being made to set in motion the process of disarmament and for securing the further and steady development of this process.

The Conference therefore urges the participating countries to take, at the forthcoming General Assembly of the United Nations, all the necessary steps for the holding of such a conference and of any other special conference for the conclusion of special agreements on certain measures of disarmament.

The Conference urges all nations to join in the co-operative development of the peaceful use of atomic energy for the benefit of all mankind; and in particular, to study the development of atomic power and other technical aspects in which international cooperation might be most effectively accomplished through the free of such scientific information.

MILITARY PACTS, FOREIGN TROOPS AND BASES

The Conference reiterates its conviction that the existence of military blocs, Great Power alliances and pacts arising therefrom has accentuated the cold war and heightened international tensions. The Non-Aligned Countries are therefore opposed to taking part in such pacts and alliances.

The Conference considers the maintenance or future establishment of foreign military bases and the stationing of foreign troops on the territories of other countries, against the expressed will of those countries, as a gross violation of the sovereignty of States, and as a threat to freedom and international peace. It furthermore considers as particularly indefensible the existence or future establishment of bases in dependent territories which could be used for the maintenance of colonialism or for other purposes.

Noting with concern that foreign military bases are in practice a means of bringing pressure on nations and retarding their emancipation and development, based on their own ideological, political, economic and cultural ideas, the Conference declares its full support to the countries which are seeking to secure the evacuation of foreign bases on their territory and calls upon all States maintaining troops and bases in other countries to remove them forthwith.

The Conference considers that the maintenance at Guantanamo (Cuba) of a military base of the United States of America, in defiance of the will of the Government and people of Cuba and in defiance of the provision embodied in the Declaration of the Belgrade Conference, constitutes a violation of Cuba's sovereignty and territorial integrity.

Noting that the Cuban Government expresses its readiness to settle its dispute over the base of Guantanamo with the United States on an equal footing, the Conference urges the United States Government to negotiate the evacuation of this base with the Cuban Government.

The Conference condemns the expressed intention of imperialist powers to establish bases in the Indian Ocean, as a calculated attempt to intimidate the emerging countries of Africa and Asia and an unwarranted extension of the policy of neo-colonialism and imperialism.

The Conference also recommends the elimination of the foreign bases in Cyprus and the withdrawal of foreign troops from this country, except for those stationed there by virtue of United Nations resolutions.

THE UNITED NATIONS: ITS ROLE IN INTERNATIONAL AFFAIRS, IMPLEMENTATION OF ITS RESOLUTIONS AND AMENDMENT OF ITS CHARTER

The participating countries declare:

The United Nations Organization was established to promote international peace and security, to develop international understanding and co-operation, to safeguard human rights and fundamental freedom and to achieve all the purposes of the Charter. In order to be an effective instrument, the United Nations Organization must be open to all the States of the world. It is particularly necessary that countries still under colonial domination should attain independence without delay and take their rightful place in the community of nations.

It is essential for the effective functioning of the United Nations that all nations should observe its fundamental principles of peaceful co-existence, co-operation, renunciation of the threat or the use of force, freedom and equality without discrimination on grounds of race, sex, language or religion.

The influence and effectiveness of the United Nations also depends upon equitable representation of different geographical regions in the various organs of the United Nations and in the service of the United Nations.

The Conference notes with satisfaction that with Resolution 1991 (XVIII), the General Assembly has taken the initial positive step towards transformation of the structure of the United Nations in keeping with its increased membership and the necessity to ensure a broader participation of States in the work of its Organs. It appeals to all Members of the United Nations to ratify as speedily as possible the amendments to the Charter adopted at the XVIIIth Session of the General Assembly.

The Conference recognises the paramount importance of the United Nations and the necessity of enabling it to carry out the functions entrusted to it to preserve international co-operation among States.

To this end, the Non-Aligned Countries should consult one another at the Foreign Minister or Head of Delegation level at each session of the United Nations.

The Conference stresses the need to adapt the Charter to the dynamic changes and evolution of international conditions.

The Conference expresses the hope that the Heads of State or Government of the States Members of the United Nations will attend the regular Session of the General Assembly on the occasion of the 20th anniversary of the Organisation.

Recalling the recommendation of the Belgrade Conference, the Conference asks the General Assembly of the United Nations to restore the rights of the People's Republic of China and to recognize the representatives of its Government as the only legitimate representatives of China in the United Nations.

The Conference recommends to the States Members of the United Nations to respect the resolutions of the United Nations and to render all assistance necessary for the Organization to fulfil its role in maintaining international peace and security.

ECONOMIC DEVELOPMENT AND COOPERATION

The Heads of State or Government participating in this Conference,

Convinced that peace must rest on a sound and solid economic foundation,

that the persistence of poverty poses a threat to world peace and prosperity,

that economic emancipation is an essential element in the struggle for the elimination of political domination,

that respect for the right of peoples and nations to control and dispose freely of their national wealth and resources is vital for their economic development;

Conscious that participating States have a special responsibility to do their utmost to break through the barrier of underdevelopment;

Believing that economic development is an obligation of the whole international community,

that it is the duty of all countries to contribute to the rapid evolution of a new and just economic order under which all nations can live without fear or want or despair and rise to their full stature in the Family of Nations,

that the structure of world economy and the existing international institutions of international trade and development have failed either to reduce the disparity in the per capita income of the peoples in developing and developed countries or to promote international action to rectify serious and growing imbalances between developed and developing countries;

Emphasizing the imperative need to amplify and intensify international co-operation based on equality, and consistent with the needs of accelerated economic development;

Noting that as a result of the proposals adopted at Belgrade in 1961 and elaborated in Cairo in 1962, the United Nations Conference on Trade and Development met in Geneva in 1964;

Considering that while the Geneva Conference marks the first step in the evolution of a new international economic policy for development and offers a sound basis for progress in the future, the results achieved were neither adequate for, nor commensurate with, the essential requirements of developing countries;

Support the Joint Declaration of the "Seventy-Seven" developing countries made at the conclusion of that Conference, and PLEDGE the co-operation of the participating States to the strengthening of their solidarity;

Urge upon all States to implement on an urgent basis the recommendations contained in the Final Act of the United Nations Conference on Trade and Development and in particular to co-operate in bringing into existence as early as possible the new international institutions proposed therein, so that the problems of trade and economic development may be more effectively and speedily resolved;

Consider that democratic procedures, which afford no position of privilege, are as essential in the economic as in the political sphere;

that a new international division of labour is needed to hasten the industrialization of developing countries and the modernization of their agriculture, so as to enable them to strengthen their domestic economies and diversify their export trade, that discriminatory measures of any kind taken against developing countries on the grounds of different socio-economic systems are contrary to the spirit of the United Nations Charter and constitute a threat to the free flow of trade and to peace and should be eliminated;

Affirm that the practice of the inhuman policy of apartheid or racial discrimination in any part of the world should be eliminated by every possible means, including economic sanctions;

Recommend that the target of economic growth set for the development Decade by the United Nations should be revised upwards,

that the amount of capital transferred to developing countries and the terms and conditions governing the transfer should be extended and improved without political commitments, so as to reinforce the efforts of these countries to build self-reliant economics,

that a programme of action should be developed to increase the income in foreign exchange of developing countries and, in particular, to provide access for primary products from developing countries to the markets of industrialized countries, on an equitable basis and for manufactured goods from developing countries on a preferential basis,

that the establishment of a Specialized Agency for industrial development should be expedited,

that members of regional economic groupings should do their utmost to ensure that economic integration helps to promote the increase of imports from the developing countries either individually or collectively,

that the recommendation of the United Nations Conference on Trade and Development to convene a conference of plenipotentiaries to adopt an International Convention to ensure the right of landlocked countries to free transit and access to the sea be implemented by the United Nations early next year, and that the principles of economic co-operation adopted by the United Nations Conference on Trade and Development in relation to the transit trade of landlocked countries be given consideration;

Call upon participating countries to concern measures to bring about closer economic relations among the developing countries on a basis of equality, mutual benefit and mutual assistance, bearing in mind the obligations of all developing countries to accord favourable consideration to the expansion of their reciprocal trade, to unite against all forms of economic exploitation and to strengthen mutual consultation;

Call upon the members of the "Seventy-Seven" developing countries, who worked closely together at the United Nations Conference on Trade and Development of 1964 in Geneva to consult together during the next session of the General Assembly of the United Nations in order to consolidate their efforts and harmonize their policies in time for the next Conference on Trade and Development in 1966.

Convinced that progress towards disarmament increases the resources available for economic development;

Support proposals for the diversion of resources now employed on armaments to the development of underdeveloped parts of the world and to the promotion of the prosperity of mankind.

448

CULTURAL, SCIENTIFIC AND EDUCATIONAL COOPERATION AND CONSOLIDATION OF THE INTERNATIONAL AND REGIONAL ORGANIZATIONS WORKING FOR THIS PURPOSE

The Heads of State or Government participating in the Conference:

Considering that the political, economic, social and cultural problems of mankind are so inter-related as to demand concerted action;

Considering that co-operation in the fields of culture, education and science is necessary for the deepening of human understanding, for the consolidation of freedom, justice and peace, and for progress and development;

Bearing in mind that political liberation, social emancipation and scientific advancement have effected fundamental changes in the minds and lives of men.

Recognising that culture helps to widen the mind and enrich life; that all human cultures have their special values and can contribute to the general progress; that many cultures were suppressed and cultural relations interrupted under colonial domination; that international understanding and progress require a revival and rehabilitation of these cultures, a free expression of their identity and national character, and a deeper mutual appreciation of their values so as to enrich the common cultural heritage of man;

Considering that education is a basic need for the advancement of humanity and that science not only adds to the wealth and welfare of nations but also adds new values of civilisation;

Appreciating the work of the international and regional organisations in the promotion of educational, scientific and cultural co-operation among nations;

Believing that such co-operation among nations in the educational, scientific and cultural fields should be strengthened and expanded;

Recommend that international co-operation in education should be promoted in order to secure a fair opportunity for education to every person in every part of the world, to extend educational assistance to develop mutual understanding and appreciation of the different cultures and ways of life through the proper teaching of civics, and to promote international understanding through the teaching of the principles of the United Nations at various levels of education;

Propose that a free and more systematic exchange of scientific information be encouraged and intensified and, in particular, call on the advanced countries to share with developing countries their scientific knowledge and technical knowledge so that the advantages of scientific and technological advance can be applied to the promotion of economic development;

Urge all states to adopt in their legislation the principles embodied in the United Nations Declaration of Human Rights;

Agree that participating countries should adopt measures to strengthen their ties with one another in the fields of education, science and culture;

Express their determination to help, consolidate and strengthen the international and regional organisations working in this direction.

SPECIAL RESOLUTION

I

The Conference of Heads of State or Government of Non-Aligned Countries meeting in Cairo from October 5 to 10 1964;

Considering their common will to work for understanding between peoples and for international co-operation;

Reaffirming their solidarity with the African States fighting for the consolidation of their independence and the total emancipation of their continent, through concerted action and close co-operation;

Noting with satisfaction that in that historic document, the Charter of Addis Ababa, adopted on 29 May 1963, and in subsequent decisions, the African States members of the Organisation of African Unity have unreservedly adhered to the positive policy of non-alignment in relation to all great blocs;

Firmly resolved to unite their efforts and actions in fight colonialism, neo-colonialism and imperialism by all appropriate means;

Considering the outstanding work for peace and harmony which the Organisation of African Unity has accomplished, since its recent creation, in the interest of both the African Continent and the international community as a whole;

(1) *Express* their conviction that the establishment of the Organization of African Unity is an important contribution to the strengthening of world peace, the triumph of the policy of non-alignment, and the fundamental values laid down by this policy.

(2) *Decide* to coordinate and concert their efforts with those of the Organisation of African Unity, with a view to safeguarding their joint interests in economic, social and cultural development and in international cooperation.

SPECIAL RESOLUTION

II

The Heads of State or Government attending the Second Conference of Non-Aligned Countries are happy to express their warmest appreciation to the brave people, the Government and the distinguished President of the United Arab Republic, His Excellency Gamal Abdel Nasser, for the superb way in which they organized this Conference, both materially and morally, and for the generous and most brotherly hospitality extended to all delegations.

They wish to say how deeply satisfied they are with the astounding success of the Conference, which opens up new prospects for positive action and general advancement towards mutual understanding, active solidarity and the strengthening of cooperation between nations dedicated to freedom, peace and justice.

JOINT COMMUNIQUE
OF THE TRIPARTITE MEETING BETWEEN
TITO-NASSER-INDIRA GANDHI

The President of the Socialist Federal Republic of Yugoslavia, His Excellency Mr. Josip Broz Tito, the President of the United Arab Republic, His Excellency Mr. Gamal Abdel Nasser, and the Prime Minister of India, Shrimati Indira Gandhi, met in New Delhi from October 21 to 24, 1966.

The following communique was issued at the end of the meetings:

The two Presidents and the Prime Minister examined the present world situation and exchanged views on international problems as well as on the further strengthening of cooperation in all fields of interest to their respective countries. These talks were held in an atmosphere of complete frankness, mutual understanding and cordiality and confirmed the concordance of views characteristic of the close friendship between the Governments and the peoples of the three countries.

The two Presidents and the Prime Minister expressed their deep concern at the increasing threat to world peace due to the violation of the principles of peaceful coexistence and the principles and purposes of the Charter of the United Nations. They noted in particular the increasing interference, intensified use of force, and the exercise of pressures on the part of some Powers against the newly independent and other developing countries. They believe that the main source of persisting difficulties is the opposition of imperialist and neo-colonialist forces to the aspirations and the struggle of many peoples and countries towards achievement of complete political and economic emancipation.

The two Presidents and the Prime Minister noted with satisfaction that there is a strong determination among the peoples of the world to safeguard peace and intensify their struggle for political and economic independence. They welcomed the encouraging trend of an increasing number of countries taking an independent and active stand with regard to world problems, thus contributing to the maintenance of international peace and security. Further, they noted favourable developments in Europe and expressed the hope that these would have a beneficial effect on international relations as a whole.

The two Presidents and the Prime Minister consider that recent trends and developments which have taken place in the world in general confirm the validity of the policy of nonalignment. They note with satisfaction that the principles of non-alignment as formulated at Belgrade and Cairo are gaining more and more ground among independent countries which are exerting efforts towards the achievement of peace and progress in the world.

The policy of non-alignment stands against every form of imperialism, hegemony or monopoly of power and military alliances. The aim of non-alignment is to strengthen international peace, not through division of the world but through the expansion of areas of freedom, independence and co-operation on the basis of equality and mutual benefit.

The two Presidents and the Prime Minister remain resolutely opposed to colonialism and neo-colonialism in all their forms and manifestations, which seek to curb the freedom of action of newly independent countries, distorting their national goals, and to exploit their natural and human resources. They depreciate the use of economic and financial assistance as an instrument of pressure, and note with satisfaction that many developing countries have resisted such pressures. Furthermore, they believe that as problems of growth and development multiply and become more difficult, ways and means should be devised to initiate and further expand areas of cooperation among the developing countries in the fields of trade and development.

The two Presidents and the Prime Minister reiterated their conviction that the universal acceptance and application of the principles of peaceful co-existence are essential if international peace and security are to be safeguarded.

The two Presidents and the Prime Minister view with deep concern the dangerous situation in South-East Asia, more particularly the escalation of the military operations in Vietnam, which threatens to develop into a wider war. The sufferings of the Vietnamese people, the loss of human life and the material damage cannot but cause great anxiety to all peace-loving peoples of the world. They reiterate that the bombing of North Vietnam should be ended immediately without any pre-conditions.

They firmly believe that the implementation of the Geneva agreements of 1954 and the withdrawal of all foreign forces would lead to peace and enable the Vietnamese people to decide their future themselves, free from all external interference. They recognise that the participation of the South Vietnamese National Liberation Front would be necessary as one of the main parties in any efforts for the realisation of peace in Vietnam.

The two Presidents welcomed the Tashkent Declaration as a significant contribution to the cause of peace.

The two Presidents and the Prime Minister welcome the progressive developments in Asia and Africa leading to the independence of a large number of countries and their emergence as a powerful new factor for peace and international cooperation.

They note, however, that colonialism still persists in certain parts of the world. They reiterate their firm opposition to colonialism and neo-colonialism in all their forms and manifestations. They fully support the just struggle of the peoples of Zimbabwe, South-West Africa, Angola, Mozambique, the so-called Portuguese Guinea, Aden and the Protectorates. They equally reaffirm their opposition to racialism as practised in South Africa, South-West Africa and Southern Rhodesia. They consider it imperative that these oppressed peoples should recover their freedom and independence in the immediate future. They condemn the alliance between the forces of colonialism and racialism and are confident that these forces shall be defeated.

The two Presidents and the Prime Minister fully support the legitimate rights of the Palestinian Arabs and their struggle for the realisation of their aspirations in accordance with the declaration of the Cairo Conference of Non-aligned Countries.

The two Presidents and the Prime Minister reiterated their conviction that the intensification of the arms race poses a serious threat to international peace and security, and that an early agreement on general and complete disarmament under effective international control constitutes one of the most urgent problems facing the international community. They reaffirmed their support for the convening of a world disarmament conference to which all countries should be invited.

They emphasised the serious dangers inherent in the spread of nuclear weapons and called for the early conclusion of a treaty on non-proliferation of nuclear weapons in accordance with the principles approved by the United Nations General Assembly at its XX Session.

The two Presidents and the Prime Minister reiterated their faith in the vital role of the United Nations for the promotion of international cooperation, peace and security. They pledge their continuing support to make the world organization more effective in discharging its responsibilities in accordance with the Charter. They support the principle of universality of the United Nations. They urge the restoration of the legitimate rights of the People's Republic of China in the world organization.

The two Presidents and the Prime Minister consider that rapid economic progress of the developing countries is a pre-requisite for safeguarding their political and economic independence. They reviewed the struggle of developing countries to break the shackles of poverty and technological backwardness, and noted with concern that the rate of economic growth of the developing countries has fallen short even of the target envisaged for the development decade. They recognized that the responsibility for development rests primarily with the developing countries themselves. The developing countries have made strenuous efforts to mobilise domestic resources and over the past decade and a half appreciable progress has been made in social welfare and economic development. However, self-sustaining growth has yet to be attained and in the meanwhile the disparity between the developed and developing countries of the world continues to widen, resulting in increase of social, economic and political tensions.

The two Presidents and the Prime Minister feel that a principal obstacle to rapid economic growth is the insufficiency of external resources. The modest target of 1% of gross national product set by the United Nations for the transfer of net resources from developed to developing countries has not been reached and the terms and conditions for the transfer of these resources impose fresh burdens on the limited capacity of weaker economies. The policies followed by affluent

453

countries in relation to prices of primary products and their reluctance to provide satisfactory conditions for the increase in imports of processed and finished products from developing countries have made it difficult for these countries to augment their foreign earnings.

The two Presidents and the Prime Minister accordingly consider that the creation of more favourable international conditions for development remains one of the vital prerequisites for promoting economic progress of developing countries. They highly appreciate the concerted efforts that led to the convening of the United Nations Conference on Trade and Development; they regretted that effective measures have not been taken to implement its recommendations and expressed the hope that development policies of both developed and developing countries would be guided by the Final Act.

The two Presidents and the Prime Minister are convinced that the 77 developing countries will strengthen their unity and consolidate their efforts to ensure the success of the Second Conference when it meets in the autumn of 1967.

The two Presidents and the Prime Minister consider that it is necessary for developing countries to initiate new measures and to co-ordinate their individual efforts to face the challenge posed by the slackening in their rate of growth. They are resolved to take practical steps in this direction and trust that all developing countries would join in the effort to expand the area of mutual co-operation, increase trade exchanges among themselves, pool technical and scientific experience, and undertake joint endeavours to develop beneficial patterns of trade and development.

The two Presidents and the Prime Minister expressed satisfaction that friendship and understanding between their countries, based on common objectives and a common approach to world problems, as well as close co-operation in the economic, technical and cultural spheres, has continued to grow stronger over the years. They discussed the further steps to be taken by their Governments and agreed that their concerned Ministers meet at an early date to examine the possibilities of co-operation between their Governments in technical, commercial and industrial fields.

They appreciated that their three countries have continued to draw closer together and have strengthened bonds of warm friendship and brotherhood, reflecting the sentiments and common aspirations of their peoples towards lasting peace and economic progress.

The two Presidents and the Prime Minister agreed to work together to strengthen the forces of non-alignment in the changing world context and to co-operate with other countries in the task of promoting world peace and security in conditions of freedom and equality of all countries.

President Josip Broz Tito and President Gamal Abdel Nasser expressed to President Sarvepalli Radhakrishnan and to Prime Minister Indira Gandhi their great appreciation for the warm reception and hospitality accorded them throughout their stay in New Delhi by the Government and people of India.

454

CHARTER OF ALGIERS

The representatives of developing countries, assembled in Algiers in October 1967 at the Ministerial Meeting of the Group of 77, united by common aspirations and the identity of their economic interests, and determined to pursue their joint efforts towards economic and social development, peace and prosperity,

Having reviewed the work of the international community for economic progress since the adoption of the Joint Declaration of the 77 Developing Countries at the conclusion of UNCTAD I in 1964,

Have decided to chart a common course of action as conceived in the African Declaration of Algiers, the Bangkok Declaration of Asian countries and the Charter of Tequendama of Latin American countries,

Deem it their duty to call the attention of the international community to the following facts:

I

The lot of more than a billion people of the developing world continues to deteriorate as a result of the trends in international economic relations;

The rate of economic growth of the developing world has slowed down and the disparity between it and the affluent world is widening;

While the developed countries are adding annually approximately 60 dollars to the per capita income of their people, the average increase of per capita income in the developing world amounts to less than 2 dollars per annum;

The share of the developing countries in total world exports declined from 27 per cent in 1953 to only 19.3 per cent in 1966. In the first half of the 1960's total world exports grew at an average annual rate of 7.8 per cent and exports of developing countries, excluding oil exports, grew at an average rate of 4 per cent only. While the value of exports of manufactures from industrial countries increased between 1953/54 and 1965/66 by 65 billion dollars and from socialist countries by 10 billion dollars, the increase from developing countries amounted to only 3 billion dollars;

The purchasing power of exports from developing countries has been steadily declining. In the mid-1960's the developing countries have been able to buy, for a given volume of their traditional exports, one-tenth less imports than at the beginning of this period. The loss in purchasing power amounted annually to approximately

2½ billion dollars, which represents nearly half of the flow of external public financial resources to developing countries;

This has aggravated the problem of the increasing indebtedness of developing countries. The external public debt alone has increased from 10 billion dollars in 1955 to 40 billion in 1966. While the debt service payments averaged half a billion dollars annually in the mid-1950's, these have already increased to 4 billion dollars and may offset the entire transfer of resources before the end of this decade if present trends continue; they already equal the entire amount of grants and grant-like contributions;

Although modern technology offers developing countries great possibilities to accelerate their economic development, its benefits are largely by-passing them due to its capital and skill intensive nature, and is drawing away from them such limited skills as are developed;

The virtual stagnation in the production of foodstuffs in developing countries, in contrast with the rapid increase in population, has aggravated the chronic conditions of undernourishment and malnutrition and, combined with the distortion of production and trading patterns by artificial means, threatens to give rise to a grave crisis.

II

The concern over these economic and social trends and the joint efforts of the developing countries to correct them have progressively led the international community to embark on a series of initiatives culminating in the Final Act adopted in 1964 by UNCTAD I; however, the promise held out by the Final Act has not been realized. In fact, in spite of the provisions of the Final Act of UNCTAD I:

— no new commodity agreement on primary products of interest to developing countries has been concluded;

— the standstill has not been observed by the developed countries and they have increased the degree of protection in many of those agricultural products in which developing countries are more efficient producers;

— while the average prices for primary products exported from developing countries have decreased by 7 per cent since 1958, those for primary products exported from developed countries increased by 10 per cent in the same period;

— heavy fiscal charges continue to levied on products of export interest to developing countries;

— the proliferation and promotion of synthetic substitutes in developed countries has resulted in shrinking markets and falling prices for competing natural products produced by developing countries;

— insufficient progress has been made by developed countries in dismantling import tariffs on tropical products without prejudice to the interests of certain developing countries;

— little or no progress has been achieved in the relaxation of quota restrictions that are applied particularly to industrial products imported from developing countries; nor did the situation improve for some temperature zone products whose access to the developed countries is governed by restrictive measures and policies applied by the developed countries;

— the implicit discrimination in tariff policies towards developing countries has been further intensified as a result of the process of economic integration among some developed countries and also as a consequence of the Kennedy Round of negotiations;

— no progress has been made by developed socialist countries on the recommended transferability of credit balances held with them by developing countries;

— the wide disparity between domestic selling prices of goods imported by socialist countries from developing countries and the import prices of such goods creates unfavourable conditions for increases in consumption and import of such goods from developing countries;

— in spite of the unanimously agreed target of 1 per cent of national income of financial resources to be provided to developing countries, actual disbursements have levelled off in absolute terms and declined as a proportion of gross national product of developed countries. While in 1961 the flow of development financing to developing countries amounted to 0.87 per cent of gross national product of developed countries, it come down to 0.62 per cent in 1966;

— with a few notable exceptions, the terms and conditions of development finance are becoming more and more onerous; the proportion of grants is declining; interest rates are increasing; repayment periods are shortening and development loans are becoming increasingly tied;

— discriminatory practices and arrangements in the field of shipping and increasing freight rates have aggravated further the balance-of-payments position and hindered the effort to promote the exports of developing countries.

III

The international community has an obligation to rectify these unfavourable trends and to create conditions under which all nations can enjoy economic and social well-being, and have the means to develop their respective resources to enable their peoples to lead a life free from want and fear.

In a world of increasing inter-dependence peace, progress and freedom are common and indivisible. Consequently the development of developing countries will benefit the developed countries as well.

Developing countries reiterate that the primary responsibility for their development rests on them.

Developing countries are determined to contribute to one another's development.

However, a fuller mobilization and more effective utilization of domestic resources of developing countries is possible only with concomitant and effective international action.

Traditional approaches, isolated measures and limited concessions are not enough. The gravity of the problem calls for the urgent adoption of a global strategy

457

for development requiring convergent measures on the part of both developed and developing countries.

The establishment of UNCTAD and the dialogue which has taken place within it constitute a step towards a new and dynamic trade and development policy. What is needed now is to move from the stage of deliberation to the plane of practical action.

Developing countries expect that UNCTAD II will concentrate on a common endeavour for accelerated economic and social development. The agreement which has recently emerged on the basic issues to be negotiated reflects the general feeling in this respect.

To this end the representatives of developing countries at the Ministerial Meeting of the Group of 77 have considered carefully the present state of affairs and suggest the following programme of action as the most urgent and immediate step to be taken by UNCTAD II.

Part Two

PROGRAMME OF ACTION

A. COMMODITY PROBLEMS AND POLICIES

1. *Commodity Policy*

(a) *Commodity arrangements*

(i) Commodity problems should, where appropriate, be dealt with by international commodity arrangements negotiated on a commodity-by-commodity basis;

(ii) Producing developing countries should consult and co-operate among themselves in order to defend and improve their terms of trade by effective co-ordination of their sales policies;

(iii) A Cocoa Agreement should be concluded before the end of 1967 and an Agreement on Sugar early in 1968;

(iv) Commodity arrangements for oil seeds and vegetable oils, bananas, rubber, tea, sisal and hard fibres should be concluded at the earliest possible date;

(v) Appropriate action should be taken on an urgent basis in respect of iron ore, nickel, tobacco, cotton, wine, citrus fruit, manganese ore, pepper, mica, shellac and tungsten.

(b) *Buffer stocks*

Buffer stock techniques as a short-term measure for market stabilization should, where appropriate, be one of the methods adopted for international commodity arrangements, and international financing institutions and developed countries should participate in their pre-financing, while with regard to its regular income producing and consuming countries should devise a formula ensuring an equitable distribution of costs.

(c) *Diversification programmes*

Developed countries and the appropriate international financial institutions should make available additional financial and technical assistance to developing countries, including specific funds, in order to facilitate the carrying out of diversification programmes, highest priority being given to diversification in the programmes on inter-regional, regional and sub-regional levels in the process of trade expansion and economic integration among developing countries. These specific funds for diversification should be one of the features of commodity agreements.

(d) *Pricing policy*

The main objectives of pricing policy should be: (i) elimination of excessive price fluctuations; (ii) the highest possible earnings from the exports of primary products; (iii) maintenance and increase of the purchasing power of the products exported by developing countries in relation to their imports; and (iv) that developed countries undertake to assist in achieving more stable and higher prices for unprocessed and processed commodities from developing countries by applying adequate domestic taxation policies.

2. *Trade liberalization*

(a) *Standstill*

No new tariff and non-tariff restrictions should be introduced by developed countries and those introduced since UNCTAD I should be eliminated by 31 December 1968.

(b) *Removal of barriers*

(i) All restrictions and charges applied by developed countries to primary commodities including semi-processed primary products originating exclusively from developing countries should be removed;

(ii) A programme of specific commitments should be elaborated with a view to eliminating tariff and non-tariff barriers, including duties and revenue charges, on all products;

(iii) Pending the elimination of internal duties and revenue charges a system of partial refund should be introduced to lead progressively on an annual basis to full refund;

(iv) The tariff reductions offered during the Kennedy Round of negotiations on primary products of export interest to developing countries should be implemented without phasing and without reciprocity in favour of all developing countries.

(c) *Preferences*

The representatives of the developing countries at the Ministerial Meeting of the Group of 77, (i) bearing in mind the desire expressed by all members of the Group of 77 to apply recommendation A. II. 1, Section II, paragraph 3 and 6 concerning the elimination of preferences, adopted unanimously at UNCTAD I, and noting that the abolition of preferences requires that the developed countries grant equivalent advantages to the countries which at present enjoy such preferences; (ii) noting that the developed countries have not so far taken effective measures

459

for the implementation of this recommendation; (iii) considering that, in the case of certain commodities, the special preferences in force could be reduced or even abolished through international agreements:

Decided to request the Secretary-General of UNCTAD and the regional groups to undertake studies, commodity-by-commodity and country-by-country on the effect of the abolition of the special preferences in force and the steps necessary to ensure that countries which at present enjoy such preferences receive advantages at least equivalent to the losses resulting from abolition.

(d) *Minimum share of markets*

(i) Where products of developing countries compete with the domestic production of developed countries, the latter should allocate a defined percentage of their consumption of such products to developing countries; in any case, a substantial share of any increase in domestic demand for primary commodities in the developed countries should be reserved for the output of the developing countries. This allocation should be arrived at on a country-by-country and commodity-by-commodity basis, through multilateral negotiation; developed countries should agree to establish maximum ratios of domestic production so as to guarantee to developing countries adequate conditions of access for their exports;

(ii)) The developed countries should adopt measures to discourage uneconomic production of commodities which compete with those originating from developing countries and should abolish subsidies on such competing products.

(e) *Surpluses and reserve stock disposal*

The existing machinery for consultation on surplus disposal should be widened and reinforced and suitable machinery should be established, where such arrangements do not exist, in order to ensure that disposal of production surpluses or strategic reserves does not result in the depression of international prices, and does not adversely affect the exports of developing countries or the intraregional trade and agricultural development of developing countries and the position of developing countries receiving those surpluses as assistance.

(f) *Use of escape clauses*

Objective criteria should be adopted under a multilateral institutional arrangement for identifying situations on which restrictions are applied by virtue of safeguard clauses and the unilateral application of restrictions should be avoided.

3. *Synthetics and substitutes*

(i) Special measures in the field of finance, technical assistance and marketing, including financing of research, abolition of subsidies and granting of preferences should be taken to improve the competitive position of natural products of developing countries that are affected by the competition of synthetics and substitutes originating from developed countries;

(ii) The provision of Special Principle Nine of the Final Act cf UNCTAD I on dumping should be implemented with special reference to the marketing of synthetic products.

460

1. *Principles for a general system of preferences*

The following principles should be adopted in order to implement a general system of preferences. They should be accepted simultaneously as complementary and indivisible measures.

(a) At UNCTAD II there should be negotiations which should lead to the conclusion of an agreement on a general system of tariff preferences on a non-discriminatory and non-reciprocal basis. The agreement should provide for un-restricted and duty-free access to the markets of all the developed countries for all manufactures and semi-manufactures from all developing countries;

(b) Without prejudice to the general provisions contained in paragraph (a) above, the escape clause actions as envisaged below may be taken; in particular special treatment may be granted by developed countries to the less developed among the developing countries;

(c) The manufactures and semi-manufactures covered by the preferential system should include all processed and semi-processed primary products of all developing countries;

(d) All developed countries should grant such preferences to all developing countries;

(e) The form of the escape clause action, the objective criteria which should govern the application of escape clause action by developed countries and the procedures that should be followed in such cases must be agreed upon internationally. Such action must however be temporary in nature and be subject to international consultation, approval and review;

(f) The preferential system must be conceived in such a way as to make it possible for the least advanced among developing countries to share in its benefits. Accordingly any time limits of the system should be flexible so that countries at present in very incipient stages of developing will also be able to reap its advantages. Escape clause actions limiting or excluding particular exports should not apply to the less competitive products from less advanced countries. Specific commitments should be taken for technical and financial assistance in the establishment of export oriented industries in least advanced countries, with a view to markets both in the developed world and in other developing countries.

(g) The new system of general preferences should ensure at least equivalent advantages to developing countries enjoying preferences in certain developed countries to enable them to suspend their existing preferences on manufactures and semi-manufactures. From the beginning, provisions should be incorporated in the system of general preferences, for the developed countries to redress any adverse situation which may arise for these developing countries as a consequence of the institution of the general system of preferences;

(h) In order to achieve the objective of the general preferential system the arrangement should last long enough to enable all developing countries to benefit from it. Initially the arrangement should last for 20 years and should be reviewed

461

towards the end of this initial period. In any event the preferential treatment should not thereafter be abruptly terminated;

(i) In order that the general system of preferences makes adequate contribution to the balance of payments of the developing countries, the developed countries should not reduce their aid to them or nullify or impair the benefits of preferences through other measures.

(j) Suitable machinery within UNCTAD should be established to supervise and ensure the effective implementation of a general system of preferences in accordance with the foregoing paragraphs.

2. *Liberalization of trade in manufactures and semi-manufactures*

(a) The developed countries should implement immediately, without phasing, in favour of all developing countries, concessions agreed on during the Kennedy Round of trade negotiations, on products of export interest to the latter countries;

(b) The developed countries should state at UNCTAD II that all concessions agreed on during the Kennedy Round of trade negotiations on products of export interest to developing countries would be extended at the time of implementation to all developing countries whether or not members of the GATT, without reciprocity;

(c) At UNCTAD II both developed and developing countries should on the basis of the evaluation of the Kennedy Round being prepared by the UNCTAD and GATT secretariats and those prepared by governments themselves identify all outstanding issues for further negotiations. The principles of the most-favoured-nation treatment and reciprocity should in no way be introduced in these negotiations. In these negotiations all developing countries should be allowed to participate if they so desire;

(d) The developed countries should implement the agreements reached at UNCTAD I on liberalization for manufactures and semi-manufactures of export interest to the developing countries, particularly as regards the principle of the standstill;

(e) The developed countries should establish at UNCTAD II a concrete programme for the removal of quantitative restrictions at an early date, particularly those which are applied by them inconsistently with their international obligations, and also give an undertaking not to renew existing restrictions or impose new quantitative restrictions, nor adopt any other measures having equivalent effects on products of export interest to developing countries;

(f) Developed countries should supply all relevant information to the UNCTAD secretariat in respect of non-tariff barriers other than quantitative restrictions applied in the markets of the developed countries for examination at UNCTAD II;

(g) Objective criteria should be established for the application of restrictions to trade in products from developing countries under escape clauses relating to "market disruption" and other "special circumstances" applied by developed countries, so that such situations may be defined, provisions may be laid down specifying what measures restrictive of trade can legitimately be applied when such a situation is found to exist, and compensation may be fixed which corresponds to the loss or damage suffered by the developing countries.

Multilateral consultative and supervisory should be set up for that purpose. The developed countries should undertake measures for anticipatory structural readjustments and other measures for bringing about such changes in their production patterns as to eliminate the possibility of resorting to restrictive trade policies or escape clause actions on ground of market disruption in relation to products of export interest to developing countries in order to establish a new international division of labour that would be more equitable. The developed countries should not promote the development in their territories of industries of particular interest to the developing countries. In those cases where developed countries have invoked escape clauses on grounds of market disruption, they should make the appropriate domestic structural adjustments;

(h) The developed countries should take appropriate action to carry out readjustments in the tariff nomenclatures of their countries so as to facilitate the granting of duty-free entry on products exported by and large by developing countries;

(i) The machinery which would be established to supervise the effective implementation of a general system of preferences should also supervise the programme for the elimination of tariff and non-tariff barriers, and the application of escape clauses, in particular any such barriers which prejudice or nullify the scheme of general preferences.

3. *Trade with socialist countries*

The socialist countries should grant concessions to the developing countries whose advantages are at least equivalent to the effects of preferences which would be granted by the developed countries with market economies.

The socialist countries should:

(a) Adopt and implement measures designed to increase the rate of growth of the imports of manufactures and semi-manufactures from developing countries, and to diversify such imports in consonance with the latter's trade and development requirements;

(b) Undertake to contribute to the maintenance of remunerative and stable prices for the exports of developing countries by the inclusion of suitable provisions in their trade agreements with these countries;

(c) In drawing up their national and regional development plans take due account of the production and export potential in developing countries;

(d) Abolish customs duties and other trade restrictions on goods imported from and originating in developing countries;

(e) Eliminate the margin between the import price and the domestic selling price of the goods imported from developing countries;

(f) Refrain from re-exporting the goods purchased from developing countries, unless it is with the consent of the developing countries concerned;

(g) Encourage conclusion of industrial branch agreements for the supply of plant and equipment on credit to the developing countries, accepting repayment of such credits in particular with the goods manufactured by such plant in the developing countries concerned;

463

(h) Multilateralize, to the extent possible, among the socialist countries of Eastern Europe, payments arrangements with developing countries to facilitate increase of imports from the latter;

(i) Grant preferential access conditions for products originating from developing countries. These conditions should include the establishment, in their international purchasing policies, of margins of tolerance in favour of the developing countries with regard to prices and delivery terms;

(j) Within the framework of UNCTAD to set up permanent consultative machinery through which socialist countries and developing countries may promote mutual trade and economic co-operation, and solve the problems and obstacles which may arise.

4. *Trade promotion*

(a) Diversification of production of manufactures and semi-manufactures of developing countries should be carried out within the framework of a new and more equitable international division of labour between developing and developed countries;

(b) Developed countries should abstain from harming the interests of developing countries by fostering production of commodities produced principally by developing countries, and, in that regard, they should encourage the establishment in the developing countries of export industries processing primary commodities produced by the latter;

(c) Developed countries and international agencies should channel more, and more effective, technical and financial assistance in order to improve the productivity of the developing countries' industries and their competitiveness in international markets;

(d) International co-operation should also be secured with a view to the dissemination of trade information, particularly with regard to the opportunities offered by the developed countries' markets. To that end, the developing countries should support the establishment of the joint UNCTAD-GATT trade promotion centre and obtain the financial and technical support of the developed countries for its operation. Also a close and continuing co-operation between UNIDO and UNCTAD should be promoted, on the general understanding that, as stated in General Assembly resolution 2152 (XXI), "the former shall be competent to deal with the general and technical problems of industrialization, including the establishment and expansion of industries in developing countries, and the latter with the foreign trade aspects of industrialization, including the expansion and diversification of exports of manufactures and semi-manufactures by developing countries". Furthermore, developing countries should take into consideration the possibility of the establishment of a single export promotion centre within the United Nations family under the auspices of UNCTAD.

1. Flow of international public and private capital

(a) Each developed country should comply with the target of a minimum 1 per cent of its gross national product for net financial flows, in terms of actual disbursements, by the end of the Development Decade. A separate minimum target, within this goal, and progressively increasing, should be established for the official component of aid flows, net of amortization and interest payments;

(b) Any gaps remaining in the 1 per cent transfer each year should be made good by additional government transfers;

(c) Resources of the International Development Association (IDA) should be immediately replenished and augmented;

(d) Developed countries and financial institutions should extend and intensify their support to regional development banks;

(e) The International Bank for Reconstruction and Development (IBRD) should be made a Development Bank for developing countries exclusively. Total repayment of current loans by developed countries in advance of maturity should be secured. Such released funds should be used to augment resources of IBRD and IDA to finance development of developing countries;

(f) There should be no discrimination by international lending institutions against the public sector, in particular in industry;

(g) Special consideration should be given to developing countries which have not so far received adequate international aid;

(h) Private investments should be of permanent benefit to the host developing country. Subject to nationally-defined priorities and within the framework of national development plans, private investments may be encouraged by incentives and guarantees;

(i) No developed countries should decrease the existing level of their aid to developing countries, especially those forms of aid granted through negotiations.

2. Terms and conditions of development finance

(a) By 1968, the norms of lending laid down by General Assembly resolution 2170 (XXI) and the Development Assistance Committee of OECD should be reached;

(b) Beyond a date to be internationally agreed, all development lending should be on terms currently applied by IDA. In regard to earlier loans or loans on other than IDA terms, the interest should be subsidized by governments of developed countries;

(c) Pending the general adoption of IDA terms, there should be a considerable lowering of interest rates and a considerable increase in maturities and grace periods;

(d) A Multilateral Interest Equalization Fund should be created to cover the interest margin between loans obtained on international capital markets and concessional development loans;

(e) Development finance should be rapidly and progressively untied, with a view to reaching the goal of total untying by a specific date; excess costs incurred through tying should be subsidized by creditor countries; procurement in developing countries should be freely permissible, especially within the same region;

(f) External finance should be made available both for programmes and for projects and should include local costs where necessary;

(g) Development finance commitments should be on a continuing basis to cover plan programmes over a period of years;

(h) Appropriate steps should be taken to improve the administration of development finance;

(i) An intergovernmental group with equitable representation of developed and developing countries should be established to deal with all aspects of commercial credits, including suppliers' credits.

3. *Problems of external indebtedness*

Suitable measures should be adopted for alleviating the debt-servicing burdens of developing countries by consolidation of their external debts into long-term obligations on low rates of interest. In case of imminent difficulties, speedy arrangements should be made for refinancing and re-scheduling of loans on "soft" terms and conditions.

4. *Mobilization of financial resources*

Developing countries recognize that they should to the fullest extent possible consistent with smooth economic growth and social stability continue to mobilize their domestic resources for financing their development process. They recall, however, that the utilization of these resources cannot be fully effective without the necessary external assistance.

5. *Supplementary financing*

UNCTAD II should negotiate an agreement for early implementation of a scheme of supplementary financing on the basis of a consensus to be reached after considering the report of the Intergovernmental Group on Supplementary Financing on the World Bank study.

In no case should the scheme involve internal policy commitments which prejudice the sovereignty of any member country as defined by that country, the means for achieving this objective to be further discussed at the forthcoming meeting of the Inter-Governmental Group on Supplementary Financing and negotiated at UNCTAD II. These discussions and negotiations should take account, *inter alia*, of the positions expressed in the regional declarations of the developing countries.

6. *Compensatory financing facility*

The developing countries ask that:

(a) drawings on the International Monetary Fund under the Compensatory Financing Facility should be immediately available up to 50 per cent of the countries' quotas in the Fund, and that such drawings are not subject to any conditions;

466

(b) the formula for calculating shortfalls be modified, taking as the basis the exports of each of the countries concerned either during three normal years or more, preceding the payment of compensation;

(c) due consideration should be given to refinancing debts incurred by developing countries during periods of persistent shortfalls in their export earnings, including a revision of current repurchase time limits.

7. *International monetary issues*

(a) Developing countries should participate from the outset in all discussions on international monetary reform and in the operation of the new arrangements for Special Drawing Rights in the International Monetary Fund;

(b) A link between development finance and additional liquidity should be forged as urged by the developing countries;

(c) The developing countries are intimately concerned with the policies of international financial organizations relating to use of their resources, voting power and the improvement of machinery for balance of payments adjustments.

D. INVISIBLES, INCLUDING SHIPPING

Developing countries reaffirm the competence of UNCTAD in shipping matters.

1. *International shipping legislation*

(a) Developing countries ask that UNCTAD II should include "international shipping legislation" in the work programme of the Committee on Shipping which should use such technical and expert advice as may be necessary;

(b) In accordance with the obligations undertaken by the international community, all developed countries should give full co-operation to the UNCTAD secretariat by providing complete information for studies being carried out by it in the field of shipping including freight rates, conference practices, adequacy of shipping services, etc;

(c) These studies should take into account the implications of technical advances in shipping in respect of the organization and structure of conferences, cost levels, rate structure and techniques of port organization and operations as well as the implications of technical advances for the expansion of merchant marines of developing countries.

2. *Freight rates and conference practices*

(a) Immediate steps are needed at UNCTAD II to provide a basis for future action on freight rates which are not only continuing to rise but are still discriminatory and restrictive vis-a-vis the developing countries;

(b) Developed countries should press freight conferences and shipowners to abolish the widespread practice of fixing special high freight rates for the transport of non-traditional products of the developing countries and to lower freight rates applied to traditional exports of the developing countries;

(c) Developing countries ask UNCTAD II to adopt the following principles:

(i) the right of developing countries to take part in any freight conference affecting their maritime traffic on an equal footing with shipowners of developed countries;

(ii) freight conferences to have representation in developing countries;

(iii) publication of information, including advance publication of any proposed changes on freight rates and other cargo arrangements by freight conferences affecting the foreign trade of developing countries.

(d) Developing countries should intensify their co-operation amongst themselves, *inter alia* on a regional basis, to secure maximum benefits and better bargaining positions in the field of shipping, in particular regarding freight rates.

3. *Expansion of merchant marines*

(a) Developing countries affirm their unquestionable right to establish and to expand their merchant marines in the context of rising freight rates and the prospects of their foreign trade;

(b) Developed countries and international agencies should extend financial and technical assistance to developing countries for the establishment and expansion of national and regional merchant marines and related facilities. Such assistance should include the training of personnel in the economic, managerial, technical and other aspects of shipping. Financing arrangements should be in favour of national enterprises;

(c) All countries should recognize the right of developing countries to assist their merchant marines, including the right to reserve a fair share of the cargo transported to and from those countries;

(d) The regulations enacted by developing countries with a view to achieving the objectives aforementioned should not be considered justification for the adoption of retaliatory or other measures by the developed countries and their shipping conferences which may have the effect of rendering ineffective the measures taken by the developing countries;

(e) Developing countries should be enabled to make the maximum use of their shipbuilding industries and expand them.

4. *Consultation machinery*

(a) Specific action should be taken by UNCTAD in collaboration with UNDP and the regional economic commissions to give effect to the resolution of the Committee on Shipping on the establishment of national and regional consultation machinery in various parts of the world in accordance with the provisions adopted;

(b) Financial and technical assistance should be given to developing countries for the establishment of such machinery where necessary.

5. *Port improvements*

(a) Practical measures should be devised at UNCTAD II for financing and giving technical assistance to developing countries for port development and allied works and programmes relating to port operation, taking into account technical advances in shipping;

(b) Measures should be devised at UNCTAD II for ensuring that savings achieved by the improvement of port facilities in shipping operations are utilized to the advantage of developing countries through reduction of freight rates in respect of the port achieving such improvement.

6. *Insurance and re-insurance*

(a) Developed countries should reduce the cost of re-insurance to developing countries;

(b) A substantial part of the technical reserves of the insurance and re-insurance companies should be retained in the countries where premium incomes arise for re-investment in those countries;

(c) Developing countries should be technically and financially assisted in building up their own insurance and re-insurance facilities.

7. *Tourism*

(a) Developed countries and financing institutions should extend credits on easy terms to developing countries for promoting tourism;

(b) Developed countries and international credit institutions should make investments in infrastructure in tourism in developing countries;

(c) Passenger fares to developing countries should be concessional and attractive and other facilities should be provided in order to encourage tourist traffic.

E. GENERAL TRADE POLICY ISSUES

1. *Principles governing international trade relations and trade policies conducive to development*

(a) UNCTAD II should review the implementation of the principles governing international trade relations and trade policies conducive to development;

(b) In compliance with recommendations A. I. 1 and A. I. 3 of the Final Act of UNCTAD I which leave open the completion of these principles, UNCTAD II may elaborate new principles. However, principles already adopted would not be subject to re-examination.

2. *Trade relations among countries having different economic and social systems*

(a) The expansion of trade between developed socialist countries of Eastern Europe and developed market economy countries should not unfavourably affect the trading possibilities of developing countries but on the contrary should lead to a rising trade between them and the latter. In pursuance of this objective the socialist countries should provide in their economic development plans and trade policies measures for accelerated increase of their imports of primary commodities and manufactures and semi-manufactures originating from developing countries;

(b) Socialist countries should also reaffirm the assurances given by them in UNCTAD I that they will refrain from re-exporting the goods purchased from the developing countries unless it is with the consent of the developing countries concerned;

(c) Socialist countries should adopt the necessary measures to reduce the gap between import and sales prices of products originating from developing countries in order to promote the consumption of these commodities; the establishment in the import policies and trade programmes of the socialist countries of margins of tolerance with regard to prices, delivery dates and other conditions relating to exports from developing countries would greatly contribute to the increase of trade between these countries and the socialist countries;

(d) Credit extended by socialist countries for financing public and private projects in developing countries should be adapted to the particular conditions of the countries concerned; and where possible provisions should be made for repayment by the export of the products of those or other projects;

(e) In case of contracts, concluded between the enterprises in the developing countries and the relevant agencies in the socialist countries, due attention should be given to the periods covered by those contracts in order to enable the enterprises to plan and execute with greater efficiency their investment, production and delivery programmes.

3. *Impact of regional economic groupings*

(a) Regional economic groupings of developed countries should avoid discriminating against the exports of developing countries of manufactures, semi-manufactures and of primary products, particularly temperate and tropical agricultural commodities;

(b) The expansion of these groupings should not increase the incidence of any discrimination; ·

(c) Regional economic groupings of developed countries should take measures with a view to ensuring freer access of the exports of developing countries.

4. *International division of labour*

A new and dynamic international division of labour should be applied whereby developed countries avoid taking protective measures affecting agricultural exports of developing countries in fields in which they are more efficient and duplicating investments already made or about to be made by developing countries in industry. Conditions should be created for industrialization in developing countries to make the fullest use of their available resources. The diversification of production of developing countries should also be carried out within a framework of a division of labour that would enable the greatest flow of trade on the one hand among developing countries and on the other hand between these countries and others.

5. *The world food problem*

It was agreed that, in the light of the fact that the item had only recently been introduced, consultations would be pursued within the Group of 77 with a view to adopting a common position on the world food problem for UNCTAD II.

6. *Special problems of the land-locked countries*

A group of experts should be established in order to carry out a comprehensive examination of the special problems involved in the promotion of trade and economic development of the land-locked developing countries, with special reference to the high costs involved in the execution of their development programmes and trade expansion programmes. In the light of this examination, adequate financial and technical assistance should be extended by international financial institutions to minimize the cost of the factors involved. The international financing agencies should also give priority to such technical and financial assistance programmes as the land-locked developing countries may propose in connexion with the special problems of their trade and development and, in particular, with the development and improvement of their transport infrastructure.

7. *Transfer of technology, including know-how and patents*

(a) The developed countries should encourage the transfer of knowledge and technology to developing countries by permitting the use of industrial patents on the best possible terms which will enable products manufactured in developing countries to compete effectively in world markets;

(b) They should also promote the elimination of restrictive practices, relating to market distribution and price-fixing, which are imposed by enterprises in developed countries in granting licences for the use of patents and trade-marks in developing countries;

(c) The developed countries should provide guidance to their industrial entrepreneurs regarding investment opportunities in the export industries of the developing countries and familiarize them with legal, political, economic and other relevant information on the situation in the developing countries.

F. TRADE EXPANSION AND ECONOMIC INTEGRATION] AMONG DEVELOPING COUNTRIES

(a) The developing countries reaffirm that trade expansion and economic co-operation among themselves is an important element of a global strategy for development, and they are therefore determined to make their own contribution toward the fulfilment of the objectives of UNCTAD II by stepping up their efforts in this respect. Such action can in no way be regarded as a substitute for larger and more remunerative exports to developed countries or for a greater contribution by the latter countries. However, trade expansion and economic integration among developing countries raises special problems and difficulties as compared with similar processes among developed countries. Action with regard to trade barriers

471

will therefore not be enough, but must be combined with suitable measures in other fields in particular investment matters and payments. In this connexion, the availability of appropriate external financing and technical assistance would be an important contribution for enabling developing countries to achieve more rapid progress in trade expansion and integration efforts. This international support should however be granted in a manner that would fully respect the determination of developing countries to follow their own methods of approach when expanding trade and advancing towards integration among themselves.

(b) The developing countries will inform UNCTAD II of the efforts they are making or planning to make, in order to increase their trade and strengthen their economic co-operation, particularly in the field of inter-regional, regional and sub-regional co-operation.

(c) Since the joint efforts of the developing countries cannot be fully successful without financial and technical aid from the developed countries, the latter should at the same time make a formal declaration of support for the developing countries' efforts at co-operation and integration, specifying the nature and the volume of financial assistance they are prepared to render to those efforts.

(d) At UNCTAD II a special working group should be set up to study the practical problem related to:

(i) trade expansion, economic co-operation and integration among the developing countries, including consideration of the special problems of the least developed countries;

(ii) the establishment of improvement of multilateral payments systems between developing countries;

(iii) The practical measures for the implementation of an international policy which would support these joint efforts with particular reference to financial and technical assistance.

Regional or sub-regional groups of developing countries should be invited to participate in the working group.

(e) UNCTAD II should establish a permanent Committee whose task would be to study all questions relating to trade expansion and economic integration among developing countries, with particular reference to ways and means of enabling the developing countries participating in such groupings to derive equitable benefits therefrom.

This Committee should, in particular, undertake the following activities:

(i) The study, centralization and dissemination of information and data on the experience acquired by developing countries in dealing with specific problems of sub-regional, regional or inter-regional co-operation and integration, and the organization of symposia on such problems for national and regional officials;

(ii) Studies relating to the possibility of establishing export and import groupings by commodity, or by group of commodities, among developing countries;

(iii) Studies for the improvement of the infrastructure of transport and communications among developing countries;

(iv) Study the possibility of establishing national and regional information and trade promotion centres in developing countries;

472

(f) Consideration should be given to the establishment under the auspices of UNCTAD, and of other specialized agencies, of a special centre to train experts, particularly from developing countries, in the field of economic co-operation and integration among developing countries;

(g) The international information and trade promotion centre which is being established under the sponsorship of UNCTAD and GATT should give due importance to the question of promoting exports among developing countries.

G. SPECIAL MEASURES TO BE TAKEN IN FAVOUR OF THE LEAST DEVELOPED AMONG THE DEVELOPING COUNTRIES

Owing to the varying stages of economic development existing among the developing countries and to the varying factors responsible for their development, the trade and financial policy measures required to accelerate the pace of economic development would differ from one developing country to another. It is therefore essential to devise a global strategy of convergent measures in order to enable the least developed among the developing countries to derive equitable benefits so that all the developing countries would gain comparable results from international economic co-operation of member countries of UNCTAD, particularly that with the developed countries.

The individual measures recommended by UNCTAD I and those that would be recommended by UNCTAD II should be viewed as components of an integrated policy of co-operation for achieving the over-all objectives of trade and expansion and accelerated development. All these measures are inter-related.

While the appropriate mix of the convergent measures required for the least developed countries cannot be determined at this stage, these measures may be devised from the spheres of:

(a) commodity policy, including measures of financial and technical assistance for diversification programmes;

(b) preferences in trade of manufactures and semi-manufactures;

(c) development finance;

(d) regional economic integration;

(e) invisibles;

(f) trade promotion.

With regard to commodity policy the following actions should be recommended to be taken by UNCTAD II:

— Special consideration of the need of the least developed countries in relaxing tariff and non-tariff barriers affecting access to the markets both in tropical and temperate products;

— Temporary refunds, at least in part, of revenue charges and duties on commodities of particular interest to least developed countries.

With reference to manufactures and semi-manufactures, the recommendation on the general scheme of preferences contained in this document under section B (Expansion of exports of manufactures and semi-manufactures) should be taken into consideration and adopted. This should take place independently of the principle

473

in virtue of which substantial advantages may be granted to the least developed among the developing countries under systems of regional or sub-regional integration; while the latter, where appropriate, attain perfection in the matter of customs duties.

For the purpose of designing special measures for the least developed countries it does not seem to be desirable or convenient to attempt an abstract general definition of such countries nor, at this stage, an *a priori* strict listing of such countries applicable to specific measures considered. Hence this could be better undertaken, in due course, in a form agreed upon by the developing countries.

In order to give effect to the provisions of section G, the Ministerial Meeting decides to establish a working group. The function of the working group shall be to make a special study of the arrangements to be made on the matters referred to in the third paragraph of this section.

Composition of the working group: it is agreed that each regional group shall be represented on this group by five members.

The working group shall meet at Geneva on or about 1 December 1967. It shall submit its report to the countries members of the Group of 77 not later than 15 January 1968.

PART THREE

A. FUTURE ACTIVITIES OF THE GROUP OF 77

The representatives of developing countries of the Group of 77 are firmly decided to maintain and further strengthen the unity and solidarity of the group of developing countries. They agree to maintain continuous consultations and contacts in order to further that objective.

The Group of 77 should meet at the ministerial level as often as this may be deemed necessary, and in any case always prior to the convening of sessions of the United Nations Conference on Trade and Development, in order to harmonize the positions of developing countries and to formulate joint programmes of action in all matters related to trade and development. It can also meet at any other level, as required by the needs of developing countries.

In all matters relating to the preparation for Ministerial Meetings of developing countries, and, during the intervals between these Ministerial Meetings, and for the formulation of joint positions on issues within the purview of UNCTAD, the competent authority of the Group of 77 is the Group of 31 developing countries. This Group of 31 is composed of the developing countries, members of the Trade and Development Board, and should normally meet concurrently with the Trade and Development Board. For all matters related to their specific fields of activities the developing countries members of the Committee of the Board are fully competent.

The Co-ordinating Committee of the Group of 77 as established in Geneva in October 1966, should be continued until the New Delhi Conference with the following terms of reference:

474

(a) to assist in making appropriate arrangements for visits of Goodwill Missions;

(b) to transmit to Member Governments of the Group of 77 the reports of the Goodwill Missions received from the President of the Ministerial Meeting;

(c) to undertake any other work that may be entrusted to it by the Group of 77 in Geneva.

Informal co-ordinating groups of the 77 should be established in all headquarters of the various United Nations specialized agencies.

B. GOODWILL MISSIONS

The representatives of developing countries participating in the Ministerial Meeting of the Group of 77 have decided to send high-level Goodwill Missions to countries belonging to other groupings of member countries of UNCTAD. These missions, entrusted with the task of informing and persuading, shall acquaint the respective governments of the countries to be visited of the conclusions of the Meeting so as to contribute to the creation of the best possible conditions for negotiations on the programme of action at UNCTAD II.

There will be six high-level Goodwill Missions to visit capitals of developed and socialist countries, composed of at least one, and if possible, two special envoys accredited by Heads of States from each of the three regional groups within the Group of 77. Each mission will be headed by one of its members so as to ensure that each regional group provides two mission leaders.

Necessary steps will be taken immediately to contact the respective Governments to fix suitable dates for the visits of the missions in such a way as to ensure the completion of all visits before the end of November 1967.

Each mission will submit its report to the President of the Ministerial Meeting who, in his turn, in co-operation with the Co-ordinating Committee, will forward these reports to all the developing countries members of the Group of 77 as soon as possible.

The President of the Ministerial Meeting of the Group of 77 was requested to present the Charter of Algiers to the General Assembly of the United Nations and to the Secretary-General of the United Nations. The President of the Ministerial Meeting, in his turn, invited the Rapporteur General of the Ministerial Meeting and the Chairmen of the four main Committees of the Meeting to accompany him on this mission. He also invited the Vice-Presidents of the Ministerial Meeting to accompany him if their duties permit them to do so.

COMMUNIQUE ON THE CONSULTATIVE MEETING OF SPECIAL GOVERNMENT REPRESENTATIVES OF NON-ALIGNED COUNTRIES

A Consultative Meeting of Special Government Representatives of Non-Aligned Countries was held in Belgrade from July 8 to 12, 1969.

The governments of the following countries participated at the meeting: Afghanistan, Algeria, Burma, Burundi, Cambodia, Cameroon, the Central African Republic, Ceylon, Congo Brazzaville, Cyprus, the Democratic Republic of Congo, Ethiopia, Ghana, Guinea, India, Indonesia, Iraq, the Islamic Republic of Mauritania, Jamaica, Jordan, Kenya, Kuwait, Laos, Lebanon, Liberia, Libya, Malawi, Mali, Morocco, Nepal, Nigeria, Senegal, Sierra Leone, Somalia, Sudan, Syria, Chad, Tunisia, Uganda, the United Arab Republic, Yugoslavia and Zambia.

The governments of the following countries were represented by observers: Argentina, Bolivia, Brazil, Chile, Trinidad-Tobago, Uruguay and Venezuela.

The agenda of the Consultative Meeting was as follows:

1. The role of the policy of non-alignment in the present-day world, with special reference to the problems of peace, independence and development.

2. Consideration of possibilities for intensifying consultations, cooperation and joint activities by the non-aligned countries in various spheres.

The special representatives of the governments participating in the Consultative Meeting expressed their points of view on the questions on the agenda in an atmosphere of sincerity and mutual respect. They reaffirmed the dedication of their States to the principles of the policy of non-alignment as expressed in the declarations of the Belgrade and Cairo Conferences of Heads of State and Government of the non-aligned countries. These principles continue to be valid in the conditions of the present-day world and the policy of non-alignment has asserted itself as a significant and lasting factor in international relations.

Participants in the Consultative Meetings observed that present trends in the world are characterized by the confrontation between peoples struggling for their political, economic, social and cultural independence on the one hand, and forces of imperialism, colonialism, neo-colonialism and all other forms of foreign domination on the other, which are with increasing frequency resorting to power politics and pressure, including armed intervention, subversive activities and interference in the internal affairs of others, thereby violating and menacing the sovereignty and territorial integrity of many independent States.

476

The participants have taken note of the efforts being made by the big powers with the aim of preventing a direct armed conflict among themselves as well as their tendency to have recourse to negotiation. However, the participants stressed that this does not in itself ensure peace and independence for all and that the solution of international problems requires due respect for both the interests of the countries concerned and of those of the international community at large as well as participation in world affairs on a footing of equality by all countries. The determination of the non-aligned countries to be an active factor in solving international problems, found expression at the Consultative Meeting.

It was pointed out that so far no notable progress had been towards achieving security through disarmament, as a result of which the independence and sovereignty of peoples and their accelerated economic advancement is being permanently exposed to difficulties and dangers.

In their remarks, the participants laid special stress on the existence of areas of international crisis and crucial problems in the contemporary world.

Declaring their support for the heroic struggle the people of Vietnam have been waging for years for their freedom and independence, the participants expressed the hope that the Paris talks would lead as promptly as possible to a lasting settlement which would enable the people of Vietnam to decide their own destiny themselves. In this connexion they stated that immediate and unconditional withdrawal of all foreign troops from South Vietnam constitutes the precondition to any solution of the problem.

Unanimously pledging their support for the national liberation movements, the representatives of governments participating in the Consultative Meeting observed with indignation that the process of the liquidation of colonialism was stagnating. In Africa, the situation in the countries still subject to colonial domination is marked by the intensification of imperialist, colonialist racist forces especially in Zimbabwe, in South Africa and in Portuguese-held territories, thus constituting a grave menace to international peace and security. The Consultative Meeting reaffirms the inalienable rights of the people in these countries to independence and pledges to support them materially and morally. The participants in the Consultative Meeting demand that concrete measures be taken to assure the complete and prompt implementation of the Declaration of the United Nations on Independence for the Colonial Peoples still under colonial domination.

Having heard the representatives of the Palestinian Liberation Organization, the participants reaffirmed the resolution of 1964, in which the Heads of State and Government of the non-aligned countries, in conformity with the United Nations Charter, endorsed the full restoration of the rights of the Arab people of Palestine to their usurped homelands. Participants declared full support to the Arab people of Palestine in their struggle for liberation from colonialism and racism and for the recovery of their inalienable rights.

In reviewing the present international situation they considered that the continued occupation of territories of three countries, members of this group, constitutes a violation of the principles of the United Nations, a challenge to the aims of non-alignment and a grave threat to peace. Consequently, they reaffirm the inadmissibility of the acquisition of territory by war and call for the withdrawal of foreign troops from all the Arab territories occupied since June 5, 1967, in accordance with the Resolution of the Security Council of November 22, 1967.

The representatives of governments participating in the Consultative Meeting consider that the economic situation of the developing countries is deteriorating because the terms of their economic and trade relations with the developed countries are unfavourable. Such a state of affairs has increased the economic dependence of these countries which are thus exposed to pressure and external interference of all kinds which is conducive to neo-colonialist undertakings and thus constitutes an impediment to the economic and social development of the people of these countries and a threat to peace. The participants were encouraged by the various measures already taken by the non-aligned countries to promote regional economic cooperation in their regions. They emphasized the need for urgent action on measures such as increasing access to the markets of developed countries, development finance, commodity stabilization agreements, international support for diversification of their economy and the scheme for supplementary financing. They stressed that unless appropriate measures are taken in conformity with the Charter of Algiers, the new technological revolution which opens up considerable prospects for mankind would only widen the existing gap between the developed and developing countries.

The participants underscored the need for intensifying joint political action by the non-aligned countries for the purpose of greater mobilization particularly in the preparations for the Second UN Development Decade and in the future activities of UNCTAD. To that end, they supported the proposal of countries belonging to the Organization of African Unity to hold a meeting of ministers of the 77 developing countries.

Participants in the Consultative Meeting reaffirmed their adherence to the principles of the UN Charter and agreed that the consolidation and assertion of the UN requires, as an addition to the universality of this Organization, the restoration to the People's Republic of China of its legitimate rights and the adaptation of the structure of the UN in such a way as to allow all states to play their full role. The UN would then become a more representative and effective instrument for the regulation of international relations in the lasting and long-term interests of all countries. They are of the opinion that the tendencies to bypass the UN, lack of respect for its Charter and non-implementation of UN resolutions, as well as the failure to achieve universality, were negative in their effects on the role of the UN and that this tends to undermine its effectiveness. They agreed to intensify their activities in the world organization and to join efforts, especially at the forthcoming General Assembly session and the session celebrating the 25th anniversary of the UN, in achieving such results as would contribute to the further assertion of the UN and its role in international affairs.

The participants in the Consultative Meeting were gratified at the growing interest in non-aligned policy in the world and considered that the present international situation was such as to call for intensified activation by the non-aligned and all forces willing to lend their support to full respect for independence and sovereignty, to the exclusion of threat or use of force in the solution of disputes between independent states, to the right of each people, independently and without outside interference, to decide on the ways and means of their own development, to the liquidation of colonialism and racial discrimination, to accelerated economic development and equitable international relations and co-operation.

In this connection the need was stressed for the non-aligned countries to strengthen and develop their mutual relations and cooperation, so that their relations may serve as an example of the application of the principles they advocate.

The participants in the Consultative Meeting reaffirmed their adherence to the rights of each people to decide freely on their own path of development. They feel that the elimination of colonialism and abolition of discrimination would strengthen the cooperation between their countries and other developing countries and also lead to the establishment of international relations on the basis of equality and the true interest of all nations.

Participants in the Consultative Meeting were agreed on the need for a more active approach by the non-aligned countries on the international scene and concerted efforts within UN frameworks. In this connection, they exchanged views on various forms and possibilities for more regular and comprehensive consultations and cooperation, and on the desirability of holding, with adequate preparation, a conference of Heads of State and Government of non-aligned countries.

The desire was expressed at the Consultative Meeting that those interested countries that proclaim their adherence to the policy of non-alignment and particularly those who had won their independence after the Cairo Conference and all members of the OAU should also be invited to the future gatherings of the non-aligned countries in accordance with the principles and criteria observed at the Belgrade and Cairo Conferences.

LUSAKA DECLARATION
ON PEACE, INDEPENDENCE, DEVELOPMENT, CO-OPERATION AND DEMOCRATIZATION OF INTERNATIONAL RELATIONS

The Third Conference of Heads of State or Government of the following Non-aligned countries was held in Lusaka, Zambia from 8th to 10th September, 1970. The following countries were present:

Afghanistan, Algeria, Botswana, Burundi, Cameroun, Central African Republic, Ceylon, Chad, Congo (Brazzaville), Congo (Kinshasa), Cuba, Cyprus, Equatorial Guinea, Ethiopia, Ghana, Guinea, Guyana, India, Indonesia, Iraq, Jamaica, Jordan, Kenya, Kuwait, Laos, Lebanon, Lesotho, Liberia, Libya, Malaysia, Mali, Mauritania, Morocco, Nepal, Nigeria, Rwanda, Senegal, Sierra Leone, Somalia, South Yemen, Singapore, Sudan, Swaziland, Syria, Tanzania, Trinidad and Tobago, Togo, Tunisia, Uganda, United Arab Republic, Yemen Arab Republic, Yugoslavia, Zambia.

The following countries attended as observers:

Argentina	Brazil	Peru
Austria	Chile	Republic of South Vietnam
Barbados	Equador	(Provisional Revolutionary Government)
Bolivia	Finland	Uruguay
		Venezuela

The Secretary-General of the Organization of African Unity also attended as an observer.

The following national liberation movements addressed the Conference as guests:

African National Congress (South Africa)
Afro-Asian Peoples Solidarity Organisation
Frelimo (Frente de Libertação de Moçambique)
Pan-African Congress
MPLA (Movimento Popular de Libertação de Angola)
UNITA (União Nationale para á Independencia Totale de Angola).

They exchanged views on the significance and the role of non-aligned countries in the present-day world with particular reference to safeguarding and strengthening world peace and security, ensuring national independence and full sovereignty of all nations on a basis of equality, on the need to realize the fundamental right of all peoples to self-determination, as well as democratization of international relations, promoting the rapid economic growth of the developing countries and considering possibilities for greater consultation and co-operation among the non-aligned countries and strengthening the United Nations.

2. Two and a half decades ago, the peoples of the United Nations inscribed in the Charter their desire to save succeeding generations from the scourge of war; to reaffirm faith in fundamental human rights, in the dignity of the human person, in the equal rights of nations, large and small; to establish conditions under which justice and respect for obligations arising from treaties and other sources of international law can be maintained and to promote social progress and better standards of life in larger freedom for all. The intervening period has confirmed the historic merit of these ideals and aspirations but, it has likewise demonstrated that many expectations have not been fulfilled and many problems have not been solved, notwithstanding the efforts of the non-aligned countries.

3. The policy of non-alignment has emerged as the result of the determination of independent countries to safeguard their national independence and the legitimate rights of their peoples. The growth of non-alignment into a broad international movement cutting across racial, regional and other barriers, is an integral part of significant changes in the structure of the entire international community. This is the product of the world anti-colonial revolution and of the emergence of a large number of newly-liberated countries which, opting for an independent political orientation and development, have refused to accept the replacement of centuries-old forms of subordination by new ones. At the root of these changes lies the ever more clearly expressed aspiration of nations for freedom, independence and equality, and their determination to resist all forms of oppression and exploitation. This has been the substance and meaning of our strivings and actions; this is a confirmation of the validity of the Belgrade and Cairo Declarations. At a time when the polarization of the international community on a bloc basis was believed to be a permanent feature of international relations, and the threat of a nuclear conflict between the big powers an ever-present spectre hovering over mankind, the non-aligned countries opened up new prospects for the contemporary world and paved the way for relaxation of international tension.

4. Our era is at the crossroads of history; with each passing day we are presented with fresh evidence of the exceptional power of the human mind and also of the dangerous paths down which its imperfections may lead. The epoch-making scientific and technological revolution has opened up unlimited vistas of progress; at the same time, prosperity has failed to become accessible to all and a major section of mankind still lives under conditions unworthy of man. Scientific discoveries and their application to technology have the possibility of welding the world into an integral whole, reducing the distance between countries and continents to a measure making international cooperation increasingly indispensable and ever more possible: yet the states and nations comprising the present international community are still separated by political, economic and racial barriers.

These barriers divide countries into developed and the developing, oppressors and the oppressed, the aggressors and the victims of aggression, into those who act from positions of strength, either military or economic, and those who are forced to live in the shadow of permanent danger of covert and overt assaults on their independence and security. In spite of the great progressive achievements and aspirations of our generation, neither peace, nor prosperity, nor the right to independence and equality, have yet become the integral, indivisible attribute of all mankind. Our age, however, raises the greatest hopes and also presents the greatest challenges.

5. The immediate danger of a conflict between the superpowers has lessened because their tendency to negotiate in their mutual relations is strengthening, however, it has not yet contributed to the security of the small, medium-sized and developing countries, or prevented the danger of local wars.

6. The practice of interfering in the internal affairs of other states, and the recourse to political and economic pressure, threats of force and subversion are acquiring alarming proportions and dangerous frequency. Wars of aggression are ragging in the Middle East and in Indo-China and being prolonged in South Viet-Nam and extended to Cambodia and the presence of foreign forces in Korea is posing a threat to national independence and international peace and security. The continued oppression and subjugation of the African Peoples in southern Africa by the racist and colonial minority regimes, apart from being a blot on the conscience of mankind, poses a serious threat to international peace and security. This situation is becoming dangerously explosive as a result of the collusion between certain developed countries of the West and the racist minority regimes in that part of the world. The continuing arms race is causing alarm and concern and rendering nuclear detente extremely precarious and serves as a spur to limited wars. The balance of terror between the superpowers has not brought peace and security to the rest of the world. There are welcome signs of a growing detente between the power blocs but the abatement of the cold war has not yet resulted in the disintegration of the military blocs formed in the context of great power conflicts.

7. International relations are entering a phase characterized by increasing interdependence and also by the desire of States to pursue independent policies. The democratization of international relations is therefore an imperative necessity of our times. But there is an unfortunate tendency on the part of some of the big powers to monopolize decision-making on world issues which are of vital concern to all countries.

8. The forces of racism, apartheid, colonialism and imperialism continue to bedevil world peace. At the same time classical colonialism is trying to perpetuate itself in the garb of neo-colonialism — a less obvious, but in no way a less dangerous, means of economic and political domination over the developing countries. These phenomena of the present day world tend not only to perpetuate the evils of the past but also to undermine the future; they retard the liberation of many countries still under colonial domination and jeopardize the independence and territorial integrity of many countries, above all of the non-aligned and developing countries, hampering their advancement, intensifying tension and giving rise to conflicts.

9. The economic gap between the developed and the developing countries is increasingly widening — the rich growing richer and the poor remaining poor. The developing countries are being denied their right to equality and to effective participation in international progress. The technological revolution, which is now the monopoly of the rich, should constitute one of the main opportunities for progress of developing countries. World solidarity is not only a just appeal but an overriding necessity; it is intolerable today for some to enjoy an untroubled and comfortable existence at the expense of the poverty and misfortune of others.

10. Concerned by this state of affairs in the world, the participants in this Conference have agreed to take joint action, and to unite their efforts towards that end.

11. The participants in the Conference of Non-Aligned Countries reaffirm and attach special importance to the following principles: the right of the peoples who are not yet free to freedom, self-determination and independence; respect for the sovereignty and territorial integrity of all States; the right of all States to equality and active participation in international affairs; the right of all sovereign nations to determine in full freedom, the paths of their internal political, economic, social and cultural development; the right of all peoples to the benefits of economic development and the fruits of the scientific and technological revolution; refraining from the threat or use of force, and the principle of peaceful settlement of disputes.

12. The Conference declares that the following continue to be the basic aims of non-alignment: the pursuit of world peace and peaceful coexistence by strengthening the role of nonaligned countries within the United Nations so that it will be a more effective obstacle against all forms of aggressive action and the threat or use of force against the freedom, independence, sovereignty and territorial integrity of any country; the fight against colonialism and racialism which are a negation of human equality and dignity; the settlement of disputes by peaceful means; the ending of the arms race followed by universal disarmament; opposition to great power military alliances and pacts; opposition to the establishment of foreign military bases and foreign troops on the soil of other nations in the context of great powers conflicts and colonial and racist suppression; the universality of and the stating of strengthening of the efficacy of the United Nations; and the struggle for economic independence and mutual co-operation on a basis of equality and mutual benefit. What is needed is not redefinition of non-alignment but a rededication by all non-aligned nations to its central aims and objectives.

13. The participants in the Conference solemnly declare that they shall consistently adhere to these principles in their mutual relations and in their relations with other States. They have accordingly agreed to take the following measures:

(a) To achieve full solidarity and to initiate effective and concrete measures against all forces that jeopardize and violate the independence and territorial integrity of the non-aligned countries and or this purpose to co-operate with and consult each other as and when necessary.

(b) to continue their efforts to bring about the dissolution of great power military alliances in the interest of promoting peace and relaxing international tensions, under circumstances ensuring the security of all states and peoples; to safeguard international peace and security through the development of social, economic, political and military strength of each country.

(c) to assert the right of all countries to participate in international relations on an equal footing which is imperative for the democratization of international relations.

(d) to offer determined support to the intensification of the work of all international bodies concerned with problems of disarmament, particularly in the preparations for and implementation of the programme of the Disarmament Decade as an integral part of general and complete disarmament.

(e) to intensify and unite efforts among the developing countries and between them and the developed countries for the carrying out of urgent structural changes in the world economy and for the establishment of such international co-operation as will reduce the gap between developed and developing countries.

(f) to intensify joint efforts for the liquidation of colonialism and racial discrimination: to this end to pledge their utmost possible moral, political and material support to national liberation movements and to ensure implementation of international decisions, including measures by the Security Council in accordance with the relevant provisions of the United Nations Charter.

(g) to continue their efforts toward strengthening the role and efficacy of the United Nations, to promote the achievement of the universality of the United Nations and the urgent need for giving the People's Republic of China her rightful place in the organization and the admission of other countries.

While at the same time examining the modalities of enabling all countries outside the United Nations including those which are divided to participate in the activities of the Organization and its Agencies.

(h) to strengthen steadily, and expand the domain of mutual co-operation within the international, regional and bilateral frameworks.

(i) to ensure the continuity of action by holding periodic consultations of representatives of non-aligned countries at different levels and by convening summit conferences more frequently depending on the prevailing international situation.

14. The Heads of State or Government and leaders of participating countries resolve that this Declaration as well as the statements and resolutions issued by this Conference shall be forwarded to the U.N. and brought to the attention of all the member States of the world organisation. The present Declaration shall also be forwarded to all other states.

15. The participants in the Conference appeal to all nations and governments, all peace and freedom-loving forces and to all people the world over for co-operation and joint efforts for the implementation of these objectives. At the same time, they declare that they shall support all international actions that are initiated in the interests of the progress of mankind.

LUSAKA DECLARATION ON
NON-ALIGNMENT AND ECONOMIC PROGRESS

The Heads of State or Government of non-aligned countries, united by common political and economic aspirations

Expressing the determination of the non-aligned countries to achieve economic emancipation, to strengthen their independence and to make their contribution to world peace and to economic and social progress for the benefit of all mankind;

Reviewing the lack of progress in the implementation by the international community of the policies and objectives declared by them at Belgrade and Cairo, and those enshrined in the Charter of Algiers;

Disturbed by the rapidly widening gap between the economies of the rich and the poor nations, which constitutes a threat to the independence of developing countries and to international peace and security;

Noting with concern the negative trends which exclude developing countries in particular the decline in the share of developing countries from the mainstream of world economic life despite their endeavour to participate in contemporary progress;

Noting in particular the decline in the share of developing countries in world export trade from one third in 1950 to 1/6th in 1969;

Noting further with regret the decline in financial flows in terms of percentage of GNP from developed to developing countries and the increase in financial flows from developing to developed countries by way of payments of account of debts, dividends, and royalties, and financial and commercial services;

Believing that the poverty of developing nations and their economic dependence on those in affluent circumstances constitute a structural weakness in the present world economic order;

Convinced that the persistence of an inequitable world economic system inherited from the colonial past and continued through present neo-colonialism poses insurmountable difficulties in breaking the bondage of poverty and shackles of economic dependence;

Realizing that the occupation of parts of territories of non-aligned developing countries and dependent nations by aggressors or minority governments deprives

485

these groups of their natural resources and constitutes a hindrance to their development;

Considering that the gap in science and technology between the developing and developed countries is widening and the need for preventing the emergence of technological colonialism is pressing;

Recognizing that the massive investments in the economic and social progress of mankind can be made if agreements are reached to reduce expenditure on armaments;

Conscious of the increase since the meeting in Belgrade, in the capability of non-aligned countries to plan, organise, and manage their own economic development, both individually and within a multi-national co-operative framework, and the progress made by them during the sixties;

Convinced that the second United Nations Development Decade provides an opportunity to bring about structural changes in the world economic system so as to meet the pressing needs of poor nations, to strengthen their independence, and to provide for a more rapid and better balanced expansion of the world economy;

HEREBY

A. *PLEDGE THEMSELVES*

(i) to cultivate the spirit of self-reliance and to this end to adopt a firm policy of organising their own socio-economic progress and to raise it to the level of a priority action programme;

(ii) to exercise fully their right and fulfil their duty so as to secure optimal utilisation of the natural resources on their territories and in adjacent seas for the development and welfare of their Peoples;

(iii) to develop their technology and scientific capability to maximise production and improve productivity;

(iv) to promote social changes to provide increasing opportunity to each individual for developing his worth, maintaining his dignity, making his contribution to the process of growth and for sharing fully in its fruits;

(v) to promote social justice and efficiency of production, to raise the level of employment and to expand and improve facilities for education health, nutrition, housing and social welfare;

(vi) to ensure that external components of the developmental process further national objectives and conform to national needs; and in particular to adopt so far as practicable a common approach to problems and possibilities of investment of private capital in developing countries;

(vii) to broaden and diversify economic relationships with other nations so as to promote true inter-dependence;

486

B. *DECIDE*

to foster mutual co-operation among developing countries so as to impart strength to their national endeavour to fortify their independence;

to contribute to each other's economic and social progress by an effective utilization of the complimentarities between their respective resources and requirements;

to intensify and broaden to the maximum extent practicable, the movement for co-operation and integration among developing countries at sub-regional, and inter-regional levels for accelerating their economic growth and social development and take into account the necessary measures required to guarantee that the peoples of developing countries concerned receive the benefit of the integration and not the foreign companies operating within the integrated area;

and to this end, to adopt the following Programme of Action in the field of:

I. PLANNING AND PROJECTION

(a) to identify products and countries in which production can be stimulated and expand with a view to increasing existing income and trade exchange;

(b) to identify projects and programmes for which import requirements capable of being met from developing countries are likely to arise, and

(c) to define as closely as possible financing and technological requirements to secure increases in production and to support expansion of trade flows amongst developing countries.

II. TRADE, CO-OPERATION AND DEVELOPMENT

(a) to organize exchange of information in regard to products of export interest to developing countries;

(b) to provide adequate access to products of export interest to other developing countries, especially by preferential reduction of import duties;

(c) to negotiate long-term purchases and sale agreements in respect of industrial raw materials and to orient policies of official procurement organisations in favour of developing countries;

(d) to evolve payment arrangement to support expansion of trade exchanges amongst developing countries;

(e) to facilitate transit traffic for the diversification and the expansion of the external trade and landlocked countries;

(f) to facilitate international traffic across overland transit highways crossing international borders amongst developing countries; and

(g) to encourage travel and tourism amongst developing countries.

III. INDUSTRIAL, MINERAL, AGRICULTURAL AND MARINE PRODUCTION

(a) to exchange information on needs and resources of different developing countries in respect of technical know-how, research, consultancy services, experts and training facilities; and

(b) to institute and intensify programmes of co-operation at bilateral, regional and inter-regional levels to combine needs and resources of developing countries for furthering one another's production programmes and projects.

(c) to co-ordinate through policies and measures for the utilization in their national interest their mineral and marine resources and for the protection of the maritime environment;

IV. DEVELOPMENT OF INFRASTRUCTURE

(a) to facilitate mutual co-operation in preparing preinvestment investment surveys and in executing projects for the development of one another's infrastructure in the field of road and rail communication, irrigation and power; and

(b) to concert measures for transforming the prevailing systems of communications, transport and commercial services previously designed to link metropolitan countries to their dependent territories so as to promote direct commerce, contact and co-operation amongst developing countries.

V. APPLICATION OF SCIENCE AND TECHNOLOGY

(a) to organize means and measures to share one another's experience in the application of science and technology to processes of economic and social development;

(b) to institute schemes of co-operation for the acquisition of skills relevant to their situation and in particular to promote exchange of trainees and experts and thus provide for optimum use and efficiency of their specialised technological and scientific institutions; and

(c) to devise programmes for adoption of technology to the special needs of countries in different stages of development, and to provide for its widest possible diffusion to developing countries and for the conservation of their technical skills and personnel in consonance with their needs and conditions.

VI. MECHANISM

to facilitate contact, exchange of information, co-ordination and consultations among Governments and concerned organizations and institutions to further mutual co-operation and integration for implementing the programmes of action;

C. URGE THE UNITED NATIONS

to fulfil the objectives enshrined in the Charter "to promote social progress and better standards of life in larger freedom";

to employ international machinery to bring about a rapid transformation of the world economic system, particularly in the field of trade, finance and technology so that economic domination yields to economic co-operation and economic strength is used for the benefit of the world community;

to view the developmental process in a global context and to adopt a programme of international action for utilization of world resources in men and materials, science and technology, benefiting developed and developing countries alike;

to adopt at their Commemorative Meeting a Declaration on the international strategy providing for the following:

I. GOALS AND OBJECTIVES

(a) International co-operation for economic development is not a one sided process of donor-donee relationship; the development of developing countries is a benefit to the whole world, including the more advanced nations;

(b) The aim of international economic co-operation should be to provide a dynamic combination of the world's production, market and technological factors to promote a rational division of labour and a humane sharing of its fruits; international co-operation should strengthen the capability of developing countries to exercise fully their sovereignty over their natural resources;

(c) A rapid transformation of the world economic system should be achieved through the adoption of convergent and concomitant policies and measures so that the developing and developed countries become partners, on a basis of equality and mutual benefit, in a common endeavour for peace, progress and prosperity;

(d) The essential purpose of development is to provide equal opportunity for a better life to everyone; the aim should, therefore, be to accelerate significantly the growth of gross product per head so that it is possible to secure for everyone a minimum standard of life consistent with human dignity;

II. POLICIES AND MEASURES

(a) Since primary commodities constitute a preponderant source of foreign income for most developing countries, provision should be made for maximising their consumption, diversifying their utilisation, securing for producers a fair and equitable return, organising their production on the basis of endowment factors, and securing for developing countries an increasing share of the growth in consumption; unfinished action to conclude commodity agreements should be completed by 1972;

(b) International action should be taken to promote processing of primary products in areas of production and to provide access to consuming markets of processed products, free from all tariff and non-tariff barriers;

489

(c) The scheme of non-discriminatory non-reciprocal preferences in favour of products of developing countries is implemented without further delay;

(d) Other measures should be undertaken to secure for developing countries an increasing share of international trade in manufactured and semi-manufactured goods, especially through adjustment of production structures in developed countries;

(e) A distinction should be made between transfer of resources intended to promote development of developing countries and commercially motivated investments;

(f) The new flow of financial transfers from developed to developing countries should correspond, by 1972, to a minimum of 1 per cent of the GNP of each developed country, 3/4 of which should be from official sources;

(g) Financial transfer for development should be untied and provided on terms and conditions compatible with the efficiency of the developmental progress;

(h) Appropriate measures should be adopted to alleviate the burden of debts on developing countries;

(i) A link between Special Drawing Rights and development finance should be established by 1972;

(j) Steps should be taken to enable developing countries to extend their merchant marines, to develop their shipbuilding industries, and to improve and modernize their ports. Urgent action is needed to restrain the alarming increase in freight rates and to eliminate discriminatory and restrictive elements from it. Consultation machinery for the solution of difficulties of shippers from developing countries needs to be improved to increase its efficiency;

(k) Concerted measures should be undertaken to bridge the widening gap in the technological skills between developing and developed countries, to facilitate diffusion of technology, patented and non-patented, on reasonable terms and conditions, and to ensure that transfers of technology are free from illegitimate restraints. An appropriate international mechanism should be devised to implement these measures;

(l) Provision should be made to expand research and development on materials with which developing countries are endowed. Arrangements should also be made for their nationals and institutions to build up scientific capabilities;

(m) Within the framework of international development strategy, special measures should be taken to improve the productive capacities and develop the infrastructure of least developed, including land-locked countries so as to enable them to derive full benefit from convergent and concomitant measures; and

(n) Mutual contact and co-operation amongst developing countries is an indispensable element in the global strategy. The developed countries should support the initiatives of developing countries in this regard and pay special attention to concrete proposals that may be put forward by them to this end.

D. *DECLARE THEIR DETERMINATION*

(a) to undertake sustained and continuous endeavours within the United Nations system to secure faithful implementation of international development policies and programmes;

(b) to further the unity and solidarity of the Group of 77 at all levels including the convening of a ministerial meeting to prepare for UNCTAD 3;

(c) to review and appraise periodically the progress of mutual co-operation in the field of development in pursuance of the programme of action;

(d) to seek ways and means for strengthening the capabilities of the United Nations system, to fulfil its commitments to social and economic progress.

INDEX

*

BIOGRAPHICAL & GEOGRAPHICAL GUIDE

INDEX

A

African states — attitude towards Biafra's secession 90
Afro-Asian conference, preparation for it 324
aggression, Japanese, against China 70
aggression against Egypt (1956)
  — U.S. attitude 78
  — U.S.S.R. attitude 78
Agreement at Bled, Yugoslavia, three western powers, foodstuffs 207
Agreement between U.S.S.R. and Hitler's Germany (1939) 203
Agreement on economic relations U.S.S.R. — Hitler's Germany 18
Agreement on Friendship and Cooperation between U.S.S.R. and Yugoslavia 180, 181
Agreement on Non-Proliferation of Nuclear Armament, first draft of superpowers, opposition to 299, 300
Agreement on the entrance of Soviet units into Yugoslavia 197
Agreement with Italy in Rapallo 203
agricultural equipment, underdeveloped countries 158
agricultural produce, underdeveloped countries, output, advance, need of 160
agriculture
  — India, modernization 171
  — underdeveloped countries
    — economic activity, share 159
    — intensification 160
    — modernization, labour market 171
    — productivity 159, 160
aid
  — grants 358
  — irretrievable grants 355
  — to India 355
  — to Yugoslavia 355
Algier's Charter
  — Algier's conference of underdeveloped countries 281
See also 171, 354
Algier's conference of underdeveloped countries, Algier's Charter 281
alignment
  — Latin America, military dictatorships, exponents 132

495

C

500

E

506

F

Fascism 23, 62, 66, 67, 194
Federal Executive Council, Yugoslavia, ratification of the memorandum on abolishing the Free Territory of Trieste 209
— memorandum on abolition 209
See also 192
feudal relations, colonies 135
finished products, exports, rate of growth 154
Finno-Soviet War 18
First Balkan War 22
First World War 10, 12, 29, 33, 43, 53, 54, 57, 60, 61, 145, 147, 148, 166, 180, 193, 355
foodstuffs
— underdeveloped countries, consumption 157
foreign bases, nonaligned countries, demand for removal 263
foreign markets, underdeveloped countries, dependence on 125
Free Territory of Trieste
French Revolution 127
Friendship pact between U.S.S.R. and Hitler's Germany 18, 24

G

Gandhism 68
GATT — see General Agreement on Tariffs and Trade
General Agreement on Tariff and Trade
— activity 267
— foundation 267
— world trade 269
See also 278
Geneva Agreement 1954, Vietnam 100
Genoa Conference (1922) 204
German militarism, possible renewal 31
German question, deterioration 196
great powers
— behaviour
— China factor 334, 335, 337
— trends in the world, influence 334
— equilibrium, tendencies to maintain 328
— nonaligned countries, influence, attempts 337, 338, 339
— tension, relaxation, nonaligned countries, role 341
— third world
— attitude 358
— influence, expansion, attempts 358
gross domestic products (in the fifties)
— Burma 38
— Venezuela 38

507

industrial output
- Japan 337
- West Germany 36, 337
industrial revolution
- Australia, indigenous population, extermination and disenfranchisement 145
- British, overseas countries, settlement 145
- Central Europe 144
- England 144
- Europeans, western, overseas countries, settlement 145
- expansion through colonization and economic penetration 147
- expansion through the transfer of experience and knowledge 147
- France 144
- New Zealand, indigenous population, extermination and disenfranchisement 145
- North America, indigenous population, extermination and disenfranchisement 145
- original 167
- steam energy, its uses 145
- the United States 144
- underdeveloped countries, endeavours 170
- Western Europe 144
industrialization
- China, socialist revolution, importance of 146
- Eastern Europe (prior to World War I) 145
- foundations 41
- Russia, socialist revolution, importance of 145
- underdeveloped countries, trade-development, relationship 272
industry, steel; industrial revolution, importance of 144
industry, textile; industrial revolution, importance of 144
Islam
- Arab countries, influence on politics 54
See also 134
Institute for Strategic Studies, London 305
Institute for World Economy and International Relations of the U.S.S.R. 85
Institute of International Politics and Economics, Belgrade, Symposium on nonalignment 90
Institute of the U.S.S.R. Academy of Sciences, for World Economy and International Relations 332
Intelligentsia, newly liberated countries, progressive actions 100
internal development, economics — politics, inter-action 161
internal markets, underdeveloped countries 115
international aid, underdeveloped countries, U.N. fund for capital construction 268
International Court 29
International Peace Research Institute 322
IRO, International Refugee Organization 264
ITO, International Trade Organization, foundation 267
intervention

Moscow Declaration (October 30, 1943) 21
Moslems, division of the British India 52
Moslemic League (Pakistan) 53
movements for independence, newly created countries, influences from the
    developed parts of the world 126
multilateral nuclear naval force
    — NATO 109
    — NATO member states, attitude 225
    — opposition 299
Munich, agreement 18

N

National Assembly of Yugoslavia
    — ratification of the memorandum on the abolition of the Free Ter-
    ritory of Trieste 209
    — Tito's address (April 1, 1946) 187
National Committee of the Liberation of Yugoslavia, election of Tito as
    President 183
national gross product, underdeveloped countries 149
national income
    — countries with the lowest income
        — annual growth 164
    — investment for administration, defence, economic growth, burden
        of 114
    — investment rates 114
    — underdeveloped countries
        — rate of growth 164
    See also 357
national income per capita
    — Japan 166
    — Russia — Latin America (1913) 167
    — South Africa 166
    — Southeast Asia 164
    — The United States 164
    — The U.S.S.R. 166, 167
    — underdeveloped countries, growth rate 164
    See also 275
national liberation movements, moral force 231
national problems
    — France 320
    — Great Britain 320
    — U.S., Negroes 320
national product
    — Japan 337
    — the Federal Republic of Germany 337
nationalism 342
nations
    — equality, Bandung 243

517

Nonaligned Countries, peaceful uses, demand 257
— peaceful uses, agreement 258
— race 334
— uses, agreement 304
— war uses, prohibition 329
overseas possessions
— European population 165
— exchange, preferential treatment 166

P

Pact against Comintern 19, 24, 25
Palestine problem
— Cairo Conference of the Heads of State or Government of Non-
aligned Countries 293
— Yugoslavia — U.S.S.R. 197
See also 54
Paris meeting of four powers representatives 256
Parliament, British, N. Chamberlain's speech (Sept. 1, 1939) 25
Parliament Indian 72
Parliament Indonesian, political statement of the Indonesian government 50
payments means, foreign, underdeveloped countries 125, 160, 272
Peace Conference in Paris 192
peace in the world, nonaligned countries, cooperation with all countries
desiring it 346
Peace Treaty, London tri-partite declaration 193
Peace Treaty U.S.S.R. — Finland 18
Peace Treaty with Italy
— revision, attempt 194, 203
— Yugoslavia, rejection 204
peaceful and active coexistence
— underdeveloped countries, protagonists 170
peaceful cooperation, coexistence
— agreement China—Indonesia 243
— formulation, bilateral talks India—China 242, 243
Petrograd Soviet of workers' and soldiers' deputies, Lenin's speech on
November 7, 1917 182
Poland — frontiers of interests between U.S.S.R. and Germany 24
Poland's division
— agreement between U.S.S.R. and Hitler's Germany 18
— new status quo 24
policies in agriculture, underdeveloped countries 158
polycentrism, world, growing 299, 304
population
— annual growth (1950—1960) 154
— armament race, sacrifices 331
— countries with the lowest income, growth, rate 164
— India, increase 96
— Indonesia, increase 96

521

R

527

V

West-U. S. S. R., relations before the war 18
White House — Kremlin, communication 329
White Paper of the Yugoslav Ministry for Foreign Affairs 196
workers' class
    — newly liberated countries, progressive actions 100
    — nonaligned countries 99
World conference on the peaceful uses of nuclear energy 253
world division of labour, world market 151
world economy
    — COMECON, role 278
    — eastern Europe 36, 37
    — economic disturbances 35
    — newly liberated countries 152
    — structure, changes 232
    — western Europe, role 36
world gross product, underdeveloped countries, share 163
world income
    — bloc countries, share 39
    — developed regions, share, U. N. data 35
    — Europe, share, U. N. data 36
    — underdeveloped continents, share, U. N. data 35
    — U. S., share, U. N. data 35
    — U. S. S. R., share 37
world industrial output
    — U. S. rise, U. N. data 36
    — western Europe, role 36
world market
    — and labour productivity 150
    — and new countries 33, 94
    — capital market 150
    — character 150
    — cooperation and integration 151
    — developed countries — underdeveloped countries, relationships 154
    — economies, developed, dictate 126
    — functioning, changes 232
world population, underdeveloped countries, share 163
world trade
    — developed capitalist countries, share 154
    — development 153
    — GATT 270
    — underdeveloped countries, share 154
See also 150
World Trade Conference 267
world war two
    — Yugoslavia, losses 180
See also 14, 17, 20, 22, 23, 29, 34, 42, 44, 45, 49, 55, 56, 64, 82, 99, 101, 106, 119, 130, 145, 148, 149, 167, 168, 175, 176, 189, 194, 236, 264, 285, 295, 315, 342, 349, 355, 357

Y

Z

BIOGRAPHICAL AND GEOGRAPHICAL TERMS

A

F

G

H

I

Mali 79, 113
Marshall, George 265
Marx, Karl 87
Mates, Leo 65, 130
Mboya, Tom 97.
McClintock, Charles G. 232
Mediterranean 298
Menon, Krishna 75, 103
Middle America 121
Middle East 30
Molotov, Vjačeslav Mihailovič 18, 21, 24, 28, 181, 297
Monfalcone 190
Mongolia 230
Moon 312
Morocco 288, 321
Moscow 181, 193, 196, 198, 199, 200, 202, 203, 204, 256, 318, 319, 340
Mozambique 341, 347
Munich 18, 19
Mynt, H. 114, 149, 154, 160, 161

N

Nasser, Gamal Abdel 49, 75, 228, 241, 244, 247
Near East 30, 49, 53, 54, 79, 88, 106, 128, 225, 230, 234, 292, 298, 301, 302, 329, 330, 341, 344
Nehru, Jawaharlal 32, 46, 47, 48, 50, 58, 59, 61, 62, 63, 64, 65, 66, 69, 70, 71, 72, 73, 75, 76, 77, 84, 99, 103, 187, 221, 228, 240, 241, 242, 244, 245, 247, 255, 345
Nepal 244
Netherlands 30, 50, 107
New Delhi 242, 280, 281, 282, 356
New York 228, 255, 275, 280
New Zealand 35, 37, 120, 145, 151, 165, 230, 264
Nigeria 89, 113, 128, 138, 230, 341
Nkrumah, Kwame 87, 97, 228
North 42, 230, 233, 236, 238, 304, 347
North America 119, 121, 133, 139, 144, 145, 147, 163, 323, 335
Northedge, F. S. 117
North Korea 36, 209
North Vietnam 36, 244
Norway 109
Nyerere, Julius 97

O

Oceania 37, 145
Osgood, Robert E. 84

P

Pacific 131, 341
Padmore, George 97
Pakistan 49, 52, 53, 72, 101, 121, 124, 128, 234, 235, 240, 244, 246, 286
Pakistan, eastern part 49, 96